Health and Social Care
for Vocational A level

(formerly Advanced GNVQ)

Mark Walsh,
Josephine de Souza,
Peter Scourfield, Paul Stephens
and Gareth Price

Published by HarperCollins *Publishers* Limited
77–85 Fulham Palace Road
Hammersmith
London
W6 8JB

www.**Collins**Education.com
On-line support for schools and colleges

First published 2000
Reprinted 2000, 2001 (twice)

Layout, compilation, design and illustrations © HarperCollins *Publishers* Ltd 2000
Text © Mark Walsh, Josephine de Souza, Peter Scourfield, Gareth Price and Paul
Stephens 2000

ISBN 0 00 329100 6

British Cataloguing in Publication Data.
A cataloguing record for this publication is available from the British Library.

Almost all the case studies in this book are factual. However, the persons, locations
and subjects have been given different names to protect their identity. The
accompanying images are for aesthetic purposes only and are not intended to represent
or identify any existing person, location or subject. The publisher cannot accept any
responsibility for consequences resulting from this use, except as expressly provided by
law.

Series commissioned by Charis Evans
Designed, edited and typeset by DSM Partnership
Cover designed by Patricia Briggs and Sylvia Kwan
Cover picture by Sally and Richard Greenhill
Picture research by Thelma Gilbert
Illustrations and cartoons by Barking Dog Art
Index by Julie Rimington
Project managed by Kay Wright
Production by Emma Lloyd-Jones
Printed and bound by Scotprint

www.**fire**and**water**.co.uk
The book lover's website

Contents

Acknowledgements

The authors would like to thank everybody involved in supporting them during the writing and production of this book.

Janet Phillips, Curriculum Unit Manager at Oxford College, is especially acknowledged and thanked for her contribution to Unit 1.

The authors and publisher would like to thank the following for permission to reproduce photographs and other material.

Ace Photo Agency: Sam Sloane (p. 75 centre); Mauritius (p. 75 bottom)

Age Concern England (p. 8)

BBC ONE (p. 182)

Bubbles: Frans Rombout (p. 217 left), (p. 217 right); Ian West (p. 226); Loisjoy Thurstuin (p. 232)

BUPA (p. 299)

Collections: Sandra Lousanda (pp. 74, 75 right, 229, 256); Anthea Sieveking (pp. 213, 230); Fiona Pragoff (p. 236); Roger Scruton (p. 243); Terry Simmonds (p. 257 top); Brian Shuel (pp. 341, 348); Paul Bryans (p. 351 right)

Commission for Racial Equality (p. 20)

Corbis (p. 262)

CPD: Don McCullin and Neil Godfrey (p. 6 left)

Emma Dunlop (p. 269 right)

Equal Opportunities Commission (p. 17)

Format: Paula Solloway (p. 6 right); Brenda Prince (pp. 16, 69, 81, 316); Judy Harrison (pp. 3, 36, 221, 316 top right); Ulrike Preuss (pp. 70, 97, 222); Sally Lancaster (p. 90); Raissa Page (p. 160); Lisa Woollett (p. 231); Maggie Murray (p. 264)

Hammersmith Community Health Council (pp. 61, 93)

Harry Venning, Evening Standard (p. 73)

Hearing Concern (pp. 86, 92)

Helen Evans (p. 85 top)

Hulton Getty (p. 268)

John Birdsall (pp. 54, 85 bottom, 112, 316, 351 left)

John Walmsley (p. 75 top)

Kay Wright (p. 257 bottom)

The Kobal Collection (p. 162)

Mary Evans Picture Library (p. 290)

Mother & Baby Picture Library (p. 312)

Muriel Kasner (p. 124)

Network: James Nubile (p. 15); Homer Sykes (p. 77): Jonathan Olley (p. 129); Mike Abrahams (p. 212); Mike Goldwater (p. 249)

Novosti Photo Library (pp. 269 left, 261)

PA Pictures: Matthew Fearn (p. 49)

Popperfoto (pp. 13, 14, 93)

Private Eye (p. 295 left)

Rex Features: Nils Jorgensen (p. 148)

Roger Scruton (pp. 42, 115, 210 right, 393)

Sally and Richard Greenhill: Richard Greenhill (p. 80 top and bottom) Sally Greenhill (pp. 53, 76, 80 centre, 82, 94, 209, 210 left, 225, 316)

Science Photo Library: Melissa Grimes-Guy (pp. 71, 121, 195); D Phillips (p. 244 left); James Stevenson (pp. 244 right, 273); Tim Beddon (p. 295); Stevie Grand (p. 350); Blair Seitz (p. 361); Klaus Guldbrandsen (p. 372)

Scope (p. 9)

Shout (pp. 117, 144)

Solo Syndication (p. 285)

Telegraph Colour Library: A Tilley (p.253)

Tricia de Courcy Ling (p.243)

Trip: V Kolpakov (p. 166)

Every effort has been made to contact copyright holders, but if any have been inadvertently overlooked, the Publisher will be pleased to make the necessary arrangements at the first opportunity.

Introduction

WELCOME TO ADVANCED VOCATIONAL Health and Social Care. In this first edition, we've tried to produce a textbook that is interesting, accessible and clear. The book is written primarily for students taking the advanced level vocational award in Health and Social Care (formerly GNVQ Advanced). However, we hope that students studying other courses, such as Access, BTEC National Social Care and GCE Advanced level Sociology and Psychology will also find the book useful for parts of their course.

This book covers the six compulsory units of the advanced level vocational award in Health and Social Care. The book therefore also includes coverage of the three units (1, 2 and 5) required for the advanced level Part Award in Health and Social Care. This introduction sets out the structure and requirements of the advanced level vocational health and social care course and explains how the textbook is organised. It aims to help you understand what is required of you as a student of advanced vocational health and social care and decribes how to get the most out of the book.

What does the course involve?

An advanced level vocational Health and Social Care qualification is of the same standard as a traditional A level but with a different focus. If you have achieved an Intermediate GNVQ, you will already have a good idea of what it is like to study for an advanced level vocational award. However, if you have taken GCSEs, you will find studying for a vocational award different in several ways from GCSE work, and from studying for traditional A levels.

First, as an advanced level vocational student, you take more responsibility for your own learning, for planning your work, for undertaking your own investigations, and for keeping proper records of what you have done. Your tutor will play an important part in teaching you some of what you need to know and in helping you to respond to problems and setbacks in your own investigative learning. However, in the end, you have to take responsibility for your own programme of study, just as you will take responsibility for whatever job you do in the future.

Second, much of your vocational learning will be done through carrying out your own enquiries and investigations, often in connection with assignments

agreed with your tutor. During the course, your investigations may involve:

- research in libraries and resource centres

- visits to work places and interviews with the people who work there

- meetings with local employers and care practitioners visiting your school or college

- surveys of people's activities, preferences and opinions

- studies of people, places and organisations that relate to the health and social care area

- work experience with a local care organisation.

Overall, you will be actively investigating the vocational area of health and social care and presenting your findings in various ways, including giving talks and presentations. All these activities develop skills that are essential in the modern world.

Third, some two-thirds of your work is assessed through assignments that you complete during the course. Only one third is assessed through externally set tests. Many students find that they can give a better account through coursework and assignments than in a test, but don't underestimate the amount of work involved in doing assignments. You can't leave everything to the last minute on an advanced level vocational Health and Social Care course, any more than you can when you are at work.

How is the course structured?

This depends on whether you are taking the vocational advanced level Health and Social Care as a double (12 units), single (6 units) or part (3 units) award.

The double award

In the double award there are twelve units. Six are compulsory; all students take them. Six are optional. Each awarding body has produced its own set of optional units and your centre will probably ch___ which of these you will study. In very large ___ may be offered a choice of optional units. ___ the same size. The result for your advanced ___

Health and Social Care double award is worked out by adding up the results you get on each of the 12 units that you take.

The single award

In the single award there are six units. There are three compulsory units listed in what is known as Block A,

at least one unit from Block B, and the remaining units from Block C (see Figure I.1).

The part award

In the part award you must take three specified compulsory units. These are are shown in Figure I.2.

Figure I.1: The structure of the single award

Block A – Three compulsory units

Unit	Unit title	Assessment
1	Equal opportunities and client's rights	External test
2	Communication in health and social care	Assignment
4	Factors affecting human growth and development	External test

Block B – At least one of these two units

Unit	Unit title	Assessment
3	Physical aspects of health	Assignment
5	Health, social care and early years services	Assignment

Block C - Any further one or two units from the remaining compulsory or options units not already chosen. Block C choices should bring the total up to six units.

The single, six-unit award is equivalent to a single GCE Advanced (A level) award.

Figure I.2: The structure of the part award

Unit	Unit title	Assessment
1	Equal opportunities and clients rights	External
2	Communication in health and social care	Assignment
5	Health, social care and early years services	Assignment

How will I be assessed?

A third of your award is assessed through externally set tests and the remaining two thirds is assessed through work (usually assignments) set by your tutors.

The externally set tests are short answer tests in which you have to demonstrate your knowledge and understanding of the unit contents being tested. You have two chances to pass each external test. The tests are taken in January and June each year.

The assessment of the other units is usually through assignments that are set by your tutors. The

assignments are written around the assessment criteria included in each unit specification. The work that you produce is assessed against these criteria so you should get to know them well and understand what is required of you before you begin any assessment work.

Each external test and assignment that you undertake results in a points score that is then converted into a grade from A to E. The overall grade of your award is worked out by adding up the total number of points you gain and then dividing this by the number of units that you've taken. Your average score then determines what grade you get.

About this book

This textbook covers the six compulsory units of the advanced level vocational award in Health and Social Care. The book therefore includes coverage of the three units (1, 2 and 5) required for the advanced level part award in Health and Social Care. Each compulsory unit is covered in a separate chapter in this book. The chapters all have the same structure and features.

Preview

Every unit of the book begins with a preview. This outlines the unit's main contents and focus, providing a quick introduction to the topic areas that follow.

Topic sections

These cover the subject matter of the five or six main topic areas outlined in the award's unit specifications. The topic sections are broken down into a number of subsections and provide you with the essential information, and explanation of key concepts and ideas, needed for each topic area. The topic sections are generally presented in the same order as they are found in the specification itself. There are some occasions where the order changes or where we've introduced a topic. We've done this in order to help you understand and learn about a particular subject more easily.

Activities

The activities in the text provide opportunities for you to develop and apply your understanding of the information and concepts covered in each topic section. You are encouraged to attempt the activities as they are an essential part of the 'learning process' built into the book. It is always easier to learn something by doing it rather than by just reading about it or being told about it. You might find it helpful to return to your activity notes and answers when doing revision for the external tests or preparation for your assignment work. Have a look at examples of activities on p. 6 or p. 22 now.

Case studies

Case studies are an occassional feature throughout the textbook. We've used case studies to bring to life some of the concepts and ideas presented in the main text. Where the case study is designed for you to develop or apply your understanding of a concept or topic we've included some questions. You should always try these. Where the case studies don't have questions we've used them to illustrate a point or concept or to provide extra information in the form of an example.

Build your learning

At the end of each main topic section, there is a feature called 'Build your learning'. This feature always indicates that one topic section has ended. Have a look at the example on pp. 11–12. The feature is designed to help you to check and consolidate your understanding of the topic that you've just studied. It has three parts,

- **Keywords and phrases.** This lists some of the concepts introduced in the topic section. Test your understanding by writing down what you think each term means. Check whether you've got it right, by finding where the term is explained in the book (maybe by using the index). Your knowledge of key concepts will be assessed through the external tests, so use the keywords and phrases as an opportunity to prepare yourself.

- **Summary points.** Use these to check that you have understood all the key points in the section. Again, you can use these for revision purposes.

- **Questions.** This is another way to test your own learning and develop your exam skills. You should always try to answer these questions, then check your answers by looking back at the relevant part of the unit. The answers to the questions can always be found in the book. Your answers to these questions don't count towards your result for the unit: the questions are there to help you learn, not to test you. Nevertheless you can improve your chances of passing the external tests by practising writing short answers to these questions.

It would be a good idea to keep a file of your answers to keywords and phrases and to the end of topic questions, with corrections where necessary, for revision.

Finding Information

There are references in most units to other books or research studies. You can find the full details of any publications cited in the text by turning to the alphabetical references listed at the end of each unit.

When you want to find information on a specific topic, use the index at the back of the book (see p. 403). Some coverage of the topic can be found on each of the pages referred to by the index entry. The page numbers highlighted in green provide either a detailed or very specific explanation of the topic you are looking for and may be a good place to start. Try looking up *confidentiality* as a topic to see how the index works.

Author biographies

Mark Walsh is a writer, teacher and INSET trainer. He has taught and assessed a range of care and social science-based courses in further education colleges and the NHS. As the lead author and series consultant for Collins vocational health and social care publications, Mark has written a wide range of educational resources.

Josephine de Souza is a practising barrister and lecturer. She has taught various courses in further and higher education, including early childhood studies, health studies, matrimonial law and practice and the law relating to family and children.

Peter Scourfield is an experienced teacher across a range of courses. He currently combines teaching in health and social care at a further education college in Cambridgeshire with working as a social work practitioner.

Paul Stephens is associate professor of education at Stavanger University College in Norway. He has a BSc and a PhD in sociology from London University and has written several books on sociology and education.

Gareth Price taught science and humanities for many years in a Leicestershire community college and is the author of a number of science textbooks. He currently works as a science editor.

This unit helps you to develop your knowledge and understanding of equality of opportunity principles, the law relating to equal treatment and how these affect health and social care service users and care practitioners. It will enable you to recognise unfair discrimination and will raise your awareness of the importance of an anti-discriminatory approach.

We begin with an introduction to some of the key concepts and language used in the field of equal opportunities. You are encouraged to become familiar with and use these concepts and terms in your work.

As a result of their experience of unfair discrimination and unequal opportunities, various social groups have sought and struggled to achieve legal rights to protection and fair treatment. We look briefly at the background to these struggles in order to show why the current equality of opportunity legislation has been developed.

Next we focus on the impact of unfair discrimination on the individual. We also look at its effects on the life chances, or opportunities, of members of social groups which experience most unfair treatment and discrimination. Inequality of opportunity affects members of these groups in a broad range of ways, though we concentrate on the impact it has in the areas of education and employment.

The next part of the unit is concerned with legislation, policies and codes of practice that aim to promote equality of opportunity. We begin with a brief look at the types of law that exist and that are applied in the United Kingdom. The two key areas that we focus on are legislation and case law. This general section about the law is followed by a detailed outline of specific examples of equality legislation, such as the Sex Discrimination Act 1975 and the Race Relations Act 1976, which apply to all citizens of the United Kingdom. We then focus on how care service users' rights are protected through care-related legislation, codes of practice, national charters and the internal policies of care organisations. We consider the various ways in which people can pursue a claim of unfair treatment and gain redress if they feel they have been discriminated against.

Next we are concerned with the ways in which ethical issues arise and affect service users' rights. We consider how issues such as confidentiality, risk management and the funding of care create moral dilemmas for care practitioners when they wish to ensure equal treatment for all service users but are not able to do so.

We move on to look at the ways in which equality of opportunity can be promoted. We consider the role that care practitioners and care organisations have to play in promoting equality. In particular, we look at anti-discriminatory practice and at the ways in which organisational practices and procedures can be developed to incorporate equality of opportunity principles. Finally, we outline the main sources of support and guidance on equal opportunity issues. Throughout the unit we have tried to provide a range of relevant examples from the health, social care and early years field.

1

Equal opportunities and clients' rights

Contents

Promoting equality

PEOPLE WHO LIVE IN THE United Kingdom should be able to enjoy life free from any form of prejudice, unfair discrimination or stereotyping on the grounds of their race, gender, sexual orientation, age, disability, or nationality. As people living in a democratic country, we tend to expect that we share the same rights as our fellow citizens and that we will be treated fairly and equally in our personal and professional lives. The reality for many people, however, is different. People in the United Kingdom live in an unequal society where some people are treated less favourably than others. Equality is a goal that some groups in our society struggle to achieve and which is denied them because of prejudice, stereotyping and unfair discrimination.

Terms and concepts

We begin learning about equality and clients' rights by exploring some of the key terms and concepts that inform care practitioners' efforts to promote equality and combat unfair discrimination. Understanding what these key terms mean is a necessary starting point for understanding the significance that equality and clients' rights have in a care context.

Equalities

The first thing to say about equality is that there is more than one form of it. A dictionary definition of equality says that it is simply a state of being equal. However, because there is more than one way of interpreting this, it's better to talk about equalities or to define the kind of equality that you are really referring to. In our discussion of these different forms of equality we are really talking about differences in principle. Later in the unit we look at how equality principles are, or might be, translated into practice in care settings.

The three different equality principles that we consider here are called:

- egalitarianism
- equity
- equality of opportunity.

Egalitarianism is a form of equality that is based on the idea that all people have equal rights and that there should be equal outcomes for all. For example, an egalitarian might say that all care workers who provide care for others have the right to the same pay. If they all make their best effort and play a necessary part in providing care, or in making it possible for care to be given, then they all deserve an equal reward. In reality, this doesn't happen. There is a wide range of pay rates across the care professions, even though most care practitioners make an equally valuable contribution to caring for service users.

Equity is another form of equality. It means treating people with greater needs more favourably than people with fewer unmet needs in order to equalise outcomes. For example, care workers who are poorer might, on the grounds of equity, be given more pay than care workers who are wealthier. This doesn't sound like equality at first, because it involves treating people differently rather than the same. However, it is a way of ensuring equality of outcome that some people see as fairer.

Both egalitarianism and equity involve attempts to ensure **equality of outcome**. People who advocate equality of outcome believe that everyone, regardless of background or characteristics, should obtain an equal share of society's resources such as education, health services and employment. The third approach to equality does not advocate this. The third way is to use the law and policies to ensure that people have a right to **equality of opportunity**. This usually means giving people an equal chance or equal access to opportunities and resources. Equality of opportunity works a little bit like a competitive race.

Anyone is allowed to enter the race (equality of opportunity) and everybody who enters starts from the same point and races under the same conditions. All runners enter on the same terms (equal access) and, in theory, any competitor has the chance to win. In reality it is highly likely that some competitors will do better than others, even if all entrants try their best, so there won't be equality of outcome. We look at some reasons why this is later in the unit. A key point to note at this stage is that most equality law is based on ensuring equality of opportunity not equality of outcome.

The social nature of inequality

People are born with individual differences. However, it is wrong to think that biologically based differences in physical appearance and ability and in mental capacity are the cause of the broad range of inequalities that exist in society. The causes of inequalities in society are social. This means that inequalities (rather than differences) between people result from the ways in which society is divided and structured.

British society is divided and structured according to social class, race, gender, physical ability, age and, to some extent, sexuality. Some people achieve more power and success than others because they are born, or manage to get themselves, into the social groups that have more power and advantages. In British society, people who are white, middle class, male, heterosexual and able-bodied have greater power and opportunities than people who are non-white, working class, female, homosexual or disabled.

When thinking about the role that care practitioners and care organisations have in promoting equality, you should remember that discrimination and unfair treatment are closely associated with **social or structural inequality**. Inequality is not simply the result of individual differences in physical and mental ability and unfair discrimination involves more than unacceptable behaviour by bad people.

Rights

In the same way that there are a number of forms of equality, it is possible to identify a number of types of rights. These include legal and civil rights. Equality of opportunity is closely linked to giving and enforcing legal rights. **Legal rights** are the entitlements that people can claim under the law. For example, all children in the United Kingdom have a legal right to State education between the ages of five and 16 years and women employees have a legal right to 14 weeks maternity leave after they have a baby. **Civil rights**, in contrast, refer to broader issues such as freedom of speech and freedom of movement that are taken for granted in a democratic society and that are rarely the subject of complaints or legal proceedings for most citizens.

In this unit, we are most concerned with the legal rights of health and social care service users. Many of the legal rights that people in the United Kingdom now possess have been granted as a result of the government passing laws. The development of these laws often follows organised, long-term campaigns to end unfair treatment and to improve the opportunities of particular groups in society. (The background to the struggle by various groups for legal rights and equality is outlined later in the unit on pp. 13–19.)

Prejudice

A **prejudice** is an opinion, feeling or attitude of dislike concerning another individual or group of people. Prejudices are usually unfavourable, unreasonable and unfair judgements which are not based on accurate information or fact and may be held even when proved to be unjustified or false. When people act on their prejudices they treat the targets of their prejudice in an unfair, unequal way. In the United Kingdom, prejudice against people from minority ethnic groups, homosexual men and women, women in general, people with disabilities and older people is acted on in various ways and makes the lives of the people who experience it harder.

It is very difficult to prevent people from forming and holding prejudices but, as we will see later, prejudice isn't something that people are born with (see p. 20). It is something that they learn from parents, the media, friends, teachers and work colleagues, for example (see p. 22 for case study). Nevertheless, while various prejudices are socially disapproved of, there is no law against prejudice. The law attempts to prevent people from acting on their prejudices and then punishes those who are convicted of doing so. As a result, the law focuses on unfair discrimination.

Unfair discrimination

Unfair discrimination occurs when individuals or groups are treated unfairly, or less favourably than others. Prejudice is at the root of unfair discrimination. The main focuses and forms of prejudice and unfair discrimination are:

Focus of prejudice	Form of discrimination
race, ethnicity, skin colour	racism
gender	sexism
sexuality	homophobia or heterosexism
age	ageism
disability	disablism

▲ Another example of police prejudice or another of yours?

Before we look at specific forms of unfair discrimination it's important to make a point about **fair discrimination**. This happens where there is a justifiable reason to treat people differently. There are some situations in which it is right to identify and acknowledge differences between people. For example, when several people apply for the same job the interviewers are justified in discriminating between them on the basis of who has the best qualifications, experience or talent. There are also exceptional employment situations in which it is lawful to discriminate on the grounds of **genuine occupational qualification**. Examples include:

- employment in dramatic performances or photographic modelling, where someone of a particular racial group is needed for reasons of authenticity

- employment in restaurants, where someone of a particular group is needed for reasons of authenticity (for example, Chinese waiters in a Chinese restaurant)

- employment of someone to provide personal services to a particular racial group or gender, where someone of the same racial group or gender can do the job more effectively.

There are some jobs in which it is necessary to be either a man or a woman, or to have a specific ethnic background in order to do the job. The key point about fair discrimination is that it is based on justifiable grounds and not on prejudice or unfair treatment.

ACTIVITY

Sticks and stones

Identify the words and names that were used at your primary and secondary school to insult, hurt and humiliate others. Divide them into lists of words that are about:

- gender

- ethnicity

- disability

- sexual orientation.

What were generally thought to be the most hurtful and insulting words?

What would you least like to have been called?

You will probably have come up with words and phrases that express one or more forms of prejudice. Both children and adults use sexist, homophobic, ageist and disablist language to express prejudiced beliefs that devalue, humiliate and hurt others.

Racism

The belief that one ethnic group is naturally superior to others is known as **racism**. Racists tend to make distinctions between, and judgements about, people on the basis of their physical appearance, particularly the colour of their skin. In the United Kingdom, where the majority of the population is white, racism is usually directed against minority ethnic groups. Racist beliefs are used to justify the inferior and unfair treatment of members of minority ethnic groups and to deny members of these groups equality of opportunity.

Racism is deeply rooted in the history of the United Kingdom and still profoundly affects the lives of people who have a different ethnic origin from the indigenous white population. Racial inequalities are created by, and unfortunately continue to be maintained by, people at all levels within British society.

Racism does not merely exist on an individual level and should never be seen simply as an individual's problem. Racial discrimination can be expressed through the practices, policies and procedures of institutions and organisations. This happens when an institution or organisation operates in ways that fail to give people from minority ethnic groups a fair chance or equal treatment. **Institutional racism**, as it is known, can even occur in organisations in which the organisational practices, policies and procedures are operated by people who appear to be fair minded. This was highlighted by the Stephen Lawrence inquiry, in which institutional racism was identified and acknowledged as a feature of the Police Service in England and Wales.

Sexism

The belief that one gender (usually male) is naturally superior to the other is called **sexism**. It is often used to justify the inferior treatment, and to restrict the opportunities, of women. Sexism stems from the belief that a person's gender automatically limits and defines his or her abilities and determines how he or she should be valued. The abilities and worth of women and girls have, historically, been undervalued compared to those of men. The ways in which social attitudes and employment practices are shaped by sexist beliefs can be seen in the fact that men in western societies generally have more power and obtain higher salaries than women. This situation is frequently justified in terms of women's alleged inferiority, rather than being explained by unequal and unfair treatment or the structural sexism of British society.

Sexism can occur on individual, institutional and structural levels, in the same way as racism. Some people may deliberately treat women unfairly in comparison to men through the way that they behave towards them. Organisations can also develop and apply practices, policies and procedures that put women at a disadvantage in comparison to men. Such **institutional sexism** is a particular concern in care organisations,

Figure 1.1: UK population by ethnic group and age, 1996

Great Britain	Percentages				
	Under 16	16–34	35–54	55 and over	All ages (=100%) (thousands)
White	20	27	27	26	52,942
Black Caribbean	23	36	24	17	477
Black African	28	43	23	6	281
Other Black	49	38	12	–	117
Indian	27	32	29	12	877
Pakistani	40	33	19	8	579
Bangladeshi	40	35	17	8	183
Chinese	16	40	30	15	126
Other Asian	27	31	36	6	161
Other ethnic minorities[1]	51	30	15	5	506
All ethnic groups[2]	21	27	27	25	56,267

[1] Includes those of mixed origin

[2] Includes ethnic group not stated

Source: *Key Data 97*, © Crown copyright 1997

such as the National Health Service and local authority social services departments, where the majority of employees are women but the people who get paid most and hold the most power are men. **Structural sexism** refers to the ways in which women are disadvantaged by a society that creates and maintains social expectations, practices and relationships which value and place women second to men.

Whilst women are more likely to be the victims of sexism, men can also be treated unfavourably and unfairly simply because of their gender. Nevertheless, sexism tends to be seen as prejudice against women because it is inextricably linked to the belief that women are inferior to men.

Homophobia

Webb and Tossell (1997) define **homophobia** as 'the fear and resulting contempt for homosexuals that is expressed by some people who are heterosexual'.

Because of the deep hostility that exists towards people who are lesbian or gay, many men and women are fearful of disclosing their sexual orientation. People who are lesbian or gay have few specific legal rights to protect themselves against the unfair discrimination and harassment that they experience because of their sexual orientation.

Awareness and rights campaigns by organisations representing lesbian and gay people (such as Stonewall, the Campaign for Homosexual Equality and Outrage!), have achieved a shift towards greater social acceptance of people who are lesbian or gay. This has been assisted by the relatively recent practice of coming out, in which people publicly declare their gay or lesbian sexual orientation. Nonetheless, this shift in acceptance by some parts of society has not had much impact on the legal restrictions and inequalities that lesbian and gay people experience in comparison to people who are heterosexual (see p. 36). Gay men and lesbians also continue to experience violence, harassment and intimidation as a result of homophobic prejudice about their sexual orientation.

Ageism

Unfair discrimination against people on the basis of their age is known as ageism. There can be prejudice against older or younger people for a variety of reasons. However, ageism is usually a problem experienced by older and middle-aged people, especially in terms of employment, rather than by younger people. Organisations like Age Concern, a charity that works with and for older people, have identified a range of areas and issues in which ageist attitudes have a

THE FIRST THING SOME PEOPLE NOTICE IS HER AGE.

AGE *Concern*

LET'S MAKE AGE DISCRIMINATION A THING OF THE PAST.

▲ Age Concern's controversial poster makes an ironic statement about the way people are stereotyped by age

negative effect on the lives and opportunities of older people.

There is currently no specific law aimed at preventing age discrimination. However, age discrimination is a significant and sensitive issue in health and social care. Many vulnerable older people are health and social care service users. Age discrimination goes directly against the values and principles of the value base that informs care practice.

Disablism

Language and terminology are important in the field of disability. The ways in which individuals and their circumstances are described is a sensitive and hotly contested issue. It is important, initially, to distinguish between **impairment** and **disability**. The term impairment is used to refer to any loss or abnormality of psychological, physiological or anatomical structure or function. The term **disability** is used to refer to any restriction on the opportunities of people with impairments to participate equally in the normal life and activities of a community.

▲ People are disabled by the barriers and attitudes which separate them from the rest of society

In Webb and Tossell (1997), the British Council of Organisations of Disabled People stresses that:

while we agree that some people have impairments, it is not these impairments which disable them. What disables us are the barriers and attitudes which separate us from the rest of society.

The language used to describe people with mental, physical and sensory impairments has traditionally expressed prejudices that have labelled, stereotyped and devalued people with impairments. Terms such as lunatic, spastic and cripple were all commonly used to indicate that the people they referred to were less than whole, normal or acceptable human beings. Given such attitudes, it is not surprising that people who have some form of impairment are highly likely to experience social disadvantage, unequal opportunities and unfair discrimination. Prejudice and less favourable treatment on the grounds of a person's physical, mental or sensory impairment is referred to as **disablism**.

Until relatively recently, it was generally accepted that people were disabled by their impairments and imperfections and that they had to find ways, or accept help, to overcome their disabilities. A lot of care practice and care legislation aimed at helping people with impairments has been based on this assumption. There has been little or no expectation or requirement that society should adapt to meet the different and varying needs of people with impairments. People with physical, mental and sensory impairments have not so far benefited from the kind of legislation that requires individuals and organisations to take into account, and adapt to, the diverse needs of different ethnic groups or the different needs of men and women, for example.

Tokenism

Later in the unit we consider the laws and strategies that can be used to prevent unfair discrimination and which give the right of redress to people who feel that their rights have been infringed. Health and social care organisations often seek to act in positive anti-discriminatory ways to ensure that groups which experience unfair discrimination and which are underrepresented in society become visible and gain influence in the organisation. These attempts to redress unfair discrimination must be real or the organisation may be seen as engaging in tokenism.

Tokenism occurs where people of a minority group, or an aspect of their culture, are included in the background or in unimportant roles in written or visible materials, but never as main characters doing important things or playing prominent roles in the organisation or its business.

Ford reverses into a row by changing black faces

Caroline Davies

Black workers at Ford were more than happy to appear in an advertising photograph with white colleagues to promote the multi-ethnic nature of the car company's Dagenham plant. When the same photograph appeared on the cover of the firm's Credit Options brochure, however, the black workers noticed a slight change. The alterations were first noticed by Noel Sinclair, a worker at the plant, who walked into a showroom in Essex to buy a car for his mother. He immediately recognised the photograph. 'I laughed and told the salesman some of my friends were in the picture. But when I looked for Patricia, I realised something was wrong. It was her body but not her face. Then I looked and realised that all their faces had been changed. Their overalls were there, even the rings on their fingers matched the original. But the faces were different and, without exception, white.'

One of the black workers, Douglas Sinclair, 56 – who has worked at Ford for 30 years – said: 'When I saw the brochure I didn't notice immediately. Then I looked again. My body was there dressed in my overalls, the rings on my fingers were still there, but the next thing I knew I had glasses on and a white face.' Patricia Marquis, 30, saw herself seated, wearing the same T-shirt and trousers, but with a face that had aged 20 years, put on 10lbs and was also white. 'My first reaction was what a cheek they had after they had asked us to do the campaign. I felt humiliated and really angry,' she said.

'I wanted an explanation from them. They had changed my face, for God's sake. What on earth did they think they were doing?' Keith Thomas, 40, found that not only had his face been erased and replaced, but his arms too. And George Pinto, sitting in his overalls, had not only become white but had moved from one side of the group to the other to replace a dummy. 'I immediately thought it was racist. Why didn't they just use a different picture in the first place? But to

actually make it white was a racist act,' Mr Thomas told the London Evening Standard. 'They wanted me in the picture when they wanted to show the mix of ethnic groups in Ford's workforce, but then I wasn't good enough.'

Of the six in the original photograph whose black faces were erased, at least four, who work in the paint, trimming and assembly section of the plant, have received apologies from Ford and £1,500 compensation for the distress caused them. A spokesman said: 'When the mistake was discovered, immediate action was taken to withdraw the brochure. The reason for the picture being altered was investigated and we explained fully what had happened to the employees and to the trade unions.' Van Leeuwen, managing director of Ford Credit added: 'We believe that we have explained to the unions that there was absolutely no racial motive. I apologise again for any offence.'

Daily Telegraph, 1996

ACTIVITY

Identifying types of unfair discrimination

Read through these examples of unfair discrimination in employment situations. Identify the particular type of prejudice that may be involved in each case.

- A man with a visual impairment is told that he is not capable of working as a receptionist.

- A woman is overlooked for promotion because she is pregnant.

- A man not being sent a job application form because of his age.

- A woman is not given an opportunity to do a job because it entails travelling to countries such as Saudi Arabia and Iran.

- An advertisement stipulates that only those of a particular age and appearance should apply, saying that applicants 'must be physically fit, attractive and 19–25 years of age'.

- A man earns more money than a woman with the same qualifications, doing the same job.

- Workers at a company do not want to associate with two other employees because they suspect that they are gay men.

BUILD YOUR LEARNING

Keywords and phrases

You should know the meaning of the words and phrases listed below. If you are unsure about any of them, go back through the last ten pages of the unit to refresh your understanding.

- Ageism
- Disability
- Disablism
- Egalitarianism
- Equality of opportunity
- Equality of outcomes
- Equity
- Fair discrimination
- Genuine occupational qualification
- Homophobia
- Impairment
- Individual discrimination
- Institutional discrimination
- Legal rights
- Prejudice
- Racism
- Sexism
- Structural inequality
- Structural discrimination
- Tokenism
- Unfair discrimination

Summary points

- Equality is a concept that can be interpreted in a number of ways. The different forms of equality focus on equality of opportunity or equality of outcome.

- Egalitarianism and equity are forms of equality of outcome.

- Equality law is based on the right to have equality of opportunity or access to goods, services and resources.

- Social, or structural, inequality is a feature of British society. Whilst some social groups have more power, success and opportunities, others are disadvantaged by their unequal access to power and resources.

- Unfair discrimination occurs when people act on their prejudices to treat others in an unfair and unfavourable way.

- Prejudice and unfair discrimination against disadvantaged social groups maintain inequality and deny some people equality of opportunity.

- There are a number of laws in Britain that aim to prevent and challenge unfair discrimination against individuals.

- Prejudice can be expressed at an individual, organisational (institutional) or structural level. Laws primarily aim to prevent and combat unfair treatment by individuals and institutions.

- Women, people from minority ethnic groups, lesbians and gay men, older people and people who are disabled tend to experience less favourable treatment to the extent that they do not enjoy equality of opportunity.

QUESTIONS

1 What does egalitarianism mean? In your answer explain how this is different to equality of opportunity.

2 Explain what a prejudice is.

3 Describe three ways in which unfair discrimination (racism, sexism or disablism, for example) can occur.

4 What is a genuine occupational qualification?

5 What does it mean to say that the United Kingdom is a multicultural and multiethnic society?

The struggle for equal rights

SOCIETIES WORLDWIDE HAVE generally recognised that everyone has basic human rights and that there is a need for people to live together irrespective of differences in race, colour, gender, sexual orientation or disability. The development of equality principles and rights, though occurring only very slowly, has become an important influence on the way members of society think and feel about others from diverse social and cultural backgrounds.

An understanding of equal opportunities issues needs to be based on a good knowledge of the social and historical contexts that lie behind the struggle for equality in British society. In the section that follows, we briefly consider the background to the struggle for equality and the extent to which progress towards equal rights has been achieved for women, people from minority ethnic groups, lesbians and gay men and users of health and social care services.

Women's struggle for equality

Women have fought to improve their unequal social position and legal rights in relation to men for a long time. The goal of an equal society and equality of opportunity for women is one that many women feel still hasn't been achieved. Support for the emancipation, or liberation, of women dates back more than a century. From the late nineteenth century onwards there have been organised campaigns to improve women's legal rights. In what is sometimes referred to as the first wave of feminism, at the beginning of the twentieth century women mounted campaigns that succeeded in:

- obtaining the right to vote

- improving educational opportunities

- gaining the legal right for married women to own property

- making it easier for women to get divorced.

Women have struggled for significant improvements in their legal rights throughout the twentieth century. A guiding principle of the women's battle for equality has been to challenge the idea that women could be treated unfavourably in comparison to men because they were assumed to be lesser in some way.

▲ The suffragettes campaigned for equality in the face of considerable opposition

Young women who have grown up in a society that is now more used to the idea of equality between men and women may find it hard to believe that it was once generally accepted that girls and women should not enjoy the same opportunities as boys and men. As recently as the 1960s and 1970s, women were campaigning on issues such as education, abortion and equal pay. This second wave of feminism led to greater public awareness of how these issues affected women's lives and resulted in some important legislative changes. Laws like the **Equal Pay Act 1970** and the **Sex Discrimination Act 1976** have been particularly important landmarks in the sex equality struggle. Nevertheless, women as a social group remain less powerful than men and still have to struggle to obtain and enforce their legal rights to equality and to achieve equality of opportunity.

The growth of multicultural Britain

Britain is a multicultural society, particularly as the result of British colonisation of the Indian subcontinent and the West Indies. However, people of African-Caribbean and Asian origin were already present in the centuries before Britain obtained its colonial empire. For example, the Roman armies which invaded Britain in the first century AD included many black soliders.

Many of the black people who arrived in Britain in the eighteenth and nineteenth centuries came to work as soldiers, servants and sailors. Others were brought forcibly and kept as slaves until slavery was abolished in Britain in 1838. The economic and military needs of Britain have been important factors influencing immigration to the United Kingdom. The end of both World Wars saw an increase in the black population in Britain, as people from Commonwealth countries and America who had fought for Britain settled here.

▲ Caribbean immigrants arriving in the UK in the 1950s aboard the Windrush

Figure 1.2: Regions of residence of ethnic minorities in UK, 1991 census

	White		Ethnic minorities	
	Residents	Percentage of GB population	Residents	Percentage of GB population
South east	15,513,800	29.9	1,694,700	56.4
Greater London	*5,332,900*	*10.3*	*1,346,800*	*44.8*
East Anglia	1,983,700	3.8	43,300	1.4
South west	4,546,900	8.8	62,700	2.1
West Midlands	4,727,200	9.1	422,900	14.1
West Midlands MC	*2,179,200*	*4.2*	*372,500*	*12.4*
East Midlands	3,764,500	7.3	188,800	6.3
Yorks & Humberside	4,261,200	8.9	215,200	7.2
North west	6,000,400	11.6	243,200	8.1
Greater Manchester	*2,351,900*	*4.5*	*147,500*	*4.9*
Merseyside	1,378,300	2.7	25,300	0.8
North	2,989,000	5.8	37,800	1.3
Tyne and Wear	*1,075,500*	*2.1*	*19,700*	*0.7*
Wales	2,773,900	5.4	41,200	1.4
Scotland	4,934,500	9.5	64,000	2.1
Total	**51,843,900**	**100.0**	**3,006,500**	**100.0**

Source: Commission for Racial Equality Factsheet, Ethnic Minorities in Britain (1999)

While multicultural Britain has a long history, most black immigration has occurred since 1945. In the early 1950s, people from the Commonwealth nations such as India, Pakistan and the West Indies were invited to Britain to work on the reconstruction of Britain's damaged housing, railways, hospitals and factories when indigenous British workers were in short supply. Sir Winston Churchill visited Jamaica in the West Indies and spoke to the British subjects there in ringing tones of their motherland and urged them to come and rebuild it. Many of them were skilled workers, such as teachers, nurses and civil servants, who gave up their jobs, homes and families to come to the United Kingdom, only to be treated with hostility by members of the indigenous population who were not used to living with people of a different colour.

A great number of these new communities suffered a great degree of racial discrimination, to the point where they experienced difficulties obtaining work and accommodation. This was hardly the welcome they expected from the motherland. As the immigrant population grew in the early 1950s, parts of the British population became more discontented. The then Labour government saw fit to create laws that would eventually restrict the number of people moving to Britain from other countries, rather than to pass legislation promoting racial equality.

▶ Lesbian and gay people have been very active in campaigning for equal rights since the Stonewall riot in 1969

Lesbian and gay rights in Britain

Homophobia and unfair discrimination against lesbians and gay men has a long history and remains widespread in British society. The gay liberation movement began in the United States of America in 1969 following the so-called Stonewall riots. This incident happened when a group of gay people retaliated against police intimidation outside the Stonewall Inn in New York.

The gay rights movement subsequently developed through the work of gay organisations that effectively challenged prejudice and unfair discrimination to improve the social acceptance and legal rights of gay men and women. The gay rights movement in Britain has followed a similar pattern and has achieved similar success in gradually shifting public attitudes, and increasing awareness of prejudice and unfair discrimination against gay people.

Whilst homophobic prejudice and unfair discrimination against gay people have been challenged on an attitudinal level, the gay rights movement in Britain has had less success in actually improving the legal rights of gay people. Many areas of unequal treatment still exist (see p. 37).

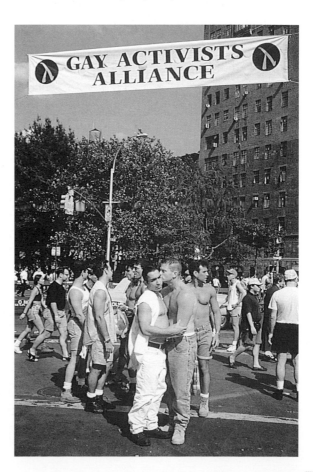

The disability rights and user involvement movement

▲ Protestors demanding equal rights for disabled people

People with physical, mental and sensory impairments have never enjoyed equal treatment and social acceptance in British society. Until the late twentieth century people with impairments were often removed and segregated from mainstream society in large rural institutions, colonies and special schools. The twentieth century saw a gradual change in this policy, as a general move away from long-term institutionalisation occurred.

Awareness of the needs of people with impairments was raised during the Second World War, when significant numbers of soldiers returned home with injuries that reduced or removed their ability to work and to function independently. The **Disabled Persons (Employment) Act 1944** was one of the first pieces of legislation to address their specific needs and to attempt to improve the employment rights of people with disabilities.

Despite some basic provisions, like the above Act, traditional political parties and mainstream sources of power and influence have failed to significantly address the needs of people with impairments. Equality of opportunity and equal rights for people with impairments were not issues that were high on the political agendas of any government in the twentieth century. The real pressure for equality of opportunity and better legal rights has come from people with impairments themselves.

In the last quarter of the twentieth century a disability rights movement run by people with impairments themselves has grown in power and influence. Encouraged by the success of women and black people in getting anti-discrimination laws passed, the disability movement has tried to raise awareness of the prejudice and unfair discrimination that people with impairments experience and has had some success in doing so. It has begun to challenge the attitudes and practices of policy makers, care practitioners and the general public towards disability. Equal opportunities and anti-discrimination rights for people with impairments are now a relatively important political issue.

In the care sector, a greater awareness of equal opportunities issues has led to a shift in the way in which care relationships are understood, particularly in relation to the distribution of power and the process of decision-making. Greater 'user involvement' in decision-making and the provision of care services has developed out of the general disability rights movement. User involvement is now particularly strong in mental health and physical disability areas of service provision. Many new organisations of, rather than for, disabled people have developed out of the shift towards independent living, equal opportunities and improved rights.

The European influence

The various groups which experience prejudice and unequal treatment have done a lot to improve their own position and to gain legal rights and protection. However, since the mid-1970s the UK government's approach and response to unfair discrimination has been strongly influenced and shaped by the growing significance of European law.

The **European Union (EU)** has its origins in a need, and wish, for economic and social co-operation between European States. The European Union began formally with the Treaty of Rome 1958. The United Kingdom did not become a member of the European Economic Community (EEC), as the European Union was then called, until 1974. Since that time, Europe has had a formal and important influence on the development of laws that affect people in the United Kingdom (see p. 29).

Equality has always been an important principle in European Union initiatives. The EU, and its predecessor the EEC, has consistently sought to improve the rights and employment conditions of groups which experience less favourable treatment. Europe has played an important role in forcing British governments to change domestic laws to improve equality of opportunity for women, lesbians and gay men and equal treatment of employees generally. The EU currently supports several equality initiatives that aim to challenge prejudice, reduce unfair discrimination and improve opportunities for women, people with impairments and other socially excluded groups.

- The Now programme is aimed at women. It seeks to support job creation and self-employment, access to areas of work that women have traditionally been excluded from (for example, engineering), and work in areas of new technology.

- The Horizon programme aims to develop and support employment opportunities for people with disabilities. The programme supports training, job creation and self-employment initiatives.

- The Youthstart programme is targeted at people under 25. Programmes involve job training, work placements and job search programmes.

- The Integra programme focuses on the inclusion of socially excluded groups such as migrants, travellers, refugees and ethnic minority groups. One of the aims of the programme is to challenge racism and xenophobia.

Migration processes and social change have created a more culturally diverse society in the United Kingdom. As a result of the changing nature of our society, and the pressure from various communities for equality, it has become important for the government to protect individual rights and to promote equality of opportunity for everyone, irrespective of colour, nationality, ability, race, gender or sexual orientation. In the following pages, you will learn about the legislation, codes of practice, organisational policies and charters that have been developed to achieve this aim.

▼ This campaign poster draws attention to the fact that, in the UK, women's wages still lag behind those of their male counterparts

EQUAL OPPORTUNITIES COMMISSION

Prepare your daughter for working life.

Give her less pocket money than your son.

After 29 years of equal pay law, women's wages are still 20% lower than men's. www.eoc.org.uk

BUILD YOUR LEARNING

Keywords and phrases

You should know the meaning of the words and phrases listed below. If you are not sure about any of them, go back through the last eight pages of the unit to refresh your understanding.

- European Economic Community
- European Union
- First wave of feminism
- Immigration
- Integra project
- Migration
- Multicultural
- NOW programme
- Second wave of feminism
- Stonewall riots
- Treaty of Rome
- User involvement
- Youthstart programme

Summary points

- Historically, socially disadvantaged groups, including ethnic minorities, women and disabled people have struggled to raise awareness of prejudice and unfair discrimination against them.

- Legislative changes have granted some of these groups some protection from specific forms of unfair discrimination.

- Women have fought for equality of opportunity with men. The equality campaigns and feminist movement achieved significant improvements in women's legal rights during the twentieth century. The Equal Pay Act 1970 and the Sex Discrimination Act 1976 were important landmarks in women's equality struggle.

- Britain's ethnic minority population grew significantly in the 1950s, as immigration from the Caribbean and Indian subcontinent was encouraged by British governments eager to recruit more workers.

- The hostility and discrimination suffered by ethnic minority groups and their reactions against this eventually led to the Race Relations Act 1975. This offered some legal protection against unfair discrimination.

- Lesbians and gay men have actively campaigned for equal treatment and anti-discrimination laws since the 1960s. The gay rights movement has raised awareness of lesbian and gay issues but there is still no legislation making unfair discrimination on the grounds of sexual orientation unlawful.

- Disability discrimination has become an important political issue. Recent statutes such as the Disability Discrimination Act 1995 have improved the legal rights of disabled people in a number of areas.

- The European Union has introduced a range of initiatives to promote equality and improve the rights of marginalised groups. This has contributed to the improvement of equality rights in employment situations.

QUESTIONS

1 How did the first wave of feminism improve women's position in British society?

2 Where did most migrants to the United Kingdom during the 1950s originally come from?

3 What are the Stonewall riots said to have initiated?

4 What effect has the disability rights movement had on the relationship between carers and disabled people?

5 When did Europe's influence on the development of equal opportunities law in the United Kingdom begin?

The impact of unfair discrimination

WE LOOK NEXT AT WHAT CAN happen to people when they are unfairly discriminated against. On an individual level, the impact of unfair discrimination can have a profound psychological effect, though it is also the case that people experience unfair discrimination differently. We consider how an individual's self-esteem and sense of empowerment can be affected by the experience of unfair discrimination.

As well as having an impact at an individual level, unfair treatment and prejudice at an institutional and structural level has the effect of limiting the life chances and opportunities of whole social groups. We review evidence that shows that prejudice and unequal treatment have a negative effect on the educational, employment and health experiences of people from minority ethnic groups, women, people with impairments and older people as whole social groups.

Learning to discriminate

We begin by briefly reflecting on the origins of unfair discrimination. At the beginning of the unit (see p. 5) we said that people aren't born prejudiced, but that they learn their prejudices from others.

Babette Brown (1985) provides good reinforcement of this point when she begins her book *Unlearning Discrimination in the Early Years* with a quote from Nelson Mandela:

No one is born hating another person because of the colour of his skin or his background or his religion. People must learn to hate, and if they can learn to hate, they can be taught to love, for love comes more naturally to the human heart than its opposite.

Babette Brown left South Africa when it still had a regime that imposed **apartheid**. This was a racist system of deliberately and openly enforcing a strict segregation of black, coloured and white people. When Babette Brown came to Britain she says she found a different kind of racism. 'It was much more subtle, not entrenched by law, but very deeply rooted.' Brown established the Early Years Teachers Anti Racist Network (EYTARN) to challenge racism in early years work and continues to provide training and support for people to

▼ What point do you think this Commission for Racial Equality poster is making?

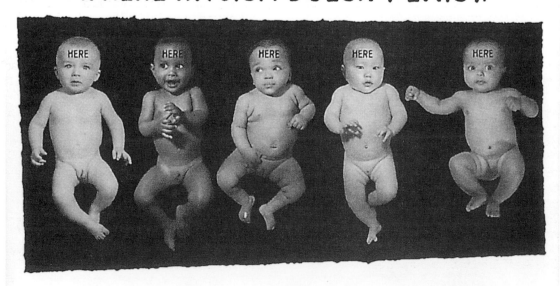

THERE ARE LOTS OF PLACES IN BRITAIN WHERE RACISM DOESN'T EXIST.

Figure 1.3: Sources of prejudice

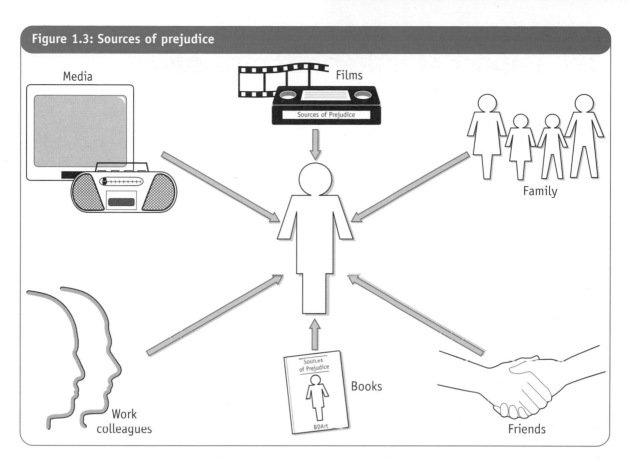

actively counteract the learning of prejudice and unfair discrimination.

The United Kingdom has never had an overt system of forced segregation between people like the apartheid system. Nevertheless, British society is divided, structured and unequal. People in less powerful social groups are more likely to experience prejudice and be the victims of unfair discrimination. How did the prejudices that exist in British society develop? What are the sources of the 'subtle but deeply rooted' racial prejudices that Babette Brown refers to?

People acquire their prejudices partly as a result of the messages and teaching they receive from their family, friends and work colleagues, from the media and from other sources of information such as books and films. During infancy, childhood and adolescence, people are socialised into the accepted attitudes and values of the groups and the broader society in which they live. The actions and attitudes of people who are influential in our development during infancy and childhood have an important effect on the range and depth of prejudices that we learn. However, as we mentioned earlier, prejudice and unfair discrimination are also rooted in and learnt from the ways in which organisations operate and the ways in which broader society is structured. In *Unlearning Discrimination in the Early Years*, Babette Brown says that:

Black children growing up in a racist society, receiving verbal and non-verbal messages that they are less valued and that less is expected from them, may not be motivated to learn. If they are constantly being presented with a 'white' world, they may find it more difficult to develop a sense of identity and feelings of personal worth. The pride and sense of belonging which they draw from their families and communities will limit the extent of the damage but, like all children, if they are not encouraged, valued, praised and expected to achieve, they many give up and stop trying.

This quote is a good indication of how deeply racial prejudice is rooted and of the powerful impact that this can have. Think about the various ways in which children also receive verbal and non-verbal messages that:

- men are more valued than women

- being able-bodied is better than being disabled

- being young is better than being old

- being lesbian or gay is unacceptable and shameful.

It is possible to understand how prejudices are learnt by the way that society operates.

ACTIVITY

Learning to discriminate unfairly

In 1963 Jane Elliott, a teacher in a small primary school in the United States of America, carried out an experiment. She divided the children in her class into two groups based on the colour of their eyes. On the first day of the exercise the blue-eyed children were told that they were the better group and were treated more favourably. They had more privileges, such as second helpings at lunchtime and five minutes extra playtime. Jane Elliott also ridiculed the brown-eyed children and continually put them down during the first day. On the second day she made the brown-eyed children the better group. This time they had all of the advantages and the blue-eyed children were told that they were the bottom group.

Imagine you were one of the children in Jane Elliott's class.

- How would you have felt on the day you were in the bottom group?

- How do you think you would have felt when you were told you were stupid because of the colour of your eyes?

- How do you think you would have reacted towards your friends when they were in the better group?

- How do you think you would you have felt when you were in the better group'?

The results of Jane Elliott's exercise were remarkable. The children reacted very strongly. Children of different eye colour who had previously been friends fought each other and joined in with putting each other down because of the colour of their eyes. When Jane Elliott carried out maths and word tests, the children who were in the better group did very well but the same children then did very badly when they were in the bottom group. The conclusions drawn from the experiment were that the children's self-image and self-esteem had been affected by the unfair discrimination that they had experienced. They performed badly when on the receiving end of eye-colour prejudice and better when they felt that they were a member of a better group of people.

Being aware of, and commenting on, difference is a normal part of children's cognitive development. Children do notice and point out physical differences between themselves and other children and adults. However, they don't naturally make the assumption that some features are better than others. They learn this from what they hear others say and what they observe. It is a mistake not to acknowledge difference but it is equally important to promote a sense of pride and positive self-worth rather than of superiority in terms of identity and background. We consider the negative emotional and psychological effects of prejudice and unfair discrimination next.

The effects of unfair discrimination on the individual

ACTIVITY

Bullying

Have you ever been bullied? Have any of your friends ever been affected by bullying? Either on your own or in pairs, write down what happened, how you felt then and how you feel about it now.

Do you remember feeling:

- angry?
- undermined?
- insecure?
- put down?
- hurt?
- insignificant?
- belittled?
- vengeful?
- defenceless?
- small?
- resentful?
- patronised?

Now think how it would feel if you were bullied all the time. How do you think it would affect you when you were at work or when you were trying to make friends or when you were at home with your family? Briefly reflect on how you think you would feel about yourself and other people.

Ford worker was racism victim

Peter Foster

Ford was again defending itself against charges of racism at its Dagenham car plant yesterday after admitting to an industrial tribunal that an Indian employee was repeatedly harassed on account of his colour.

Sukhjit Parma, 34, described how he had suffered almost four years of systematic racial abuse at the hands of his foreman and group leader while working at the east London engine plant. Mr Parma, a production operator, said senior staff had ignored his complaints as he was subjected to racist graffiti including the word 'Paki' daubed across his payslip and death threats accompanied by Ku Klux Klan symbols scrawled on a lavatory wall.

After complaining, he said he was made to work in an oil-spraying booth without protective clothing until he was sick, and was threatened with broken legs if he persisted with his allegations. His lunch was also kicked out of his hand by a colleague who objected to Indian food.

Bill Morris, General Secretary of the Transport and General Workers' Union, which assisted Mr Parma's case against Ford, said it was one of the most 'vicious and disturbing' encountered in the union's history. He said: 'Ford have been aware of the harassment and abuse Mr Parma has suffered but it was not until last Friday that two people were eventually disciplined, one being sacked and the other demoted.'

Yesterday, after a 30 minute hearing in Stratford, east London, at which Ford admitted liability, the company issued a brief statement of apology to Mr Parma. A second, similar case is being brought by another Dagenham worker.

Daily Telegraph, 24 September 1999

Being bullied is one example of how people are treated unfairly and less favourably in comparison to others. The emotional and psychological effects of bullying on the individual can be profound. A person's **self-image** and sense of **self-worth** can be reshaped, almost always in a negative way, by the experience of being bullied. If the bullying is an isolated incident, or is quickly dealt with, the person may only be affected temporarily. If the bullying or another form of unfair discrimination is experienced over a long period, the person's **self-confidence** and **self-esteem** is damaged by it.

The wider social effects of unfair discrimination

Research evidence suggests that prejudice and unfair discrimination have a negative effect on access to educational and work opportunities for a number of socially disadvantaged groups. Educational achievement and satisfying work roles are closely linked to people's sense of self-worth and self-esteem, regardless of the links that they have to practical factors, like income, that affect quality of life.

Racial prejudice and discrimination

Official government statistics regularly show that people from minority ethnic groups are more likely to be unemployed than white people (see Figure 1.4).

Figure 1.4 shows that in 1997–98 fewer than 7 per cent of white people were unemployed compared to 20 per cent of people who were black and 16 per cent of

Figure 1.4: Unemployment rates, 1997–98

	Percentage	
	Men	**Women**
White	6.5	5.0
All minority ethnic groups	14.1	13.1
Black	20.5	14.8
Indian	7.4	8.4
Pakistani/Bangladeshi	15.9	22.1
Other	15.0	14.0

Unemployment rates are for Great Britain, 1997–98.
Note that the sample size was too small to make accurate estimates of unemployment rates amongst Chinese people.
Source: Office for National Statistics, 1998

people from a Pakistani or Bangladeshi background. Research carried out by Colin Brown and Pat Gay (1985) found that when black, Asian and white people applied for the same jobs, there was a large difference in the rate of positive responses that they received. Ninety per cent of white applicants gained positive responses, while only 63 per cent of Asian and 63 per cent of African-Caribbean applicants received a positive response.

Black, Pakistani and Bangladeshi school pupils tend to do less well in achieving educational qualifications than others in the population (see Figure 1.5). The Swann Committee report, *Education for all* (1985),

revealed that white students gained the most from education, followed by African and Indian Asian students. Students of Bangladeshi and African-Caribbean origin gained the fewest qualifications and the least access to degree-level higher education. Lower natural ability and cultural (especially language) differences are not the reason for these differences. Bernard Coard (1971) has argued that the British education system fails black children, giving them an inferiority complex and a poor self-image. This is a very controversial claim that is both supported and contradicted by other, subsequent research investigations into racism in the education system.

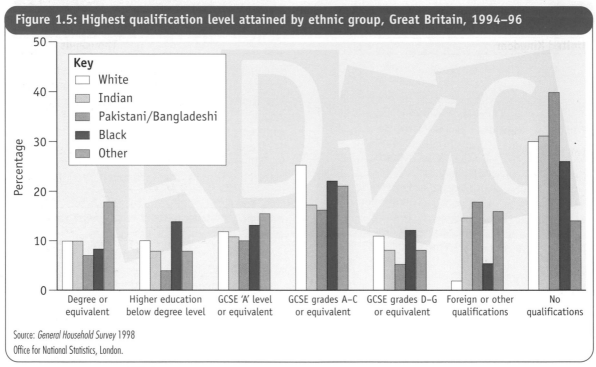

Figure 1.5: Highest qualification level attained by ethnic group, Great Britain, 1994–96

Source: *General Household Survey* 1998
Office for National Statistics, London.

Questions that may end pay gap

By Alexandra Frean

Working women are to be encouraged to ask male colleagues how much they earn as part of a campaign to eliminate the pay gap between men and women within 20 years.

Julie Mellor, chairwoman of the Equal Opportunities Commission, said that it was high time to lift the 'great British taboo' of talking about pay. The pay differential between men and women remains stuck at about 20 per cent. An EOC survey showed that more than three-quarters of employees had never asked colleagues what they earned.

Although women's earnings have risen by 24 per cent in real terms over the past ten years – compared with 14 per cent for men's earnings – the average weekly wage for women is £326, against £442 for men. Ms Mellor said that employers still assume that women are not main breadwinners and do not need as much as men.

Sunday Times,
27 October 1999

The impact of sex discrimination

Sexism and unfair discrimination against women has led to inequality of opportunity and under-representation of women in high status, higher paid jobs. Despite equal pay legislation (see p. 7) women still earn, on average, only about 80 per cent of what men earn. This is partly due to their overrepresentation in lower status, lower paid jobs and to the fact that women are more likely to work part time.

More women than ever are now in employment outside the home. Despite this, they still experience greater:

- vertical discrimination – within the same professions women are more likely to be in lower paid, lower status jobs than men and they are found lower down the same career ladder.

- horizontal discrimination – within all occupational areas women are overrepresented in low paid, low status service areas, including care work.

Educational opportunities for girls improved significantly during the 1970s and 1980s and deliberate efforts were made to break down gender bias and divisions in subject choice. Academically, girls generally

Figure 1.6: Enrolments in further education by subject group and gender, 1993–94

United Kingdom					Thousands
	Full time		Part time		All enrolments[1]
	Males	Females	Males	Females	All
Further education					
Combined and general[2]	131	141	200	359	831
Languages/humanities	35	57	111	251	453
Business and finance	60	84	79	206	429
Engineering and technology	76	5	213	18	312
Sciences	33	59	62	94	248
Education	8	6	25	42	81
Social Sciences	3	14	10	46	73
All enrolments[3]	360	379	720	1,033	2,494
Higher education					
Combined and general	61	74	8	11	154
Languages/humanities	66	96	10	14	186
Business and finance	77	76	67	64	285
Engineering and technology	124	23	70	8	225
Sciences[4]	145	121	40	111	416
Education[5]	21	58	15	35	128
Social Sciences	57	66	15	21	159
All enrolments[6]	550	514	282	319	1,664

1 Includes students in further education in Scotland whose gender is not recorded.
2 Includes GCSE, CSE and GCE courses.
3 Includes enrolments on unspecified courses.
4 Part time includes nursing and paramedic enrolments at Department of Health establishments.
5 Includes teacher training.
6 Part time includes Open University for which there is no subject breakdown.

Source: *Social Trends 26*, © Crown copyright 1996

do better than boys at school. However, there are more pronounced gender differences at higher education level with a clear gender imbalance in some subject areas (see Figure 1.6). Men significantly outnumber women at postgraduate level, with one in three men going on to postgraduate studies, compared to only one in five female students.

People with impairments

People with impairments experience a disproportionate amount of social deprivation. This results from their large-scale exclusion from paid employment and, to a lesser though still significant extent, from educational opportunities. In a study of employers' attitudes to people with impairments Morrell (1990) found that 91 per cent believed that employing people with impairments would be problematic, about two-thirds believed that the work they had was unsuitable for people with impairments, and just over 50 per cent believed that their premises were unsuitable. It is probably no surprise then that the unemployment rate for people with impairments is about three times as

high as for the general population and that the main source of income for three-quarters of people with impairments is State benefits. As the value of State benefits is only about 20 per cent of average earnings, people with impairments are much more likely than the general population as a whole to be living in poverty.

Children and young people with impairments have, historically, experienced poorer educational opportunities than other children. A separate system of 'special' education for children with impairments was developed in Victorian times and continues to exist, despite efforts to integrate children with impairments into mainstream schools and colleges. The segregated special school system denies children social and academic opportunities, particularly in respect of taking mainstream qualification courses. Robert Drake (1999) argues that many mainstream schools into which children with impairments are integrated have facilities that are inaccessible. He also argues that they adopt educational approaches and teaching practices that neglect the specific learning needs of children with impairments, but favour those pupils who can achieve high grades and league table points for their schools.

BUILD YOUR LEARNING

Keywords and phrases

You should know the meaning of the words and phrases listed below. If you are not sure of any of them go back through the last eight pages of the unit to refresh your understanding.

- Apartheid
- Horizontal discrimination
- Self-confidence
- Self-esteem
- Self-image
- Self-worth
- Vertical discrimination

Summary points

- Prejudice is not something that people are born with. It is learned from family, friends, work colleagues and the culture in which people live.

- When prejudice is expressed as unfair and less favourable treatment, abuse or harassment it can have a deep and damaging effect on the self-esteem, confidence and self-image of those at whom it is targeted.

- The broader impact of institutional and structural discrimination can be seen in the unequal and generally poorer achievements in education and employment of minority ethnic groups, women, and people with disabilities.

QUESTIONS

1 Identify three ways in which people learn to be prejudiced.

2 Describe the psychological effects that an experience of unfair discrimination might have.

3 Why are men more likely to gain highly paid, high status jobs than women? Use the terms horizontal and vertical discrimination somewhere in your answer.

4 How can the concept of institutional discrimination help to explain the lack of employment opportunities available to people with disabilities in the United Kingdom?

Legislation, policies and codes of practice

HEALTH, SOCIAL CARE AND EARLY years practitioners in the United Kingdom work within a **legal and ethical framework**. This means that care practitioners must follow and put into practice a range of laws, policies, codes of practice and charters in their work with service users. We look next at the different sources of equality law and the various methods through which these laws, and ethical values about what is right and wrong, and good and bad behaviour, are implemented by care organisations and care practitioners.

Sources of equality law in the United Kingdom

The laws that promote equality and protect equal rights in the United Kingdom come from a number of different sources. These sources include legislation passed by the British and European parliaments and decisions made by judges in British and European courts.

Legislation is the term given to **Acts of Parliament**, or **Statutes**, that have been passed by Parliament in the United Kingdom. A number of important pieces of legislation relating to equal opportunity and clients' rights have been enacted, or passed, by the United Kingdom Parliament. These include the Sex Discrimination Act 1975 and the Race Relations Act 1976. The way in which this kind of parliamentary legislation is developed is outlined in Figure 1.7.

Acts of Parliament set down the basic principles of law on particular issues, such as racial discrimination, in a formal, precise way. These legal principles are gradually tested and clarified when people bring cases of alleged unfair discrimination before courts of law. Judges then have to look at the facts of individual cases and decide whether and how the legal principles of the Act of Parliament can be applied. When a judge makes a decision that establishes a new legal principle, perhaps because a new situation or set of circumstances has arisen, they establish a **precedent**. This precedent, or decision, then applies to all cases in which the facts are the same as those of the original case. The series of precedents that have been established are collectively known as **case law**. The law on sex discrimination, racial discrimination and equal pay is now contained both in Acts of Parliament (The Sex Discrimination Act, Race Relations Act and Equal Pay Act, respectively) and in the case law that has been built up around each Act.

When the United Kingdom joined the European Economic Community (EEC) in 1974, European legislation and European Court of Justice decisions became new sources of law affecting equality of opportunity issues. There are three different classes of European law affecting equal opportunities issues.

- **Regulations**, which must be applied directly and in their entirety by all Member States of the European Union. They are the strongest forms of European law.

- **Directives**, which must be applied by Member States to make their national laws compatible with all other Member States on particular issues.

- **Decisions**, which are the decisions of the European Court to whom an individual or organisation has appealed against a decision of the courts in the United Kingdom. A decision of the European Court of Justice must be followed by courts in the United Kingdom.

The EEC has now become the European Union (EU). An important legal consequence of the United Kingdom's membership of the European Union is that European law now takes precedence over the domestic law of the United Kingdom. This means that whenever there is a conflict between EU law and UK law, European law will prevail. For example, in the case of *Marshall* v. *Southampton and South-West Hampshire Area Health Authority* [1986], Marshall claimed that the health authority sexually discriminated against women by adopting a policy that employees should retire at the state pension ages of 60 for women and 65 for men. Although this policy was legal under domestic, United Kingdom law, it was argued and agreed by the European Court of Justice, that it was contrary to the European law (Equal Treatment Directive 76/207) on the same issue.

European law has been a major influence in the development of equality and anti-discrimination law in the United Kingdom since the 1970s. Governments in the United Kingdom have been forced to introduce a variety of measures that have improved the employment rights and opportunities of women in particular (see Figure 1.8).

Care organisations and care practitioners have to abide by and incorporate into their work the various parts of the law that seek to promote equality of opportunity and to protect the rights of individuals. They do this in a variety of ways. For example, care organisations produce policies and charters that set out

Figure 1.7: How legislation is developed

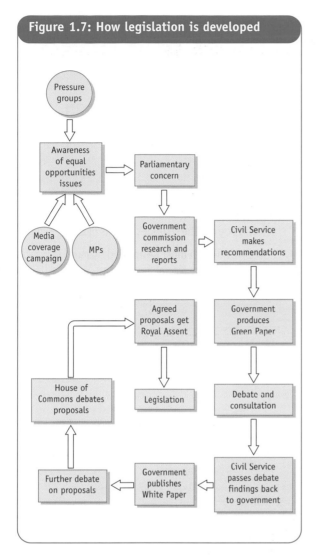

how they intend to offer their services and conduct their business. Care practitioners then have to make sure that they put the policies into practice in their work (see Figure 1.9). Policies, charters and codes of practice are discussed in more details later in the unit. Next we look at what the legislation relating to discrimination and rights actually says.

Figure 1.8: European legislation to improve women's employment rights

European legislation	Provisions
Equal Treatment Directive 76/207	Prevents discrimination on the grounds of 'marital or family status'
Employment Protection (Part-time employees) Regulations 1995	Gives all workers the same legal rights, regardless of the number of hours that they work
Pregnant Workers Directive 92/85	Gives all women the right to a minimum amount (14 weeks) of paid maternity leave regardless of their length of service
Equal Pay (Amendment) Regulations 1983	Allows women to claim equal pay for doing work that is of equal value to men employed in other jobs

Figure 1.9: Sources of law affecting women carers

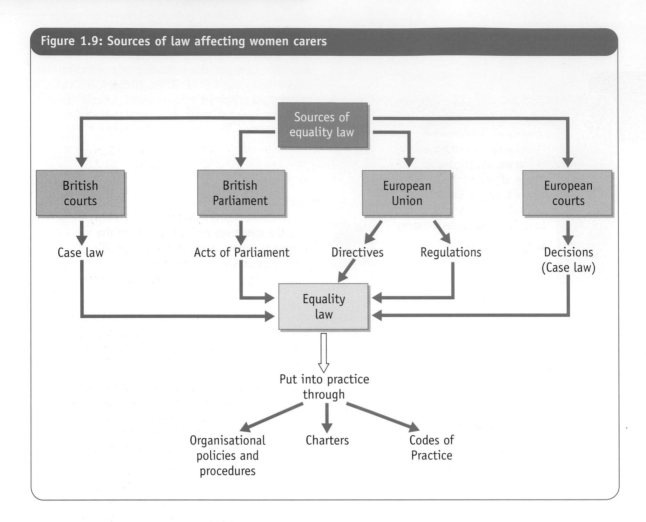

BUILD YOUR LEARNING

Keywords and phrases

You should know the meaning of the words and phrases listed below. If you are unsure about any of them, go back through the last four pages of the unit to refresh your understanding.

- Act of Parliament
- Case law
- Code of practice
- Decision
- Directive
- European Economic Community
- European Union
- Legal and ethical framework
- Legislation
- Organisational policy
- Precedent
- Regulation
- Royal Assent
- Statute

Summary points

- In the United Kingdom the right to equal treatment is enshrined in legislation and case law.

- Legislation refers to the Acts of Parliament, (such as the Sex Discrimination Act 1975) and the directives and regulations of the European Union, that set out the specific principles on which most equality of opportunity and anti-discrimination law is based.

- Case law refers to the decisions or precedents that are made when a feature of equality legislation is tested in a British court or in the European Court of Justice.

- A lot of United Kingdom law on equal rights and equal treatment has been developed as a result of decisions made in the European Court of Justice and the directives and regulations passed by the European Union.

- European Union law now takes precedence over UK legislation and case law. When a decision or directive on an equality issue is made in the European Union, UK law has to be changed to accommodate it.

- Health and social care organisations have to produce policies on equality of opportunity issues. These organisational policies are supposed to incorporate the key points of equality law.

QUESTIONS

1 Care practitioners work within a legal and ethical framework. Explain what this means.

2 What is legislation? Give two examples of anti-discrimination legislation in your answer.

3 What is a legal precedent? Use the term case law and explain who makes precedents in your answer.

4 Identify two forms of European legislation that are part of equality law in the United Kingdom.

Legislation about discrimination and rights

THE MOST SIGNIFICANT RECENT legislative developments in the area of anti-discrimination and equal rights have been the Sex Discrimination Acts 1975 and 1986, and the Race Relations Act 1976. These statutes outlawed unfair discrimination in employment on the basis of gender and race. There are a number of other Acts protecting everyone's equality interests and a number that protect the rights of specific groups who use care services. Examples of such Acts are shown in Figure 1.10.

We look first at the impact of equality legislation on citizens of the United Kingdom generally and then at how specific provisions are used to protect the rights of users of care services.

Legislation relating to equal rights is based on the principle of **equality of opportunity**. That is, individuals should be treated equally and fairly in comparison with others regardless of their physical or social characteristics, apart from in specifically excepted circumstances (see p. 6). We are going to look in detail at equality of opportunity law in relation to race, sex and disability.

Race relations law

The **Race Relations Act 1976** is the key statute promoting racial equality and making racial discrimination illegal. It defines racial discrimination as less favourable treatment on racial grounds and identifies several ways in which such treatment may occur. A person racially discriminates against another if:

- he or she treats the person less favourably than he or she treats, or would treat another person on racial grounds or

- he or she applies a requirement, or condition to that other person which is such that the proportion of the person's racial group which can comply with it is considerably smaller than the proportions of persons not of their racial group; and

- which he or she cannot show to be justified irrespective of the colour, race, nationality or ethnic or national origins of the person to whom it is applied and

- which is to the detriment of certain people because they cannot comply with it.

The Race Relations Act 1976 aims not only to eradicate racial discrimination but also to promote equal opportunities. Under the Act, it is unlawful for employers to discriminate unfairly in the selection of staff, the arrangements made for recruitment, promotion, training or transfer, and in the terms and

Figure 1.10: Equality legislation

General equality legislation	Care-related 'rights' legislation
The Disabled Persons (Employment) Acts 1944 and 1958,	The Chronically Sick and Disabled Persons Act 1970
The Equal Pay Act 1970 The Equal Pay Act 1975	The Education (Handicapped Children) Act 1981
The Employment Protection Act 1975,	The Mental Health Act 1983 The Mental Health (Scotland) Act 1984
Sex Discrimination Act 1975 and 1986	The Data Protection Act 1984
Race Relations Act 1976	The Access to Personal Files Act 1987
The Disabled Persons (Services, Consultation and Representation) Act 1986	The Access to Health Care Records Act 1990
The Disability Discrimination Act 1995	The Children Act 1989 The Children (Scotland) Act 1995
	The NHS and Community Care Act 1990

conditions of employment and dismissal that they apply. The Race Relations Act 1976 identifies several ways in which such unfair, discriminatory treatment may occur.

Direct discrimination

To treat a person less favourably than another person is or would be treated in the same or similar circumstances on racial grounds is known as **direct discrimination**. The motive or intention behind such treatment is irrelevant. For example, it would be unlawful for a nursing home or any residential care setting to refuse to admit a person as a resident simply because he or she is black, white or Asian or because of the colour of his or her skin. It is also unlawful for a residential home or care setting to set quotas for people from specific ethnic groups or to reserve places on a racial basis.

Segregation

Section 1(2) of the Race Relations Act 1976 makes it unlawful for a person to be **segregated** from others on racial grounds. This would amount to less favourable treatment. For example, grouping people for activities or arranging attendance at day centres according to racial group, and for no other reason, would be unlawful.

Indirect discrimination

Section 1(1) (b) of the Race Relations Act 1976 says that applying a requirement or condition which, although applied equally to all racial groups, means that only a considerably smaller proportion of a particular racial group can comply with it, is unlawful. The Act says that such a condition would be to that group's detriment and is unfair discrimination if the condition cannot be justified on grounds that are not racial. For example, in the much publicised case of *Mandla* v. *Dowell Lee* [1983], a school made it compulsory for pupils to wear a cap as part of the school uniform. This rule had the effect of excluding Sikh boys, who are required by their faith to wear a turban. The House of Lords decided that the rule was not justifiable and that it constituted unlawful and **indirect discrimination**.

Another example of indirect racial discrimination occurred when an employer told an employment agency that his care setting only wanted people who spoke good English without a foreign accent. Although the employer did not specify that he would employ white people only, the effect of the condition was to exclude many people from minority ethnic groups and was unlawful.

Victimisation

People are unfairly discriminated against if they are **victimised**. Section 2 of the Race Relations Act 1976 states that people are victimised if they:

- are treated less favourably than others in the same circumstances because it is suspected or known that they have taken action against an employer or another person under the Race Relations Act or

- have given evidence or information in a situation where discrimination has allegedly occurred.

For example, to refuse a child a nursery place because his or her parents have complained previously about racial discrimination at the nursery would be unlawful. Similarly, to refuse an employee promotion because he or she had complained about a particular incident relating to alleged discrimination would also be unlawful.

The definition of racial discrimination that is given on p. 33 refers to less favourable treatment on racial grounds. **Racial grounds** means discrimination on the basis of colour, race, nationality, or ethnic or national origin.

Incitement of racial hatred

It is a criminal offence to use threatening, abusive, or insulting words in a public place. It is also an offence to publish or distribute threatening, abusive or insulting written material in circumstances in which racial hatred is likely to be stirred up. It does not matter whether the person accused intended to incite people to racial hatred or not. A person who feels so affected must bring an action under the **Crime and Disorder Act 1998**. Under this Act, judges are obliged to take note of any cases with racial overtones and if it is found that there is any degree of racism in the facts, punishment will be reflected in the sentence.

Sexual equality law

The **Sex Discrimination Acts 1975** and **1986** are the key statutes promoting sexual equality and making sexual discrimination illegal. They define sexual discrimination in a similar way to racial discrimination, as less favourable treatment on grounds of gender or marital status. They identify the same ways in which less favourable treatment may occur (direct and indirect discrimination). The Acts apply to both men and women. Women have benefited most from them as they face greater prejudice and experience more unfair discrimination on grounds of gender than men.

Applying equal opportunities law

Jenny Lopez is a health visitor who is planning to return to work after a three-year career break to have a child. She tells you that she is going to put an advertisement in the local paper and the newsagent's window for a Spanish-speaking childminder.

■ Is Jenny discriminating unfairly against childminders who do not speak Spanish?

■ Will Jenny be breaking the law relating to racial discrimination?

NECESITAMOS NIÑERA!

Spanish-speaking childminder required to care for lively, but well-behaved toddler – weekdays only, 9 – 6.
Call Jenny 01812 307465

The inclusion of marital status was an important feature of the Sex Discrimination Act 1975. The reason for including this alongside gender is to prevent employers from making, and acting upon, assumptions that married women are more likely to have childcare responsibilities, and are therefore less reliable or less committed employees, than unmarried women.

The Sex Discrimination Act 1986 brought Britain's sex equality laws into line with the rest of Europe. The original Sex Discrimination Act 1975 was amended in 1986 so that sex discrimination in employment in private households, in small firms, and in retirement age was outlawed.

Sexual harassment

Sexual harassment is one of the most offensive and demeaning experiences an employee can suffer. It conflicts fundamentally with the principle of equal treatment of men and women at work. Both men and women are victims but overwhelmingly, it is women who are victims of sexual harassment.

The European Commission's code of practice on sexual harassment defines it as unwanted conduct of a sexual nature or other conduct based on sex affecting the dignity of women and men at work. Examples of unacceptable behaviour include, physical or non-verbal conduct of a sexual nature, conversations or comments of a sexual nature, public display of sexually offensive material and actions which ridicule or denigrate people because of their gender. The European Commission code of practice states that sexual harassment may be an unlawful breach of the Equal Treatment Directive and that it may also be a breach of criminal law.

Sexual harassment policies

Prevention of sexual harassment should be seen as an integral part of good management practice in any care or business organisation. Managers should aim to ensure that their staff are treated with dignity and respect. Many health and social care organisations are committed to creating environments in which all employees can seek, obtain and hold employment without any form of unfair discrimination or harassment. In this regard, most operate a sexual harassment policy that is an extension of their commitment to equal opportunities. This policy should outline the responsibility of the organisation, senior management and all employees with respect to sexual harassment in order to promote a healthy working environment. It should aim to assist managers and employees in dealing effectively with problems of sexual harassment at work.

Pay and employment protection

The **Equal Pay Act 1970** is designed to prevent unfair discrimination between men and women with regard to the terms and conditions of employment. Where a woman is employed in like work or in work that is of equal value to that of a man, she should be given equal treatment as regards pay.

Equal pay has been the subject of a significant proportion of industrial tribunal cases. An **industrial tribunal** is a special form of court that hears cases that relate specifically to employment situations. Equal pay has also become one of the major areas where European Union law has been used, with many cases being taken to the European Court of Justice.

▲ It is illegal to dismiss a woman employee simply because she is pregnant

Coupled with the Equal Pay Act is the **Employment Protection (Consolidation) Act 1978 (EPCA)** which also aims to protect the rights of employees. Under this Act, a female employee has the right not to be dismissed simply because of pregnancy. Section 60 of the EPCA 1978 provides that a dismissal is automatically unfair if the reason for the dismissal is pregnancy or any other reason connected to it, (such as a miscarriage for example), unless the employer can prove that:

- the woman was incapable of doing her work adequately because of her pregnancy or

- that she could not carry on working without breaking other legal rules relating to women or

- that there was no suitable alternative work for her to do.

The EPCA 1978 also provides that women must be allowed to return to work after paid maternity leave, having notified the employer of a return date.

In the past, employees were expected to be in the same employment for a continuous period of two years before taking action against an employer for unfair dismissal. Recent legislation has reduced this to one year in the same continuous employment.

The legal position of lesbian and gay people

Lesbians and gay men have the same legal rights as heterosexuals under general equality laws such as the Sexual Discrimination Acts and the Race Relations Act. However, while members of the lesbian and gay community do experience unfair discrimination and harassment because of their sexual orientation there are no specific laws to outlaw this or to protect them specifically. The laws relating to lesbians and gay men actually impose restrictions on them and thereby cause them to have unequal rights in comparison to heterosexual people (see Figure 1.11).

Disability legislation

People with physical, mental and sensory impairments have the same legal rights as any other person under the provisions of general anti-discriminatory legislation such as the Sex Discrimination Act 1975 and the Race Relations Act 1976. However, until recently there have been few legal provisions outlawing unfair discrimination of the basis of disability. The key piece of legislation that now offers some legal protection, and makes unfair discrimination in certain areas unlawful on the specific grounds of disability, is the **Disability Discrimination Act 1995**.

The Act introduced new rights to reduce unfair discrimination on the grounds of disability (what we call impairment). The Act concentrated on rights in the three main areas of employment, access to goods and services and the sale or rental of land or property.

Employment

Under the Act, it became unlawful for employers to treat people less favourably because of their physical, mental or sensory impairment. Unfortunately this part of the Act only applies to employers who employ 20 or more people. As this amounts to less than 10 per cent of employers in the United Kingdom, most cannot be prevented from discriminating unfairly on the grounds of impairment.

Figure 1.11: Restrictions of the rights of lesbians and gay men

Area of legal rights	Heterosexual rights	Lesbian/Gay restrictions
Age of consent	16 for both men and women	18 for gay men. There is no legal rule regarding gay women
Marriage	Men and women can legally marry after the age of 16	Same-sex partners cannot legally marry at any age
Adoption of children	Married opposite sex partners can jointly legally adopt a child	Same-sex partners cannot jointly legally adopt a child
Taxation	Married men and women can claim additional tax allowances	Same-sex partners cannot claim married person's additional tax allowance
Pension rights	Married person acquires the pension right/benefits of partner on their death	Same-sex partners have no legal rights to partner's pension benefits
Next of kin status	Married couples have the right to act as each other's next of kin	No legal right to next of kin status
Employment in the armed forces	Heterosexuality is an acceptable form of sexual expression in the armed forces	Until 28 September 1999 it was a criminal offence to be a practising or 'out' gay person in the armed forces
Immigration	Opposite-sex married couples have legal rights to obtain entry to UK for their non-British partner	Same-sex non-British partners have no legal right of entry on grounds of their relationship
Promotion of sexuality	Heterosexuality is promoted in schools as the natural and best form of sexual orientation	It is an offence under Section 28 of the Local Government Act 1988 to 'intentionally promote homosexuality' as an acceptable form of sexual orientation in schools

Access to goods and services

Refusal to serve people or to supply them with goods because they have a physical, mental or sensory impairment is unlawful under the Act. It is also unlawful to offer such people a lower standard of service or poorer quality goods or terms of sale.

Selling or letting land or property

It is unlawful under the Act for people who are selling or letting land or property to treat people with impairments less favourably because of their impairment.

The Act also set up the National Disability Council (see p. 64) and gave it advisory powers to support the implementation of the key provisions.

The **Disabled Persons (Employment) Acts 1944 and 1958** made provision for the employment rights of people with impairments. The Acts provided that where there were more than 20 people employed in any one company or firm, it was incumbent upon the employer to make sure that at least three per cent of the workforce were considered 'disabled'. Employers were exempt from prosecution if they could show that there was no suitable employment for people with impairments, or that people with impairments had not applied. The provisions of the Acts were not actively applied and were hardly enforced through court cases. Drake (1999) explains that only ten prosecutions were ever brought under the Act and that government departments were among the worst offenders. In 1994, the Department of Health employed 68 people with impairments, a mere 1.4 per cent of its staff. The quota provisions of these Acts were abolished by the Disability Discrimination Act 1995.

The **Disabled Persons (Services, Consultation and Representation) Act 1986** requires local authorities to provide potential service users and their relatives with information about the services and facilities for people with impairments that are available in their area. The aim is to give such people the opportunity to take full advantage of them and continue to live independent lives in the community. Under the Act, local authorities have a duty to:

- identify the people with impairments in their area

- assess their needs

- provide resources and facilities to meet those needs

- monitor and review needs and service provision.

The **Chronically Sick and Disabled Persons Act 1970** and the **Education (Handicapped Children) Act 1981** both include provisions that aim to protect the rights and promote equality for people with specific forms of impairment in care-related settings. The details are outlined next, as we move on to look at service users' rights in care settings.

ACTIVITY

Why is it unlawful?

Read through each of the following scenarios and then, using your understanding of equal rights legislation, decide whether the action taken breaches the legal rights of the individual or people concerned. If you think that it does, explain why.

- A local bus driver refuses to stop and let people standing outside the local psychiatric hospital on to the bus because he says they're not right in the head and they don't always pay.

- A shopkeeper won't allow an older woman who is a wheelchair user into his shop until after 7 p.m. because he says she's too slow and that she holds everyone up during the day.

- A zoo won't allow a group of children with severe physical and learning disabilities to enter, on the grounds that they will frighten the animals.

- A landlord charges a woman an additional wear and tear fee on top of her deposit when he lets her a ground floor flat, because she is a wheelchair user.

- A woman's application to legally adopt her same-sex partner's daughter is refused by social services.

BUILD YOUR LEARNING

Keywords and phrases

You should know the meaning of the words and phrases listed below. If there are any that you are not sure about, go back through the last six pages of the unit to refresh your understanding.

- Chronically Sick and Disabled Persons Act 1970
- Crime and Disorder Act 1998
- Direct discrimination
- Disability Discrimination Act 1995
- Disabled Persons (Employment) Acts 1944 and 1958
- Disabled Persons (Services, Consultation and Representation) Act 1986
- Education (Handicapped Children) Act 1981
- Employment Protection (Consolidation) Act 1978
- Equal Pay Act 1970
- Indirect discrimination
- Industrial tribunal
- Race Relations Act 1976
- Racial grounds
- Segregation
- Sex Discrimination Acts 1975 and 1986
- Sexual harassment
- Victimisation

Summary points

- The Sex Discrimination Act 1975 and Race Relations Act 1976 were major landmarks in the area of employment-related equality law. Since this time a number of statutes have outlawed unfair discrimination in other areas and have introduced rights to protect users of care services.

- The Race Relations Act 1976 outlawed direct and indirect discrimination on racial grounds. It also outlawed segregation and victimisation on racial grounds.

- The Crime and Disorder Act 1998 made incitement of racial hatred a criminal offence.

- The Sex Discrimination Act 1975 made unfavourable treatment on the grounds of a person's sex unlawful in employment situations.

- Women have also benefited from legislation on the issues of equal pay and maternity rights.

- Lesbians and gay men have the same general rights as heterosexual people but do not currently have specific protection from unfair discrimination and harassment on grounds of their sexual orientation.

- Laws actually impose restrictions on lesbians and gay men, causing them to have unequal rights in comparison to heterosexual people.

- The Disability Discrimination Act 1995 made less favourable treatment on grounds of disability unlawful. This Act extended the specific rights and protection of people with disabilities.

QUESTIONS

1 Name the four different forms of unfair discrimination that are outlawed by the Race Relations Act 1976.

2 Give two examples of the less favourable treatment of women in employment situations that was made unlawful under the Sex Discrimination Act 1975.

3 Can a woman be legally dismissed from her job when she becomes pregnant? Refer to appropriate legislation in your answer.

4 What is sexual harassment?

5 What is the key statute that makes less favourable treatment of people with impairments unlawful?

Service users' rights and care law

PEOPLE WHO USE HEALTH, social care and early years services now do so in the belief that care practitioners, and the organisations they work for, will put service users' interests first and will not mistreat or unfairly discriminate against them. Users of care services have become more aware of their rights over the years and their expectations of care services are now much higher than previously. Care service users' rights and interests are now protected through:

- the law – specific statutes have been enacted on a range of care-related issues

- government charters, such as the Patients' Charter

- codes of practice and codes of conduct of regulatory bodies such as the United Kingdom Central Council for Nursing, Health Visiting and Midwifery and the College of Occupational Therapists

- organisational policies and procedures.

Care-related legislation

The protection of clients' rights in care situations is an area of considerable importance within care work. These are some of the statutes that exist to protect the rights and interests of health and social care service users.

- The Mental Health Act 1983 and the Mental Health (Scotland) Act 1984 protect people who are experiencing mental illness from the risk of harm to themselves and from harming other individuals and groups in society.

- The Children Act 1989 and the Children (Scotland) Act (1995) protect the welfare and safety of children.

- The Data Protection Act 1984 protects access to information and confidentiality of personal information.

- The Access to Personal Files Act 1987 deals with access to and confidentiality of information.

- The Access to Health Care Records Act 1990 gives service users the right of access to their medical information and files.

- The NHS and Community Care Act 1990 ensures that service users are sufficiently catered for in the community. It incorporates the principles of empowerment, risk assessment and the preservation of independence.

All care practitioners owe service users a duty of care and are under a legal obligation to ensure that they observe the requirements of the legislation listed above. We look next at the main provisions of statutes that are designed to protect users of care services from any infringement of their rights.

Child protection law

Issues relating to children's rights are covered by legislation that includes a number of specific legal provisions. Childcare law was brought together and simplified by the **Children Act 1989** in England, Wales and Northern Ireland and by the **Children (Scotland) Act 1995**. These statutes have the primary aim of strengthening the legal position of children by giving them certain legal rights whilst imposing legal duties on parents and childcare workers to protect children from any form of abuse and to promote their welfare.

The Children Act 1989 aims to protect those children who are felt to be in need or at risk. These are children whose health and welfare may suffer significantly without support from social services. All children with disabilities are included in this definition. Local authorities are required to ensure that children's welfare is protected and that appropriate services are provided to meet their identified needs. The **paramountcy principle** is a key feature of the Children Act 1989. It means that the rights, wishes and feelings, interests and welfare of children should be given paramount (the most) importance and should always be put first by their family, social services and the courts. Where children are mature or old enough to express their wishes, they have a right to be consulted about what they actually want.

Mental health legislation

Mental illness and learning disability are very different and require significantly different care provision and intervention approaches from care practitioners. However, the law and many ethical issues relating to service users who have a mental illness or learning disability is very similar.

The **Mental Health Act (1983)** and the **Mental Health (Scotland) Act (1984)** are the key statutes affecting care and treatment and service users' rights in these areas. The two Mental Health Acts only affect service users who are compulsorily admitted to or detained in hospital. The majority of people with mental health problems or learning disabilities are not detained against their will. This process is often described as **sectioning**, as the key provisions that allow detention and treatment against a person's will are contained in the various sections of the Acts. The key sections of each Act and the conditions associated with them are outlined in Figure 1.12.

The Mental Health Acts have a number of safeguards built into them to protect the rights of service users who are particularly vulnerable because of their mental impairment or illness. For example, an application to detain a person in hospital can only be made by the person's nearest relative, an approved social worker (ASW), or a mental health officer (as they are called in Scotland). Usually, the person can then only be compulsorily admitted on the recommendation of two specially qualified medical practitioners after they have carried out a detailed assessment of the person's mental state.

The compulsory treatment of people with mental illness and people with learning disability is an area that raises major ethical issues. Depriving people of their liberty involves a major infringement of their normal rights. Compulsory treatment goes against the ethical principle of gaining informed consent and obtaining permission before any intervention can take place. As a result, the Mental Health Acts contain a

▲ Health records must always be treated as confidential

number of provisions that give service users the right to appeal against their detention in hospital to a body called the **Mental Health Review Tribunal**. The **Mental Health Act Commission**, and the **Mental Welfare Commission in Scotland**, are government bodies that also have the role of ensuring that the legislation is applied and implemented properly and that service users' welfare is given appropriate consideration.

Access to information

Health and social care service users have the statutory right to see their records. There are a few circumstances in which access to personal files compiled and held by care professionals can be denied, but generally service users have the right to know what information their records contain.

The **Data Protection Act 1984** established clear principles about the use of, and access to, automated (computerised) records. **Data users**, such as NHS trusts and local authority social services departments, are

Figure 1.12: Key provisions allowing detention and treatment of mentally ill people

Mental Health Act (1983) (England, Wales and Northern Ireland)

Section	Purpose of detention	Length of time it applies	Right of appeal
2	Assessment	28 days	Yes, within 28 days
3	Treatment	6 months	Yes, at any time
4	Emergency	72 hours	
5 (2)	Doctors holding power	72 hours	
5 (4)	Nurses holding power	6 hours	

Mental Health Act (Scotland) 1984

Section	Purpose of detention	Length of time it applies	Right of appeal
18	Application through Sheriff Court		6 months
24	Emergency admission	72 hours, can be extended to 28 days	

required to register their records and use of service users' personal data with the Data Protection Registrar. They must then comply with the following Data Protection Act principles. Personal data must be:

- collected and processed fairly and lawfully

- only held for specific, lawful registered purposes

- only used for registered purposes or disclosed to registered recipients

- adequate and relevant to the purpose for which it is held

- accurate and, where necessary, kept up to date

- held no longer than is necessary for the stated purpose

- surrounded by appropriate security

- subject to a right of access by the data subject (to records held about him or herself).

Service users are entitled to know whether any information about them is being held by a care organisation. If it is, they have the right to apply to see and be given access to a copy of the information. Access to health records can be denied where the disclosure of the contents would:

- be likely to cause serious harm to the physical or mental health of the data subject

- reveal the identify of others (not including care professionals) who have provided information in confidence and who have not consented to it or their identity being disclosed.

Permission to see personal health records has to be sought from and given by the medical practitioner who is responsible for service users' care. Applications must be made in writing and a fee must be paid. Unless the exception principles apply, applicants are entitled to a copy of the information contained in their records within 40 days of application. If this is not forthcoming they can go to court to enforce their legal right or obtain enforcement from the Data Protection Registrar.

The **Access to Medical Reports Act 1988** gives health service users the right to see and correct their medical records in cases where an employer or insurance company has applied for a medical report on them. Access can be denied for the same reasons as in the Data Protection Act 1984.

The **Access to Health Records Act 1990** filled a rights gap left by the Data Protection Act, which only covered automated records. The 1990 Act gave statutory access rights to records that are produced and held in manual (non-computerised) form. This actually applies to most health records. In general, the 1990 Act

does not give right of access to records produced before 1 November 1991, when it came into force. It should also be noted that the 1990 Act does not apply to other non-health records, such as those held by social services departments.

The following people have the right of access to their own or another person's health records:

- the service user (or data subject) whom the record is about

- a person authorised in writing to make an application on the service user's behalf

- a person who has parental authority over a service user who is under 16 years of age

- a person appointed by a court to manage the affairs of a service user

- the executor of a deceased person's estate.

A record can be kept from a service user if:

- it is a medical record that was written before 1 November 1991, unless it helps to explain something written after that date

- the record holder believes that access is likely to cause the patient or another person serious physical or mental harm

- the record would disclose that a person had been born as a result of treatment within the meaning of the Human Fertilization and Embryology Act 1990

- the record contains information that the patient expressly stated must not be revealed

- the record related to anybody other than a doctor or health professional unless his or her consent has been given

- the record holder thinks that a patient under 16 cannot understand what the application to see records means.

The **Access to Personal Files Act 1987** is the statute which covers housing and social services records. Application procedures and rights are very similar to those of the 1990 Act and access to records can be denied on similar grounds.

Ideally, health and social care professionals would disclose all relevant information to service users and keep them informed about all matters relating to their care or treatment. It should not really be necessary for service users to have to make a formal application to see their records. They can be granted access informally. As there are relatively few formal applications to see health and other personal care files, it would appear that this is what happens in practice.

BUILD YOUR LEARNING

Keywords and phrases

You should know the meaning of the words and phrases listed below. Go back through the last four pages of the unit to refresh your understanding.

- Approved social worker
- Children at risk
- Children in need
- Data user
- Data subject
- Mental Health Act Commission
- Mental health officer
- Mental Health Review Tribunal
- Mental Welfare Commission
- Paramountcy principle
- Sectioning

Summary points

- The rights of users of care services are contained in a number of statutes that aim to give them specific legal protection against unfair treatment.

- The Children Act 1989 is the key statute that aims to protect children who are in need and at risk. It introduced the paramountcy principle in order to ensure that the welfare and wishes of the child are always put first.

- Mental health legislation aims to protect the rights of service users and give protection to mental health workers and the general public. The Mental Health Acts set out the law on compulsory detention in hospital and rights of appeal against detention.

- A number of statutes give health and social care service users the right to access records containing information about them that are held by care organisations. These legal rights are enforceable in court, except where there is a justifiable reason to deny service users access to part or all of their records.

QUESTIONS

1 What is the paramountcy principle?

2 Why are some people sectioned under the Mental Health Acts?

3 What happens when a person is sectioned under the Mental Health Act 1983?

4 Name two organisations that exist to monitor the welfare and protect the rights of people detained in mental hospitals.

5 Which pieces of legislation give you the right to apply to see the medical records about you which are produced and held by your GP?

Putting equality law into practice

The laws that promote equal rights and equality of opportunity principles are incorporated in a number of different types of document that can be found in care settings and which are widely used by care practitioners in their work. These include:

- government charters that identify entitlement to services and define national standards of care that service users can expect to receive

- codes of practice produced by bodies such as the Commission for Racial Equality and the Equal Opportunities Commission

- codes of conduct, produced by bodies such as the UKCC, which regulate the work of registered care professionals

- organisational policies produced by individual care organisations and which apply to all of their employees.

Each of these types of document imposes responsibilities on care practitioners and the managers of care organisations. Failure to implement, or breaches of, their provisions can lead care practitioners and care organisations to face a variety of possible sanctions or punishments.

Charters and national standards

The government has produced national guidelines setting out the rights and standards of service that all users of public services in England and Wales can expect to receive. The Citizen's Charter aims to improve standards of public service at all levels and to give the public more information about government departments and statutory organisations. Under the Citizen's Charter we can expect public services to:

- set out and publish minimum standards of service

- be more open and provide more information

- provide choice and consult service users where possible

- provide polite and helpful service at all times

- put things right when they go wrong

- give value for money.

The Patient's Charter puts the Citizen's Charter into practice in the National Health Service and social services settings. It aims to help service providers to:

- listen to, identify and respond to service users' views and needs

- set clear standards of service

- provide services that meet those standards.

Under the provisions of the Patient's Charter, all statutory health and care agencies such as health centres, hospitals and clinics must provide the general public with services of a specified standard.

▲ The Patient's Charter ensures equal access to care

The Citizen's and Patient's Charters are based on equality of opportunity principles. They implicitly incorporate the principle of equal and fair treatment of all people regardless of race, gender, sexual orientation, ability or age.

Charters give assurances to service users that certain services will be provided by care organisations within given time scales and to specified quality standards. They do not, however, give legal rights and are not enforceable in court. Complaints about the failure of an organisation to fulfil its charter promises have to be dealt with by using the organisation's complaints procedures.

Codes of practice

In a care context, codes of practice are sets of rules or guidelines that aim to ensure that care staff implement specific policies, procedures or pieces of legislation. **Codes of practice** are drawn up by individual care organisations and by bodies such as the Commission for Racial Equality and the Equal Opportunities Commission as part of their remit under the law.

The Commission for Racial Equality and the Equal Opportunities Commission both produce codes of practice that outline sets of procedures for implementing equal opportunity policies in employment. These codes of practice do not, in themselves, impose any legal obligations on employers. However, failure to observe the guidance within them may result in breaches of the law where an employer's or employee's action or failure to do something falls within any of the specific prohibitions of the Race Relations Act or the Sex Discrimination Acts. For example, employers must take steps that are outlined in the codes of practice to prevent their employees committing acts of unlawful discrimination.

Codes of conduct are guidelines for professional and ethical practice that are produced and issued by the regulatory bodies of the various care professions. They aim to define principles of best practice, serve to protect service users' rights and ensure that they receive the highest possible standards of care. The United Kingdom Central Council for Nursing, Health Visiting and Midwifery (UKCC) code of conduct (see Figure 1.13) is an example of this kind of professional guideline. All registered nurses are required to be aware of and work within the ethical framework of the UKCC code of conduct. Other care professions that run a registration scheme, such as doctors, occupational therapists and physiotherapists, have similar codes of practice. Professionals who fail to follow, or who deliberately breach their professional body's code of conduct can be brought before a disciplinary hearing. In some circumstances the practitioner can be struck off the register and be prevented from practising.

The role of organisational policies

In order to ensure that service users' legal rights are observed, and that a high standard of care is provided to all service users, health and social care organisations devise policies for care practitioners to follow. Service users' legal rights and equality of opportunity principles are written into these documents to promote anti-discriminatory practice and reduce the possibility of unfair or unlawful treatment.

A **policy** is a detailed statement of the approach that an organisation will adopt towards a particular issue. It is like a statement of intent and it details what the organisation aims to achieve. For example, an equal opportunities policy is a statement of belief and a plan of intended action on the broad issue of equality of opportunity within a particular organisation. Equal opportunities policies should include the following:

- a statement of the organisation's position on equal opportunities

- definitions of unfair discrimination, victimisation and harassment

- statements of the organisation's policy on:

  – employment terms and conditions

  – recruitment, promotion and training

  – how harassment and victimisation will be dealt with

- details of who is responsible for the specific implementation of the policy.

A **procedure** is a written instruction about what must happen in a certain situation. Care organisations write procedure manuals to give employees specific instructions on how to implement the organisation's policies.

Organisational policies and procedures are affected by legislation that details what is legally required in specific circumstances. For example, care organisations are required by law to establish policies and procedures on equal opportunities, service users' access to their records, notification and reporting of accidents and incidents in the workplace and the safe storage of dangerous substances and controlled drugs.

The implementation and effectiveness of all policies and procedures should be monitored and evaluated on a regular basis. Health and social care organisations now tend to collect and analyse data on the social and cultural characteristics of their staff for equal opportunities purposes, on the number and type of complaints and disciplinary actions, and on health and

Figure 1.13: UKCC code of professional conduct

Each registered nurse, midwife and health visitor shall act, at all times, in such a manner as to:

- safeguard and promote the interests of individual patients and clients

- serve the interests of society

- justify public trust and confidence

- uphold and enhance the good standing and reputation of the professions.

As a registered nurse, midwife or health visitor, you are personally accountable for your practice and, in the exercise of your professional accountability, must:

- act always in such a manner as to promote and safeguard the interests and well-being of patients and clients

- ensure that no action or omission on your part, or within your sphere of responsibility, is detrimental to the interests, condition or safety of patients and clients

- maintain and improve your professional knowledge and competence

- acknowledge any limitations in your knowledge and competence and decline any duties or responsibilities unless able to perform them in safe and skilled manner

- work in an open and co-operative manner with patients, clients and their families, foster their independence and recognise and respect their involvement in the planning and delivery of care

- work in a collaborative and co-operative manner with healthcare professionals and others involved in providing care, and recognise and respect their particular contributions within the care team

- recognise and respect the uniqueness and dignity of each patient and client, and respond to their need for care, irrespective of their ethnic origin, religious beliefs, personal attributes, the nature of their health problems or any other factor

- report to an appropriate person or authority, at the earliest possible time, any conscientious objection which may be relevant to your professional practice

- avoid any abuse of your privileged relationships with patients and clients, and of the privileged access allowed to their person, property, residence or workplace

- protect all confidential information concerning patients and clients obtained in the course of professional practice and make disclosures only with consent, where required by the order of a court or where you can justify disclosure in the wider public interest

- report to an appropriate person or authority, having regard to the physical, psychological and social effects on patients and clients, any circumstances in the environment of care which could jeopardise standards of practice

- report to an appropriate person or authority any circumstances in which safe and appropriate care for patients and clients cannot be provided

- report to an appropriate person or authority where it appears that the health or safety of colleagues is at risk, as such circumstances may compromise standards of practice and care

- assist professional colleagues, in the context of your own knowledge, experience and sphere of responsibility, to develop their professional competence and assist others in the care team, including informal carers, to contribute safely and to a degree appropriate to their roles

- refuse any gift, favour or hospitality from patients or clients currently in your care which might be interpreted as seeking to exert influence to obtain preferential consideration

- ensure that your registration status is not used in the promotion of commercial products or services, declare any financial or other interests in relevant organisations providing such goods or services and ensure that your professional judgement is not influenced by any commercial considerations.

Notice to all registered nurses, midwives and health visitors

The code of professional conduct for the nurse, midwife and health visitor is issued to all registered nurses, midwives and health visitors by the United Kingdom Central Council for Nursing, Midwifery and Health Visiting. The council is the regulatory body responsible for the standards of theses professions and it requires members of the professions to practise and conduct themselves within the standards and framework provided by the code.

safety incidents and accidents. Many organisations also have audit staff who monitor and evaluate the effectiveness of procedures and who sometimes conduct service user and staff satisfaction surveys to assess whether the policies are working effectively.

Pursuing a case of unfair discrimination

What can you do if you feel that you have experienced unfair discrimination and that your legal rights have been infringed? There are a number of possible ways of pursuing a case of unfair discrimination in order to **obtain redress**, or justice. Unfair discrimination complaints can be pursued:

- within an organisation through its internal complaints and disciplinary procedures
- by implementing trade union procedures
- through hearings held by professional and regulatory bodies
- in an industrial tribunal or a court.

The route taken depends on the nature of the complaint for which the person seeks redress and upon whether the complainant is a service user or an employee.

Disciplinary procedures

Health and social care organisations have internal complaints and disciplinary policies and procedures to enable them to deal with alleged breaches of equal opportunity policy. These complaints and disciplinary policies should enable both staff and service users to pursue a complaint of unfair discrimination against an employee of the organisation.

Most complaints of unfair discrimination are initially dealt with internally, through the use of a written complaint and disciplinary hearing system. If the matter cannot be resolved in this way, the complainant has to take the case further. For a service user this means making a formal complaint to a care practitioners' regulatory body or an ombudsman, or pursuing the case in a court of law.

A member of staff who makes an unfair discrimination complaint may initially try to resolve it internally in an informal way. If this fails, he or she has the option of making a formal complaint and of pursuing the case internally with the help and support of the trade union, or of pursuing the complaint externally in a court or industrial tribunal.

The role of trade unions

Trade unions and professional associations are organisations made up of groups of people with similar jobs. These organisations aim to protect the employment rights and working conditions of their members. Trade unions and professional association representatives are usually consulted by employers to seek their views and gain agreement on policies relating to contracts of employment, disciplinary procedures and equal opportunities issues. In employer/employee disputes and unfair discrimination cases they can provide valuable information, legal support and advice to their members.

Trade union or professional association membership is one way of ensuring representation by a recognised body at grievance or disciplinary hearings. There are a number of different trade unions and professional associations representing the interests of health and social care workers. For example, nurses tend to belong to the Royal College of Nursing or Unison; health visitors tend to belong to the Health Visitors' Association and doctors to the British Medical Association.

Regulatory bodies

In the care context, **regulatory bodies** are organisations that are set up to monitor and regulate the behaviour and standards of practice of the registered members of a profession. We've mentioned some of these and their role earlier (see p. 46). The United Kingdom Central Council for Nursing, Health Visiting and Midwifery (UKCC), the General Medical Council (GMC) and the College of Occupational Therapy (COT) are three important regulatory bodies responsible for monitoring the professional standards and behaviour of large numbers of health and social care practitioners. Regulatory bodies have complaints and disciplinary procedures to deal with allegations of unlawful and unprofessional practice by their members. The ultimate sanction, or punishment, available to a regulatory body is to remove a care practitioner from the professional register if the allegations against them are proven. This means that they are unable to practise legally in their particular area of care until they are re-admitted to the register.

Industrial tribunals and the courts

A complaint about unfair discrimination in the field of employment must be brought to an industrial tribunal within three months. Tribunals hear cases concerning equal pay, redundancy, unfair dismissal, sex discrimination, race discrimination, and many other aspects of discrimination relating to contracts of employment and other aspects of industrial training and employment rights. Cases usually commence by completing the ITi form – the originating application. In it, the employee describes the grounds of the application as briefly as possible. Detailed evidence is saved until the final hearing.

In employment-related cases, the courts are used as a last resort for the resolution of unfair discrimination disputes. In England and Wales, cases are heard in a **county court** or an appropriate industrial tribunal such as the employment tribunal. In Scotland, cases are heard in the **sheriff courts**. Any complaints that are not related to employment are dealt with in a county court. If the individual wins the action and intentional direct or indirect discrimination is proven, they are awarded **damages**. This is a sum of money awarded as compensation for the unfair discrimination. If the direct or indirect discrimination is shown to be unintentional, the tribunal or court can only make recommendations and cannot award damages.

ACTIVITY
Sex discrimination gets the red card

In September 1999 a case of sex discrimination was brought before Judge Brian Knight sitting at the Central London County Court. It concerned Britain's only female football agent, Rachel Anderson, who had been barred from attending the Professional Footballers' Association awards dinner because she was a woman. The judge ruled that the players' body had breached the Sex Discrimination Act 1975 and awarded maximum damages in a landmark decision.

Using the language of the Sex Discrimination Act 1975 (see p. 35) explain why you think Rachel Anderson won her case.

An appeal against the decision of a county court or a tribunal can be made, on a point of law, to the **employment appeals tribunal (EAT)**. Further appeal can be made to the House of Lords and then to the European Court of Justice, though such appeals are very rare.

The **European Court of Justice** in Luxembourg is the final court in which redress on all equal opportunities issues relating to equal pay, race and sex discrimination may be sought. It was set up in 1952 and aims to protect individuals and groups from abuses of their human rights. Before an individual can bring an action before the Court of Justice it must be shown that all other processes of justice have been exhausted, or special permission must be sought from the House of Lords if it is to be by-passed.

ACTIVITY
Employment rights of pregnant women

A number of European Court decisions on equal opportunities issues have affected employers and employees in the United Kingdom. The case of *Dekker v. Stichting Vormingscentrum* [1991] concerned Elizabeth Dekker who was pregnant when she applied for a job at a youth centre in Holland. At the interview she told the panel that she was pregnant. After she was refused the job she claimed damages for unfair discrimination. The European Court decided that since maternity could only concern a woman, to take the pregnancy into account in justifying the refusal of a job was direct discrimination on the grounds of sex and Mrs Dekker's claim succeeded.

What other legal rights relating to maternity introduced by European legislation could Mrs Dekker look forward to claiming when her child was born?

▼ Rachel Anderson leaves court after winning her case against the Professional Footballers' Association

BUILD YOUR LEARNING

Keywords and phrases

You should know the meaning of the words and phrases listed below. If you are unsure about any of them, go back through the last five pages of the unit to refresh your understanding.

- Citizen's Charter
- Code of conduct
- Code of practice
- County court
- Damages
- Employment Appeals Tribunal (EAT)
- European Court of Justice
- Industrial tribunal
- Obtain redress
- Organisational policy
- Organisational procedure
- Patient's Charter
- Redress
- Regulatory body
- Sheriff court

Summary points

- Charters are documents that set out the standards of service that users of care services can expect to receive but do not have legal force in the way that legislation and case law does.

- The government sets out the standards of care and service that it expects public services to provide in the Citizen's Charter and the Patient's Charter.

- A code of practice is a document that sets out key principles or guidelines to help care workers to implement specific features of legislation and general good practice.

- Codes of practice do not have legal force in themselves. However, in breaching a code of practice a person may also be breaking the law or may fail to meet the expected standards of his or her profession. This can lead to prosecution and disciplinary proceedings.

- Organisational policies are statements that set out how an organisation expects its employees to approach or deal with specific issues such as equal opportunities or access to clients' records.

- Organisational policies are usually written in such a way that they incorporate the key points of law on the issue that they cover.

- Breaching or failing to follow an organisational policy can result in dismissal from employment and, in some cases, prosecution.

- A person who wants to pursue a claim for unfair discrimination has a number of potential sources of redress. These include internal, organisational enquiries and disciplinary proceedings, industrial tribunals and courts, regulatory body complaints and disciplinary proceedings, and the European Court of Justice.

QUESTIONS

1 What is the purpose of the Patient's Charter?

2 How do codes of practice help to promote equality of opportunity?

3 What is the purpose of a code of professional conduct? Use the UKCC code of conduct to illustrate your answer.

4 What role do organisational policies play in promoting equality of opportunity?

5 Briefly describe three ways in which a person can pursue a claim of unfair discrimination.

Ethical issues and rights in care settings

WE HAVE REPEATEDLY MADE the point that health, social care and early years service users have legal rights, as individuals and as users of care services, to equality of opportunity and protection from damage or harm. Care service users generally expect that health and social care practitioners will respect their rights and interests. We look next at situations in which ethical issues arise and question this principle.

Ethical issues are dilemmas concerning the best course of action or the right way to address a situation or issue. For example, health, social care and early years workers regularly have to decide whether, and how much, they should share information about service users with colleagues, other care organisations or the service users' family and friends. Ethical dilemmas place a great deal of pressure on care workers and are often not easy to resolve. Care practitioners are faced with the difficult task of having to work within the law whilst trying to ensure that the best interests of service users and the general public are met, at the same time as doing what is most ethically acceptable. As a result, ethical issues can arise and create conflicts, as the following examples show.

■ Care workers have to observe the law even where they feel it is unethical to do so. For example, health care workers cannot deny women abortions because of their own Catholic faith, or force Jehovah's Witness patients to accept life-saving blood transfusions.

■ Care workers sometimes have to go against normal ethical principles or deny service users their normal legal rights in order to act in an individual's best interests or to protect the interests and safety of others. For example, mental health staff may have to detain people in hospital against their will if they are felt to be at risk of harming themselves or others.

■ Care workers sometimes have to work with levels of resources that don't allow them to put best practice policies into action.

We look next at confidentiality, risk management and the resourcing of care as areas where ethical dilemmas frequently arise.

Confidentiality issues

Care practitioners are in a relatively powerful position in relation to service users because of their specialist skills, clinical knowledge and the privileged access that they have to information about service users' social situation and health status.

Within care relationships, the principle of **confidentiality** plays a vital role in establishing and maintaining the trust that effective relationships depend upon. Confidentiality refers to the protection of personal and private details about service users' situations or conditions. Service users generally consent to this information being made available to a restricted group of care professionals on a need-to-know basis. They also expect that care practitioners will respect the limits they place on the disclosure of the information outside of the care team or for any reason that is not related to their care. Care practitioners should not break confidentiality in situations in which:

■ service users have a right to privacy

■ their comments or behaviour do not cause anybody harm or break the law.

Disclosure of personal details or information about someone's condition must only be made with that person's explicit consent. This can present care practitioners with ethical problems. For example, if the person is in hospital, information about his or her condition must only be given to the next-of-kin, or another person whom the patient has nominated. It is neither advisable nor common practice to provide other relatives with information unless the patient gives permission to do so. This never stops relatives inquiring, and they can feel aggrieved when they are told that the information is confidential! Each hospital has a policy on giving information about patient progress, but it always includes the next-of-kin and patient consent restrictions. The policy must be adhered to strictly to avoid legal actions for breach of confidentiality.

Disclosure of confidential information can, and in some cases must, be made:

■ when required by a court order

■ during social services case conferences dealing with children or childcare matters

■ when one can justify that disclosure is necessary in the wider public interest.

Disclosing confidential information

There are times when care practitioners have to reveal what they have been told, or have seen, to a more senior person at work or to an external organisation. Clients' requests that you keep what they tell you a secret can be overridden if:

- what they reveal involves them breaking the law or planning to do so
- they tell you that they intend to harm themselves or another person
- they reveal information that can be used to protect another person from harm.

If an offence that could have been prevented by your revealing the confidence is committed, you could be brought to court to face charges. Care workers should never promise a client that what they say will be absolutely confidential. They should explain that, depending on what they are told or observe, there are times when they may have to share information with their colleagues and other authorities. In all care settings the standard of confidentiality that care practitioners are able to provide should be communicated to service users at the first point of contact and may be reinforced by leaflets and posters.

Generally, information about service users should be:

- kept secure and private, and locked in special filing cabinets
- only shared within the strict boundaries of the care team
- only used for the purpose for which it is given
- never deliberately disclosed so as to break confidentiality, other than in exceptional circumstances. Care practitioners must always be able to justify their decisions to break confidentiality.

ACTIVITY

Confidentiality and child protection

The court has a duty, under the Children Act 1989, to protect children and young people from risks of harm or significant harm. During investigations where there is suspicion of child abuse of any kind, the court will, in keeping with its duty, order that certain investigations be carried out. This may involve requiring the disclosure of confidential information about the child or the child's parents. Once the court makes such an order, a care practitioner who does not comply is in contempt of court, even if this means that he or she must disclose confidential information.

Which important principle introduced under the Children Act 1989 (see p. 41) is always applied by the court in these circumstances?

ACTIVITY

Tumbledown Day Nursery

Jane is a nursery assistant at the Tumbledown Day Nursery. She recently overheard two of the children's mothers discussing personal and confidential matters about the health of three-year-old Joel, a child at the nursery. Joel's mother wasn't present at the time. Jane has told her supervisor that she feels this wasn't right or in Joel's best interests, but that she is not sure what she should do about it.

- If you were Jane's supervisor, how would you deal with this issue?
- What would you advise Jane to do if this situation arose again in future?
- Would you discuss the matter with Joel's parents?
- Have any of Joel's legal rights been infringed here?
- Would any of Joel's legal rights have been infringed if Jane had given information to the two women about Joel's health?

Risk issues

Risk management is now a major feature of care practice in many areas of health, social care and early years work. **Risk assessment** is concerned with identifying the likely occurrence or influence of a potential hazard. In health, social care and early years settings, risk assessments are made of the care environment itself and of the likelihood that individual users of care services may behave in ways that present a risk of harm to themselves or others.

Risk is a difficult thing to assess. It is concerned with making judgements about, or predicting, the future possibilities that someone might behave in a particular way or that something might happen. Risk management is concerned with practising in ways that reduce the likelihood of a potential hazard occurring. Risk assessment and management are important in areas of care work in which service users, such as children, older people, those with physical or learning disabilities or people with mental illnesses are particularly vulnerable to harm and require forms of protection. This can be because they are unable to protect their own interests or because they may be at risk of harming others.

Ethical issues arise when care staff want to avoid being overprotective of service users whilst also ensuring that they don't let them get into situations in which they are unable to cope or to look after themselves safely. This situation might arise where a resident of a supported house for people with learning disabilities, for example, wants to go out to a local pub on his own one evening. Care staff who put equal opportunities principles into practice would want to avoid restricting the resident in order to maximise his freedom and choice. However, there are clearly some risks involved in allowing the resident to go to the pub alone. You may want to reflect on the pros and cons of agreeing to the resident's request in the situation described and then try out the following activity.

▼ Are these children at risk?

ACTIVITY

Assessing risks in care situations

What are the possible benefits and the potential risks associated with each of the following?

- Integrating children with Down's syndrome into mainstream secondary schools.

- Giving adults with long-term mental health problems the right to choose whether to take medication to control their symptoms.

- Providing home care support services on request for frail elderly people who prefer to live independently in their own homes rather than move into nursing or residential homes.

In each situation explain what you feel would be in the best interests of the people concerned. Try to balance the ethical issues raised with the goals of promoting equality of opportunity and respecting people's legal rights.

Funding and resourcing issues

Charters, organisational policies and professional codes of practice require care practitioners to provide the highest standards of care. To a large extent being able to achieve high standards depends on the availability of sufficient resources. To provide high quality health care services in hospital, for example, it is necessary to have enough appointments to accommodate everyone who wants to be seen, adequate numbers of staff to provide care, appropriate equipment and enough beds for people to be admitted to. A common complaint from health care staff at the beginning of the twenty-first century is that one or more of these resources is often not available. This presents an ethical dilemma for staff who are committed to providing health care services that meet promised and expected standards.

Care practitioners sometimes find that they are unable to provide care that reaches the standards set by charters, policies or professional codes of conduct because, through no fault of their own, they lack the resources to do so. Care practitioners should always do the best they are able to in the circumstances and should always act in the best interests of service users. However, they should also alert those who are responsible for resourcing care services, such as service managers and their professional body, about the possible consequences of the shortfall in resources.

So-called whistle blowing, where a professional draws attention to resource problems, has got some concerned professionals into trouble in the past, but it is now encouraged and supported by regulatory bodies. Care practitioners must be aware that they always face the threat of litigation by service users, and disciplinary action by their regulatory body, if they collude in providing sub-standard service.

Resolving ethical dilemmas

In many care practice situations there is no clear right or wrong answer to an ethical dilemma. Care practitioners are required to make skilled and ethically justifiable judgements and to select the best, or most correct, course of action open to them. Where the matter involves a complex ethical issue which is too difficult for an individual care practitioner to resolve, guidance should be sought from managers, professional bodies and ethics committees where such bodies exist.

BUILD YOUR LEARNING

Keywords and phrases

You should know the meaning of the words and phrases listed below. If you are unsure about any of them, go back through the last five pages of the unit to refresh your understanding.

- Confidentiality
- Disclosure
- Ethical issues
- Risk assessment
- Risk management

Summary points

- Ethical issues are dilemmas concerning the best course of action or decision in particular circumstances.

- Ethical issues arise where care workers are trying to balance conflicting demands. Care practitioners have to work within the law and the resources available to them, whilst trying to ensure that they also respect service users' wishes and rights, and protect the safety and interests of others who may be affected by their decisions.

- Confidentiality is a key ethical issue for all care workers; it is concerned with the protection and appropriate use of service users' personal and private information.

- Care workers should normally maintain the confidentiality of the information given to them by service users. The exceptions to this rule occur where disclosure is required by a court, during a child protection case conference or where the wider public interest requires disclosure.

- Risk assessment and management raise many ethical dilemmas for care practitioners. They involve identifying potential hazards or harm and taking steps to reduce the risk.

- Care practitioners are frequently faced with the difficult task of balancing service users' rights and ethical issues. There are often no clear, absolute courses of action in such circumstances.

QUESTIONS

1 Why do ethical issues regularly arise in health, social care and early years settings?

2 In your own words, explain why maintaining confidentiality is an ethical issue which care practitioners often face.

3 Identify three situations in which a care practitioner must breach confidentiality.

4 What does risk management involve?

5 Why does risk management raise ethical issues for care practitioners?

How care organisations promote equality

HOW CAN CARE ORGANISATIONS operate to promote equality? We are going to look at the different strategies which organisations can use to meet the diverse needs of their staff and clients and, in so doing, promote forms of equality.

The phrase 'promote equality' is about actions and not just ideas and beliefs. It is about actively working to ensure that everybody is fairly treated and that everyone is given the opportunity to reach his or her potential. People need different forms and levels of support to reach their potential because their needs differ. For example, one person might require additional training in particular work skills, while another might require an aid such as an adapted computer keyboard to enable him or her to work at all.

Management structures

The management structure of a care organisation is influenced by factors such as:

- the size of the organisation

- the primary aim and general purpose of the organisation

- the degree to which its work roles are specialised

- the relationship between the care organisation and other organisations.

Large organisations such as NHS trusts and local authorities tend to have **hierarchical management structures** (see Figure 1.14) in which greater management authority and decision-making power are concentrated at the top of a pyramid structure and in which work roles are very specialised. In practice this means that care workers are part of a line management structure and are responsible to a designated supervisor or manager who is partly there to support them and partly there to monitor their work.

Health and social care organisations don't always use hierarchical management structures. Smaller care organisations tend to have flatter management structures in which more of the decision-making authority and management responsibility is shared between fewer levels of staff. Other workplaces are organised into collectives in which everybody has an equal amount of responsibility, even though they have different work roles.

The main aim of an organisation's management structure is to distribute authority and decision-making responsibility in a way that enables people to work together effectively and so achieve the organisation's main goals or mission. The aim of management practice within the organisation is to promote consensus working and to stamp out negative, conflictual behaviour like unfair discrimination.

The management structure of an organisation is the means by which power and communication opportunities are distributed. Hierarchies themselves introduce some inequality because they place people at different levels within the care organisation thereby giving them unequal amounts of power and influence. It is therefore important that effective recruitment, training and promotion policies, and procedures exist to ensure that the organisation itself does not simply recreate the unequal distribution of power and opportunity that exists outside the organisation.

There is plenty of evidence to show that health and social care organisations do recreate the forms of social inequality that exist in society. For example, women, people with impairments and people from minority ethnic groups tend to be underrepresented in the higher levels of management in most health and social care organisations. The policies and procedures of many organisations also tend to assume that employees are heterosexual. Few organisations consider the issue of whether they discriminate unfairly or provide equality of opportunity on the grounds of sexual orientation.

In order to promote equality, organisations need to develop management structures and practices that are open and flexible enough to allow people with diverse backgrounds to enter and make progress in them. Equal opportunities policies may facilitate this in theory, but monitoring and evaluation of policies and procedures is necessary to ensure that the policy works in practice.

Training and professional updating

Health and social care practices and methods are continually changing as new ideas and approaches are developed and adopted, and different areas of care practice are prioritised. Health and social care professionals have a responsibility towards service users to maintain an up-to-date knowledge of good practice.

Legislation is a major area where regular updating is important, as the responsibilities of the care worker and

Figure 1.14: A hierarchical management structure

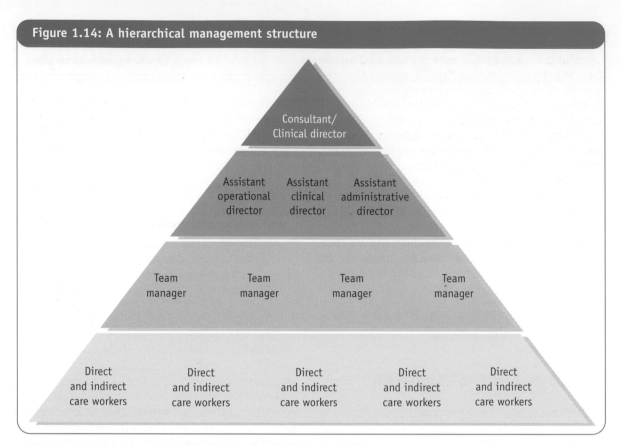

Figure 1.15: A collective collaborative management structure

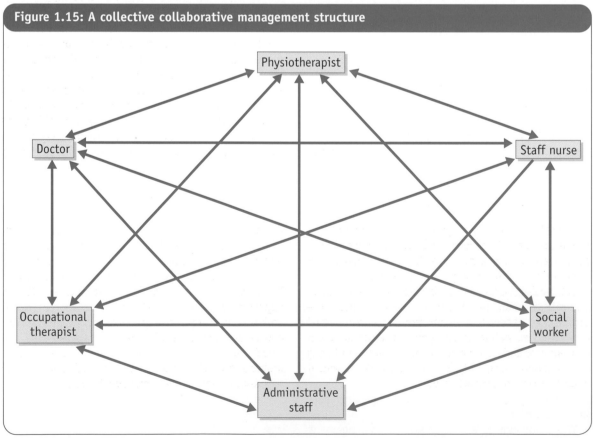

service users' rights are affected. Organisations should ensure that staff receive adequate training and that all individuals have an equal chance to attend and benefit from training opportunities. Training ensures that new guidelines for practices are enforced and that each worker has an opportunity to develop his or her understanding of the changes.

Updating of skills is also an essential aspect of health, social care and early years work. Some skills, such as first aid and resuscitation, require regular updating. As new regulations, for example on manual handling, are introduced, they become a training requirement as observing them is an essential part of the care worker's role.

Staff who receive effective training can be more positive in their approach towards clients' needs. Training also ensures that policies and procedures are followed and that the reasons for them are more apparent. Common practices between staff mean that the staff receive consistent and high level care. The standards that they can expect to experience are overt and can be monitored.

Employees have a responsibility to their employers and to the organisation to be aware of legislation and codes of practice that may be relevant to their work. Employers also have a responsibility to provide training to ensure that skills and knowledge match the requirements of the organisation. The promotion of equal opportunities and anti-discriminatory practices are important areas for training.

Improving staff knowledge

All staff in care organisations should have access to, and should know about, the policies and procedures of the organisation. Most health and social care organisations provide opportunities for staff to develop and improve their knowledge of policies and procedures through induction and refresher training programmes.

Fostering positive attitudes in staff

Organisations have a responsibility to ensure that unfair discrimination does not limit the opportunities of different groups of staff and that prejudice does not affect working relationships. There are various ways in which positive attitudes to diversity and equality of opportunity can be fostered. These include the production and implementation of an equal opportunities statement and policy, the development of awareness and training packages, regular monitoring and discussion of equality issues, and the development of anti-discriminatory practices.

ACTIVITY

Dealing with prejudice

What could you do if a new colleague made a remark that expressed prejudice against a service user or behaved in a way that unfairly discriminated against a particular person when you were working with him or her?

Think about the possible range of responses. Issues to consider include:

- the impact of the remark on the service user
- the effect on yourself, your colleagues and the service user of complaining
- the need to work within the law and to uphold high ethical standards in your care practice.
- the consequences of not doing anything.

Providing support for staff

Health, social care and early years work is sometimes difficult and pressurised. Staff who are not adequately supported in meeting the demands and challenges of their work experience stress, and prolonged exposure to stress causes burnout. This is a psychological condition that causes people to cut off from the emotional aspects of their work in order to protect themselves from its effects. They then work on automatic pilot and run the risk of not responding in an appropriate and sensitive way to service users' needs. Adequate staff support must be made available to all employees in the form of supportive supervision and counselling, workload management and debriefing opportunities.

Developing codes of practice

All care organisations should ensure that they and their employees operate and practice in ways that do not break the law. However, the laws that exist will not, on their own, bring about equality of opportunity. Progressive care organisations that take equality of opportunity seriously develop their own organisational policies, codes of practice and charters of rights for staff and service users. These take the diverse needs and backgrounds of staff and service users into account in promoting equal access to opportunities within the organisation and actively manage diversity.

Writing an equal opportunities policy

1 Design an equal opportunities policy for a day centre. Think about the equal rights law that you would want to be covered.

2 Explain how you would ensure that the policy is implemented.

3 Who would be responsible for implementing the policy?

4 How would the implementation and effectiveness be monitored and evaluated?

5 When you've written the policy, ask a colleague to critically (but constructively!) evaluate it.

Staff selection procedures

The Commission for Racial Equality, the Equal Opportunities Commission and the National Disability Council have all produced guidelines on staff selection. These give information on how to organise the whole process of deciding on who to appoint to a post. In care organisations, the procedures aim to safeguard both applicants and service users' rights by ensuring that service users' needs are central to the work of the employees and by creating an equality-based procedure that is open to scrutiny.

Anti-discriminatory care practice

Promoting equal opportunities should be a real issue for all health, social care and early years practitioners because they come face-to-face with people who experience health and social problems that are triggered or made worse by unequal access to society's resources. Promoting equal opportunities in the care setting means that health, social care and early years workers need to address their own prejudices and tackle unfair discrimination where they see this occurring. This can seem like a daunting and intimidating task to students and care workers just beginning their careers. The best way of putting equal opportunities ideas into action is through **anti-discriminatory practice**. This means developing ways of working that:

- recognise the needs of people from diverse backgrounds including those who come from minority religious or cultural backgrounds

- actively challenge the unfair discrimination that people have experienced

- counteract the effects that unfair discrimination has already had on people.

Is equal opportunities your responsibility?

As a care worker, what should or shouldn't you do to promote equality of opportunity for service users?

Think about the various aspects of this question for a while. What do you see as your personal responsibility? Do you believe that you should just do your bit? What does this involve? Perhaps you believe that you have a wider responsibility to actively try and challenge broader forms of organisational and structural discrimination. What does this mean in terms of your work as a health, social care or early years practitioner?

Most care workers would like to believe that they provide fair and equal treatment to all service users. However, some of the strategies that people use do not always support equality of opportunity in practice, even though this is the intention.

Blindness to differences

It is often impossible not to notice physical, social and cultural differences between people. It is better practice to acknowledge and accept that people are different but equally valued than to pretend not to notice difference. Being aware of cultural and identity needs is an important part of care practice. How else will you be able to meet people's individual needs?

Treating everyone the same

This is similar to not noticing difference. Treating everyone the same may seem equal and fair but it may also involve a denial of a person's identity at a time when he or she needs to have this acknowledged and affirmed. Boys and girls are not the same, neither are black, white or Chinese people. It's important to respond to the needs of individuals in a care setting. This often requires the care worker to find out about, and be skilled at, adapting to the culturally diverse needs of service users and colleagues.

It's not my responsibility

Some care workers feel that they shouldn't impose their own values on service users and colleagues and that challenging prejudice and unfair discrimination is not their responsibility. Acceptance, consideration for others and equality of opportunity are, however, superior values to prejudice and unfair discriminatory behaviour. Care workers should not remain silent or passive when prejudice is expressed or when unfair discrimination occurs, as this could be seen to be supporting the unequal and unacceptable treatment of an individual or group of people. As a health, social care or early years worker you can help to promote equality of opportunity for care service users by developing your own awareness, knowledge and practice.

Awareness

- Be self-aware and self-critical (within reason!). Question your own assumptions and be prepared to change your ideas and views about people.

- Continue re-evaluating and developing yourself and your ideas on equality.

- Adopt the view that people are different but of equal value regardless of their physical, mental or cultural characteristics. Don't judge people.

- Accept people's physical, social and cultural differences as a positive and interesting, rather than problematic, feature of care work.

Knowledge

- Make sure that you know how race relations, sex discrimination, equal pay and disability discrimination legislation applies to you.

- Make sure that you know about legislation affecting the rights of service users with whom you work.

- Read and become familiar with the policies and procedures of the organisation in which you work. Know how they affect your rights and responsibilities at work.

- Ask questions about, and seek advice on, how to implement the equality and anti-discriminatory policies and procedures of the organisation.

Practice

Remember that equality of opportunity for all care service users can only be achieved if care professionals approach care work in ways that challenge the prejudices, unfair discrimination and inequalities that some people experience.

ACTIVITY

Anti-discrimination strategies

How will the following activities challenge prejudice and unfair discrimination in care settings?

- Providing pamphlets and information in local community languages.

- Celebrating multicultural festivals in a nursery.

- Employing male workers to work with children.

- Encouraging service users to take part in planning their care.

- Monitoring ethnicity and impairment on application forms for jobs.

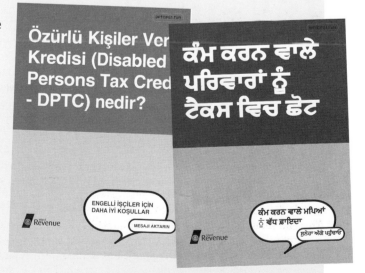

BUILD YOUR LEARNING

Keywords and phrases

You should now know the meaning of each of the key words and phrases listed below. If you are unsure about any of them, go back through the last five pages of the unit to refresh your understanding.

- Anti-discriminatory practice
- Burnout
- Hierarchical management structures

Summary points

- Health, social care and early years organisations can play a part in promoting equality of opportunity in the way that they organise and provide services.

- Care organisations should ensure that a diverse range of people are able to access positions of power and that people employed in the organisation are accessible and accountable to service users.

- Care organisations should develop and implement effective equal opportunities policies. They should provide access to training, foster positive attitudes in staff and ensure that appropriate staff selection and promotion procedures are in place.

- Complaints and disciplinary procedures, staff support and effective induction are also mechanisms for promoting equality of opportunity within care organisations.

- Care workers employed by health and social care organisations should understand and adopt anti-discriminatory strategies in their work with service users. This involves applying the care value base to their work whilst acknowledging the diverse social, cultural and care needs of all service users.

QUESTIONS

1 What is a hierarchical management structure? Explain how this can affect equality of opportunity within a care organisation.

2 How can care organisations promote equal opportunities through their training policies?

3 Why is treating everyone the same not an effective or appropriate way for care practitioners to promote equality of opportunity?

4 Describe the main features or characteristics of anti-discriminatory care practice.

5 Describe, using examples, what a care organisation could do to promote equality of opportunity through its staff selection policies.

Sources of support and guidance

SUPPORT AND GUIDANCE ON EQUAL opportunities issues is provided by a number of government-funded and independent organisations. Some government-funded bodies have a formal, legal responsibility to monitor the implementation of anti-discrimination laws and to promote equality of opportunity for minority ethnic groups, women and people with impairments. Independent sector organisations tend to have more of a campaigning role, aiming to represent the interests of, and challenge prejudice and unfair discrimination against, the groups they work for and with.

Many of the organisations referred to below produce excellent, up-to-date information on discrimination and equality of opportunity issues in both printed and online form. Contact addresses for these organisations are given at the end of the unit.

Government bodies

The organisations described below are independent, statutory bodies; in other words, they are funded by government but have an independent role to play in monitoring and advising on discrimination and equality of opportunity issues.

The Equal Opportunities Commission

▲ EOC website's homepage, you can find this at http://www.eoc.org.uk

The **Equal Opportunities Commission (EOC)** was set up under the Sex Discrimination Act 1975. It is based in Manchester and has responsibility for advising, providing information on and monitoring the workings of the Act and the elimination of sexual discrimination in England, Wales and Scotland. The key responsibilities of the Equal Opportunities Commission are to:

- promote equality of opportunity between men and women

- work towards the elimination of sex discrimination in employment, education and consumer services

- monitor the working of the Act and draw up and submit proposals to the government for amending it where this is thought to be necessary.

The Equal Opportunities Commission provides information and support to people who want to bring a complaint of sex discrimination before an industrial tribunal. It runs an Equality Exchange that has around 700 members. This enables employers to exchange information on good practice in relation to equality of opportunity.

The Commission for Racial Equality

The **Commission for Racial Equality (CRE)** was created under the Race Relations Act 1976. The CRE monitors and provides advice on the implementation of the Act, and investigates allegations of racial discrimination. Its duties include:

- working towards the elimination of racial discrimination

- promoting equality of opportunity and good relations between people of different racial groups generally

- drawing up and submitting proposals to the government for amending the work of the Act where this is thought necessary.

Like the Equal Opportunities Commission, the CRE provides information and support to people who want to bring a complaint of unfair (racial) discrimination before an industrial tribunal. Over 1,500 people formally applied for legal assistance and over 10,000 people contacted the CRE for advice about racial discrimination in 1997.

The CRE also supports the work of 91 racial equality councils that operate throughout the United Kingdom. These are voluntary bodies that seek to promote equality of opportunity and good race relations at local level in areas where there is a significant ethnic minority population.

The Disability Rights Commission

The Disability Rights Commission replaced the National Disability Council in 2000. Whereas the National Disability Council only had advisory powers with respect to the implementation of the Disability Discrimination Act 1995, the new body does have enforcement powers. The functions of the Disability Rights Commission include:

- working towards the elimination of discrimination against people with impairments

- promoting the equalisation of opportunities for people with impairments

- encouraging good practice in the treatment of people with impairments

- keeping under review the working of the Disability Discrimination Act 1995.

The Commission may, for any purpose connected with the performance of its functions:

- make proposals or give other advice to any minister of the Crown about any aspect of the law or a proposed change to the law

- make proposals or give other advice to any government agency or other public authority about the practical application of any law

- undertake, or arrange for, or support (whether financially or otherwise) the carrying out of research or the provision of advice or information.

The Council of Europe

The Council of Europe is part of the European Union organisational structure. Its main role is to strengthen democracy, human rights and the rule of law in EU member states. The Council of Europe has established a range of administrative and organisational means of achieving these aims. It has developed the European Convention on Human Rights which is designed to protect the fundamental rights and freedoms of individuals. Complaints about violations of rights are dealt with by the European Court of Human Rights.

Voluntary and independent sector organisations

A large number of independent sector health and social care organisations in the United Kingdom have an equality focus to their work. There are also a number of independent sector organisations that work specifically on equality and anti-discrimination issues. These organisations represent and campaign for improvements in the rights of, and access to equal opportunities for, people who experience significant levels of prejudice and unfair discrimination.

Disability Scotland and **Disability Wales** are both independent charitable organisations that work across their national areas to promote equality of opportunity for people with disabilities. They provide information and advice, and campaign to raise awareness. They also influence policy makers on issues relating to people with disabilities. **Disability Action** is an umbrella organisation with over 180 member groups which works to ensure that people with disabilities are given equal rights and equality of opportunity.

The **Campaign for Homosexual Equality, Stonewall**, and **Outright Scotland** are all independent sector organisations dedicated to raising awareness of homophobia and the unequal treatment of lesbians and gay men. They have clear equality agendas that aim to improve the legal rights as well as broader social acceptance of people with a lesbian or gay sexual orientation.

Age Concern and **Help the Aged** are large voluntary organisations that work with, and on behalf of, older people. Both campaign against age discrimination and for improved rights and equality of opportunity for older people.

Resources

A variety of resources are available to people who are looking for further information on unfair discrimination in the workplace and in society generally. These may be obtained from the following organisations.

Age Concern
Astral House
1268 London Road
Mitcham
London
SW16 4ER

Disability Action
2 Annadale Avenue
Belfast
BT7 3JH

Disability Scotland
Princes House
5 Shandwick Place
Edinburgh
EH2 4RG

Disability Wales
Llys Ifor
Crescent Road
Caerphilly
Mid Glamorgan
CF8 1XL

Stonewall
16 Clerkenwell Close
London
EC1R 0AA

Campaign for Homosexual Equality
PO Box 342
London
WC1X 0DU

Outright Scotland
58a Broughton Street
Edinburgh
EH1 3SA

Help the Aged
St James's Walk
London
EC1R 0BE

The Council of Europe
Point 1
The Council of Europe
67075 Strasbourg Cedex
France

The Commission for Racial Equality
Elliot House
10-12 Allington Street
London
SW1E 5EH

The CRE publishes a broad range of free and low-cost information on race discrimination issues and is able to give advice on how to pursue claims of racial discrimination.

Your local Racial Equality Council will be able to provide you with information and advice on local racial equality issues and resources. Look in Yellow Pages to find your nearest REC.

Equal Opportunity Commission
Overseas House
Quay Street
Manchester
M3 3HN

The EOC is able to give advice on and carry out formal investigations into complaints of sex discrimination. It produces a range of information in book and booklet form.

Citizens Advice Bureaux provide general advice and information on ways of seeking redress in disputes relating to issues of unfair discrimination. Look in Yellow Pages for local branches.

Law centres and community advice programmes in your local area provide free legal advice on all areas of law as it affects the individual, including unfair discrimination.

BUILD YOUR LEARNING

Keywords and phrases

You should be familiar with the key terms and phrases listed below. If you are not sure about any of them, go back through the last four pages of the unit to refresh your understanding.

- Equal Opportunities Commission
- Commission for Racial Equality
- Disability Rights Commission
- The Council of Europe
- European Convention on Human Rights

Summary points

- Support and guidance on discrimination and equality issues can be obtained from a variety of specialist government-funded and independent sector organisations in the United Kingdom.

- The Equal Opportunities Commission, Commission for Racial Equality and Disability Rights Commission are all statutory organisations that monitor and advise on equal opportunities issues and legislation.

- Independent sector organisations include charities that have a broader care role, such as Age Concern, and campaigning groups, like Stonewall, that seek to influence government and improve the legal rights of the groups of people whom they represent.

QUESTIONS

1 Which Act of Parliament led to the establishment of the Equal Opportunities Commission?

2 What is a Racial Equality Council?

3 Which organisation took over the monitoring of disability legislation from the National Disability Council in 1999?

4 Name two organisations that campaign for equal rights on behalf of lesbians and gay men.

5 Which local organisation could provide you with free general information and advice on unfair discrimination issues?

References

Brown, B (1998) *Unlearning Discrimination in the Early Years*, Trentham

Brown, C and Gay, P (1985) *Racial discrimination 17 years after the Act*, Policy Studies Institute

Coard, B (1971) *How the West Indian Child is Made Educationally Sub-normal in the British School System*, New Beacon Books

Drake, R F (1999) *Understanding disability policies*, Macmillan

Morrell, J (1990) *The employment of people with disabilities*, Department of Employment

Swann, Lord (1985) *Education for all: A brief guide*, HMSO

Webb, R and Tossell, D (1997) *Social Issues for Carers*, Arnold

This unit enables you to develop your understanding of the communication skills that are needed by people who work in health and social care settings. It is concerned with communication and interaction in health and social care settings. We begin by looking at the key elements of human communication. We discuss the types of interaction that health and social care workers become involved in and the importance of communication skills in these situations. Learning about the nature of communication should enable you to understand and evaluate communication styles and will inform your interactions when you are working in a care setting.

Next we look at the physical, emotional, social and cultural factors that help and hinder communication. Awareness of these factors, and their impact, will help you to develop and adapt your communication strategies and improve interactions with service users and colleagues.

Many health and social care students and people who are new to care work have concerns about their ability to talk to service users. We explore and offer some guidelines on verbal skills and how to manage different types of conversation with service users in one-to-one interactions.

Health and social care workers often have to communicate within group situations. To prepare yourself for working in a group it is helpful to know how groups develop and how people behave in group situations. We look at both of these topics and at the skills that are needed to take part in and run groups in care settings. By this point you will have developed a good all-round understanding of communication and interaction in care settings.

The unit ends by exploring methods of evaluating communication skills and by addressing the issue of confidentiality. The ability to evaluate your own and other people's communication strategies and interactions will enable you to monitor and improve the effectiveness of communication performance. Knowing about and promoting the principle of confidentiality will ensure that your communication and interaction skills meet the ethical standards expected of health and social care practitioners.

2

Communication in health and social care

The elements of communication

Types of interaction

WHEN PEOPLE TALK ABOUT **interpersonal interaction** in care settings they are referring to the actions, or relations, between people. Inter means between or among. Interact means to act on or in close relation with each other (Collins English Dictionary).

People who work in health or social care settings are likely to become involved in a range of different types of interaction during the working day. For example, care workers are likely to have regular interactions with:

- service users (patients or clients)

- colleagues within their own organisation

- health and social care workers from other organisations

- the family and friends of service users.

Health and social care workers interact with the above people for various reasons. For example, they may interact in order to give or receive information about care, to provide support for a service user, a member of their family or a colleague, or to carry out an assessment of an individual's care needs.

Interactions can be formal or informal. **Formal interactions** are likely to involve a health and social care worker communicating in an official capacity, typically representing their organisation or profession. In this type of interaction, the person tends to interact in role, in the sense that he or she is communicating as a manager, a doctor or an employee of a particular organisation rather than simply as him or herself. In **informal interactions**, in contrast, people are more themselves. They communicate and interact in a personal capacity rather than in their professional role. This does not mean that when health and social care workers interact with service users and colleagues at work they always do so in a formal way. Skilled communicators are able remain within their professional role and communicate in a way that is genuine and personal. One of the challenges that new health and social care workers face is to develop a communication style that best balances their professional role with just being themselves.

▼ Health and social care workers have different types of interaction during the working day

ACTIVITY

Learning to communicate in a care setting

Chloe Evans is an experienced staff nurse working on an intensive care unit (ICU). She is on a late shift, which begins at 1 p.m. and ends at 9 p.m. Chloe arrives a few minutes early for the shift so that she can have a chat with Janet, a colleague and friend, before the shift begins. They chat about the holiday that they are planning to take in Jamaica this summer. As other colleagues arrive and crowd into the ICU office, they greet each other and the conversation changes to work-related matters. Informally, Chloe asks Ian, one of the nurses on the early shift, whether it has been busy so far. Ian makes a joke about it always being busy and says he will tell them more in the handover report. Emma, a student nurse, sits quietly in the corner of the office observing this.

At 1 p.m. Ian and Jessica, the ward manager, begin the handover report. They describe the problems and care that each of the ICU patients have had that morning. Jessica says that one of the patients needs to have a chest drain removed shortly. Emma is asked to observe Chloe and the ICU doctor doing this so that she will be able to help in future. Ian and Jessica take about half an hour to go through the needs and care requirements of all of the ICU patients.

At the end of the report, Chloe has written two sides of notes, lots of it in abbreviations, symbols and jargon. She knows which patients she is allocated to look after and has a good understanding of their overall medical problems and nursing needs. In contrast, Emma leaves the office looking a little worried and feeling nervous. She feels that she didn't have time to get all the information she might need, as the handover seemed so fast. During the afternoon she is to shadow Chloe and is relying on her to explain what is going on and to help her with what she has to do.

After five years as a staff nurse, Chloe has developed a lot of confidence and is at ease with the other staff and relatives who come to the ICU. She makes her interactions appear effortless and natural but is using a lot of communication skills and experience to do so. Emma, like most new and inexperienced student nurses, feels very nervous and unskilled in this setting. One of the main differences between new carers and more experienced staff is the high level of communication skills that the latter have developed and are able to use.

1 Identify an example of a formal and and informal interaction that Chloe becomes involved in.

2 What do you think Emma has to learn in order to communicate more effectively in the ICU setting?

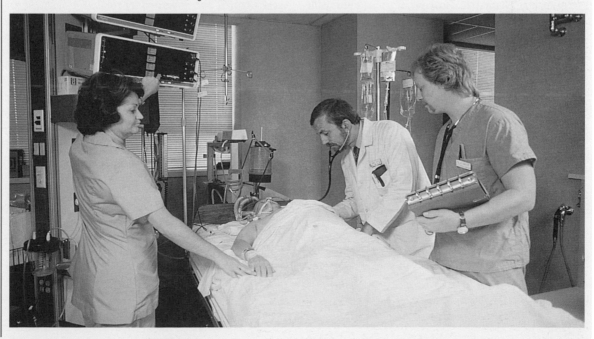

Interpersonal interaction is based on the effective use of communication skills. People who work in health and social care rely on their communication skills as much as their technical knowledge and practical care skills in order to be effective practitioners. It does seem to be true that some people are more natural communicators than others. However, as a potential care worker of the future, you should not rely on your natural communication abilities alone, or feel that you won't be very good at interacting appropriately if you currently lack confidence in your communication skills.

Health and social care workers gradually develop and improve their communication skills through training, practice and experience. Acquiring an understanding of the basic elements and characteristics of human communication is an essential part of learning how to communicate in care settings.

| The communication cycle |

Perhaps the most fundamental aspect of communication theory that you need to understand is the **communication cycle**. This term refers to the apparently simple process of sending and receiving messages. Messages are what communication is all about. Saying that communication is based on sending and receiving messages makes it sound a bit odd. For example, when you become involved in a conversation with your friends or class colleagues you probably don't consciously think 'I need to send an oral message to her in reply', or, 'I'm receiving your non-verbal messages loud and clear, thank you'. However, if you analyse your interactions with others you will find that your communication is quite organised and follows a definite pattern: the communication cycle.

Figure 2.1: The communication cycle

Sender   Feedback   Receiver

Messages are sent from one person to another through the use of an oral (spoken) or non-verbal (unspoken) methods of communication. People use their senses (sight, hearing or touch) to receive the message. An interaction is, by definition, two way. The receiver of a message prolongs the interaction by responding, or giving feedback, to the original message. The cycle then repeats and repeats. This is exactly how a conversation works. You may have noticed that conversations don't work when people interrupt (that is, don't wait their turn) or don't listen (that is, receive the message) properly. Where these kinds of disruptions to the communication cycle occur, attempts at communication become ineffective.

Communication in care settings occurs when people use verbal, non-verbal, written and graphical means of sending messages to each other. On an individual level, most of the communication that occurs between health and social care workers and service users is verbal and non-verbal. Organisational communication tends to use written, and sometimes graphical, means to convey official messages in a more formal way. Letters, memos and written files are all commonly used examples of official communication strategies. The verbal and non-verbal communication skills used in care settings are outlined below.

Verbal communication

Verbal communication occurs when a person speaks. When people talk to each other in a one-to-one or group situation, their verbal communication and interaction is structured and governed by rules. For example, the way that people begin conversations with a standard greeting, the formal ways we have of ending conversations and the turn-taking that occurs as people alternate between speaking and listening are some of the basic accepted rules of conversation.

Verbal communication is based on the use of an oral language. Languages are made up of a vocabulary of words and a set of conventions, or grammar, which define the acceptable ways of putting the words together. Speaking, or talking, is the most socially accepted and expected form of everyday oral communication.

Effective verbal communication involves a two-way process of speaking and listening. Effective listening is much harder, and requires more practice, than talking! Whilst listening is part of the communication cycle and is necessary for effective verbal communication, it is really a non-verbal act. Listening is therefore covered in more detail when we discuss non-verbal communication (see p. 74).

Talking to service users, their friends and relatives, and to colleagues is such a common, everyday

▲ Should the client's needs always take priority?

occurrence for health and social care workers that they may not even realise when they are using different verbal skills to deal with situations that require them to conduct different types of conversation. For example, a range of verbal communication skills are needed to:

- respond to service users' questions and distress

- take a clinical history or ask assessment questions

- contribute to a team or group meeting

- run a meeting

- break bad news to a patient or client or to their friends and relatives

- provide support to relatives and friends

- communicate with children

- communicate with people with hearing impairments

- communicate with people with speech impairments

- overcome second language problems

- deal with problems and complaints.

Each of these situations requires the health and social care worker who deals with them to have the practical skills to initiate and maintain effective verbal communication with other people.

ACTIVITY

The effect of dialect and accent

Dialect and accent are features of verbal communication that may have some effect on relationships between people in care settings. A dialect is a form of language spoken in a particular area. It usually involves the use of some words that have a specific local meaning. An accent is a style of pronunciation that is distinctive to a local, national or social group. For example, people from Merseyside, Tyneside and south Wales would each pronounce the same words differently because of their accents.

- How do dialect and accent affect communication?

- What assumptions do we make about people on the basis of the dialects that they speak?

- Which regional accents do you find easy or difficult to understand?

- Should people with strong regional accents modify them in care settings?

- What effect can a local dialect have on communication in care settings?

Use these questions to prompt your thinking about this aspect of communication. You may like to discuss them as a class, as a small group or in pairs. Share your ideas and views with other people.

Non-verbal communication

People continuously use their bodies and aspects of their behaviour to convey messages to others. This type of non-verbal communication is also referred to as body language. You are already skilled to some degree at reading or listening to the body language of other people. For example, have you ever thought that somebody liked or disliked you, even though he or she had never actually said so? How did you know? It was probably something about their body language that told you this. The non-verbal aspects of people's communication often convey a stronger message about whether one person likes or dislikes another than what they say. A person may not have to actually tell you that he or she likes or dislikes you. This message can be sent to you using body language, behaviour or appearance.

The main features of non-verbal behaviour that are important in human communication are:

- facial expression
- eye contact
- gesture
- posture
- proximity and touch.

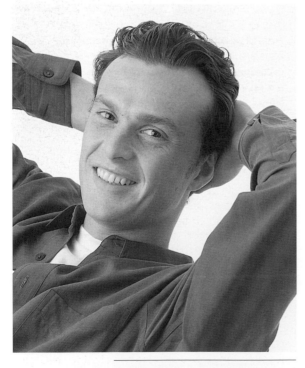

▲ This man's facial expression and open posture suggest that he is happy and relaxed

Facial expression

The human face is very expressive and is an important source of non-verbal communication. Facial expression typically reveals a person's feelings. Many people can control their facial expression to disguise their true feelings and to present what they feel is a socially acceptable face.

When we read other people's facial expressions we look at particular features:

- **Eyes.** Are the pupils dilated (large) or contracted (small)? Large, dilated pupils tend to suggest interest or excitement.

- **Skin colour.** Is the person blushing or sweating?

- **Mouth.** Is the person smiling or frowning? Is the person's mouth dry?

- **Facial muscles.** Are the muscles in the face tight or relaxed?

Different facial expressions involve very subtle changes in each of these features. Human beings make use of a very wide range of facial expressions and are very adept at reading each other's non-verbal communication in this way.

Eye contact

People's eyes, like their facial expression, can be a good barometer of their feelings or emotions. The type of **eye contact** that you make with another person communicates a particular form of non-verbal message. Long, unbroken eye contact can indicate hostility or attraction. The difference in meaning between the two messages is read in the fine detail of what the people do with their eyes and with other parts of their body, like their facial expression and posture. A person who makes eye contact for longer than is socially expected and who widens his or her eyes is likely to be perceived as friendly. This impression is confirmed if he or she smiles. A person who narrows his or her eyes whilst holding long eye contact is likely to be seen as hostile, especially if the jaw is clenched and the facial muscles are tensed.

In health and social care settings, care workers need to use eye contact, or gaze, appropriately in their interactions with service users, their relatives and colleagues. Eye contact can be used to let another person know that you wish to talk to him or her. It can be used to offer trust and reassurance and is an important way of showing interest in what somebody else is saying to you.

It is important for care workers to be aware that people's use of eye contact is influenced by their cultural background. People from European cultures tend to interpret broken, or avoidant, eye contact in a negative way (mistrusting the person) but people from other cultures may do this to show respect and deference.

Gesture

A **gesture** is a deliberate movement, usually of the hands, that is used to convey meaning. People send

▲ Gestures convey meaning

messages through the use of a variety of different gestures. Individuals from the same culture can generally understand the gestures that other members of the culture use. Gestures are a simple form of sign language. They are used to give information in a shorthand way, to emphasise meaning and to express emotion.

Health and social care workers and service will tend, like other people, to use gestures in a natural, unplanned way. Care workers need to be aware that some people use their hands very expressively when communicating and that they need to read these gestures while listening to what the person is saying.

Posture

This term refers to the way that a person sits or stands. People tend to read each other's posture in order to interpret attitude and feelings. For example, somebody

▼ This woman appears to be upset or nervous. She conveys this through her facial expression and closed posture

who is sitting or standing in a very upright, stiff way may be seen as tense or serious in attitude. **Closed postures**, in which people have their arms or legs, or both, crossed, tend to suggest defensiveness and tension. **Open postures**, in which people have their arms loose or open and lean slightly forward, tend to indicate relaxation and comfort.

Health and social care workers can use their understanding of postural messages to read people's moods and feelings. This may be important and revealing during assessment interviews and in one-to-one counselling sessions. It is always best to check your reading of a person's postural message, by sensitively asking a question about how the person is feeling, to avoid making false interpretations or reading too much into how he or she is standing or sitting.

Proximity and touch

Proximity refers to the physical closeness between people during interactions. Another term for proximity is personal space. The amount of personal space that people need during an interaction tends to depend on their cultural background, upbringing and the type of relationship that they have with the other person. People from the Mediterranean, Middle East and South America tend to make more physical contact and require less personal space when communicating than people from Western European and Scandinavian countries. The latter generally prefer only formal touching, such as brief handshakes, and plenty of personal space unless they know the other person extremely well. People tend to require less personal space when the relationship with the other person is a close or personal one. More formal relationships, as with colleagues at work, tend to demand greater physical distance for interactions to be comfortable and effective.

▲ People need varying amounts of personal space to feel comfortable

Health and social care workers are required to make judgements about personal space in many different situations. Service users, if they are able, usually adjust their proximity by moving their chair or standing position to acquire the amount of personal space they need during an interaction. However, if they are not physically able to do this, or lack the confidence to do so, care workers who are aware of the person's discomfort and the reason for it, would be able to improve the quality of the communication by adjusting their own proximity.

Non-verbal messages are an important feature of communication during interpersonal interactions. However, it is usually necessary to listen to and understand the verbal and non-verbal aspects of a message together before a person's communication can be fully understood.

Listening

Effective communication in care settings depends on the ability of health and social care workers to listen well. Service users value the efforts of those health and social care workers who really listen to what they have to say. So, what does listening involve? It is a more complex and difficult skill than many of us think. We look now at some of the main elements of the listening process.

Attending

A prerequisite, or pre-condition, for effective listening is the ability to attend. In basic terms this means paying attention to the other person appropriately. **Attending** involves focusing on the speaker and his or her communication, and being aware of what is being said, verbally and non-verbally. The listener's attention should be focused outward on the speaker. It should not be focused on the listener's own thoughts and feelings as this distracts from really listening to what the other person is communicating.

It is not realistic to think that you can, or should, always avoid focusing on your own thoughts and feelings when you are listening to another person. There are times when it is important to notice how you are being affected by what the other person is saying. This inevitably requires you to focus on your own thoughts and feelings. However, the process of switching focus, from outward on the speaker to inward on your own thoughts and feelings, should be done consciously and deliberately. The pitfall to avoid is that of lapsing into fantasy thinking about the speaker. You need to avoid making assumptions or forming your own interpretation of what is being said, as this leads to the development of unfounded theories and beliefs.

The listening process

When we **listen** effectively we hear a number of aspects of the other person's communication. Listening involves paying attention to:

- the **linguistic**, or spoken, features of what the person says
- the **paralinguistic features** of speech, including the volume, pitch, speed and accent of the person's voice
- non-verbal aspects of communication.

Effective listeners tend to be skilled at using minimal prompts to indicate to the speaker that they are focused outward and are listening. **Minimal prompts** are things like brief, subtle nods of the head, 'mm' sounds and use of affirming words like 'yes', or very brief phrases such as 'go on'. Skilled listeners are careful about their use of these prompts, ensuring that they use an appropriate variety without overusing them in general.

Egan (1986) developed the acronym **SOLER** as a reminder of the behaviours, or physical tactics, that can be used by listeners to promote communication and improve their own reception of messages.

S face the other person **S**quarely

O adopt an **O**pen posture

L **L**ean towards the other person slightly

E maintain good **E**ye contact

R try to be **R**elaxed whilst paying attention.

These are useful guidelines that are generally helpful in improving communication and listening. You shouldn't treat them as hard and fast rules that must always be obeyed. Adapt them to suit the circumstances and the speaker's particular communication needs. It is worth noting that some people find it easier to disclose their feelings or important information when they are not being focused on. For example, conversations in the car or on the train with people sitting side by side or one behind the other can take the pressure off a person who finds one-to-one conversation harder to cope with.

▼ Listening is a skill that care workers use and depend on everyday

BUILD YOUR LEARNING

Keywords and phrases

You should be familiar with the key terms and phrases listed below. If you are unsure about any of them, go back through the last eight pages of the unit to refresh your understanding.

- Attending
- Closed posture
- Communication cycle
- Dialect
- Eye contact
- Interpersonal interaction
- Formal interaction
- Gesture
- Informal interaction
- Linguistic features
- Listening
- Minimal prompts
- Non-verbal communication
- Open posture
- Paralinguistic features
- Proximity
- SOLER behaviours
- Verbal communication

Summary points

- Interpersonal interaction is a key feature of care work and of care relationships.

- Health and social care workers need to have a good understanding of, and should be able to use, a variety of communication skills in order to interact formally and informally with a variety of people in the care setting.

- Interpersonal interaction is organised around a process of sending and receiving messages. This is known as the communication cycle.

- The two key types of communication that health and social care workers use during their interactions are verbal and non-verbal communication. Verbal, or oral, communication requires language, speaking and listening skills. Non-verbal communication occurs through the use of facial expression, eye contact and gestures, for example.

- Listening is a very important feature of the communication process. It requires the individual to pay active attention to the linguistic, paralinguistic and non-verbal features of another person's communication.

- Effective listening is a skill that takes time to develop. Listening can be enhanced by using SOLER behaviours, minimal prompts and active attending skills.

QUESTIONS

1 Explain why interpersonal interaction is an important part of all care work.

2 What is the communication cycle? Use an example to illustrate and explain how the communication cycle works in health and social care settings.

3 Describe three ways in which a health, social care or early years practitioner may be required to use verbal communication skills in a care setting.

4 Explain how care and early years practitioners communicate non-verbally with service users or with their colleagues. Try to identify at least three different ways in which this can occur.

5 What skills are needed for effective listening? Describe what a health, social care or early years worker needs to do to be an effective listener.

Effective communication in care settings

THE EFFECTIVENESS, OR SUCCESS, of communication in health and social care settings is influenced by a number of interpersonal and environmental factors. Some of these factors enhance, or help, communication, whilst others inhibit, or reduce, its effectiveness. Health and social care practitioners can often overcome interpersonal and environmental barriers to effective communication by:

- being aware of possible problems and solutions associated with each factor

- adapting their interaction approach to take account of each factor

- making simple modifications to the physical environment of a care setting.

We are going to consider a number of factors that can both enhance and inhibit the effectiveness of communication in health and social care settings. The factors that we will consider are classified under the following headings:

- physical factors

- emotional factors

- social and cultural factors

- special needs factors.

Physical factors

Examples of **physical factors** that have an influence on communication in care settings include:

- a person's appearance and grooming

- his or her non-verbal behaviour

- the use of touch and proximity

- the quality and character of the physical environment

- the availability of privacy.

The first three items in the list refer to how people look and behave during interactions. The last two are aspects of the physical surroundings in which interpersonal interactions occur. We will briefly discuss each of them.

People's appearance and behaviour influence communication. The clothes and hairstyles that people choose are expressive, in that they communicate aspects of self-image, allegiance to culture or subculture, and even a sense of rebellion or conformity.

It is not unusual for people to feel that they can read the messages that another person's appearance and behaviour send out. In some ways appearance and

▲ People's appearance and behaviour has an influence on communication – you might, for example, address each of these groups of people rather differently

behaviour do communicate messages about a person's values and self-image and about how they value others. For example, a care worker who looks scruffy may send a message to service users that they aren't worth bothering with or that the care worker does not have pride in his or her work. Nevertheless, in a care setting you should never read too much into how people appear, as you may well fall into the trap of stereotyping them on the basis of a false or misleading first impression.

In health and social care settings there tend to be expected and acceptable ways of dressing and behaving. Many health and social care organisations have a policy known as a **dress code** that sets out the organisation's rules on the wearing of jewellery and make-up, and on what constitutes acceptable clothing. Sometimes it is claimed that these dress codes are justified on health and safety grounds, despite the fact that protective clothing (uniform) may only be needed temporarily. An assumption of these dress codes is that clothing and appearance are of sufficient importance to be a professional matter. This is a matter of ongoing debate. The activity below gives you an opportunity to explore this issue and to express or develop your own views.

ACTIVITY

The effects of clothing and appearance on communication

In many health and social care settings there is a clothing policy and a policy relating to standards of personal appearance and grooming. Many of these policies stipulate that members of staff should dress in ways that convey a professional image and professional standards. What do you feel about this issue?

- How does the way a person dresses affect other people's reaction to them?

- Do you think that health and social care workers should be subject to dress and appearance codes?

- What effect do you think uniforms and name badges have on the communication process in health and social care settings?

Discuss and explain your views on these questions.

It's only a nose stud

An incident over a nose stud convinced Claire Hardman that nurse leaders are out of touch with grass roots.

'In 1996 I had my nose pierced and what a fuss it caused. The nurse management did not like it, but in a politically correct world the search for incriminating evidence that wearing a nose stud was unsuitable for nurses was unfruitful and it had to consider other tactics.

'Eventually my managers produced a questionnaire and gave it to selected members of staff. They claimed the response was unanimous: nose studs for nurses were not appropriate. I asked to examine the method and results but they refused.

'All the same, I stopped wearing the stud as it made very little difference to me. Of much greater concern, however, was the management's extreme and petulant obsession with an issue that most people considered irrelevant. The nose stud incident only confirmed staff suspicions that nurse management was out of touch.'

Nursing Times, 18 August 1999

Physical surroundings

Aspects of the physical environment can affect the quality of communication and may even deter people from making efforts to communicate with each other in the first place. An environment in which there is a lot of **background noise**, either from within or from outside a building, can hamper people's efforts to communicate. Background noises are the sounds that intrude into the environment and which are not under the control of the people who want to communicate with each other. If you have ever tried to hold a conversation in a night club you will be aware that a high level of background noise can limit verbal communication. Some sections of the population, particularly older people, have difficulty in hearing certain types and levels of sound, such as low-pitched voices, and can find that their efforts to communicate are hampered by background noise

A second physical aspect of communication, the ability to see and receive another person's non-verbal signals, can be affected by the quality of light in care settings. Dark and gloomy rooms or buildings are likely to reduce people's ability to pick up the details of facial expression or of body language. The glare of lights, or the sun on windows and shiny surfaces, or the speaker standing with his or her back to the light source, has the same effect. People with a hearing impairment find that their ability to communicate with others is particularly affected by poor lighting. It reduces their ability to lip read and to pick up non-verbal communication.

Comfort is a qualitative feature of the physical environment that subtly affects communication. Comfort enables people to relax, and relaxed people are more likely to be able to use their communication skills effectively.

ACTIVITY
Promoting effective communication

You can probably think of examples of both comfortable and uncomfortable care settings from your own experience as a student or care worker or as a service user. Identify the features of one care setting that made it comfortable and of another care setting that gave it an uncomfortable quality.

The way the physical space of a care setting is used can have an impact on communication. For example, in residential and nursing home settings there are often rooms in which residents can meet to talk, watch television together or join in other shared activities. The extent to which clients are able to communicate, however, can be restricted by poor use of space. With careful thought and planning the physical space of care

▼ The physical layout of rooms can hinder communication

settings can be used to positively encourage communication. The layout of rooms, their decor, the way the room is lit and the types of furniture used can all assist communication amongst the service users.

Non-verbal communication

Non-verbal communication plays an important role in effective interaction in care settings. The ability to listen to or read the non-verbal or physical features of communication enables health and social care workers to do their jobs effectively in several ways.

- To monitor the effects of their verbal communication, care interventions and behaviour on others. For example, a service user might show pain in his or her facial expression after a physical procedure has been carried out without saying anything, or may use body language to demonstrate that they have been reassured after a chat.

- To check whether their verbal messages have been understood. For example, a person's physical response to bad news generally reveals whether the person has understood what has been said.

- To confirm the truth of the verbal statements made by another person. For example, a colleague who says that he or she is OK while crying in a distressed way may not, in fact, be telling the truth about his or her feelings.

- To convey trust, warmth and support to others, especially through the sensitive use of touch and physical contact.

- To respond sensitively to the way a service user is feeling. The ability to interpret emotions through non-verbal behaviour may make the difference between responding sensitively and insensitively to a person who is in distress.

As well as receiving the non-verbal messages of work colleagues, service users, and their friends and relatives, health and social care workers also send non-verbal messages, often without realising it, to all of the individuals with whom they have contact in their workplace. Health and social care workers can use their non-verbal behaviour in positive ways to offer support and to promote opportunities for communication. It is also possible for health and social care workers to use non-verbal behaviour to reduce opportunities for communication. This can occur where they dislike or feel unable to cope with particular service users or situations. Caring for others is a stressful activity. It is very difficult for health and social care workers to say when they are not coping well with the pressures and stress that it involves. Sensitivity to the non-verbal messages of colleagues may provide health and social care workers with the only indication that a colleague is in need of support at a particular time.

Emotional factors

Interactions are most effective where people are able to communicate in an appropriate emotional atmosphere. People communicate best when they feel relaxed in themselves and in the presence of other people; when they are able to empathise with other people; when they experience and express warmth, genuineness and sincerity; and where they give and receive respect.

Carl Rogers (1961) developed a **person-centred** approach to counselling and psychotherapy in which he identified the three conditions of genuineness, empathy and unconditional positive regard as fundamental to effective communication in therapeutic situations. **Genuineness** involves being yourself and contributing to interactions with honesty and integrity. Health and social care workers who bring genuineness to their interactions avoid being authoritarian, defensive or professionally detached.

Unconditional positive regard is a phrase that conveys the need for health and social care workers to be unconditionally warm and accepting towards other people, without approving or disapproving of them. By accepting people and not bringing reservations to an interaction, health and social care workers are better able to communicate with the real unique person they meet.

Empathy involves the ability to enter the service user's frame of reference in order to better understand their feelings and behaviour. This idea, and its importance for health and social care workers, is discussed further in the section below.

Empathy

Empathy is a critical feature of effective communication in health and social care settings. It is the ability to see life through another person's eyes. Empathy does not involve making guesses or assumptions about what the other person is really thinking or feeling. Rather, care workers who are able to empathise with service users or colleagues can put themselves in the other person's position and, because of the understanding they gain, communicate more effectively. They should still try to remain objective and should always avoid confusing empathy with sympathy.

Verena Tschudin (1982) uses the metaphor of helping a man stuck in a ditch to illustrate the difference between empathy and sympathy:

*The **sympathetic helper** goes and lies in the ditch with him and bewails the situation with him. The unsympathetic helper stands on the bank and shouts 'come on, get yourself out of that ditch!' The **empathic helper** climbs down to the victim but keeps one foot on the bank and is thus able to help the victim out of the trouble on to firm ground again.*

Health and social care workers can make their interactions with service users, their relatives and colleagues more effective by using empathy appropriately, gaining insight into the needs and experience of the service user in a careful, alert and calm way, without actually having to experience it directly. It gives the health and social care worker an effective way of communicating with the real person behind the label of service user, relative or colleague.

Social and cultural factors

People's ability to communicate in a care setting can be affected by a number of social and cultural factors. Acknowledging and responding to important features of another person's identity and cultural needs are strategies that are likely to improve communication. Health and social care workers need to develop the ability to see the real person behind the patient or client label that service users are often given in care settings. In order to do this, they must be conscious of how they are perceiving the people they are working with.

Respecting the identity and needs of others is an essential part of relationships in care settings. While most care workers would agree with this in principle, situations do occur in which the cultural assumptions of the dominant social group are taken for granted, and even imposed, within care settings. Imposing social and cultural assumptions can marginalise people who are not part of the dominant group or culture.

For example, in care settings the assumption is frequently made that the language of the dominant culture should be used in communication. In the vast majority of cases this is English and, especially where health and social care professionals are involved, may be a version of English using technical jargon peculiar to the setting or speciality. Health and social care services and individual workers who assume that all service users can understand English are making sociocultural assumptions that may inhibit the opportunities of some service users. The use of language that assumes an understanding of technical health and social care jargon can even leave service users whose first language is English confused and unable to understand.

Labelling, stereotyping and prejudice

As we saw in Unit 1, the assumptions that people make about another people or groups of people can affect their communication. **Labelling, stereotyping** and prejudice all involve usually negative assumptions and judgements about other people. Labelling and stereotyping close down communication possibilities, while prejudice is likely to make one person treat another negatively and unfairly.

The influence of roles

The roles which health and social care workers adopt can also influence the communication process. Health and social care workers and service users often relate to each other in terms of their roles when they interact in care settings. This is known as **role behaviour**. However, there is a power imbalance between relatively powerful care workers and relatively powerless service users in many care settings. This can lead to restricted forms of communication in which the parties feel that it acceptable to talk about some topics but not others and that their roles present a barrier to communicating as people rather than as patients or care professionals.

ACTIVITY

Roles and communication in GP surgeries

GP surgeries are places where people go with problems relating to health and well-being. Effective communication is important here in order that problems can be expressed, identified and dealt with. Think back to your own recent experiences of communicating at your GP's surgery and answer the following questions.

- To what extent has your ability to communicate with the administrative staff been affected by their role behaviour?

- When you see your GP do you feel that you can talk to, and communicate effectively, with him or her?

- How do expectations of patient role behaviour promote or inhibit communication with your GP?

CASE STUDY

Promoting effective interaction

Arthur Baldwin describes himself as a traditional general practitioner. Part of his traditionalism is reflected in the way he sets out his surgery and conducts interviews with patients and colleagues.

Dr Baldwin has a policy of giving every patient a five-minute consultation. He always sits behind his large oak desk, leans back in his chair and asks patients to state their symptoms. The patients sit about six feet away from Dr Baldwin and can see a desk full of files, notes and items of medical equipment and Dr Baldwin looking at them with raised eyebrows.

Dr Baldwin is not particularly interested in hearing about his patients' personal concerns but encourages them to stick to the physical or psychological symptoms. Dr Baldwin's patients complain that he sometimes seems more interested in the programme on the radio behind him, or in writing up notes from previous consultations, than in listening to them.

Produce some recommendations for Dr Baldwin that would enable him to improve interpersonal interactions with his patients. You should consider both the environmental changes that might be made and the modifications he might make to his communication skills.

Special needs factors

Health and social care service users, and indeed those who work in health and social care services, may have physical, sensory or psychological problems that affect their ability to communicate effectively. It is important for care workers to be alert to the possibility that service users or colleagues may have such a difficulty or impairment. Care workers should always try to find ways of adapting their own communication skills to the needs of others and, where appropriate, should try to adapt the care environment and provide communication aids for people with special needs. They should try and put themselves in the position of the person whose ability to communicate is restricted and work out a way of getting their messages across in appropriate ways.

People's ability to communicate can be affected by a wide range of physical and learning impairments. Conditions such as cerebral palsy, Down's syndrome and autism all tend to restrict the ability to communicate verbally, for example. Hearing and visual impairments place obvious restrictions on the ability to receive verbal and non-verbal messages.

A number of psychological factors affect the extent to which we are able to communicate effectively. Illness and social problems tend to reduce our psychological well-being. When people are unwell or have problems resulting from poverty or poor housing, for example, the stress and distress that they experience can lead to a lowering of self-esteem and a lack of confidence in social situations. This can affect the ability to communicate effectively and to maintain relationships. Health and social care workers need to take these psychological effects into account.

Different ways of adapting communication skills to the needs of people with special needs are outlined in the section on talking with service users (p. 89) and in the section on physical and emotional factors (pp. 80–84).

▼ Many care services provide facilities for people with special communication needs

Induction loop fitted. Please use `T` position on your hearing aid .

BUILD YOUR LEARNING

Keywords and phrases

You should know the meaning of the words and phrases listed below. If you are not sure about any of them, look back through the last seven pages of the unit to refresh your understanding.

- Comfort
- Background noise
- Dress code
- Empathy
- Empathic helper
- Genuineness
- Labelling
- Person-centred
- Physical factors
- Psychological factors
- Respect
- Role behaviour
- Social and cultural background
- Stereotyping
- Sympathy
- Sympathetic helper
- Unconditional positive regard
- Warmth

Summary points

- The extent to which communication in care settings is effective is influenced by a variety of physical, emotional, social and cultural factors that are a feature of the care environment and of care relationships.

- Health and social care workers need to be aware of the different ways in which these factors can be used to promote communication and also of the ways in which they can limit the effectiveness of communication.

- The appearance and behaviour of care workers and features of the physical surroundings (light, noise, comfort, privacy) are examples of physical factors that have an impact on the effectiveness of communication. Health and social care workers need to manage both themselves and the care environment to ensure the quality and effectiveness of communication.

- Qualitative features of the care relationship, such as the presence or absence of warmth, genuineness and empathy, are important in determining the effectiveness of communication within caring relationships. Unconditional positive regard and empathy enable a care worker to appreciate and address the individual needs of service users.

- Social and cultural background affect the way in which people perceive and react to others. Health and social care workers should be aware of the impact of culture on the communication process, particularly where cultural differences have the potential to cause communication problems.

- People who work in and use health and social care services may have special needs that affect their ability to communicate effectively. Health and social care workers should be aware of the ways in which physical, learning and psychological impairment can affect communication.

QUESTIONS

1 Give examples of physical factors that can have a negative effect on personal communication in health, social care or early years settings.

2 What features of a care environment can be managed or changed to improve communication and interaction?

3 What does the term unconditional positive regard mean? In your answer explain why this quality can help to promote communication in care settings.

4 Explain why empathy is a more useful and positive interaction strategy for a care practitioner than sympathy.

5 Describe some of the special or cultural needs of service users that care practitioners need to be aware of when communicating in care settings.

Talking with service users

SERVICE USERS TALK TO HEALTH and social care workers for a wide variety of reasons. As well as being able to listen (see p. 76), health and social care workers must have the skills to respond and to develop conversations with service users. We are going to look briefly at the different types of conversational skill that health and social care workers use in care settings.

Developing basic verbal skills

Although you already use talking and listening skills to the extent that you can communicate effectively in your daily life, as a health or social care worker you will need to develop these skills further so that you can use them to form and maintain effective relationships with patients, clients and colleagues. The activities that follow give you an opportunity to explore and develop your basic interactive abilities and to experience the impact of effective and ineffective listening and talking skills.

ACTIVITY

Identifying communication abilities

This activity requires you to reflect on your own strengths and weaknesses in communicating. You may benefit from sharing your thoughts and ideas with another person but you should not feel that you have to if you are uncomfortable about doing so.

Brainstorm onto a blank sheet of paper all those qualities that you feel make you the unique person you are. Include the qualities that help you in your relationships and communication with others and those that cause difficulties. Organise your list into helpful and less helpful qualities or features.

What could you do about the less helpful qualities? Think about a couple of these and suggest how they might hinder communication.

What makes a person a good communicator? Brainstorm a list of qualities and explain how they enhance communication. If possible, identify people you know of who possess them.

ACTIVITY

Experiencing ineffective listening

Listening is a very important communication skill. It takes quite a lot of time and practice to develop an effective listening ability. This activity gives you a taste of the impact of ineffective listening on a person's efforts to communicate verbally.

In pairs, sit opposite each other in chairs of equal height. Take it in turns to talk to each other on any subject for four minutes. The listener does not listen, but the talker must keep going for the whole four minutes, trying all the time to gain the partner's attention. The talker must not touch or shout at the listener. The listener must stay seated.

After each person has spoken for four minutes, take it in turns to tell each other what you liked and what you disliked about being the speaker who is not listened to. Write a short account of the exercise, explaining what happened and what it felt like not to be listened to.

ACTIVITY

Developing effective listening behaviour

In pairs, sit opposite each other in chairs of equal height. Take it in turns to talk to each other on any subject for four minutes. The listener should use the SOLER behaviours (see p. 77).

After each person has spoken for four minutes, take it in turns to tell each other what you liked and what you disliked about being the speaker and the listener. Write a short account of the exercise, explaining what happened and what it felt like to be actively listened to.

Developing responding skills

In pairs, sit opposite each other in chairs of equal height. Take it in turns to talk to each other on any subject for four minutes. The listener should use the SOLER behaviours. Every so often the listener should recap on what the speaker has said.

After each person has spoken for four minutes, take it in turns to tell each other what it felt like to be the speaker and listener in this exercise. Write a short account of the exercise, explaining what happened and what it felt like to intervene to recap and to have the listener recap every so often.

Putting skills into practice

It is often useful to try out and practice specific communication strategies in a classroom setting. There is bound to come a time, however, where you will have to put the basic listening and responding skills that you have learned into practice. Care workers develop their communication skills as they build up their knowledge and experience of care work. Over a period of time health and social care workers become aware of and develop their skills in a number of different types of conversation. Some of these are described next.

Information-giving conversations

Health and social care workers often have to give information to colleagues, to service users and to their relatives. For example, information-giving conversations happen when health and social care workers discuss the needs and situations of the service users for whom they provide care and when they explain visiting times to an inpatient's relatives. Such conversations sometimes happen in one-to-one situations and sometimes within group situations,

One of the key issues in these conversations is about how much information to give. Issues such as confidentiality (see p. 115), the complexity of the information required, the health and social care workers' role and relationship with the service users, all influence whether, and how much, information can be given. For example, if relatives request information that is personal and considered private, health and social care workers may have to refer to confidentiality and avoid disclosing the information. In contrast, if relatives ask for information about visiting times, the information can be given without restriction.

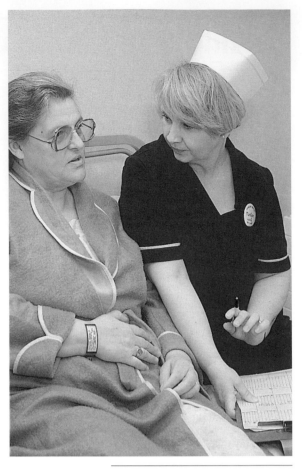

▲ Providing information in a clear, reassuring way is part of the nurse's role

As well as distinguishing between public and private information, health and social care workers need to be careful that they only give factual information, rather than information based on assumptions and opinions. It may be appropriate to make a judgement or give an opinion when asked. However, it is not good practice to offer opinions to service users unless they ask for them and then you should be very careful not to present your opinions as fact.

Helping people to talk

We said earlier that service users talk to health and social care workers about a wide variety of matters. One of the key conversational strategies that health and social care workers need to develop is the ability to help, or facilitate, service users in their efforts to talk about issues that concern them. Burnard (1992) calls this **drawing out** and says that the use of open questions, reflection, understanding checks and empathy-building statements are core components of these strategies.

- **Open questions** are questions that have no specific answer and that give the respondent a chance to talk at some length rather than to give a one word (yes or no) answer. For example, 'How are you feeling today?' is open compared to 'Are you feeling OK today?' Conversations with service users and colleagues go much further when open questions are used.

- **Reflection** is a conversational skill that takes practice and can only be developed by actually trying it out. Straightforward reflections involve reflecting, or repeating, some of the other person's words directly back to them. Health and social care workers may use reflection to check their understanding of, or to summarise part of the conversation. Selective reflection involves reflecting back the particular bits of a conversation that the other person seems to emphasise. This enables the listener to pick up and explore the key issues within a conversation a little more.

- **Understanding checks** occur when health and social care workers make a deliberate attempt to recap and summarise what has been said to them. For example, a health and social care worker might say something like 'Can I just check that you meant...'. The health and social care worker checks with the speaker that the summary is a correct account of what has been said. The value of understanding checks is that they enable listeners to avoid making their own interpretations of what has been said.

- Health and social care workers who use **empathy-building statements** in their conversations communicate to service users that they are able to understand their situation and way of seeing the world. Saying something like 'It sounds as though you are very unhappy about that', or 'You seem to find the idea of surgery quite frightening', indicates that the health and social care worker appreciates the service user's feelings and viewpoint. You will notice that the two statements begin in a tentative way. They are attempts to show an appreciation of the other person's experience. Sentences that start with phrases such as 'You seem to be...', or 'It sounds as though...' indicate empathy but also leave room for the service user to correct any misinterpretation or misunderstanding.

Making conversations therapeutic

A therapeutic conversation is one that is for the benefit of the service user. Its purpose is to help service users in some way. Burnard (1992) suggests that the characteristics of therapeutic conversations are that they:

- focus on the needs and problems of service users, not on those of health or social care workers

- make the service user feel better in some way

- are structured and managed by health and social care workers to enable service users to talk in ways, and about matters, that are helpful to them.

Health and social care workers should make time for therapeutic conversations with service users in their ordinary, everyday activities. During the conversations that they have, they need to pay attention to the way their conversations develop. The key point is to keep the focus on the service users and to make the conversation a useful and effective communication opportunity for them.

Adapting to service users' special needs

Health and social care service users often have special needs arising out of illness, impairment or developmental factors that can affect their ability to communicate and to interact. By taking account of people's special needs and adapting basic communication strategies, health and social care workers can improve the quality of their communication and interactions.

Advocacy in health and social care

Advocacy services and opportunities are increasingly regarded as basic facilities that should be offered to all users of care services, but particularly to those groups which have historically been less able to express their needs, views and wishes. Two main forms of advocacy are used in care settings. These are known as citizen advocacy and self-advocacy.

Citizen advocacy refers to the voluntary involvement of an advocate in the life of somebody with health needs or social care problems. Citizen advocates work alongside service users to represent their interests. Citizen advocacy is quite common in mental health and learning disabilities care settings. Citizen advocates usually offer to support and enable patients or clients to identify and communicate their needs and wishes to care professionals or to family members. Self-advocacy, by contrast, has been defined as 'a process whereby service users are encouraged to speak out directly for themselves' (Brandon and Brandon, 1991). Groups of service users tend to promote self-advocacy and provide

ALLIANCE ADVOCACY SERVICES

If you are an inpatient, or the friend or relative of someone in hospital, can you be sure that:

- your rights are being observed?
- your concerns and wishes are being listened to?
- your choices are being respected?

We can help you to make your voice heard. Alliance advocates are independent volunteers who visit the hospital each week on Thursday afternoons. We can provide:

- information about your rights
- help with exploring your options
- support in your meetings with professionals.

We will:

- work with you to pursue what you see as being your best interests
- work in the way that you find most helpful
- keep what you tell us confidential unless it involves harm to someone.

You can meet your Alliance advocacy service volunteer on the ward on Thursdays.

▲ Hospitals provide information on advocacy services for patients

training and support to enable members to develop the skills and confidence to speak up for themselves.

Sign language

People with hearing impairments or who have dual hearing and sight impairments, sometimes speak and listen to others through the use of specialist non-verbal forms of communication. Sign languages are also sometimes taught and used in learning disabilities settings, where service users have limited ability to use complex verbal language. Three common forms of sign language include **dactylography** or finger spelling, **British Sign Language** and **Makaton**.

Technological aids

Communication problems can often be overcome or made less disabling through the use of technological equipment and alternative communication strategies. You will probably be familiar with hearing aids and text phones, and you may have seen a videophone or an electronic communicator being used by people with speech and hearing impairments.

People who are unable to communicate in conventional ways sometimes use alternative language systems to send and receive messages. For example, people with visual impairments often use their sense of touch to read documents written in Braille or Moon letters.

▼ An example of a finger spelling chart

FINGER SPELLING CHART

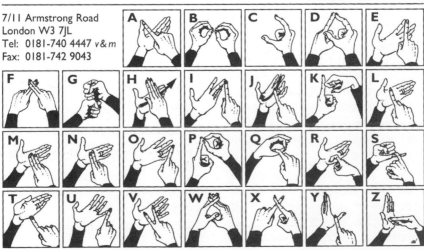

7/11 Armstrong Road
London W3 7JL
Tel: 0181-740 4447 *v & m*
Fax: 0181-742 9043

The Sympathetic Hearing Scheme (The Deaf Awareness Project of Hearing Concern)

Braille uses a series of indentations made by a special pointed stylus on one side of paper. The combinations of indentations represent letters that can be touch read by people who understand the Braille system. Moon letters are raised shapes based on the standard alphabet. They are written on special paper, using a frame and a ballpoint pen. These, and many other devices, can provide people with speech, hearing and complex physical disabilities with effective communication assistance.

of different languages. Translation services are also provided where health and social care services are used by multicultural populations.

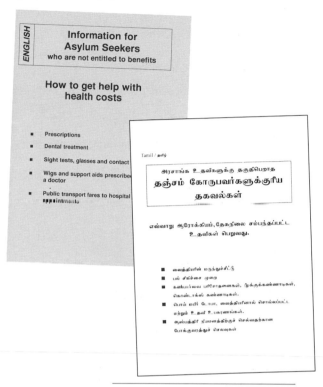

▲ Multilingual information is essential where service users do not use English as their first language

▲ Stephen Hawking uses modern technology to communicate

Second language services

People who are not able to speak or understand English or who use English as a second language find it helpful to receive information about care services in their native language. Many hospital and residential services now provide multilingual sign posting to enable people who do not speak English to find their way around the care environment, and leaflets and booklets in a range

Adapting communication skills

In addition to the specific strategies briefly outlined above, health and social care workers can take some basic steps in adapting their communication skills to the specific developmental and impairment needs of the service users they work with.

When communicating with people with hearing impairments, health and social care workers should:

- make sure they can be seen clearly

- face both the light and the person at all times

- make sure their mouth is visible

- speak clearly and slowly, repeating and rephrasing if necessary

- make sure they do not shout into a person's ear or hearing aid

- minimise background noise

- use eyes, facial expressions and hand gestures to communicate, where appropriate.

When communicating with people with visual impairments, health and social care workers should:

- speak to the person in the way that they would talk to a sighted person – there is no need to speak any louder or more slowly than normal

- say who they are somewhere in their greeting, as their voice may not be recognised

- always introduce anybody else who is with them and explain what is going on if a person with a visual impairment joins a group

- let the person with a visual impairment know when they are about to do something (like leave the room briefly or move away) that is likely to affect communication

- use an appropriate form of words to end the conversation and let the person know that they are leaving

- not assume that a person with a visual impairment wants help to sit down or move about. Ask first. On some occasions help will be appreciated whilst at other times it won't be needed.

When communicating with people with learning disabilities, health and social care workers should:

- speak directly to the person, not to a helper or carer

- keep sentences short and use straightforward, simple language without making it simplistic or patronising

- give the person plenty of time to respond and listen carefully to what he or she says. Don't put words into his or her mouth.

ACTIVITY

Role playing one-to-one interactions

Role play provides an opportunity for participants to develop and practice basic skills in a safe, simulated situation. Participants need to become as involved in their role as they can, as the purpose is to try to experience empathically something of what the situation might really be like.

Role play 1

A parent approaches a nursery nurse about securing his or her child a place at the nursery. The parent wants to know what the nursery can offer, how the child will be looked after and what costs are involved. The parent is concerned about safety and cost. The nursery nurse must provide appropriate information and reassurance.

Role play 2

A patient is waiting in his or her GP's surgery. The receptionist is aware that there is a delay of 30 minutes to all appointment times. The receptionist must try to inform and reassure the patient that he or she will get to see the doctor shortly, but that there is a delay. The patient must try to communicate irritation, restlessness and anxiety.

Both participants are allowed to speak, but they should concentrate on communicating through body language.

Role play 3

A client has comes to the housing department's homeless persons unit. The housing officer must interview the client to find out his or her details and try to understand how his or her accommodation needs can be met. The client is homeless, has no fixed abode, is reluctant to discuss his or her past and wants to get off the streets. Both parties are allowed to speak but should concentrate on the use of body language in the interaction.

Role play 4

A person has come to visit his or her partner in hospital, but the bed is stripped and empty when he or she arrives. The patient in the next bed says that the patient has been transferred to another ward. The visitor meet the staff nurse in charge of the ward and tries to find out what has happened. The staff nurse must provide information and be reassuring and supportive of the patient's partner, who is worried and concerned. Both parties are allowed to speak, but should concentrate on the use of body language in the interaction.

BUILD YOUR LEARNING

You should know the meaning of the words and phrases listed below. If you are unclear about any of them, go back through the last six pages of the unit to refresh your understanding.

- British Sign Language
- Citizen advocacy
- Dactylography
- Drawing out
- Empathy-building statements
- Information-giving
- Makaton
- Open questions
- Reflection
- Self-advocacy
- Understanding checks

Summary points

- Users of health and social care services value opportunities to talk to the health and social care workers they have contact with. Health and social care workers need to develop their natural verbal skills so that they are able to hold effective conversations with service users from a wide variety of social and cultural backgrounds.

- Effective conversational skills are developed through practice and experience. Health and social care workers need to develop both their listening and responding skills and should be able to apply them in a variety of ways.

- Health and social care workers should be able to hold information-giving and therapeutic conversations with service users and be able to help them to talk. These each require that care workers adapt and apply their communication skills in specific ways.

- A variety of strategies, adaptations and aids are used in health and social care settings to enable service users to communicate with others more effectively. Wherever possible, health and social care workers should promote awareness of and access to these sources of communication support.

- Health and social care workers should develop their awareness of the general communication needs of members of the client groups with whom they work. Simple adaptation strategies can enhance the effectiveness of their communication with children, people with sensory impairments, people with learning disabilities and older people.

QUESTIONS

1 Identify and explain two issues that health and social care workers need to bear in mind during information-giving conversations with service users or their relatives.

2 Explain how care practitioners can use different conversational strategies to help service users to express their thoughts and feelings.

3 What is a therapeutic conversation?

4 What role do citizen advocates play in promoting communication in health and social care settings?

5 What strategies or forms of equipment can be used in care situations to help service users who are unable to communicate effectively? Use an example of a service user with a specified impairment or problem to illustrate your answer.

Communication skills in groups

▲ Groups come together because they have a common purpose

AS A HUMAN BEING, YOUR LIFE has always revolved around being a member of different groups. Groups are collections of people who come together because they have a common purpose or goal and who gradually develop a shared sense of belonging, or **group identity**.

People tend to take it for granted that their various relationships require them to live and work alongside other people and may not be aware of their membership of many of the groups to which they belong. Philip Burnard (1992) classifies the many different groups into two main types. **Primary groups** involve face-to-face situations in which group members get to know each other. In health and social care settings examples might include therapy groups and relatives' meetings. **Secondary groups** have a more widely distributed membership. Many group members may never actually meet each other. Examples include trade unions and professional bodies that health and social care workers such as social workers or physiotherapists belong to.

People join different kinds of groups throughout their lives and these experiences perform important functions for them. For example, during childhood people tend to extend their membership of social groups from being part of a family to also becoming a member of a friendship group, school class or local sports group. Interaction within of all of these groups is important in providing opportunities for social, intellectual and emotional development.

Health and social care workers and service users become involved in a wide variety of group interactions. Examples include:

- report or handover meetings between care team members

- case conferences and discharge planning meetings

- support meetings for team members to share experiences and offer each other support

- therapeutic groups

- meetings with managerial staff, service users and their relatives

- educational groups and classes.

Health and social care workers need to develop communication skills that enable them to interact effectively in these groups.

You can probably appreciate by now that groups are a very important interaction context in health and social care work and have a number of advantages and benefits for participants.

- Groups can have very positive outcomes, improving members' self-esteem, behaviour, self-awareness and social skills. This is particularly the case where the group has a specific therapeutic focus or goal.

- Groups can be an effective means of problem-solving and of sharing information. This is one reason why staff work together in teams or work groups. Groups provide opportunities to share knowledge and skills with people who have a common work goal or purpose.

- Groups allow decision making and responsibility to be shared between a number of participants.

- Groups enable participants to learn from each other.

- Groups tend to command more respect and have more power than people acting alone.

- Groups provide multiple perspectives, greater depth and breadth of information and a more questioning approach to problems and decision making.

Groups are not always good experiences for members or positive, effective ways of solving problems or dealing with work and a number of problems affect interaction between group members.

- Power in a group may be held by a single person or may be misused by a small group, or **clique** of people who use it to dominate others and pursue their own agenda.

- Groups can lose sight of their primary goal and drift into an ineffective, inactive pattern of activity that is simply directed at keeping the group going for the members' own benefit.

- Groups can become beset by power struggles between members and lose sight of their real purpose.

- Groups can become leaderless, with nobody taking responsibility for their actions or activity.

- Individual ideas and identities can become lost within the group, especially if the group contains people who are relatively powerless.

- Individuals can find it difficult to challenge the assumptions, values and practices of a group that has become established. Group pressure and power is very hard to challenge and resist.

As we have seen, group members usually have a reason for meeting and getting together and this is their common goal or purpose. However, members need to have effective communication skills and an understanding of group processes and patterns of behaviour in order to maintain the interaction successfully. We look at this next.

Group formation and processes

How do groups actually form? This may seem like a question with a couple of very straightforward answers: people simply join an existing group, such as a work team, as a new member or, together with others, form a new group for a specific purpose. These answers treat the idea of group formation too superficially, however.

You will remember that earlier we said that groups are collections of people who come together because they have a common purpose or goal and who gradually develop a shared sense of belonging, or group identity. The implication of this is that every time a new set of people comes together for a specific purpose, including every time a new person joins an existing group, the group formation process begins again. Any new combination of people has to go through the process of establishing ways of communicating and working together, and of forming a new group identity.

A number of theories explain the process of group formation. Tuckman (1965) described group formation in four stages.

- **Forming** is the first stage. Group members come together and ask basic questions about the purpose and aims of the group, their role within it and consider whether they want to commit themselves to it. In this early stage of group development, members tend to feel quite anxious and disorientated in their interactions with others. A leader often emerges in this early stage.

- **Storming** is the second stage in the group's evolution. As the term suggests, this is a period of conflict within the group. Members argue over the purpose of the group, may resist or contest its aims and the authority and role of the leader. This stage is one in which power and control are the main issues. Eventually the purpose of the group and roles within it become clearer as power and control battles are won and lost.

- **Norming** is the stage at which the group's identity develops. A strong set of shared values, norms of behaviour and a group culture emerges. The group becomes more cohesive and tends to work together to resolve conflicts.

- **Performing** is the stage at which the group finally matures and gets down to working effectively at its true purpose or goal. Members tend to focus more on the overall goal rather than on their own interrelationships. Relationships have by this stage become more comfortable and are based on trust and mutual support. Leadership within the group is less directive. The norms and values are clear and shared. The group performs more effectively.

An alternative theory, developed by Schultz (1958), sees groups forming through a three-stage emotional process.

- **Inclusion** is the first stage during which most activity is directed towards relationship building between group members. Members test their relationships with each other to establish whether they want to belong to the group.

- **Control** is a stage that involves competition between members over power and status within the group. Cliques are formed and individuals compete for and establish their own roles.

- **Affection** is the final stage. The calm after the storm! Group members come together and form a more cohesive unit that develops a shared identity.

A group is more than the sum of its participants. It has an identity and life of its own that is produced and shared by the group members. The roles, relationships and aims that give a group its character and purpose provide opportunities for, and barriers to, communication and interaction between group members. We look next at the communication strategies that people use within groups. These can influence whether interaction is effective or not and whether the group is successful in achieving its purpose or goal.

Communication strategies and behaviour within groups

One of the key points that you need to know about communication and behaviour in groups is that people behave differently in group contexts compared to when they are interacting in one-to-one situations. It can sometimes be surprising to observe somebody whom you feel that you know well behaving and communicating in an unexpected way in a group situation.

Burnard (1992) makes the point that people have to make compromises within group situations. There is always a tension between the needs of the group and those of the individual. Experience in group situations shows that people do not always put group needs first. This can explain why interactions in groups can sometimes be challenging, competitive and negative whilst in other circumstances they are supportive, cooperative and productive.

R F Bales (1970) and his colleagues at the Harvard University social relations laboratory studied patterns of communication and behaviour within group situations. They identified a number of different types of communication behaviour that are used by group members.

- **Proposing** involves communications that offer new ideas, suggestions or plans of action. It tends to be positive and constructive.

- **Building** involves communications that extend or develop ideas and proposals offered by other group members. Again, it tends to be a positive, constructive group behaviour.

- **Supporting** communications offer active support for, or agreement with, the contributions of one or more other group members. They encourage group solidarity and cooperation.

- **Dominating** behaviour occurs when an individual or clique monopolises communication opportunities to gain and use power in their interactions with other group members.

- **Disagreeing** involves communicating a difference of opinion with or disapproval of the contributions or behaviour of another group member. Disagreements can be made in a constructive way or in a negative, critical way.

- **Defensive** communications usually involve group members mounting a defence of their own position, ideas or views when other group members question, disagree or attack them.

- **Attacking** communications challenge other group members' ideas or behaviour. They may be met by defensive responses.

- **Blocking** communications place obstacles or difficulties in the way of other group members' proposals or contributions. They tend to be negative manoeuvres, designed to frustrate other group members' efforts.

- **Summarising** is a communication strategy that seeks to support and maintain the work of group members. It involves a member restating or summing up the contributions and previous discussions of the group.

- **Information-seeking** communications are also constructive, in that they aim to elicit ideas and factual information from group members. Sometimes a group member may request clarification of what others say. This is also information seeking.

- **Information-giving** communications are those that contribute facts, ideas and clarification to group discussions.

- **Inclusive** behaviours and communication aim to bring group members, particularly those who are less powerful or more isolated within the group, into discussions. They usually involve seeking the views, ideas and thoughts of these group members in order to encourage interaction within the wider group.

- **Exclusive** communications have the opposite effect and intention to the above. They aim to block out other people's communication and to frustrate interaction.

Structural features of groups

Another way of understanding interaction in groups is to look at the wider, structural features that groups can have and the interaction opportunities that these provide. In effect, the quality of interaction in groups depends largely on group members having adequate opportunities to communicate with each other. Three patterns of group structure offer different possible communication networks to members.

In the hierarchical model (see Figure 2.2) communication is fed down the hierarchy. People at the bottom and top have few opportunities to interact. Hierarchies are often a feature of health and social care staff teams, particularly within inpatient settings. Decision making tends to occur where the power resides, at the top of the hierarchy.

The circular group model (see Figure 2.3) provides more opportunities for members to interact with one another. Relationships are also more equal. Circle-type structures are often a feature of community-based health and social care teams, where leadership rotates between members and decision-making is shared.

The clique is a complex type of group. The people who belong to the inner group tend to be in close contact and to communicate well with one another. The other members of the group are more isolated and find it harder to communicate and interact with the group.

In real health and social care situations, work teams can involve a combination of different group structures. For example, the multidisciplinary team in Figure 2.5 is composed of a hierarchy and circle.

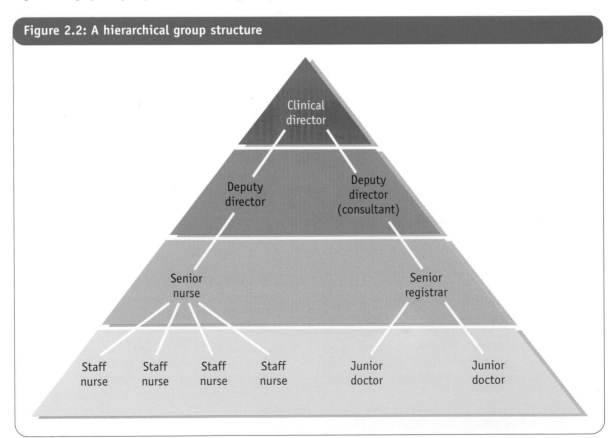

Figure 2.2: A hierarchical group structure

Clinical director

Deputy director

Deputy director (consultant)

Senior nurse

Senior registrar

Staff nurse

Staff nurse

Staff nurse

Staff nurse

Junior doctor

Junior doctor

Figure 2.3: A circular group structure

Consultant

Senior registrar

Occupational therapist

Senior nurse

Staff nurse

Figure 2.4: A clique group structure

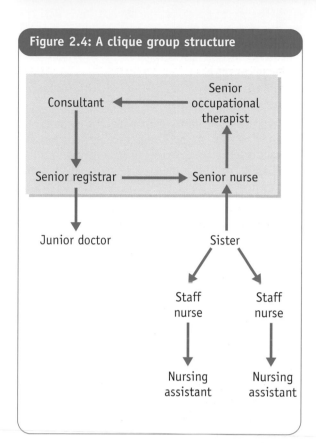

Figure 2.5: A combined group structure

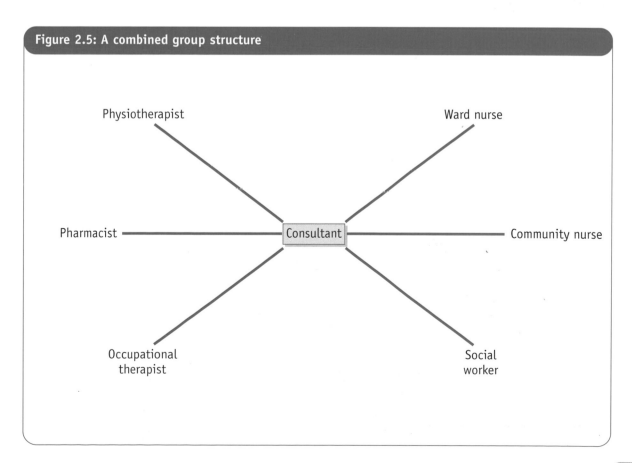

Promoting communication in groups

Group cohesion is developed and maintained through the relationships that group participants build up, through mutual support and through comfortable interaction. The group leader plays an important role in this. He or she should continually observe the dynamics of the group, watching what is happening between group members and monitoring whether the group on task. He or she should develop and facilitate opportunities for members to find out about each other's background and interests, and should ensure that members show respect and value each other's beliefs and identities.

Taking part in a group

Group communication seems to come naturally to some people. They feel confident and are able to follow and participate in the work of the group and enjoy the experience of interacting with others in this way. For others, trying to communicate in a group is a difficult, frustrating and even intimidating experience. People who dislike groups can react in various ways to their negative experience of being in the group. They can become:

- passive observers who don't contribute and who remain silent

- involved in pairing, when a couple of group members talk to each other off-task, often quietly, but still distracting attention from the work of the group

- actively involved in blocking, attacking or other negative strategies that are designed to undermine the purpose of the group.

Burnard (1992) suggests that people who are effective group members:

- make verbal contributions to the group

- listen to other group members

- are prepared to take direction from the group leader

- are prepared to be open about themselves

- stay on-task and don't set out to distract or disrupt the group

- are positive and constructive in their approach to other members and the work of the group

- arrive on time and stay until the end of the group's meetings.

If you review the different types of behaviour that occurs in groups (see p. 99) you will be able to identify and hopefully incorporate the more positive and constructive strategies into your own interactions when you are in group situations.

ACTIVITY
Contributing to a group discussion

Many employers and educational organisations which recruit trainees use group discussion as a part of their interview process. This is a typical scenario for such a discussion:

A group of applicants are gathered together to participate in an interview for a care training course. They have been asked to discuss the following questions between them.

- What do you see as the pros and cons of trainees from different care disciplines (for example, social work, nursing and medicine) having a shared training?

- What makes a person a good care worker? Is it training, experience or their natural qualities?

Identify a few people to role play course tutors. These people will observe the discussion and only occasionally intervene to help the group develop its discussion.

The remainder of the class should play the role of course applicants. The course applicants should introduce themselves at the beginning of the discussion and should all try to make contributions.

At the end of the discussion, each participant (both applicants and course tutors) should:

- write a short synopsis of their own communication contribution

- comment briefly, and in an objective, constructive way, on the communication contributions of the other participants

- indicate how they might adapt their own communication skills to improve future group discussion performances.

Setting up and running a group

There are a variety of reasons why you might want, or be asked, to set up a group in a care setting. For example, you may wish to set up leisure activities, educational or group counselling opportunities for service users. Alternatively, you may wish to set up a group for members of staff or the relatives of service users so that they can discuss and share their experiences or concerns in a supportive environment.

As part of the preparation process you should consider the following issues.

- What the key purpose of the group is and what its aims are going to be. These should be achievable but also worthwhile.

- How big the group is going to be. Too few or too many members can cause problems. Between six and 12 members is usually effective.

- The location and length of group meetings and any specific support needed. These are often referred to as domestic issues.

- What the criteria for membership of the group will be. It is important to ensure that potential group members possess the skills, ability, motivation and commitment needed to participate in, contribute to and gain from the group.

- Whether the group will be open or closed.

When running a group you should try to achieve the following.

- Start on time.

- Ensure that everyone is clear about the aims and purpose of the group.

- Make sure that participants are introduced to each other and know a little bit about one another's roles and reasons for attending the group. This can be achieved through an explicit round of introductions.

- Work to an agreed agenda or format. Sometimes an agenda is agreed in advance of the meeting. If this is the case, you should work through it methodically. If it is not, an early part of the group's work should be to set up an agenda or agree on an activity for the session. It is often helpful to agree how much time the group will spend in discussing or working on each agenda item or activity.

- Encourage contributions as group members work through the agenda or activity. It may be necessary for the group leader or other members to give quiet, passive members plenty of invitations, encouragement and opportunities to get involved and make verbal contributions.

- Invite participants to summarise how they have felt in the course of the meeting and what they feel has been achieved. One way of doing this is for everybody to say what they most liked and what they least liked about the group's session or meeting.

- Agree a date, time and location for any further meetings if this is appropriate.

- Finish on time.

BUILD YOUR LEARNING

Keywords and phrases

You should know the meaning of the words and phrases listed below. If you unsure about any of them, go back through the last seven pages of the unit to refresh your understanding.

- Affection
- Being on-task
- Circular group
- Clique
- Closed group
- Control
- Forming
- Group cohesiveness
- Group identity
- Hierarchy group
- Inclusion
- Multidisciplinary team
- Norming
- Open group
- Pairing
- Performing
- Primary group
- Secondary group
- Storming

Summary points

- Groups are collections of people who have a common goal and shared sense of belonging or identity. People belong to many groups.

- People belong to both primary and secondary groups. Primary groups are characterised by personal, face-to-face contact with other group members. Secondary groups have a more widely distributed membership and are impersonal.

- There are a number of ways of explaining how groups develop. As they evolve, groups tend to take on a life and identity of their own, with members taking on roles and forming relationships that give the group its character.

- Health and social care workers need to develop group skills as they tend to work in teams and communicate with each other in a variety of group situations in the care setting.

- Health and social care workers can benefit from being a part of a group, such as a work team, in that they can share in the decision-making process, develop a shared sense of belonging and receive support from other team members.

- Membership of a group can sometimes be a negative experience, where power and influence are too concentrated in a clique, where group members lose sight of their shared purpose, and where group pressure restricts, or stifles, the individuality and contributions of less powerful members.

- People behave and communicate differently in groups than in one-to-one situations. In groups people use a variety of positive and negative behaviours in order to make an impact on the work and communication processes of the group.

- The way in which groups are structured affects opportunities for communication. Circular groups, for example, provide more communication and interaction opportunities for group members than hierarchies or cliques.

QUESTIONS

1 What is a group? Give examples of three different groups, involving either care practitioners or service users, that can be found in health and social care settings.

2 What are the main advantages and disadvantages for effective communication associated with the team-based approach to health and social care work?

3 Describe how groups form and develop. Give examples from your own experience of your class group to illustrate the development process.

4 Explain how and why people communicate differently in groups compared to one-to-one situations.

5 Imagine that you have to set up a two-hour social group for older people. The main aim of the group is to promote conversation and interaction between group members. List the things that you would do or take into account in your role as group leader or facilitator.

Evaluating communication skills

IN ORDER TO BE AN EFFECTIVE communicator, you need to learn how to analyse both one-to-one and group interactions. Do you know whether you are an effective communicator? How can you tell whether you or your colleagues are interacting well with others? What are the different ways of judging this? There are various methods of evaluating your own and other people's communication skills. Self-awareness is a quality that plays an important part in all of these methods.

Self-awareness, reflection and self-evaluation

People who have good self-awareness have undergone a process of self-learning. That is, they have learnt a lot about their own feelings, attitudes and values. They have improved their self-understanding and know themselves in a deeper way. Self-awareness is a quality that helps health and social care workers to:

- identify and appreciate diversity and difference in people

- identify and acknowledge the differences between their own feelings and those of service users and colleagues

- acknowledge and accept other people's points of view and lifestyles without feeling threatened by them.

Developing a habit of reflecting on your thoughts and feelings is a key strategy in achieving and maintaining self-awareness. Some care workers do this by keeping a **reflective diary** in which they write down their thoughts and feelings as though they are thinking out loud. In many care settings health and social care workers develop **supervision** relationships with mentor colleagues and managers. That is, they set time aside to reflect on and talk about the issues that are affecting them and which are influencing their care practice. They may reflect about issues that concern them personally, about issues to do with service users or colleagues or about professional issues. The aim of all of these reflections is to identify and express the behaviours, thoughts and feelings that are affecting their care practice and the ways in which they are communicating with others.

---

11 December 1999

Saturday

Had a long conversation with J today. He seemed tense. Tried to put him at ease by giving information about the discharge meeting and letting him talk about his fears. Seemed to work. Tried hard to listen and empathise with his concerns. Felt I'd done this okay until he said, 'I know you don't care about what happens to me.' Tried to reassure him. Not sure what else I can do. Am I responding appropriately to his worries? Starting to feel under pressure. Need to discuss this with nurse manager before the discharge meeting next week.

You don't have to keep a reflective diary or have supervision to be reflective. If you prefer you can simply find some quiet time, when it suits you, to reflect on specific situations and interactions or on more general features of your communication performance. As well as identifying and understanding what it is that you do, think and feel, the value of reflection becomes clearer when you subsequently notice improvements in your communication skills and interaction performance.

One-to-one communication skills

There are a number of ways of evaluating, or judging, how you and others use communication skills in one-to-one situations. All rely on an understanding of what constitutes good practice and what might cause communication problems. A number of elements of good practice and some possible barriers to communication feature in the case study. Read through it and think about what makes communication effective or ineffective. Evaluate the responding skills used by answering the questions at the end.

CASE STUDY

Mrs Hart and her difficult son

Mrs Hart has come to the social services drop-in centre in her high street. She has asked to speak with a social worker about her 16-year-old son, Sean. She tells the receptionist that she can't cope and that her son is out of control. The receptionist passes on the following message to the duty social worker at the centre.

Mrs Hart, 40 years old.

Distressed – says she can't cope with son. He is out of control.

Wants social worker's advice.

The duty social worker enters the reception waiting room from a door at the far end. There are several people in the room. She looks around.

Social worker: Mrs Hart, please.

Mrs Hart: Yes..., Hello...that's me.

Social worker: Could you come through, thanks.

As Mrs Hart enters the small office the social worker gestures to a chair in front of a desk.

Social worker: Please, take a seat.

Mrs Hart: Thank you. I'm sorry about this, but I've got to talk to somebody...

Social worker: That's OK, it's no trouble...Could I just finish writing this note for a second? Sorry about this. There are a lot of people to see today.

The social worker finishes writing, smiles at Mrs Hart and moves a chair from behind the desk to face Mrs Hart. She sits facing Mrs Hart with her arms crossed across her chest.

Social worker: Right, how can I help you, Mrs Hart?

Mrs Hart: Oh, I'm not sure. It's not me, it's my son Sean, really.

Social worker: Your son...what about him?

Mrs Hart: I don't know what to do with him. We're arguing all the time, he didn't go to school at all last week. Well, he said he did but the head teacher phoned me to say he was absent. I was very annoyed with him. I told him he had to tell me what was going on. I thought he might have been in trouble or getting up to no good, you know, drugs or shoplifting or something.

Social worker: Mm, what did he say when you said this to him?

Mrs Hart: Oh, he started shouting at me, he said that he didn't want to go to school anymore. He said that I was making him go. He keeps going on about working in his uncle's garage. I'm totally exhausted worrying about what he's going to make of himself. It's making me ill. I always encouraged him and tried to help him. What can I do? I need some advice.

Social worker: Just let me check that I've understood this properly. Your son is now 16 and wants to leave school. He is very determined and you have reached a deadlock.

Mrs Hart: Yes, well, he's nearly 17 but the rest is about right. What can I do about him?

Social worker: I think that we have to think about how it is all affecting you as well as what you can do to help Sean.

Mrs Hart: What do you mean, how it all affects me?

Social worker: From what I've heard you feel angry and very worried that your son wants to finish his education too soon. You say that you can't cope with this and it's making you ill.

Mrs Hart: It's Sean who needs the help. I'd feel better if I could sort him out.

The telephone on the desk rings. The duty social worker answers it and asks the caller to come in for a second. The receptionist appears at the door.

Social worker: Could you just type these up for me, Julie? I need them for this afternoon.

Receptionist: Yes, certainly. Sorry to interrupt (looking at Mrs Hart).

Social worker: Oh, and could you hold all my calls for the next ten minutes? Thanks Julie.

The receptionist leaves and the social worker turns back to face Mrs Hart.

Social worker: Sorry about that. Where were we? Oh yes, you've told me a little bit about Sean and yourself. Can you tell me about the other members of your family?

Mrs Hart: Well, there's only my husband really. We've been married for 18 years. He's a motor mechanic. He works with his brother, they both own a garage.

He works all the hours God sends and still doesn't earn enough. He left school at 15 and it's all he's ever done. Sean idolises him. He's obsessed with cars and engines and things. Says he wants to work with his dad and his uncle in the garage. How can he though? There's hardly enough work for them, never mind him. And Sean has got eight GCSEs. He's just going to waste his ability working in a garage. Can you understand why I'm worried sick now?

Social worker: Yes, I think so. Your son wants to leave school and get a job which is making you very worried. Your husband's business has not been going well recently and, despite his qualifications, it is difficult to convince your son that studying will help him. Is that right ?

Mrs Hart: Er, well, I suppose so.

ACTIVITY

Evaluating responding skills

- Identify and explain how the social worker in the case study uses specific communication techniques to promote interaction with Mrs Hart.

- Identify and explain which factors might be responsible for inhibiting communication where this occurs.

- Suggest how the social worker could improve her communication approach to meet Mrs Hart's needs more fully.

Peer assessment and responding to criticism

Reflection on, and informal evaluation of, one-to-one communication situations can help you to gain some insight into your use of communication skills. However, the views of others and more formal structured assessments can add an external or outside view that you may also find useful as feedback on your communication style. Tools such as **evaluation checklists** can provide a useful structure and focus to these external evaluations and can be particularly helpful to new care workers and to students. Two examples of evaluation checklists are provided in Figures 2.6 and 2.7. Try using them to evaluate the your own and your colleagues' communication skills in role play (see pp. 94, 109 and 112 for role plays).

Supervision, which we mentioned earlier, is another way of obtaining or providing peer assessment and feedback on communication skills. Supervision relationships are usually one to one. However, in some care settings, team meetings are held on a regular basis so that team members can express and share their views on the way that fellow team members are working with each other and with service users. These meetings are supposed to be supportive and can provide a forum for comments and constructive criticisms about team members' use of communication skills.

It can be difficult to listen to and receive comments about your communication skills from your peers and colleagues. It is usually best to do so with an open mind, avoiding the temptation to defend yourself from what you may initially perceive as unjustified criticism. Care practitioners are always learning, no matter how experienced they are, and can usually benefit in some way from constructive comments about their care practice. With a little time for reflection, comments that initially seemed critical can often be seen in a more positive light. If you are asked to provide comments or feedback on the communication or care practice of a colleague, remember to find ways of phrasing what you have to say constructively as well as honestly!

Using role play

Role play allows you to improve on aspects of your communication skills or to practice them and receive peer feedback in a safe, supported way. Participants assume hypothetical roles to simulate realistic vocational situations. To make role play work, participants need to become as involved in their role as they can whilst they are performing it. It is always important to remember, however, that it is only a role and that the purpose is to try to empathise in the situation.

Some role play situations are provided in the activity. Try to demonstrate and develop both your communication and evaluation skills by role playing one or two of them with your class colleagues.

ACTIVITY

Evaluating interaction skills

Videotaping and peer evaluation are two ways of gaining external feedback on your use of communication skills. You are encouraged to either videotape your role plays or to obtain self and peer-evaluation by using the structured checklists (Figures 2.6 and 2.7).

- Using one or more of the following role plays (or one that you develop yourself), plan an interaction between a health or social care worker and a service user. It should be about three minutes long.

- As part of your role play performance, do your best to demonstrate appropriate verbal and non-verbal communication skills. You should show attentiveness, convey emotional responsiveness and express a message clearly.

- Either have your role play videotaped so that you and your colleagues can play it back and evaluate it later, or arrange for a couple of people to watch the performance and complete the checklists (Figures 2.6 and 2.7).

- Write a short self-evaluation of your use of communication skills in this exercise. Identify the techniques that you used and the factors that may have inhibited more effective communication.

Role play 1

A new mother is visited by a health visitor two days after the birth of her first child. The mother wants to know what the health visitor's role is and what she wants to know about her child. The parent is anxious that she is being checked up on. The health visitor must provide information and reassurance in an appropriate way.

Role play 2

A woman is waiting in the relatives' room in the accident and emergency department. Her partner has been brought in following a road traffic accident. She has been unable to see him. The A&E sister is aware that the woman is waiting for information. She knows that the man has a minor head injury and a fractured leg. The A&E sister must try to inform and reassure the woman. The woman is now quite worried, restless and anxious.

Role play 3

A confused elderly woman is brought into a day centre by a passer-by, who thinks that the woman is lost. A day centre worker must clarify what the passer-by expects the day centre staff to do and find out whether the elderly woman needs help. The elderly woman is confused and can only give her name and a description, but not the address, of where she lives.

These two checklists (figures 2.6 and 2.7) provide a structured way of evaluating aspects of your own and another person's communication skills in a role play or other observed interaction.

Figure 2.6: Non-verbal communication assessment checklist

Body message	My assessment
Approachable	
Relaxed body posture	
Physical openness	
Slight forward lean	
Good use of gaze and eye contact	
Appropriate facial contact	
Appropriate gestures	
Sensitivity to physical proximity and height	
Appropriate use of touch	
Clothing and grooming	

Figure 2.7: Interaction evaluation checklist

To what extent was the person:	My assessment
Listening?	
Giving attention?	
Using non-verbal behaviour?	
Warm and respectful?	
Empathic?	
Genuine?	
Asking open questions?	
Reflecting back?	
Summarising?	
Paraphrasing ?	
General comments on overall use of communication skills:	

Reviewing groups

Earlier in the unit we looked at the nature and development of groups and outlined a number of everyday situations in which health and social care workers use group communication skills. In the same way that it is helpful to evaluate communication skills in one-to-one situations, effective communicators in group situations need to be able to evaluate and respond to feedback on their group skills.

It is possible to use structured checklists, such as the ones in figures 2.6 and 2.7, to evaluate communication skills within group situations. They can be used to self-evaluate or to evaluate the skills of fellow group members. Alternatively, you can evaluate both your own performance and the way in which others functioned by reflecting on the group shortly afterwards. You might consider:

- whether the group's aims were achieved
- what other members liked least and most about communication within the group
- what the general communication process and individual contributions were like
- whether there were any specific communication problems in the group
- how you can respond to feedback about the group.

The review of group communication can be difficult and threatening to members' self-esteem as it is usually done when all group members are present so that problems or difficulties are aired in a public way. However, with experience and the support of other group members, evaluation opportunities provide a very good and effective way of learning about and developing group communication skills.

Sources of interaction feedback

There are a variety of ways of evaluating the use of both individual and group communication skills. Each method is based on the use of feedback information.

In order to meet the diverse needs of service users, care workers should be able to identify and use a number of different sources of **feedback** to evaluate, and if necessary adapt, their communication skills. Possible sources of feedback include:

- comments and reactions from clients
- comments and reactions from colleagues
- video footage
- personal reflections
- tape recordings of interviews and conversations
- practice role plays
- supervision.

Each source of feedback has limitations as well as strengths in terms of giving you a useful insight into the effectiveness of your communication skills. It is perhaps best to seek and respond to a variety of sources of feedback to evaluate your communication skills fully.

Limitations and strengths of feedback sources

Outline the limitations and strengths of each source of evaluation feedback on your communication skills.

Evaluation feedback source	Limitations	Strengths
Comments and reactions from clients		
Comments and reactions from colleagues		
Video footage		
Personal reflections		
Tape recordings of interviews/conversations		
Practice role plays		
Supervision		

ACTIVITY

The following role play provides an opportunity for you to take part in a group communication exercise. You can use it to practise and develop your group communication or evaluation skills.

Mrs Peters has come to the day centre to collect her mother, Mrs Hall. The deputy officer in charge of the day centre needs to talk to Mrs Peters. The day centre staff have informed the deputy that Mrs Hall now has many physical needs that she cannot meet herself. These include help in using the toilet, poor mobility, feeding and dressing needs. They feel that these needs cannot be adequately met at the day centre where the activity programme and staffing levels assume that attendees are relatively independent in these areas. Mrs Hall has many friends at the day centre but doesn't enjoy going as much as she used to. Mrs Hall has not mentioned this to her daughter but has told the day centre staff.

Roles

The job of the **deputy officer in charge** involves assessing clients' needs, ensuring that appropriate social and psychological care is provided for them at the centre, and liaising with clients' relatives about matters relating to attendance.

Mrs Peters is 32 and has three school-age children. She works in a local supermarket three days a week, when her mother attends the day centre. She has looked after her mother for the last five years and now relies on the place at the day centre to give her a break from caring for her mother and the time to go out to work.

Mrs Hall is 68 years old. She is very much a part of her daughter's family and adores her grandchildren. She moved to live with her daughter following the death of her husband five years ago. Since then her physical and mental health have gradually deteriorated. Mrs Hall has recently expressed some concern about her failing mobility and her fears of going into a home.

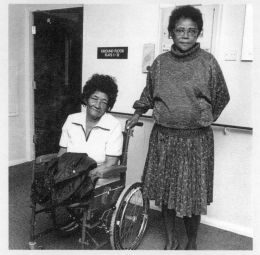

1 Work in a small group, allocating roles between yourselves. In addition to the three roles above, you may wish to develop new roles (for example, day centre staff). You may also decide to have observers who will provide feedback on communication performances.

2 In your roles, discuss the current situation and future care of Mrs Hall. You should obtain the views of all participants and express your own position on the matter. Remember to try and use a variety of interaction skills (attending, listening, empathy, open questions and responding supportively). You should spend at least ten minutes discussing the matter and should try to come to some agreement about what to do next.

3 After the meeting, take it in turns to receive feedback on your communication performances. You should also explain to the other group members how it felt to be in the role that you took. Fill out an interaction evaluation checklist for yourself and for each of the other participants.

BUILD YOUR LEARNING

Keywords and phrases

You should know the meaning of the words and phrases listed below. If you are unsure about any of them, go back through the last seven pages of the unit to refresh your understanding.

- Evaluation checklist
- Feedback
- Reflection
- Reflective diary
- Role play
- Self-awareness
- Supervision

Summary points

- The evaluation of communication skills is concerned with making judgements about the effectiveness of skills used in one-to-one and group situations.

- Health and social care workers need to develop their self-awareness and the skill of reflection in order to make self-evaluations of their communication skills.

- Individual care workers use methods such as supervision relationships and reflective diaries to develop and express their reflections and self-evaluations.

- Peer review, group supervision and role play are methods of obtaining the views and feedback of others on your use of communication skills.

- Formal evaluation checklists can be used to structure peer review feedback on the use of communication skills. Feedback should always be given in a constructive way.

- Health and social care workers should seek and use a variety of different sources of feedback on their communication skills. This will enable them to gain a broad understanding of how they use their skills and the impact that they have.

QUESTIONS

1 Explain what self-awareness is and why it is important for care practitioners to develop it.

2 What methods can care practitioners use to develop and improve their self-awareness?

3 Describe two methods that you could use to evaluate another person's communication skills and interaction abilities.

4 List the features of interaction that you would look at if you were asked to evaluate communication within a group.

5 Explain how feedback on their communication skills can benefit care practitioners in their work with service users.

Maintaining client confidentiality

▲ Confidentiality is a key value in health and social care

CONFIDENTIALITY IS A VALUE that is a part of the ethical code of practice of most professions. Lawyers, doctors, accountants and nurses all have codes of ethics that impose a **duty of confidentiality** on practitioners. Confidentiality is an important value that should be a constant consideration for health and social care workers in their interactions with their colleagues and with service users, their friends and relatives.

The meaning of confidentiality in care

As a GNVQ student you are likely to be a temporary visitor to a care setting, perhaps whilst on work placement or whilst collecting information for an assignment. You may observe or overhear things about service users, and indeed members of staff, that should remain confidential. In health and social care settings the term **confidentiality** is used to refer to the right of service users to have access to their private information restricted to people who have an accepted need to know about the content. Confidentiality is a key care value and is an important part of the NVQ care value base.

Why is confidentiality important?

People who use health and social care services are often vulnerable and anxious about the situations in which they find themselves. Despite this, service users must be able to establish appropriate relationships and communicate effectively with health and social care workers. Confidentiality is given a high value by health and social care practitioners because it is one of the foundation stones on which they build their relationships with service users. If service users do not have confidence in care practitioners' ability to keep their personal information confidential they will never be able to trust them sufficiently to establish effective relationships.

Whilst the need to establish trusting care relationships is an important reason for preserving confidentiality, there are also other practical reasons for ensuring that information about service users isn't revealed inappropriately. The security of service users' possessions (their finances and homes, for example) and their personal safety are also confidentiality issues. Disclosure of even simple details to the wrong person, such as the fact that a service user is in hospital, lives alone or has a particular condition, can expose the person to possible exploitation, theft, burglary and discrimination.

What should remain confidential?

Service users generally give health and social care workers four different types of information:

- **identification information**, including name, address and marital status

- **medical information**, including details of disease, extent of disease, treatment and past history

- **social information**, including details of housing, job, family situation, sexual preferences

- **psychological information**, including details of stress levels, emotions, sexual problems and mental state.

Identification information is less likely to be sensitive and confidential than medical, social or psychological information. However, there are always exceptions. For example, people who are admitted to psychiatric hospitals often don't want this fact confirmed to other members of their family or to close friends because they fear the social stigma attached to it. Women who have experienced domestic violence and who live in refuges will not want their address revealed to other people, even care workers, unless they have a clear need to know. As a care practitioner you should let service users decide what information about themselves they will allow you to reveal to others. Health and social care workers store, share and present information about service users in a number of different ways but should always do so in a manner that maximises their confidentiality.

Managing confidentiality

It is good practice for health and social care workers to discuss the issue of confidentiality with service users at an early point in their contact. Service users should be given an opportunity to indicate how much of their personal information they are happy to have disclosed and to say with whom, outside of the care team, the staff can share information. Care workers must always respect the confidentiality limits and preferences that service users impose and gain their permission before discussing any personal matters with their family or friends. It may be necessary at times for a care practitioner to gently but firmly refuse to discuss a service user's confidences and circumstances with other service users or even with his or her relatives. This in itself can inspire confidence that the health and social care worker can be trusted with confidential information.

Health and social care workers write down a lot of confidential information in service users' notes. You will probably be aware that your own GP keeps all of your medical notes in a file at his or her surgery. Increasingly, service users notes are produced and stored on computer. The confidentiality of service users' notes should be protected by locking all files and reports in secure cabinets, by limiting access to them, by ensuring access to computer records is protected by the use of passwords and by avoiding conversation about service users in front of non-team members.

Confidentiality dilemmas

So far we have said that confidentiality should work in favour of service users. Their private information must be protected and should not be revealed to people whom they feel don't need to know. But what about circumstances in which care practitioners are told something in confidence but feel that they ought to reveal it? There are occasions when service users can request confidentiality and put care practitioners in an untenable position. They may disclose information that indicates that they intend to do something that may put themselves or others at risk. What should you do?

In these circumstances it is important for health and social care workers to let service users know that they have a responsibility to disclose the information to other members of staff involved in their care. This might now sound confusing, or contradictory, given what we discussed earlier about protecting confidentiality and respecting service users' rights. However, confidentiality dilemmas sometimes raise difficult and controversial issues. Key confidentiality questions for all care workers to think through include:

- how much to share

- what you ought do if someone confides information to you that you feel ought to be shared

- when it is acceptable to break confidentiality.

When you think through these questions you need to remember that interactions and relationships between service users and health and social care staff are based on trust. There is a general assumption that information revealed by service users will remain confidential. At the same time it is necessary for health and social care workers to share certain pieces of information so that effective care can be given. They must also break confidentiality when they receive information that suggests that a service user or another person may be in danger or might commit an illegal act (see Unit 1, p. 43).

The key confidentiality dilemma that health and social care workers face is how to share confidential information without losing service users' trust.

ACTIVITY

What should remain confidential?

Melanie Jones is a 33-year-old woman who was admitted at 9 p.m. yesterday evening after having an epileptic fit at home. She lives locally, in council-owned property, with her two sons aged 15 and 17. Her youngest son saw her have the fit in the kitchen and phoned an ambulance. She is separated from her husband who is currently serving a prison sentence. Mrs Jones has no previous history of epilepsy. Her chest X-ray shows evidence of heavy smoking. Her brain scans reveal no significant abnormality.

During the admission interview Mrs Jones said that she was currently very concerned about Tim, her eldest son. He has recently been in trouble with the police, for burglary. She suspects that he may have been involved in some further criminal activity recently, as she has found a number of credit cards in his room and feels that he is behaving suspiciously. Because of her concerns Mrs Jones has not been sleeping well and has felt very worried about the possibility that Tim is getting into serious trouble. Mrs Jones is keen to leave hospital today, against medical and nursing advice.

■ Mrs Jones' youngest son phones, sounding upset, to ask for information about her condition.

■ During the visiting period, Mrs Jones' close friend and neighbour comes and asks whether Melanie is mentally unwell. She suggests that Tim might be the cause of her current health problems.

■ A social worker, who comes into the ward office asks about Mrs Jones' home and marital circumstances and whether you think she should talk to her about Tim.

■ The police phone the ward wanting to know if Mrs Jones is an inpatient. They say that they want to talk to her about her son, Tim whom they have just arrested.

■ You see a colleague, who is a research nurse doing a study on reasons for self-discharge against medical advice, go past the ward office.

1 What type, or level, of information do each of these people want?

2 What response options do you have in each situation?

3 What are the possible consequences of following each of these options?

4 What do you feel is the best option or response in each situation?

BUILD YOUR LEARNING

Keywords and phrases

You should be familiar with the words and phrases below. If you are unsure about any of them, go back through the last three pages of the unit to refresh your understanding.

- Confidentiality
- Duty of confidentiality
- Identification information
- Medical information
- Private information
- Psychological information
- Social information

Summary points

- Confidentiality is a care value that is concerned with protecting private information about service users.

- Service users tend to disclose four different types of information to health and social care workers. Identification information is typically less sensitive and could be thought of as public information. Medical, social and psychological information is more sensitive and should be protected by health and social care workers.

- Confidentiality is a prerequisite for establishing trust between care service users and care practitioners. It is also important on a practical level as a means of protecting the security of service users' possessions and their personal safety.

- Health and social care workers manage confidentiality by locking files and reports about service users away in secure cabinets, by limiting access to them, by ensuring that phone calls are not overheard and by avoiding talking about service users in front of non-team members.

- The confidentiality dilemma that health and social care workers always face is how much information to share without losing the trust of service users. Care practitioners must always disclose information where they are aware that service users may harm themselves or another person or where a service user is involved in illegal activity.

QUESTIONS

1 Explain what confidentiality means in the context of care relationships.

2 Why is the maintenance of confidentiality such an important principle in care work?

3 Give two examples of confidentiality dilemmas that care practitioners might face. Explain why they face a dilemma in each situation.

4 Is it ever acceptable for a care practitioner to break confidentiality?

References

Bales, R F (1970) *Personality and Interpersonal Behaviour*, New York, Holt, Rinehart and Winston

Brandon, D and Brandon, A (1991) *Staff Practice Handbook – A guide to practice in services for people with learning difficulties*

Burnard P, (1992) *Communicate!* , Edward Arnold

Egan, G (1986) *Exercises in helping skills*, Monterey, California, Brookes Cole

Hayman, M (1998) 'A protocol for people with hearing impairment', *Nursing Times*, Oct 28, Volume 94, No 43, 1998

Rogers, C (1961) *On Becoming a Person: A therapist's view of psychotherapy*, Constable

Schultz, W (1958) *FIRO: A Three-Dimensional Theory of Interpersonal Behaviour*, New York, Holt, Rinehart and Winston

Tschudin, V (1982) *Counselling skills for nurses*, Bailliere Tindall

Tuckman, B W (1965) 'Developmental sequences in small groups', *Psychological Bulletin*, 63, 384–99

Useful addresses

The Council for the Advancement of Communication with Deaf People, Pelaw House, School of Education, University of Durham DH1 1TA

Royal National Institute for the Blind (RNIB), 224 Great Portland Street, London WC1N 6AA

Royal National Institute for the Deaf (RNID), 105 Gower Street, London WC1E 6AH

Skilled care workers use information given by their clients and the results from their tests to make many routine, but important, health care and treatment decisions. Underpinning all of these decisions is a good understanding of how the human body works. Knowledge of normal functioning alerts the care practitioner to abnormalities. A simple cough in a frail, elderly care home resident can lead to a very serious illness if it is part of a more serious chest infection and is not picked up early enough. For young children in nursery school, a few hours delay in recognising that their headache, bruising and sensitivity to light may be symptoms of a dangerous form of meningitis could put them in a life-threatening situation.

This unit looks at the major body systems and shows how they work together to keep the body healthy. This knowledge is essential for you to interpret comments made by your clients and results from any tests you carry out. It will also help you to understand some of the advice given to you and those in your care by senior staff.

The unit begins with a description and explanation of the structure and function of human body systems. The respiratory, cardiovascular, digestive, renal, nervous and endocrine systems are each covered in turn. We look at how each system works, what normal functioning involves and describe how body systems relate to one another. The unit then moves on to cover the topic of homeostasis. Homeostasis is the name given to the idea that all factors within the body are kept within safe limits. We consider how homeostatic mechanisms for blood glucose levels, body temperature, heart rate, respiratory rate and water content maintain the body's internal environment. Finally, the unit covers the general topic of physiological measurements in care settings. In particular, we look at how measurements of the pulse, blood pressure, temperature, respiratory rate and peak flow are taken and what the results can reveal about people's state of health. We also consider safe practice, accuracy and the analysis of results.

3

Physical aspects of health

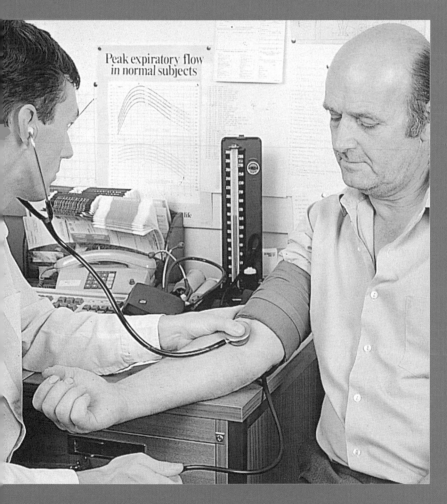

Peak expiratory flow
in normal subjects

How does the human body work?

IF AN ENGINEER WERE TO LOOK at the human body as if it were a machine, he or she could ask two questions: what is it made of and what do the different parts do? The first question gives an answer about **structures**. The body is made up of cells, such as red blood cells; organs, such as the liver or heart; and systems, such as the respiratory system. The second question gives an answer in terms of **functions**. The body's functions include moving oxygen into the body, growing, repairing cells and maintaining body temperature.

These answers are linked. Particular structures carry out particular functions. The heart and blood vessels transport oxygen around the body and the muscles allow us to move around. Sometimes the body uses a collection of many separate structures to carry out one function. Maintaining body temperature depends on structures in the brain, the skin and the muscles. Often one structure may have a part to play in many different functions. Biologists tend to link the structures that are involved in a particular major function into a **system**.

Figure 3.1: Major body systems

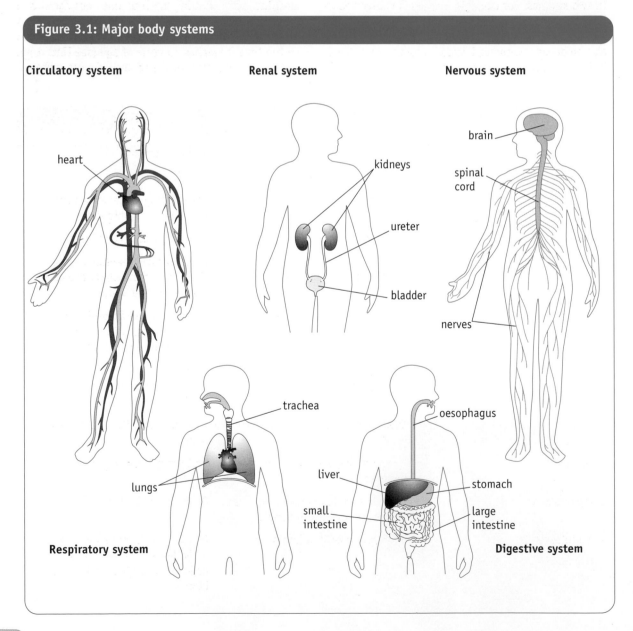

Circulatory system — heart

Renal system — kidneys, ureter, bladder

Nervous system — brain, spinal cord, nerves

Respiratory system — trachea, lungs

Digestive system — oesophagus, liver, stomach, small intestine, large intestine

The cardiovascular system, for example, includes the heart and all the blood vessels. It moves blood around the body. The renal system includes the kidneys, the bladder and the tubes that carry urine out of the body. It removes waste products from the blood and passes them out of the body.

A system includes a number of organs. An **organ** is a separate, recognisable body part, for example the liver or heart. Organs are made up of many different tissues. A **tissue** is a group of cells of the same type. The cells lining the inner surface of the gut form a tissue, for example, and muscle cells in a muscle form a tissue. An organ contains more than one type of tissue, just as a system contains more than one organ.

Sorting the structures of the body into systems is not always easy because some organs have a part to play in two systems. For example, the penis is involved in both the reproductive and the excretory systems. The pancreas is a part of the digestive system. However, it also produces a hormone, insulin, to control sugar levels in the body, so it is also part of the endocrine system.

Is the skin part of the immune system (it protects against foreign bodies), the sensory system (it is full of sensitive nerve endings) or the excretory system (it produces small amounts of urea in sweat)?

It is also important to understand that the body is not simply a collection of separate systems, although it is often treated in this way to make it easier to understand. The overlap between systems means that changes or damage to one organ can show signs in many systems and functions. For example, damage to the liver makes the skin look yellow. Damage to the nervous system may show itself as a lack of movement – an apparent failure of the musculoskeletal system.

Finally, it is important for you to understand that the body is not a machine. This is because both its structure and function change over time. A non-living machine like a washing machine does not age into a tumble drier – and it certainly cannot repair itself! A human baby will have changed many of its structures by the time it reaches 70 years of age (see Unit 4 pp. 217–222). It will have repaired damaged parts, switched

Figure 3.2: Body structures and functions

System	Main organs	Main functions
Respiratory	Lungs, trachea, nose and mouth	Breathing
Circulatory	Heart and blood vessels	Transporting materials around the body in the blood
Digestive	Gut, liver and pancreas	Digesting and absorbing food
Endocrine	Pituitary gland, adrenal glands, thyroid gland, pancreas, testes and ovaries	Coordinating conditions *within* the body – particularly chemical changes in the body
Nervous	Brain, spinal cord and nerves	Controlling and co-ordinating the body – often to do with reacting to events *outside* the body
Renal	Kidney, bladder and ureters	Excreting waste materials from the body
Sensory	Eyes, ears, nose, taste buds, skin	Detecting conditions outside the body
Immune	Lymph nodes, spleen, white blood cells	Protecting the body against illness
Reproductive	Penis and testes in males, vagina, uterus and ovaries in females	Producing offspring
Musculoskeletal	Muscles, bones and joints	Muscles and bones move the body; bones also help to protect delicate body parts and produce blood

on reproductive systems at the beginning of puberty and switched off growth in height at the end.

So, the question 'how does the body work?' needs many answers. There will be an answer in terms of structures (it has a heart and a brain). There will also be an answer in terms of functions (it carries out respiration and it grows). There will be another answer in terms of how the body is working at this moment. In a young baby, the reproductive system is not functioning, in a mature adult the body is not growing in height. Finally, there will be an answer in terms of relationships (different parts of the body working together at in different ways at different times to keep the whole body healthy). So, the ovaries in a small child are not actively at work. From puberty onwards they are releasing eggs for reproduction and producing a selection of hormones to control the growth of many body parts. During pregnancy they have yet another function and after the menopause they change function yet again.

▲ The living body is much more than its parts. This woman has matured from a baby (centre of family group) through childhood into adolescence, survived a World War, borne six children and become a great grandmother.

BUILD YOUR LEARNING

Keywords and phrases

You should know the meaning of the words and phrases listed below. If you are unsure about any of them, go back through the last three pages of the unit to refresh your understanding.

- Cells
- Functions
- Organ
- Structure
- Tissue
- System

Summary points

- The human body is made up of cells.

- Many cells are specialised for a particular function. Cells of the same type are grouped together into a tissue.

- A group of different tissues may link up to form an organ, which is part of a system.

- The system is responsible for a major function within the body.

- All systems are linked together and disruption to any system can have serious effects on other systems.

- The human body is not just a collection of different systems – it is an integrated, organised whole. Many organs take part in more than one system and change their role over life.

QUESTIONS

1 Write a sentence to explain the scientific meaning of each of the following terms:
   - tissue
   - cell
   - system
   - organ.

2 Complete the following table.

System	Main function
Cardiovascular	
	To remove waste products from the blood
Endocrine	
	To break down complex molecules into smaller ones which can then be absorbed into the bloodstream
Respiratory	

3 The parts of the body cannot be sorted easily into separate systems. Why not?

4 Bronchitis is an infection of the tubes leading into the lungs. What effect do you think this would have on the body? Explain the reasons for your answer.

5 Think of two similarities and two differences between a living thing like a human being and a machine like a motor car.

The body and energy

ENERGY IS THE ABILITY to do work. Nothing happens without energy and the body needs a constant supply of energy to stay healthy, yet energy is constantly leaving the body as heat. What stops the body from running out, rather like a battery in a torch? The answer is that the body can transfer energy from food to keep itself alive. The chemical reaction which performs this function is termed respiration.

The body uses energy to:

■ **grow** – building new tissues needs energy to convert raw materials into the chemicals found in new cells

■ **repair itself** – damaged cells need energy to be repaired

■ **move** – muscles need a supply of energy to move (remember this includes not just the movements you can see but also the muscles of the heart and the gut inside the body)

■ **build new chemicals** – these include the many chemicals made inside the body that you cannot see.

■ **send nerve impulses** – nerve tissue requires a constant supply of energy and dies very quickly if energy is not available.

In short, nothing happens in the body without a supply of energy and that energy always comes from food.

What is respiration?

The word respiration can be used in two different ways. Some people use respiration to mean breathing; so, when you respire you are breathing. The respiratory rate is the rate of breathing and the respiratory system includes the body parts involved in breathing.

However, more and more people nowadays use the word respiration to mean a chemical reaction that goes on inside every living cell. **Respiration** is the breakdown of glucose, a kind of sugar, to release energy in a form the body can use. This is sometimes called **cellular respiration**. All living things, including animals, plants and microorganisms respire in this way. In this textbook we will only use respiration to mean the chemical reaction going on in the cells of all living things. We will use the words **breathing** or **ventilation** to mean moving air into and out of the lungs.

Respiration chemistry

Energy stored in food must be converted into a form the body can use. Respiration is the only way to do this. Human bodies use two types of respiration. **Aerobic respiration** needs oxygen and produces the most energy from food. It is the system that is used whenever possible. **Anaerobic respiration** produces less useful energy from the same amount of food but does not need oxygen. It is only used when oxygen is in short supply.

Aerobic respiration is:
$$C_6H_{12}O_6 + 6O_2 \longrightarrow 6CO_2 + 6H_2O$$
Glucose + oxygen   (carbon dioxide + water + energy)

Anaerobic respiration is:
$$C_6H_{12}O_6 \longrightarrow 2C_2H_4OH.COOH$$
Glucose   (lactic acid + energy)

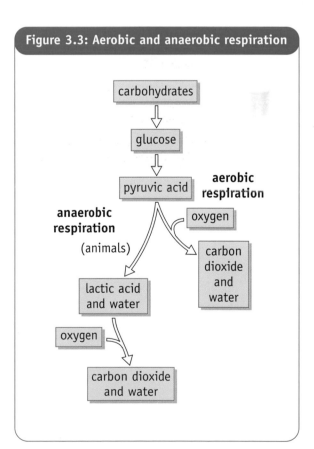

Figure 3.3: Aerobic and anaerobic respiration

carbohydrates

glucose

pyruvic acid

aerobic respiration

anaerobic respiration

(animals)

oxygen

carbon dioxide and water

lactic acid and water

oxygen

carbon dioxide and water

The equations summarise a complex series of reactions. In aerobic respiration, a carbon atom in a glucose molecule passes through more than ten different chemicals before it eventually reaches carbon dioxide. However, the complex reactions can be split into three major pathways:

- glycolysis
- Krebs cycle
- electron transfer chain.

Glycolysis splits the glucose molecule into two smaller molecules. It produces a small amount of energy in this reaction and does not need oxygen. The **Krebs cycle** splits the small molecules from glycolysis into carbon dioxide and produces a great deal of energy. It also feeds chemicals to the **electron transfer chain** which produces water and releases more energy. The electron transfer chain needs oxygen to produce water.

Mitochondria

The mitochondria are small sacs of enzymes found in human cells that carry out respiration. Mitochondria use membranes to organise the various chemicals needed for respiration into separate compartments. This makes the overall reaction much more efficient. Figure 3.4 gives you an overview of the essential components.

Adenosine triphosphate (ATP)

Cells use a molecule called **adenosine triphosphate (ATP)** to transfer energy between reactions. ATP is a bit like a rechargeable battery. When it is fully charged it holds three phosphate groups. When ATP releases one of its phosphate groups it becomes **adenosine diphosphate (ADP)**. The spare phosphate group sticks onto a molecule that needs the supply of energy. The molecule can then use the energy to do something – perhaps it allows a muscle cell to contract or an enzyme to build a complex chemical in the body.

When the reaction is over, the phosphate group is released, as its energy has been transferred into movement or another chemical. The cell then uses more energy from respiration to build fresh supplies of ATP from ADP and the loose phosphate group. A cell can charge up 38 molecules of ATP from a single glucose molecule by aerobic respiration.

How quickly can the body make ATP?

The levels of ATP in a cell are surprisingly low. For example, a muscle cell in the arm would only need to contract for about five seconds to use up its complete store of ATP. So, how does the muscle keep going when it runs out? Creatinine phosphate is a molecule that stores high energy phosphate groups for ATP. Creatinine phosphate can give its phosphate group to ADP to form

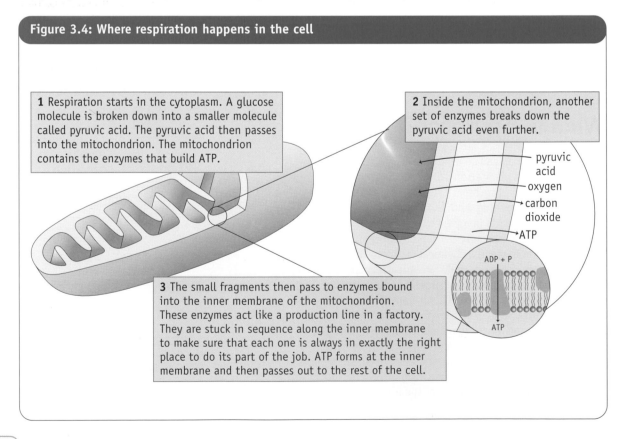

Figure 3.4: Where respiration happens in the cell

1 Respiration starts in the cytoplasm. A glucose molecule is broken down into a smaller molecule called pyruvic acid. The pyruvic acid then passes into the mitochondrion. The mitochondrion contains the enzymes that build ATP.

2 Inside the mitochondrion, another set of enzymes breaks down the pyruvic acid even further.

pyruvic acid
oxygen
carbon dioxide
ATP

ADP + P

ATP

3 The small fragments then pass to enzymes bound into the inner membrane of the mitochondrion. These enzymes act like a production line in a factory. They are stuck in sequence along the inner membrane to make sure that each one is always in exactly the right place to do its part of the job. ATP forms at the inner membrane and then passes out to the rest of the cell.

ATP very quickly. This would keep the muscle going for about another 25 seconds. After this, all of the creatinine phosphate has been used up.

The next system to kick in is anaerobic respiration. This produces small amounts of ATP but it can start quickly. However, it cannot carry on forever because it produces lactic acid as a waste product. Lactic acid is toxic and would eventually damage the cell.

Finally, the aerobic system starts to produce ATP. This takes anything from 30 seconds to two minutes to get up to speed. When aerobic respiration is working it produces large amounts of ATP and can keep going until all the food and oxygen in a cell is used up (and then you die!).

What is an oxygen debt?

After the activity is over, the body uses aerobic respiration to replenish its store of creatinine phosphate. It also needs to clear away any lactic acid left over from anaerobic respiration. Lactic acid can be broken down into carbon dioxide and water which can be passed out of the body. To break down lactic acid, the body needs a supply of oxygen. The amount of oxygen needed to clear out the accumulated lactic acid and to rebuild the creatinine phosphate is called the **oxygen debt**

During active exercise all the oxygen taken in by the body is used for aerobic respiration. The body has to wait until the exercise is over before it can get any spare oxygen to clear away the lactic acid. This is why people often continue to breathe deeply even after a race. They need plenty of oxygen for aerobic respiration to replenish the creatinine phosphate and to clear away the lactic acid.

▲ It's not just athletes who build up large amounts of lactic acid

---

Figure 3.5: The energy continuum

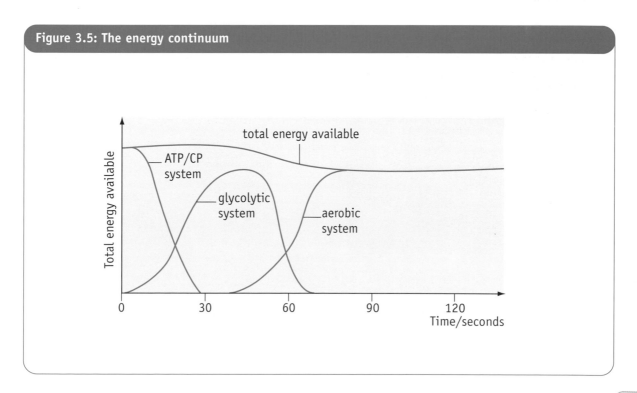

BUILD YOUR LEARNING

Keywords and phrases

You should know the meaning of the words and phrases listed below. If you are unsure about any of them, go back through the last three pages of the unit to refresh your understanding.

- Adenosine triphosphate (ATP)
- Adenosine diphosphate (ADP)
- Aerobic respiration
- Anaerobic respiration
- Breathing
- Cellular respiration
- Creatinine phosphate
- Electron transfer chain
- Glycolysis
- Krebs cycle
- Lactic acid
- Oxygen debt
- Ventilation

Summary points

- Respiration is the breakdown of glucose, a kind of sugar, to release energy in a form the body can use.

- Aerobic respiration requires oxygen and breaks down glucose into carbon dioxide and water. Anaerobic respiration does not need oxygen and breaks down glucose to carbon dioxide and lactic acid. It releases less energy than aerobic respiration.

- Adenosine triphosphate (ATP) is the chemical that transfers energy between respiration and reactions in the cell.

- The body uses a variety of systems to respond to sudden demands for energy; an anaerobic respiration, creatinine phosphate and finally aerobic respiration.

- The oxygen needed to clear away the lactic acid produced during a burst of intense activity is called the oxygen debt.

QUESTIONS

1 Write a sentence to explain the scientific meaning of each of the following terms:

- energy
- respiration
- ventilation
- anaerobic
- oxygen debt.

2 Draw a flow chart to show how ATP can supply energy to a process in a cell. Make sure your flow chart shows what happens to the ATP after it has passed on its energy.

3 Where does each of the following processes occur in the cell?

- Glucose is split into two smaller molecules (glycolysis).
- Carbon dioxide is produced.
- The electron transfer chain harvests energy from electrons.

The respiratory system

THE RESPIRATORY SYSTEM HAS two main functions: to collect oxygen from the air and to get rid of carbon dioxide made by the body. The **respiratory system** includes the lungs, trachea, nose and mouth. It moves air into and out of the lungs to allow the body to absorb oxygen and give out carbon dioxide. The respiratory system works with the **cardiovascular system** to make sure every cell in the body has a supply of oxygen and can get rid of waste carbon dioxide.

Any damage to the respiratory or circulatory systems is serious. The body needs a constant supply of oxygen. If the oxygen supply to the brain is cut for more than four minutes it will die. Compare this with your need for food and drink – people can survive for days without water and for weeks without food.

What are the lungs made of?

A typical pair of human lungs weigh just over a kilogram and fit into a space that measures less than 40 cm from top to bottom. However, they contain over 80 m² of surface area for gaseous exchange. The skin surface area in the same person is roughly two square metres. The enormous surface area in the lungs depends on 500 million small sacs called alveoli. **Alveoli** (singular, alveolus) are balloon-like swellings on the ends of **bronchioles**. An alveolus is made of a thin membrane covered with tiny blood vessels. The bronchioles are the thinnest tubes in the lungs. They carry air directly into the alveoli. Bronchioles connect to the bronchi rather like the branches on a tree. The bronchi join together to form the **trachea**, also called the windpipe. Rings of stiff cartilage help to keep the trachea and bronchi from being squashed flat by the breathing movements. The **ribs** and **sternum** protect the lungs and heart.

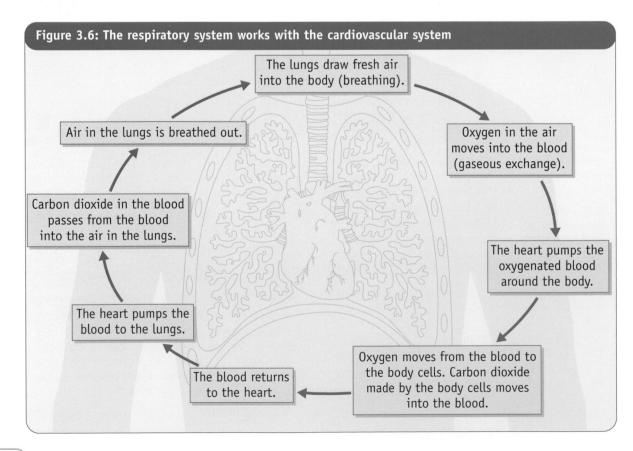

Figure 3.6: The respiratory system works with the cardiovascular system

The lungs draw fresh air into the body (breathing).

Air in the lungs is breathed out.

Oxygen in the air moves into the blood (gaseous exchange).

Carbon dioxide in the blood passes from the blood into the air in the lungs.

The heart pumps the oxygenated blood around the body.

The heart pumps the blood to the lungs.

The blood returns to the heart.

Oxygen moves from the blood to the body cells. Carbon dioxide made by the body cells moves into the blood.

Figure 3.7: The respiratory system

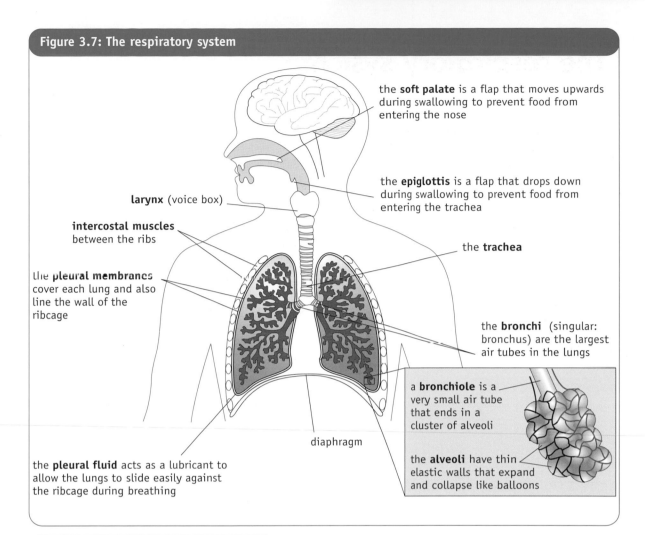

the **soft palate** is a flap that moves upwards during swallowing to prevent food from entering the nose

the **epiglottis** is a flap that drops down during swallowing to prevent food from entering the trachea

larynx (voice box)

intercostal muscles between the ribs

the **pleural membranes** cover each lung and also line the wall of the ribcage

the **trachea**

the **bronchi** (singular: bronchus) are the largest air tubes in the lungs

a **bronchiole** is a very small air tube that ends in a cluster of alveoli

diaphragm

the **pleural fluid** acts as a lubricant to allow the lungs to slide easily against the ribcage during breathing

the **alveoli** have thin elastic walls that expand and collapse like balloons

CASE STUDY

Cystic fibrosis and lung function

Cystic fibrosis (CF) is one of the commonest genetic diseases in the UK with roughly one in 2,500 babies born with the illness. CF is caused by a damaged gene, which means the sufferer cannot control the movement of salt into and out of body cells properly. This has effects in the lungs, pancreas and lower gut particularly, but can lead to problems all over the body.

In the lungs, the mucus that normally protects the internal surfaces becomes quite thick and sticky. This makes it difficult to move, so it clogs up the small tubes and can act as a reservoir for infection. Children with CF often suffer from repeated chest infections, which can make them weak and slow their growth. Damage to the pancreas can affect appetite and could lead to diabetes mellitus (see p. 171). Again, this can lead to slow growth and general lack of well being. Care staff often refer to this general condition as 'failure to thrive'.

Recently, new treatments have improved the health of people with CF enormously. A high-calorie diet with added vitamins (A, D, E and K) and a package of enzymes help with growth. Antibiotics can keep lung infections under control and should be given as soon as the slightest sign of infection occurs.

Recent trials have used genetic engineering techniques to insert undamaged genes into the cells of the lung lining. These genes 'teach' the cells how to control salt movement across the cell membranes. This reduces the thickness of the mucus and so helps to prevent build up of infection. In the future this may provide a cure for CF.

ACTIVITY

Treating cystic fibrosis

Look back at the case study on page 133. What does the term 'failure to thrive' mean?

Children with cystic fibrosis are given physiotherapy every day. They lie on their front and a trained nurse taps them on their back to loosen mucus in the lungs. The child then coughs up the mucus to help to clear the lungs. How will this treatment help to prevent lung infections?

Look at the lab report for this cystic fibrosis sufferer. By referring to the table below, choose a suitable antibiotic for this patient.

NAME:	John Smith
DoB:	2/10/56
Ref:	4456233/9
Culture:	sputum
Date collected:	24/9/99

Results

Staph aureus (penicillin sensitive)	–
Staph aureus (penicillin resistant)	–
Strep (group A)	–
Strep pneumoniae	
Enterococcus faecalis	–
E. coli	–
Klebsiella species	–
Pseudomonas aeruginosa	+++
Bacteriodes fragilis	–
Clostridium difficile	–

− no trace   + infection present

	P	A	C	I	E	Ca	T	Ch	Tr	M	Ci	Co
Staph aureus (penicillin sensitive)	1	2	2	0	2R	2R	2R	2R	0	R	0	2
Staph aureus (penicillin resistant)	R	R	2	2	2R	2	2R	2R	0	R	0	2
Strep (group A)	1	2	2	2	2R	2	R	2R	0	R	R	2
Strep pneumoniae	1	1	2	2	2R	R	2R	2R	R	R	R	2
Enterococcus faecalis	R	1	R	2	0	R	R	R	0	R	R	2
E. coli	R	1R	2	2	R	R	R	R	1R	R	2	2
Klebsiella species	R	R	2	2	R	R	R	R	1R*	R	2	2
Pseudomonas aeruginosa	R	R	R	2	R	R	R	R	R	R	1	R
Bacteriodes fragilis	R	R	R	2	R	2	0	2R	R	1	R	2
Clostridium difficile	0	0	0	0	0	0	0	0	1	0	0	0

Key

I	susceptible, first choice
2	second choice
R*	resistance is rare in most cases
R	resistance likely
0	usually inappropriate

P	Penicillin V+G
A	Ampicillin
C	Cefradine
I	Imipenem
E	Erythromycin
Ca	Clindamycin

T	Tetracyclines
Ch	Chloramphenicol
Tr	Trimethoprim
M	Metronidazole
Ci	Ciprofloxacin
Co	Co amoxiclav

What causes breathing movements?

The air in the lungs would soon run out of oxygen if it was not changed regularly. Breathing, sometimes also called ventilation, is the movement of air into and out of the lungs. Breathing in humans uses three movements:

- the liver piston
- the diaphragm
- the rib cage.

The liver piston

The liver fits neatly under the rib cage. When the muscle walls of the abdomen relax, the liver and gut drop or sag slightly. The liver pulls the floor of the lungs downwards and sucks air into the lungs. When the abdomen muscles tighten, the liver and gut are pushed back up under the ribs and air is squeezed out of the lungs.

The diaphragm

The diaphragm is a sheet of muscle that stretches across the base of the rib cage. The diaphragm is used for deeper breathing. When the muscles of the diaphragm relax it is shaped like a dome pushing up into the lung space. If the muscles contract, the diaphragm is pulled flat and the floor of the lungs is pulled down with it. This sucks air into the lungs in the same way as the liver piston.

The rib cage

The rib cage is used for the most powerful breathing movements. The ribs can move up or down when muscles pull on them. The muscles between the ribs are called **intercostal muscles**. When the external intercostal muscles contract they pull the ribs upwards and outwards. This pulls on the surface of the lungs and sucks air into the lungs. When the internal intercostal muscles contract the ribs are pulled down. This squeezes air out of the lungs.

Lung capacity

The amount of air that passes through your lungs every minute is called the **pulmonary ventilation** or the **minute volume**. This volume depends on the:

- number of breaths you take per minute
- volume of air moved per breath.

The number of breaths per minute is called the **breathing rate**. In a resting adult male this can be roughly 12 breaths per minute. In times of stress it can rise to 25 or 30 breaths per minute.

How much can you take in a breath?

The total amount of air in your lungs is called the **total lung capacity**. In a healthy adult male this can be about six litres. When he is resting and breathing normally, about 0.5 l of this air is changed at every breath. This volume is called the **tidal volume** – the air goes in and out like the tide every breath. If he takes a deep breath he can suck in about another 3.5 l. This extra volume is called the **inspiratory reserve volume**. If he tries to breath out as much as possible he can only squeeze out another litre from his lungs compared with normal tidal breathing. This extra breathing out is called the **expiratory reserve volume**. So, the maximum amount of air the healthy adult male can move in and out of his lungs in one breath is:

Inspiratory reserve volume (maximum breath in)	=	3.5 l
Tidal volume (normal breathing)	=	0.5 l
Expiratory reserve volume (maximum breath out)	=	1.0 l
Total	=	5 l

This maximum breath is called the **forced vital capacity**. Notice that it does not reach the total lung capacity. This is because the man can never completely empty his lungs of air. The volume of air always left inside his lungs is called the **residual volume** and in the figures above must be roughly 1 l.

Figure 3.8: Spirometer trace of lung volume

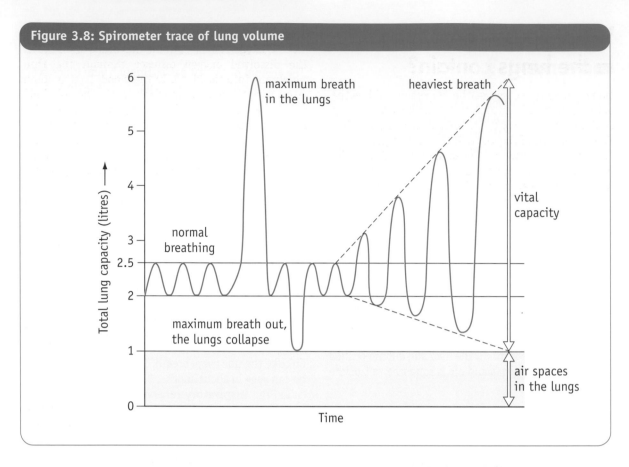

ACTIVITY

Lung volumes and fitness

Physical activity depends on a good supply of energy, and so a good supply of oxygen. So, is it fair to say that athletes have larger lungs? How could you test the idea that training increases your lung volume?

Plan an investigation to find out if training increases your lung volume. You will need to explain:

- how you will choose your test group
- how the spirometer trace will help with selection of experimental groups
- what you will measure
- how you will measure it
- what training system you will use to try to produce the lung volume increase
- how you will make sure your investigation is fair
- how you will interpret your results.

Figure 3.9: Gases in inhaled and exhaled air

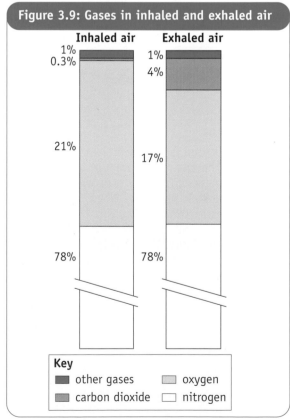

What does the air in the lungs contain?

Many people think we breathe in oxygen and breathe out carbon dioxide. In fact, the air we breathe out still contains enough oxygen to keep someone else alive. This is the basis of the kiss of life used in resuscitation. The difference between inhaled and exhaled air is the proportion of different gases they contain. Exhaled air contains more carbon dioxide and less oxygen than inhaled air (see Figure 3.9).

How does oxygen get into the blood?

Gases move into the blood by diffusion. **Diffusion** is the random movement of molecules from areas of high concentration to areas of low concentration. The rate of diffusion is normally quite slow and is slowed down even more if there is a barrier between the two areas (see Figure 3.10).

The movement of oxygen and carbon dioxide between the air in the lungs and the blood by diffusion is called **gaseous exchange**. At the surface of the **alveoli**, oxygen dissolves in the thin lining of moisture. The dissolved oxygen diffuses through the thin membrane into the blood. In the blood, haemoglobin reacts with the oxygen and locks it into the red blood cells to be carried around the body. Since the blood is always moving, oxygenated blood is always being carried away from the alveoli. At the same time, deoxygenated red blood cells from the body are always arriving. This maintains a steep concentration gradient for oxygen to encourage rapid diffusion. The blood that arrives at the alveoli is rich in carbon dioxide. This diffuses out of the blood into the air in the lungs and can then be breathed out.

Smokers are often breathless because cigarette smoke can cause a disease that destroys the alveoli of the lungs. The loss of alveoli means the surface area available for gaseous exchange drops and less oxygen gets into the blood. This means the lungs and heart have to work harder to make up for this inefficiency. This strain causes the early death from lung and heart disease in smokers.

Figure 3.10: Controlling the rate of diffusion

	To speed up diffusion	To slow down diffusion
Barrier	Make it as thin as possible and easy for the particles to pass through. Example: the material of a teabag.	Make it thick or impossible for the particles to pass through. Example: the plastic lining of a waterproof jacket.
Surface area	As large as possible to give space for particles to move across. Example: the surface in a kidney machine.	As small as possible. Example: a ball of wet paper dries out much more slowly than the same paper rolled out flat.
Concentrations of diffusing particles	Have the largest possible difference in concentration between the two areas. Example: wet clothes dry much more quickly on a dry day than a wet day – even if it is quite cold.	Diffusion stops if the concentration of particles in both areas is the same. Example: once a strong smell has filled a room it will not move around in the room any further.

BUILD YOUR LEARNING

Keywords and phrases

You should know the meaning of the words and phrases listed below. If you are unclear about any of them, go back through the last six pages of this unit to refresh your understanding.

- Alveoli
- Breathing rate
- Bronchioles
- Diaphragm
- Diffusion
- Expiratory reserve volume
- Forced vital capacity
- Gaseous exchange
- Inspiratory reserve volume
- Intercostal muscles
- Minute volume
- Oxygenated blood
- Pulmonary ventilation
- Residual volume
- Respiratory system
- Rib cage
- Sternum
- Tidal volume
- Total lung capacity
- Trachea

Summary points

- The respiratory system collects oxygen from the air and gets rid of carbon dioxide.

- The lungs contain millions of tiny air sacs called alveoli. Gaseous exchange takes place across the surface of the alveoli. The other parts of the lungs keep the airways open and ensure a constant supply of fresh air to the alveoli.

- Breathing movements depend on the intercostal muscles, the diaphragm and the abdominal muscles.

- The total lung capacity is the amount of air in the lungs. The volume of air breathed in and out at rest is called the tidal volume. The largest volume that you can breath out in one breath is called the forced vital capacity.

- All gaseous exchange in the lungs occurs by diffusion. Diffusion depends on the random movement of particles. It always occurs from areas of high concentration to areas of low concentration.

- The difference in concentration between the areas is called the concentration gradient and the steeper the gradient the faster the rate of diffusion.

- The surface area available also affects diffusion – the larger the surface area the faster the rate of diffusion.

QUESTIONS

1 **Write a sentence to show that you know the meaning of the following terms:**

  - intercostal muscles

  - minute volume

  - forced vital capacity

  - diffusion

  - surface area.

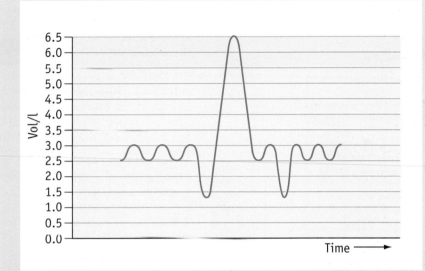

2 **From the spirometer trace, work out the:**

  - tidal volume

  - inspiratory reserve volume

  - expiratory reserve volume

  - forced vital capacity.

3 **List three factors that will increase the rate of diffusion across a membrane.**

4 **Draw a flow chart to show how oxygen gets from the air outside the body into the red blood cells.**

5 **The following adaptations allow the lungs to work efficiently. Explain why each one is an essential feature of the lungs.**

  - Large surface area.

  - Good blood supply.

  - A mechanism for moving air into and out of the lungs.

  - Systems which clear dust and dirt from the lung surfaces.

The cardiovascular system

THE CARDIOVASCULAR SYSTEM'S function is to move substances around the body. The main substances it moves are the respiratory gases (carbon dioxide and oxygen) and food (see Figure 3.11).

The cardiovascular system includes:

- the transport medium – the blood
- the pump to move it around the body – the heart
- the vessels or tubes to control the flow of the transport medium – the arteries and veins.

Blood

A normal adult male has about six litres of this precious fluid and it comprises about eight per cent of his total body weight. The **blood** is a complex mixture of substances and its different components do different jobs. For example, the red cells carry oxygen around the body while the white cells protect against disease. Figure 3.12 shows the main components of the blood and their functions.

Figure 3.12: Blood components and functions

White cells protect the body against infection. They are colourless and have a nucleus. They are larger than red cells but there are fewer of them, and they only spend about 10% of their time in the blood. White cells are made in the bone marrow and in the lymph nodes. There are different types of white cell.

 Lymphocyte

 Granulocyte

 Monocyte

15µm

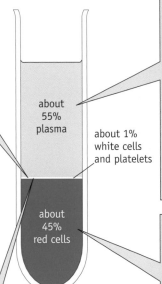

about 55% plasma

about 1% white cells and platelets

about 45% red cells

Plasma is a clear, pale yellow liquid that is 90% water. The remaining 10% contains many substances including:

- glucose, amino acids, fats, calcium and other nutrients from food
- urea, carbon dioxide and other waste products
- hormones to control the way the body works
- antibodies to destroy microbes
- fibrinogen for clotting.

Serum is the clear liquid that is left over after blood has clotted. It contains no cells, platelets or fibrinogen.

Red cells carry oxygen from the lungs to the tissues. They are made in the bone marrow. As they develop, the nucleus disappears, so mature red cells have no nucleus. The life span of a red cell is about 100–120 days. Worn-out red cells are removed in the liver or spleen and replaced by new ones from the bone marrow.

 2µm
cross section

7µm

Red cells are shaped like a disc and are concave on each surface; this shape is called a biconcave disc. They can fold and bend as they pass through the smallest blood vessels.

Platelets help the blood to clot. They are much smaller than red cells and vary in shape. They are produced by 'budding off' from special cells in the bone marrow.

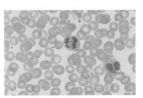

*This **blood smear** has been stained with a dye to show the white cells. There are two of them. The tiny spots are platelets.*

Figure 3.11: Substances carried by the blood

Substance	Moved from	Moved to	Notes
Oxygen	Lungs	Every cell in the body	For use in respiration
Carbon dioxide	Every cell in the body	The lungs	To pass out in exhaled air
Food substances	The gut	Every cell in the body	To be used for energy or to build up the body
Hormones	Endocrine gland	Target organs	To control the way the organs work
Urea	The liver	The kidneys	To be excreted in the urine
Antibodies	Lymph glands	Infected areas	Protect against disease
Heat	Hotter areas	Cooler areas	To equalise temperature across the body

The blood is constantly monitored by the body to make sure every single component remains within safe limits. It is a dynamic system with old parts being destroyed and cleared away at the same rate as new parts are made to replace them. No cell in the body is more than 1 mm away from the blood. This means that any poisons that get into the blood spread rapidly and dangerously throughout the body.

The heart

The **heart** has four chambers joined together to make one large block of muscle (see Figure 3.13). In a resting adult human it beats about 70 times per minute and will complete 2.5 million beats in an average lifetime. Despite this enormous task, a healthy heart can continue to beat for many years after some other body organs have worn out. Even though heart disease is one of the greatest killers in the western world this is probably to do with our stressed and sedentary lifestyle. Heart disease seems to be one of the great, preventable causes of early death.

Why doesn't the heart get tired?

The heart is made of muscle. However, heart muscle is slightly different to other muscles in the body. It can contract and relax regularly without any nervous stimulation and seems able to go on forever without tiring. An **electrocardiogram (ECG)** plots the electrical impulses that control the contraction of heart muscles.

Figure 3.14 shows that for much of a heart beat the heart muscle is actually relaxing. This may be part of the reason why the heart does not tire. However, as the heart rate rises the amount of time spent resting is reduced. This means more strain is placed on the heart. If the heart is strained too much the muscle can fail and a heart attack occurs.

What can go wrong with the heart?

Like every other muscle in the body, the heart needs a constant supply of food and oxygen, and to get rid of carbon dioxide. The blood flowing through the heart cannot do this efficiently enough, so the muscles of the heart have their own blood supply.

The coronary artery delivers oxygenated blood to the muscles of the ventricles. Any blockage in the coronary artery will starve the heart muscle of blood and lead to serious damage – possibly even death.

Cholesterol is a fatty substance that is needed by the body to build cells and nerves (see Figure 3.15). However, if our diet is too high in fats, particularly animal fats, the concentration of the cholesterol in the blood rises above a safe level. This encourages the formation of fatty deposits called **plaques** on the inside walls of arteries. These plaques slowly close down the space in the artery where the blood flows – effectively the artery 'furs up' with fat. If this happens in the coronary artery, it cannot carry enough blood to the heart muscles.

Figure 3.13: The human heart

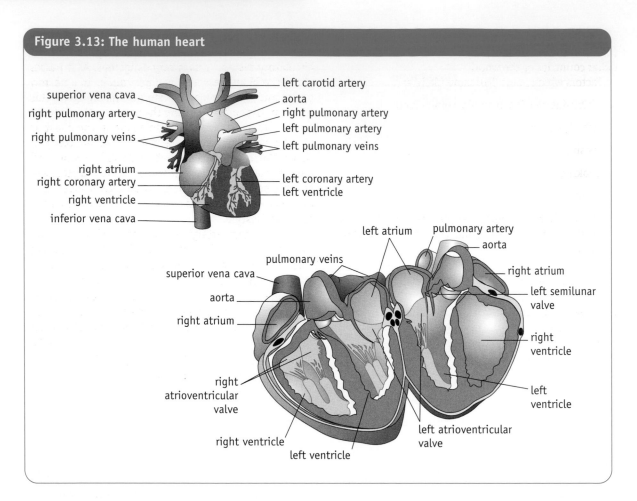

Figure 3.14: An electrocardiogram

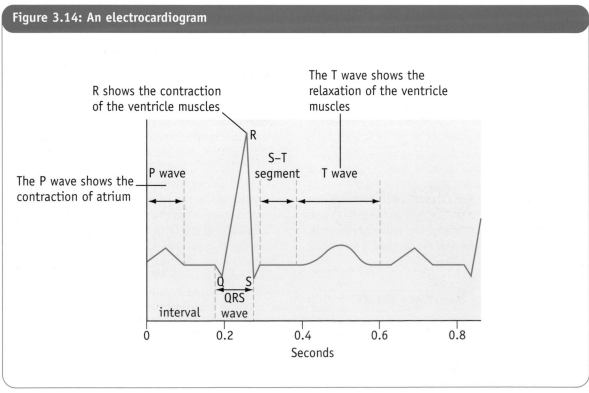

This condition is called **coronary heart disease (CHD)** and is one of the major causes of death in the richer countries of the world.

Factors which make CHD more likely are:

- a high-fat diet (particularly animal fats)
- lack of exercise
- obesity
- smoking
- stress
- genetic factors – some people seem to inherit a greater chance of suffering from CHD from their parents.

The good news on CHD is that almost all of the risk factors are under our control. We can eat a healthier diet, take more exercise and, if we smoke, we should stop. Even stress responds well to being healthy. People who have a good diet, take plenty of exercise and who look after themselves seem to cope much better with stress than people who are overweight and unfit.

Sometimes a piece of plaque breaks off from the side of an artery and starts to move through the blood circulatory system. This is very dangerous. As it passes along the blood vessels it can get caught in a narrow vessel and block it completely and instantly. If this occurs in the coronary artery the person suffers a heart attack. He or she feels a terrible pain in the chest as muscles in the heart are starved of food and oxygen. Unless the blockage clears or it affects only a very small area of muscle, the patient will die. Many doctors say that the best way to survive a heart attack is not to have one in the first place! That means sticking to a healthy diet and lifestyle.

The coronary artery can also be blocked by blood clots. Blood normally only clots when it is in contact with air. This happens at a cut or wound. Surgery involves cutting the body and so produces clots. Doctors often give patients special anti-clotting drugs (some derived from rattlesnake venom and rat poison!) to prevent clots forming. Of course, these drugs also mean that wounds take longer to seal and bleeding cannot be allowed to go on forever, so they must be used under carefully controlled conditions.

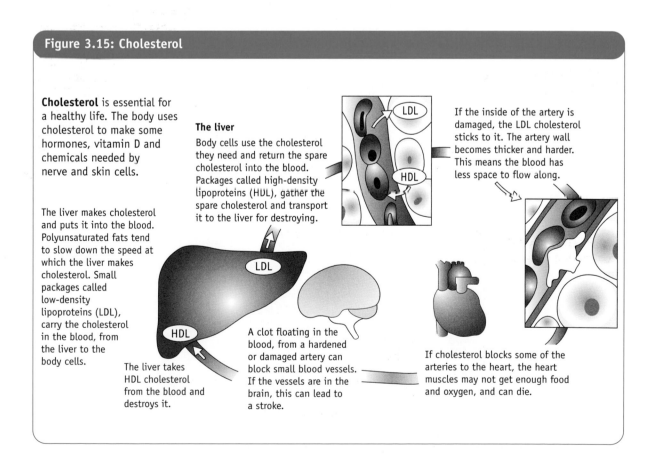

Figure 3.15: Cholesterol

Cholesterol is essential for a healthy life. The body uses cholesterol to make some hormones, vitamin D and chemicals needed by nerve and skin cells.

The liver makes cholesterol and puts it into the blood. Polyunsaturated fats tend to slow down the speed at which the liver makes cholesterol. Small packages called low-density lipoproteins (LDL), carry the cholesterol in the blood, from the liver to the body cells.

The liver

Body cells use the cholesterol they need and return the spare cholesterol into the blood. Packages called high-density lipoproteins (HDL), gather the spare cholesterol and transport it to the liver for destroying.

The liver takes HDL cholesterol from the blood and destroys it.

A clot floating in the blood, from a hardened or damaged artery can block small blood vessels. If the vessels are in the brain, this can lead to a stroke.

If the inside of the artery is damaged, the LDL cholesterol sticks to it. The artery wall becomes thicker and harder. This means the blood has less space to flow along.

If cholesterol blocks some of the arteries to the heart, the heart muscles may not get enough food and oxygen, and can die.

Arteries and veins

Arteries are the tubes that carry blood away from the heart around the body. **Veins** are the tubes that carry blood from the body back towards the heart. Both arteries and veins can get wider or narrower to control the flow of blood to different organs. When they get wider or **dilate**, more blood flows but when they get narrower or constrict, the blood supply drops. Every major body organ has its own artery and vein.

All the arteries branch off the **aorta**. When the left **ventricle** of the heart contracts it pushes a surge of blood into the aorta. The aorta stretches slightly to reduce the effect of the surge. When the ventricle is filling with blood the walls of the aorta spring back and squeeze on the blood. This stretching and contracting helps to smooth out the flow of the blood. It cannot stop it completely. When an artery runs over a bone or near to the surface of the body you can feel the surges through the skin. We call this the **pulse**. Every pulse beat corresponds to a heart beat. Parts of the body where you can feel a pulse are called the **pulse points**.

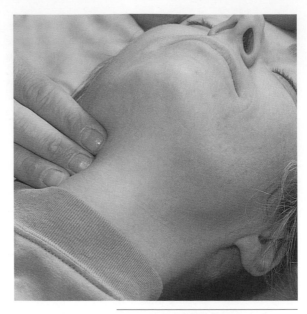

▲ First aiders and paramedics often feel for a carotid pulse to establish signs of life.

Figure 3.16: Blood vessels compared

Vessel	Cross section	Direction of flow	Pressure	Oxygen content	Inner diameter	Presence of valves	Properties of wall
Arteries		away from heart	high when an artery is cut, blood spurts out with each heart beat	high blood is bright red except in pulmonary artery	relatively small blood flows rapidly and at high pressure	no	thick elastic tissue and muscle layer allows the wall to expand and then return to its original size with each heart beat
Veins		back to heart except in hepatic portal vein	low when a vein is cut, blood oozes out, sometimes quickly, but it never spurts	low blood is dark red except in pulmonary vein	relatively large blood moves slowly so there are more veins and they have larger cavities	yes	thin, stretches easily
Capillaries	single layer of cells	through organs and tissues	medium	oxygen diffuses through wall	small, about the diameter of one red blood cell	no	one cell thick

☐ connective tissue
☐ smooth muscle and elastic fibres
— lining is a single layer of cells
■ central passageway for blood

The pressure of blood pushes the valve open and allows the blood to flow through.

When pressure is low the valve closes and stops blood flowing back.

Taking the pulse is a routine part of medical care. Abnormally high or low pulse rates are signs of dangerous conditions that need treatment. An irregular or weak pulse also suggests that something is wrong. When taking the pulse it is important to remember that the **pulse** rate changes very easily during exercise or excitement. More details about the best way to take and interpret pulse readings are given on p. 201.

Capillaries

Capillaries are the smallest blood vessels in the body and have walls that are only one cell thick. Capillaries join arteries to veins. They carry blood into every part of the body and allow food and oxygen to pass from the blood to the body tissues. Waste products pass the other way. No cell in the body is more than a millimetre away from a capillary.

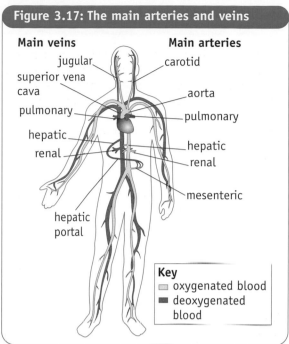

Figure 3.17: The main arteries and veins

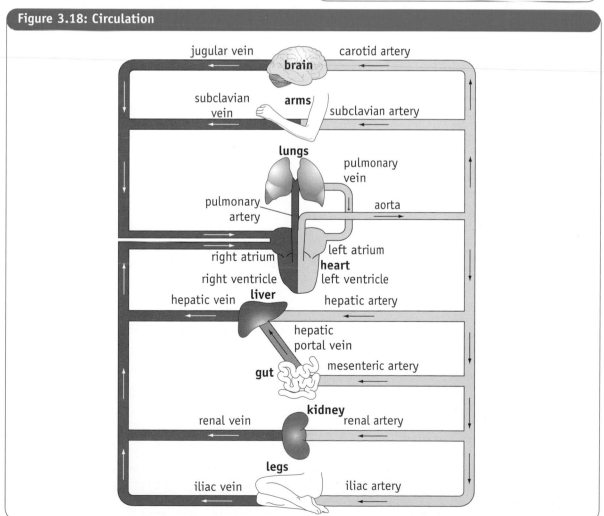

Figure 3.18: Circulation

BUILD YOUR LEARNING

Keywords and phrases

You should know the meaning of the words and phrases listed below. If you are unsure about any of them, go back through the last six pages of the unit to refresh your understanding.

- Aorta
- Arteries
- Blood
- Capillaries
- Cardiovascular system
- Cholesterol
- Coronary heart disease (CHD)
- Dilate
- Electrocardiogram
- Heart
- Plaque
- Pulse
- Pulse points
- Veins
- Ventricles

Summary points

- The cardiovascular system includes the blood, the heart and the arteries, capillaries and veins.

- The heart is a muscular pump with a resting rate of about 70 beats per minute. It beats without nervous stimulation but changes in heart rate depend on the nerves and some hormones.

- The coronary artery supplies blood to the muscles of the heart. Coronary heart disease (CHD) is any blockage or narrowing of this artery. CHD is serious and may lead to a heart attack.

- CHD is more likely to occur in people who have a high-fat diet, take little exercise, smoke, suffer from stress and who have a family history of CHD.

- Arteries carry blood away from the heart under high pressure. Veins carry blood back to the heart under lower pressure. Capillaries are tiny blood vessels that connect arteries to veins.

QUESTIONS

1 Write a sentence to explain the scientific meaning of each of the following terms:

- electrocardiogram (ECG)
- coronary artery
- cholesterol
- dilate
- pulse point.

2 Copy out the table below and fill in the gaps.

	Moved from	Moved to	Notes
Oxygen			For use in respiration
Food substances			To be used for energy or to build up the body
Antibodies		Infected areas	
Hormones			
	The liver		To be excreted in the urine
	Hotter areas		
	Every cell in the body		To pass out in exhaled air

3 Which part of the blood carries:

- oxygen?
- carbon dioxide?
- glucose?

4 Explain what coronary heart disease is and list five factors which make coronary heart disease more likely.

5 David's family has a history of heart trouble. His grandfather and father both died of heart attacks at a relatively early age. His older sister is receiving treatment for angina. David is significantly overweight and smokes 25 cigarettes a day. Give three ways David could reduce his chances of suffering from coronary heart disease.

6 Draw up a table to show three differences between arteries, capillaries and veins.

The digestive system

THE HUMAN GUT IS A MUSCULAR tube roughly 8.5 metres long folded into the space between the bottom of the ribs and the top of the legs. At the top of the gut is the stomach. It produces a solution of hydrochloric acid so strong that it can dissolve steel wool, and yet in normal situations it does not digest itself! The longest part of the gut, called the small intestine, is five metres long but has an internal surface area of about 200 square metres! If you papered a wall with the pages of a telephone directory it would take eight complete books to cover the same area! It is this combination of strong chemicals and enormous surface area that allows the gut to carry out its functions of digestion and absorption.

The digestive system has two functions:

- to break down food into simple chemicals
- to absorb these simple chemicals into the body.

What is food?

Food is a complicated mixture of chemicals. These chemicals must have come originally from a living organism, whether plant or animal, and are the same stuff that living things are made from. Food chemicals, sometimes called **nutrients**, fall into seven groups:

- carbohydrates
- fats
- proteins
- vitamins
- minerals
- fibre or roughage
- water.

The food we eat is called our **diet**. A healthy diet must contain a supply of all of these nutrients, though we need some more than others. The body needs food for energy and to provide raw materials for repair and growth.

The digestive system includes the gut and a series of glands attached to it. The **gut** is a long muscular tube that can force food along itself so that the glands can secrete enzymes onto the food to break down the chemicals they contain. **Enzymes** are special protein molecules that speed up chemical reactions in the body. There are many types of enzymes, one for each reaction. Over a dozen different digestive enzymes act on food in the gut. Each part of the gut is adapted for its particular task so, although the basic structure is the same throughout, individual areas can look very different.

▲ The human stomach is capable of dealing with most of the abuses dealt to it, although a diet of nuts, bolts and screws would give most people severe indigestion

Figure 3.19: Food groups

Food group	Main source	Main use in the body
Carbohydrates	Potatoes, bread, root vegetables	Respired to provide energy.
Fats	Butter and dairy fats, vegetable oils, nuts	Fat is essential for cell membranes and many structures in the body. It is also a very good energy store.
Proteins	Meat, fish, nuts	Used to build and repair body parts, particularly muscles. Excess protein is broken down into urea and carbohydrate. The urea is passed out of the body and the carbohydrate can be respired for energy.
Vitamins	Leafy vegetables, fresh fruit, milk	Vitamins have a range of uses in the body. Vitamin C is essential for healthy teeth, skin and gums. Vitamin K is essential for blood clotting. Vitamin D helps to build strong bones.
Minerals	Milk, red meat, leafy vegetables	Minerals are needed for particular tasks in the body. Calcium helps to build strong teeth and bones. Iron is needed to make red blood cells. Iodine is used to make the hormone thyroxin.
Roughage	Leafy vegetables, bran, brown bread, porridge	Roughage cannot be digested. It helps to keep food moving through the gut.
Water	Drinks of any sort and foods like melons and fruit	Water is needed to maintain the concentration of solutions in the body.

How does the digestive system work?

The digestive system works on food in a particular sequence.

Physical digestion. This is the grinding up of large lumps of food into smaller particles. It is done by the teeth and increases the surface area of the food particles.

Chemical digestion. This involves breaking large molecules down into molecules small enough to be absorbed into the body. Enzymes produced by the gut and the glands linked to it do this job.

Absorption. This involves taking the small molecules produced by chemical digestion into the bloodstream. Most of this is done in the lower part of the gut after digestion is complete.

Sorting. Absorbed food molecules are carried by the bloodstream to the liver for sorting. Some are passed on to the rest of the body, some are broken down or changed in chemical reactions and some are stored. Once food molecules are loaded into the blood they can

Figure 3.20: The digestive system

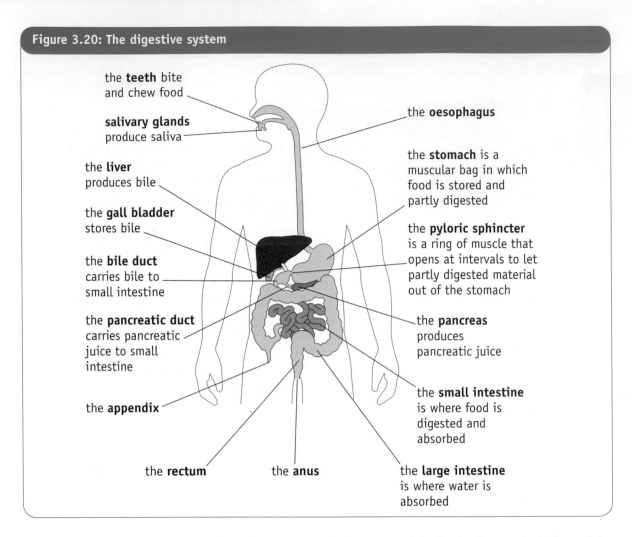

the **teeth** bite and chew food

salivary glands produce saliva

the **liver** produces bile

the **gall bladder** stores bile

the **bile duct** carries bile to small intestine

the **pancreatic duct** carries pancreatic juice to small intestine

the **appendix**

the **rectum**

the **anus**

the **oesophagus**

the **stomach** is a muscular bag in which food is stored and partly digested

the **pyloric sphincter** is a ring of muscle that opens at intervals to let partly digested material out of the stomach

the **pancreas** produces pancreatic juice

the **small intestine** is where food is digested and absorbed

the **large intestine** is where water is absorbed

be used anywhere in the body to build new body parts or to be respired for energy.

How does food move through the gut?

The muscles of the gut can squeeze the food along inside it, rather like toothpaste being squeezed along a toothpaste tube. Circular muscles behind a portion of food contract while the circular muscles in front of the food relax. This forces the food along. Muscles running lengthways along the gut help to move the food as well. This collection of coordinated muscle movements is called peristalsis (see Figure 3.21) All movement of the food in the gut from swallowing to passing it out of the anus depends on peristalsis.

Figure 3.21: Peristalsis

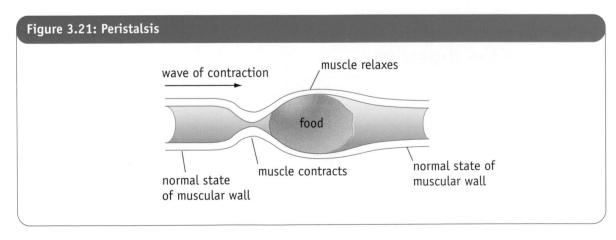

wave of contraction

muscle relaxes

food

normal state of muscular wall

muscle contracts

normal state of muscular wall

BUILD YOUR LEARNING

You should know the meaning of the words and phrases listed below. If you are unsure about any of them, go back through the last three pages of the unit to refresh your understanding.

- Absorption
- Carbohydrates
- Chemical digestion
- Diet
- Digestive system
- Enzymes
- Fats
- Gut
- Minerals
- Nutrients
- Peristalsis
- Physical digestion
- Proteins
- Roughage
- Vitamins

Summary points

- The digestive system breaks down food into simple chemicals, which can then be absorbed into the body.

- Food is a complex mixture of chemicals including carbohydrates, proteins, fats, vitamins, minerals, roughage and water. These food groups are sometimes called nutrients.

- Enzymes are proteins that can speed up a chemical reaction in the body. The gut uses digestive enzymes to break down large food molecules into smaller, simpler ones.

- Food is moved along the gut by peristalsis. This happens automatically and needs no conscious control.

QUESTIONS

1 Write a sentence to explain the scientific meaning of each of the following terms:

- digestion
- nutrient
- diet
- peristalsis
- absorption.

2 What are the four stages all food goes through before the chemicals it contains can be used by the body?

3 Copy out the table below and fill in the gaps.

Food group	Main source	Main use in the body
		Respired to provide energy
Proteins		
	Butter and dairy fats, vegetable oils, nuts	
Minerals	Milk, red meat, leafy vegetables	
		Vitamins have a range of uses in the body
	Drinks of any sort and foods like melons and fruit	
Roughage		

4 What are enzymes and what does the digestive system use them for?

5 An endoscope is an instrument that can be inserted into the gut to check for damage. Suggest a material an endoscope could be made from for use in the stomach. Why is steel probably not suitable for the stomach endoscope but quite safe to look at the lower gut?

The renal system

THE RENAL SYSTEM INCLUDES the kidneys, the ureters, bladder and urethra. The kidneys are about 11 cm long, 6 cm wide and 4 cm thick. They are higher in the body than most people imagine, tucked under the bottom of the rib cage near the spine.

The renal system has two functions; to remove waste materials (such as urea, made by the liver) from the blood and pass them out of the body in urine (**excretion**); and to control the level of water in the body to make sure the concentration of solutions in the body is kept within safe limits. This is called **osmoregulation**.

We have a great deal of spare capacity in the kidneys and people can live very healthy and active lives with only one working kidney – or even less. This is fortunate, because damage to the kidneys is very serious. Since they have the job of cleaning the blood, complete kidney failure means that the blood becomes more and more toxic as waste materials build up. Eventually the body is poisoned from within if the blood isn't cleaned.

Urea is a white, crystalline substance made in the liver. The body does not store protein so it converts it to glucose and respires it for energy. Converting protein to glucose produces waste products containing the amino group ($-NH_2$). This group of atoms is toxic and must be removed from the body. The liver uses a complex series of reactions called the **ornithine cycle** (see Figure 3.23) to build urea (chemical formula $CO(NH_2)_2$) to tie up these dangerous chemical groups. The urea can then be passed safely out of the body. Any excess amino acids in the diet are also converted to glucose and urea.

How does the kidney excrete waste?

The kidney works on the principles of ultrafiltration and selective reabsorption. This is a bit like someone looking for something in a large bag full of rubbish. The first

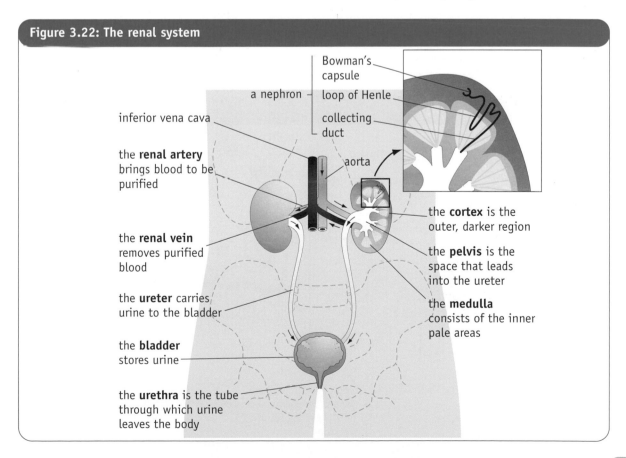

Figure 3.22: The renal system

- Bowman's capsule
- a nephron
- loop of Henle
- collecting duct
- inferior vena cava
- aorta
- the **renal artery** brings blood to be purified
- the **cortex** is the outer, darker region
- the **renal vein** removes purified blood
- the **pelvis** is the space that leads into the ureter
- the **ureter** carries urine to the bladder
- the **medulla** consists of the inner pale areas
- the **bladder** stores urine
- the **urethra** is the tube through which urine leaves the body

Fig: 3.23: The ornithine cycle

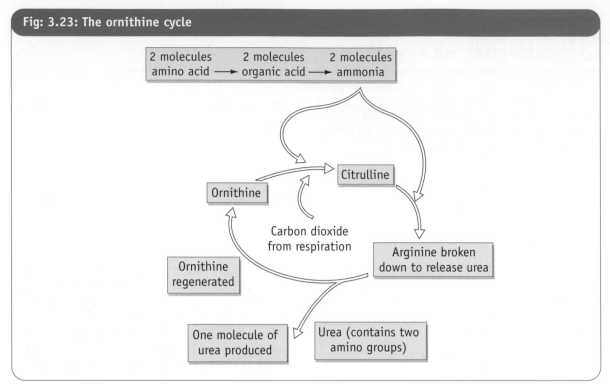

2 molecules amino acid → 2 molecules organic acid → 2 molecules ammonia

Citrulline

Ornithine

Carbon dioxide from respiration

Ornithine regenerated

Arginine broken down to release urea

One molecule of urea produced

Urea (contains two amino groups)

job is to empty the bag out onto a table – this is equivalent to **ultrafiltration**. Then you take back the thing you want to keep –   this is **selective reabsorption**. This strategy means the kidney can get rid of almost anything introduced into the body, even if it does not recognise it, (for example, a poison or a drug). It goes out by ultrafiltration. Only chemicals recognised by the kidney as useful will be taken back into the body by selective reabsorption. To carry out these tasks the kidney uses tiny tubes called **nephrons**. Each kidney contains over one million nephrons with a total length of over 100 km. Altogether the nephrons process about 1,300 ml of blood every minute to make 1 ml of urine and return 1,299 ml of clean blood back to the body.

Figure 3.24: Structure of a nephron

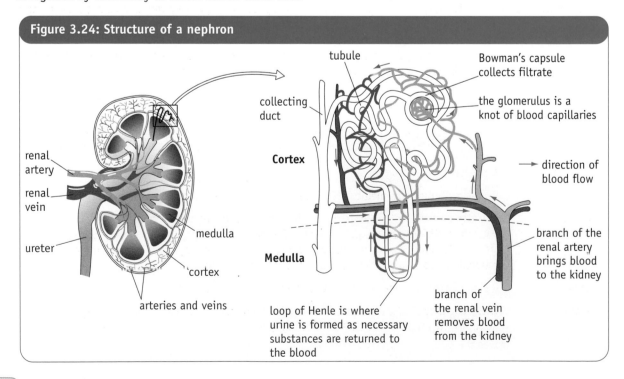

tubule

collecting duct

Bowman's capsule collects filtrate

the glomerulus is a knot of blood capillaries

Cortex

renal artery

renal vein

ureter

medulla

cortex

arteries and veins

direction of blood flow

branch of the renal artery brings blood to the kidney

Medulla

loop of Henle is where urine is formed as necessary substances are returned to the blood

branch of the renal vein removes blood from the kidney

Where does ultrafiltration occur?

Ultrafiltration takes place in the Bowman's capsule. A branch of the renal artery carries blood into a small, tangled ball of capillaries called the glomerulus tucked inside the Bowman's capsule. The blood is under pressure and most of it is squeezed through the wall of the capillaries into the space of the Bowman's capsule. The remaining blood drains away from the glomerulus along a branch of the renal vein.

Selective reabsorption

The fluid that collects in the Bowman's capsule is called the glomerular filtrate. It passes along a tube and eventually drains into the bladder to become urine. However, it contains many useful chemicals and a very large amount of water, so the body takes these things back as it passes towards the bladder. This taking back of useful chemicals is the process of selective reabsorption. Figure 3.25 shows the changes in the fluid as it passes along the nephron. Notice that urine contains no glucose or protein in a healthy person – these useful substances have been reabsorbed.

How does the kidney control water balance?

Adult humans produce something like 1.4 litres of urine every day and 96 per cent of this is water. You already know that if you drink a lot of fluids you produce a lot of very dilute urine. On hot, dry days where you do not drink enough, the volume of urine you produce falls but its concentration rises. How does the body control the amount and concentration of urine it produces? Water is forced out of the blood by ultrafiltration and is

Figure 3.25: Reabsorption by the body

	Filtered into nephrons per day	Excreted in urine per day
Blood proteins	trace	0.0 g
Glucose	144 g	0.0 g
Salt	570 g	15 g
Urea	64 g	30 g
Water	180 l	1.4 l

reabsorbed by the kidney tubules. The amount of water reabsorbed depends on how much water the body needs to conserve. On days when you have had plenty to drink, very little water is reabsorbed and you produce a lot of dilute urine. On a hot day when you have lost a lot of water through sweat, the kidneys absorb a lot of water and you produce very little concentrated urine.

What do urine tests tell us?

Urine is a very useful measure of the state of health of the body. Any imbalances or unusual chemicals in the body show up very quickly in urine. Athletes who have taken anabolic steroids to increase their performance have been caught out with simple urine tests. Some companies in the USA reserve the right to test employees for illegal drugs like cannabis and LSD during working hours. A simple urine test is often the first step in checking whether employees are fit for work.

Medical staff regularly use urine tests to detect abnormalities in the body.

Figure 3.26: Urine tests

Test for:	A positive result suggests:
Glucose	People with diabetes mellitus (p. 171) often show glucose in their urine.
Protein	This can be a sign of an infection in the renal system and needs rapid treatment with a suitable antibiotic. In pregnant women protein in urine can be a sign of pre-eclampsia. This needs bed rest and careful monitoring or it will develop into a kind of epilepsy called eclampsia which can be fatal for both mother and baby.
Blood	A sign of kidney stones or possibly cancer in the urinary tract.
Ketones	These chemicals are present if someone has been starving or slimming or if they suffer from diabetes that is not being treated properly.

BUILD YOUR LEARNING

Keywords and phrases

You should know the meaning of the words and phrases listed below. If you are unsure about any of them, go back through the last three pages of the unit to refresh your understanding.

- Bowman's capsule
- Excretion
- Glomerulus
- Glomerular filtrate
- Nephrons
- Osmoregulation
- Selective reabsorption
- Ultrafiltration
- Urea

Summary points

- The renal system includes the kidneys, ureters and bladder.

- The renal system removes waste materials from the blood and then passes them out of the body in urine. The kidneys also control water levels in the body.

- Urea is a white crystalline substance made in the liver from excess amino acids. It is passed to the kidneys in the bloodstream and then excreted in urine.

- Kidneys use ultrafiltration and selective reabsorption to ensure waste products are excreted.

- Nephrons are small tubules that filter wastes from the blood. Most of the water filtered into the nephrons is later reabsorbed by the body.

- The amount of water reabsorbed from the nephrons is used to control the level of water within the body.

- Urine tests, using simple dipsticks, provide useful indicators of a wide range of conditions.

QUESTIONS

1 Write a sentence to explain the scientific meaning of each of the following terms:

- excretion
- osmoregulation
- urea
- ultrafiltration
- selective reabsorption.

2 What are the two functions of the renal system?

3 Where is urea made? What is it made from? How is it passed out of the body?

4 List three substances that the kidney reabsorbs into the bloodstream from the glomerular filtrate. Explain the benefit to the body of this reabsorption. Name one substance that is not reabsorbed by the body and explain why it is not reabsorbed.

5 Name three conditions that could be detected by a simple urine test.

The nervous and endocrine systems

THE NERVOUS SYSTEM AND ENDOCRINE SYSTEMS work together to control conditions within the body and respond to changes outside the body. The nervous and endocrine systems have similar functions and share some structures. However, the way they carry out their tasks is quite different.

The nervous system

The nervous system includes the:

- brain and spinal cord (the central nervous system or CNS)

- nerves running through the body (the peripheral nervous system) and the autonomic nervous system (this controls the heart rate, contraction of smooth muscle in the gut and some endocrine glands)

- sense organs (for example, the eyes and ears)

- internal sense organs (chemoreceptors that can detect chemicals like carbon dioxide in the blood).

The **central nervous system (CNS)** includes the brain and spinal cord. It contains two main types of tissues. Grey matter, which is made up of the cell bodies

of nerve cell and white matter, which includes all the fibres running between nerve cells and other organs. The grey matter in the brain covers the outer surface and has the job of thinking. It is our grey matter that makes us smart.

Different parts of the brain do different jobs but they all depend on good connections. These connections are the nerve fibres. They carry nerve impulses across the nervous system. Each fibre is insulated from the ones next to it by a thin covering of myelin. It is the myelin that makes the white matter look white.

The **peripheral nervous system** includes the nerves that run out of the spine. These nerves are paired, so that nerves leaving on the right hand side of the spine match nerves leaving on the left.

What is a nerve?

An individual nerve is a bit like a telephone cable with many separate lines running along it. Each line consists of a single cell, so a nerve running from the toe to the brain may have a number of cells that are nearly two metres long! An individual cell can only carry impulses in one direction. This means that the brain is connected by individual cells to every area in the body.

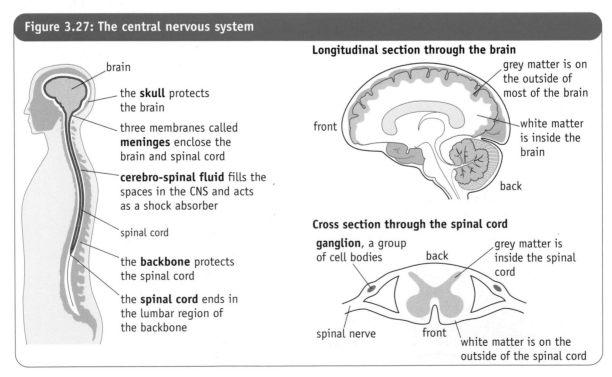

Figure 3.27: The central nervous system

brain

the **skull** protects the brain

three membranes called **meninges** enclose the brain and spinal cord

cerebro-spinal fluid fills the spaces in the CNS and acts as a shock absorber

spinal cord

the **backbone** protects the spinal cord

the **spinal cord** ends in the lumbar region of the backbone

Longitudinal section through the brain

grey matter is on the outside of most of the brain

front

white matter is inside the brain

back

Cross section through the spinal cord

ganglion, a group of cell bodies

back

grey matter is inside the spinal cord

spinal nerve

front

white matter is on the outside of the spinal cord

Nerve cells are very delicate and mature nerve cells cannot reproduce themselves. This means that the nerve cells you are born with are the ones you have to manage with for the rest of your life. To make matters worse they die as you get older, so the total number of cells starts dropping at age 20! However, we are born with millions of nerve cells which, barring accidents and illness, will keep us going for well over a hundred years.

Since nerves cannot repair themselves any damage is effectively permanent. Damage may be due to:

- illness, such as polio, meningitis or cancer

- chemicals, such as drugs or poisons

- accidents, such as car crashes, falling or sporting injuries.

Testing for nerve damage

If the spinal cord has been cut, the connection between the brain and all body parts below the cut has been lost forever. The nerves of the spinal cord cannot regrow and the person is paralysed below that point.

If a person seems to have some nerve damage it is possible to locate which nerves are affected by carefully mapping out what the body can do. Since each muscle group has its own nerve supply, it is possible to find out which nerves are damaged by asking a patient to move a particular muscle. So, if the muscles of the lower leg are reacting strangely it may be because the sciatic nerve has been damaged. The femoral nerve supplies the muscles of the thigh and damage to this nerve will only affect these muscles.

Sensory nerves carry messages from the sense organs to the central nervous system. Again, different senses and body parts have their own nerve connections. If someone cannot feel anything on the outside of his or her lower leg it may be that a branch of the lateral cutaneous nerve of the sacral plexus may be damaged. By carefully noting which muscles can move and which parts of the body are sensitive it is possible to build up a clear picture of any damage to nerves deep in the body.

Although nerves cannot regenerate once cut, they can recover from some minor conditions. The bones of the spine have small holes for nerves to pass through. As people get older these holes can begin to close up and this puts pressure on the nerves. The pressure prevents the nerves working properly and some people notice some clumsiness and lack of muscle control, particularly in the legs. Surgery to widen the holes gives the nerves room and cures this condition.

Figure 3.28: Structure of a nerve

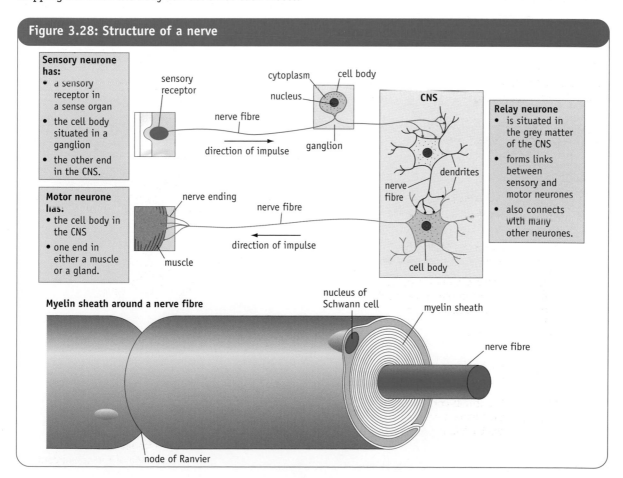

Sensory neurone has:
- a sensory receptor in a sense organ
- the cell body situated in a ganglion
- the other end in the CNS.

Motor neurone has:
- the cell body in the CNS
- one end in either a muscle or a gland.

Relay neurone
- is situated in the grey matter of the CNS
- forms links between sensory and motor neurones
- also connects with many other neurones.

sensory receptor · cytoplasm · cell body · nucleus · nerve fibre · direction of impulse · ganglion · CNS · dendrites · nerve fibre · cell body

nerve ending · nerve fibre · direction of impulse · muscle

Myelin sheath around a nerve fibre

nucleus of Schwann cell · myelin sheath · nerve fibre · node of Ranvier

Voluntary actions

Most of what we do we choose to do. So, if you want to put down this book and go for a walk your brain tells muscles in your arm to put down the book and muscles in your legs to take you out of the room. Almost all of the work done by the brain is unconscious. You are not aware of the complex coordination required to get all the muscles working together to take even a few steps – you just make the decision and your brain organises the rest.

The brain uses the peripheral nervous system to deliver the instructions, all carefully controlled and timed, to the muscles. These muscles are the voluntary muscles and you can read more about them on page 181. Even though you may not be consciously aware of the complex organisation task carried out by the brain, you do need to be conscious to make the decision. If someone seems to be having trouble making a decision or controlling complex movements then it suggests some problems with the brain. Alcohol is a chemical that has a temporary but significant effect on the CNS – making it less efficient. This explains why drunks often become confused, fall over, talk nonsense and can make very foolish decisions.

Reflexes

A **stimulus** is something in the external environment that produces a response from the body. A response is something the body does. So, if you begin to feel hot you may decide to remove your jumper. In this case, the stimulus is the rise in temperature and the response is to remove your jumper. Much of what we do is a response to things that happen to us – whether we are consciously aware of them or not.

Reflexes are simple responses to particular stimuli. A common reflex is the response of the eye to a bright light – the pupil contracts automatically to prevent you from being dazzled and the eye being damaged. If you touch a hot object you withdraw your hand automatically and rapidly – often before you realise that the object is hot. Reflexes are:

- **innate** – you do not need to learn them

- **rapid** – they often occur before you realise they have happened

- **protective** – they are often to do with protecting the body from danger.

▼ Coordinating a complex action like ballet dancing or tightrope walking needs a number of different nerve cells to work together; damage to any part of the central nervous system or the peripheral nerves that connect it with the rest of the body will make this activity impossible

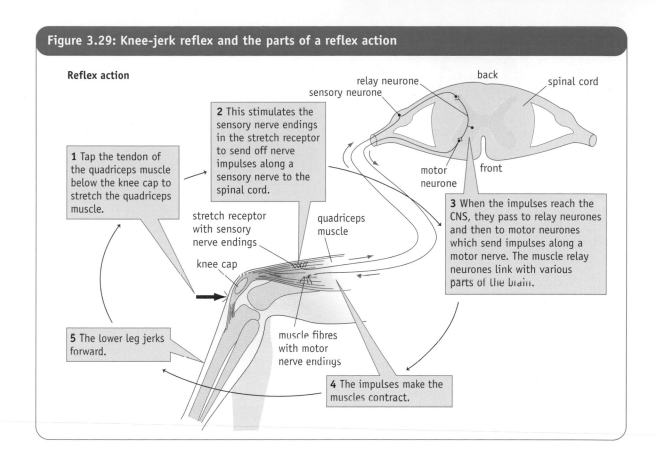

Figure 3.29: Knee-jerk reflex and the parts of a reflex action

Reflex action

relay neurone
sensory neurone
back
spinal cord

1 Tap the tendon of the quadriceps muscle below the knee cap to stretch the quadriceps muscle.

2 This stimulates the sensory nerve endings in the stretch receptor to send off nerve impulses along a sensory nerve to the spinal cord.

stretch receptor with sensory nerve endings

quadriceps muscle

motor neurone
front

3 When the impulses reach the CNS, they pass to relay neurones and then to motor neurones which send impulses along a motor nerve. The muscle relay neurones link with various parts of the brain.

knee cap

5 The lower leg jerks forward.

muscle fibres with motor nerve endings

4 The impulses make the muscles contract.

Testing reflexes

Many reflexes do not involve the brain at all. The knee-jerk reflex depends on only three nerve cells and none of these are in the brain. This means that the reflex will work even when a spinal injury has cut the link between the brain and the legs. It is possible to assess the level of nerve damage by testing reflexes. These tests work on people who are unconscious, or with babies who are too young to cooperate with a doctor. So, scratching the sole of the foot produces a response (the foot curls towards the scratch) in a healthy person. If someone does not produce this response a doctor may have cause for concern. A lack of a reflex is a very bad sign, worse even than a lack of voluntary responses, since reflexes can work even if the spinal cord is cut.

The autonomic nervous system

Both voluntary actions and reflexes depend on the nerves of the peripheral nervous system and are to do

with changes outside the body and our reactions to them. Another nervous system, called the **autonomic nervous system**, controls changes within the body. We do not have any conscious control over these changes and sometimes they can do damage. For example, stress or fear can lead to an increase in heart rate which could, in turn, lead to a heart attack. Strangely, it is possible for people to be frightened to death.

The autonomic system is divided into two parts.

■ The sympathetic system prepares the body for action. These are the nerves that act when we are under stress. Look at the effects of the autonomic system and compare them with the effects of adrenaline on page 182. Both help to prepare the body for fight or flight.

■ The parasympathetic system is antagonistic to the sympathetic system. This means it has the opposite effect, so the parasympathetic system helps to calm us down and prepare us for rest.

The endocrine system

The endocrine system consists of a collection of endocrine glands that secrete chemicals called hormones directly into the bloodstream and the **pituitary gland** in the brain. This helps to link the nervous and endocrine systems together. Different parts of the endocrine system are found all over the body and can work together, provided blood flows through both of them.

Hormones are chemicals produced by endocrine glands that travel in the bloodstream to another organ and change the way it works. The organ where the hormone has an effect is called the **target organ**. For example, antidiuretic hormone (ADH) is produced by the pituitary gland and changes the amount of water in the urine produced by the kidney. So, the kidney is the target organ.

▲ The shower scene from Psycho shows that film makers have known how to control our autonomic nervous system for years. The music, the lighting and the atmosphere of a scary film act on our autonomic nervous system to make our hearts race, our palms sweat and the hairs on the back of our necks stand up

Figure 3.30: The autonomic nervous system

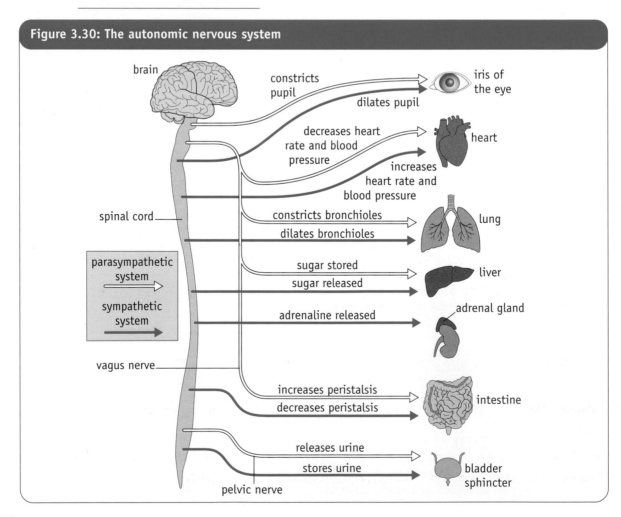

brain

constricts pupil

dilates pupil

iris of the eye

decreases heart rate and blood pressure

heart

increases heart rate and blood pressure

spinal cord

constricts bronchioles

dilates bronchioles

lung

parasympathetic system

sugar stored

sugar released

liver

sympathetic system

adrenaline released

adrenal gland

vagus nerve

increases peristalsis

decreases peristalsis

intestine

releases urine

stores urine

bladder sphincter

pelvic nerve

Figure 3.31: Endocrine glands and their hormones

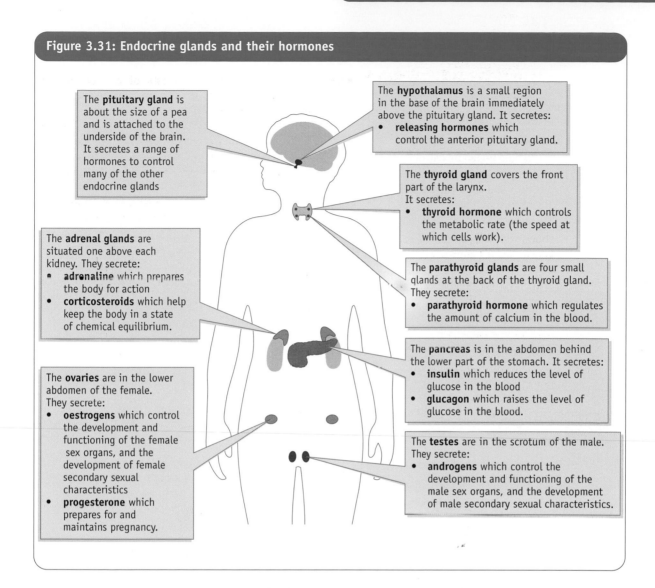

The **pituitary gland** is about the size of a pea and is attached to the underside of the brain. It secretes a range of hormones to control many of the other endocrine glands

The **hypothalamus** is a small region in the base of the brain immediately above the pituitary gland. It secretes:
* **releasing hormones** which control the anterior pituitary gland.

The **thyroid gland** covers the front part of the larynx.
It secretes:
* **thyroid hormone** which controls the metabolic rate (the speed at which cells work).

The **adrenal glands** are situated one above each kidney. They secrete:
* **adrenaline** which prepares the body for action
* **corticosteroids** which help keep the body in a state of chemical equilibrium.

The **parathyroid glands** are four small glands at the back of the thyroid gland. They secrete:
* **parathyroid hormone** which regulates the amount of calcium in the blood.

The **pancreas** is in the abdomen behind the lower part of the stomach. It secretes:
* **insulin** which reduces the level of glucose in the blood
* **glucagon** which raises the level of glucose in the blood.

The **ovaries** are in the lower abdomen of the female. They secrete:
* **oestrogens** which control the development and functioning of the female sex organs, and the development of female secondary sexual characteristics
* **progesterone** which prepares for and maintains pregnancy.

The **testes** are in the scrotum of the male. They secrete:
* **androgens** which control the development and functioning of the male sex organs, and the development of male secondary sexual characteristics.

How do the systems differ?

The nervous and endocrine systems work together to control and coordinate the body. Why does the body use two different systems to do the same thing? In fact, each system acts in a slightly different way. They share some of the same organs but they work in different ways. Coordination by the nervous system involves rapid responses to events outside the body, while coordination by the endocrine system usually involves longer-term changes, often to do with growth, which modify body parts to improve chances of survival. These characteristics are summarised in Figure 3.32.

Figure 3.32: Comparing the nervous and endocrine systems

Characteristic	Nervous system	Endocrine system
Reaction time	Very rapid	Slow
Responses	Can be very focused	Tend to occur over a wide area
How long does the response last?	Over and done with quickly	Can last for hours or days

BUILD YOUR LEARNING

Keywords and phrases

You should know the meaning of the words and phrases listed below. If you are unsure about any of them, go back through the last six pages of the unit to refresh your understanding.

- Autonomic nervous system
- Central nervous system
- Chemoreceptors
- Endocrine system
- Hormones
- Nervous system
- Peripheral nervous system
- Pituitary gland
- Target organs

Summary points

- The nervous and endocrine systems work together to coordinate the body. The endocrine system generally responds to changes within the body while the nervous system responds to events outside the body.

- The nervous system includes the central nervous system (brain and spinal cord), the peripheral nerves, the autonomic nervous system and the sense organs (internal and external).

- Nervous tissue is grey (the cell bodies) or white (the fibres wrapped in myelin). Nerve cells cannot usually repair themselves when damaged, so damage to nerve tissue is almost always permanent.

- Damage to the nervous system can be assessed by monitoring responses to particular stimuli.

- Reflexes are automatic, rapid responses to particular stimuli. They are not under the control of the conscious brain and are usually to do with protecting the body.

QUESTIONS

1 Write a sentence to explain the scientific meaning of each of the following terms:

- coordination
- stimulus
- response
- reflex
- hormone
- target organ.

2 Copy the table below and fill in the gaps

Hormone	Produced by	Target organ	Effect
ADH		Kidney	
Thyroxin		All cells in the body	Increases the rate of reactions in cells
	Islets of langerhans in the pancreas	All body cells	
Adrenaline		Many parts of the body	

3 List the main parts of the central nervous system.

4 Why should you never move anyone whom you think may have broken their spine?

Homeostasis

STAYING ALIVE AND HEALTHY is a constant battle! You need a constant supply of food, fresh water, and oxygen. You can last weeks without food and for days without water, but only minutes without oxygen. You also need to get rid of waste products like carbon dioxide. Your body is constantly monitoring itself and its internal chemistry to make sure it has all the things it needs and to prevent dangerous substances from building up in your cells. The processes going on inside your body to keep you alive are:

- respiration to provide energy for the body to do things
- breathing to gather oxygen and get rid of carbon dioxide
- digestion to break down food and absorb it into the body

- excretion to get rid of toxic waste products
- repair of any damaged body parts.

These processes do not occur by accident or randomly. They all need to be controlled and organised. That is the job of the homeostatic control mechanisms of the body.

No matter how cold you feel in the middle of winter waiting for a bus in the snow, the temperature of the main organs in your body never drops much below 36°C. Even on the hottest day in the summer and after running a 400 metre race, the same organs will still be at little more than 37°C. Whatever happens to the external environment, your body tries to keep its internal environment within very narrow limits. This close control of the internal environment of the human body is called homeostasis. Almost every aspect of your

▲ You can be sure this will give a shock to the system but the core body temperature will change very little as these brave adventurers in Murmansk, Russia, plunge into icy water

body's chemistry is controlled by a homeostatic mechanism to stop it drifting outside these limits.

Homeostasis does not mean that the body tries to keep everything constant. Homeostatic control mechanisms only start to work when a particular factor strays beyond the acceptable range. For example, blood sugar level is kept between 70 and 110 mg/100 ml of blood. Anywhere within that range is safe or **normal**. It is only when the level rises above the upper **threshold** that the body reacts and tries to force it back down into the safe range.

So, when looking at a factor like blood sugar, or temperature, remember that it will probably be controlled by a homeostatic mechanism and that it will have a normal range. Some ranges are very narrow. For example, even a drop of 0.5°C in the temperature of the brain is very serious. A similar drop in the fingers would be quite safe and even normal on cold winter days when you have forgotten your gloves!

Figure 3.34: A selection of normal values

Factor	Normal range
Blood sugar	70–110 mg/100 ml
Blood pH	7.35–7.45
Body temperature	36.3°–37.1°C
O_2 conc	>10.6 kPa
CO_2 conc	4.7–6 kPa
Haemoglobin (male)	13–18 g/dl
Haemoglobin (female)	11.5–16 g/dl
White cells (all types)	4–11 x 109/l
Cholesterol	4–<6 mmol/l
Protein	60–80 g/l
Urea levels	8–25 mg/100 ml
Heart rate at rest	70 bpm
Breathing rate at rest	12–15 breaths/min

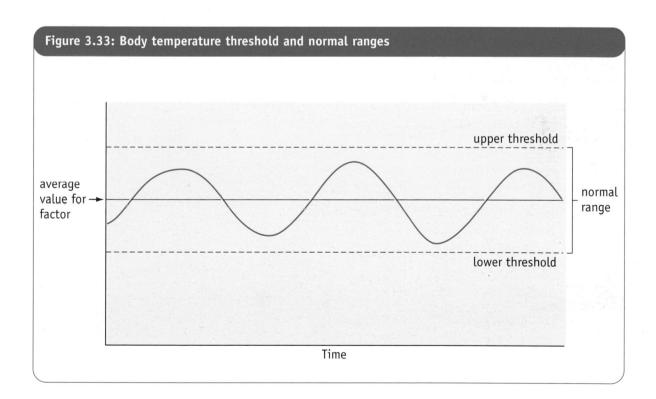

Figure 3.33: Body temperature threshold and normal ranges

What is negative feedback?

In **negative feedback**, a system will respond to any change by doing something which reduces the effect of the change on the system. For example, when you start to feel cold your body shivers. Shivering generates heat that warms the body up. If you drink a lot of water your body responds by making lots of dilute urine which passes out of the body and so reduces water content. If you hold your breath the carbon dioxide level in your blood rises. Your brain responds by forcing you to breathe more quickly as soon as you stop, so reducing the carbon dioxide level again. Even if you pass out when you hold your breath (and this is fortunately very difficult to do!) your brain takes over and forces you to breathe as soon as you lose consciousness.

Systems that show negative feedback tend to be stable and settle into a predictable pattern. Most biological systems show negative feedback. It keeps them safely within healthy limits. All of the homeostatic control mechanisms on the next few pages show negative feedback.

What is positive feedback?

Positive feedback is very rare in biological systems. In **positive feedback**, a system responds to any change by doing something which increases the effect of the change. Some people can suffer from asthma attacks due to positive feedback. They may have forgotten their inhaler and so worry about having an attack. This makes them nervous and they start to breathe more quickly. This can make the tubes in the lungs begin to tighten up and makes them feel a little breathless. This worries them more and so they start breathe more quickly and this could push them into an asthma attack.

BUILD YOUR LEARNING

Keywords and phrases

You should know the meaning of the words and phrases listed below. If you are unsure about any of them, go back through the last three pages of this unit to refresh your understanding.

- Homeostasis
- Negative feedback
- Normal
- Positive feedback
- Threshold

Summary points

- A threshold is a level of some factor that marks the outer limits of the acceptable range for a system. When a factor moves beyond the threshold value the system responds in some way.

- The word normal, when applied to biological systems, tends to describe a range of values rather than a single value.

- Homeostatic mechanisms in the body only act when a factor strays beyond the threshold value.

- Positive feedback occurs when a change in a factor tends to make the system change more rapidly. It is very rare in biological systems.

- Negative feedback occurs when a change in a factor tends to make the system respond by doing things that will reduce the change. Negative feedback is very positive in biological systems.

QUESTIONS

1 Write a sentence to explain the scientific meaning of each of the following terms:

- positive feedback

- internal environment

- threshold

- normal range.

2 'Homeostasis means keeping everything at the same level'. Explain why this is a poor explanation of the term and write a better one, giving two examples of body factors that are controlled homeostatically.

3 What is the normal range for:

- blood sugar

- body temperature

- cholesterol in the blood

- breathing rate.

Blood glucose

GLUCOSE IS A SUGAR MOLECULE found in human blood. Every cell in the body needs a constant supply of glucose for respiration (see p. 127). The normal range of blood glucose level extends from 70–110 mg/100 ml of blood and is controlled by two hormones, **insulin** and **glucagon**. These hormones act antagonistically to each other. This means they reverse the effects of each other. Insulin is produced by the islets of Langerhans in the pancreas and tends to reduce the level of glucose in the blood, while glucagon tends to raise the level of glucose in the blood.

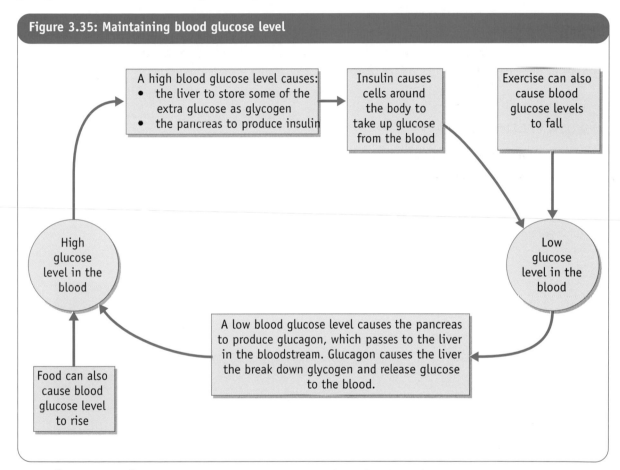

Figure 3.35: Maintaining blood glucose level

A high blood glucose level causes:
- the liver to store some of the extra glucose as glycogen
- the pancreas to produce insulin

Insulin causes cells around the body to take up glucose from the blood

Exercise can also cause blood glucose levels to fall

High glucose level in the blood

Low glucose level in the blood

A low blood glucose level causes the pancreas to produce glucagon, which passes to the liver in the bloodstream. Glucagon causes the liver the break down glycogen and release glucose to the blood.

Food can also cause blood glucose level to rise

Dealing with a diabetic hypo

About 2 per cent of people in Britain suffer from sugar diabetes (diabetes mellitus). They cannot produce enough insulin and so their blood glucose level can rise above the safe level. To try to prevent this happening they avoid sugary foods and may inject insulin when they know their blood glucose is rising. Insulin is usually injected two to four times a day, and meals and snacks are carefully planned to keep blood sugar within safe limits. The diabetic has to consciously do some of the work that the pancreas does automatically in a person without the disease.

Sometimes the control goes wrong. Maybe the diabetic injected a little too much insulin, or the meal was delayed, or some unexpected physical activity used up the store of sugar in the blood. All of these things drive the blood sugar down below the safe level and a **hypoglycaemic coma** or hypo can occur. Hypo means 'too low' and glycaemic means 'glucose in the blood', so a hypoglycaemic coma is produced by a blood glucose level that is too low. The person feels sweaty, pale, possibly aggressive and can fall into a coma. A coma is a sudden, deep sleep that the person does not wake easily from. A diabetic in a hypo should be given some sugary food or drink immediately. Even a teaspoonful of jam or honey will help to boost their blood sugar. Fortunately, sugar can be absorbed directly through the lining of the mouth. This usually leads to a quick recovery.

A **hyperglycaemic coma** is caused when the level of

glucose in the blood has been too high for a few days. Hyper means too high. The high levels of glucose mean that the person excretes a lot of urine and can become dehydrated. The dehydration is very dangerous and can cause a sudden collapse and a coma. Diabetics who go into a hyperglycaemic coma usually need hospital treatment before they recover.

ACTIVITY

Blood sugar level by time of day

1 What is the normal range for blood glucose levels?

2 Look at the graph below. When did the person eat:

- breakfast
- lunch
- dinner?

3 What might have caused the slight rise in blood sugar level at 3.30 in the afternoon?

4 The person played tennis for an hour at some point during the day. When do you think this happened? Give a reason for your answer.

5 Explain how each of the following would affect the level of blood glucose:

- an injection of insulin
- an injection of glucagon
- a glucose drip.

6 Describe how the body responds to a fall in blood glucose levels.

7 What should a care worker do if he or she finds a diabetic who is suffering from a hypoglycaemic attack?

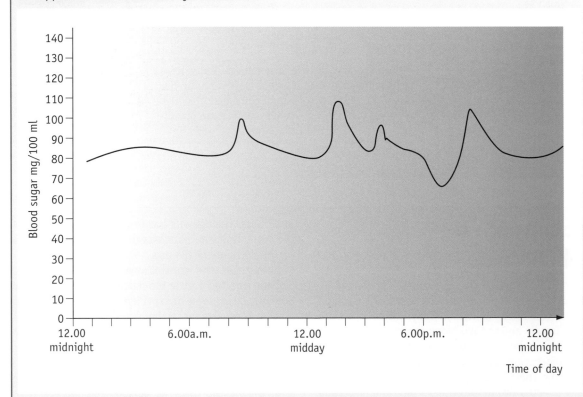

BUILD YOUR LEARNING

Keywords and phrases

You should know the meaning of the words and phrases listed below. If you are unclear about any of them, go back through the last two pages of the unit to refresh your understanding.

- Coma
- Diabetes mellitus
- Glucagon
- Glucose
- Hyperglycaemic
- Hypoglycaemic
- Insulin

Summary points

- Normal blood glucose level is in the range 70–110 mg/100 ml blood.

- Blood glucose level is controlled by the two hormones glucagon and insulin.

- Glucagon raises the level of glucose in the blood, insulin reduces the level of glucose in the blood.

- Glucagon and insulin are hormones secreted by the islets of Langerhans in the pancreas.

- Blood sugar can also be raised by the hormone adrenaline in times of stress or excitement.

- Diabetes mellitus is a disease in which the body cannot secrete enough effective insulin. This means that the levels of blood glucose can vary beyond safe limits.

- A hypoglycaemic coma is caused when blood sugar levels fall too low. It can be treated by drinks or food containing glucose.

- A hyperglycaemic coma occurs when the level of blood glucose is above the upper safe threshold for a few days. This causes dehydration and this causes the coma. A hyperglycaemic coma needs hospital treatment.

QUESTIONS

1 Write a sentence to explain the scientific meaning of the following terms:

- blood glucose

- hypoglycaemia

- glucagon.

2 What are the effects of a sudden fall in blood sugar levels?

3 What would be the safest thing to do with a person showing the symptoms you described above?

4 How would you treat a person who had accidentally injected too high a dose of insulin?

5 Many diabetics carry a small medal or bracelet to show that they are diabetic. Explain how this simple item could save their life.

Body temperature

HUMAN BEINGS HAVE A constant body temperature that is usually above the temperature of their environment. This temperature costs a great deal of energy to maintain, so why do we do it?

A constant temperature means that the reactions in the body take place at a constant, predictable rate and this helps to keep conditions in the body stable. But why at a temperature that is so high? The rate of a chemical reaction changes with temperature. As the temperature rises the rate of reaction rises. A rise of 10°C can lead to a doubling of reaction rate. By maintaining the body temperature at roughly 37°C the body helps its essential reactions go fast enough. In this section we show what happens to these reaction rates if the temperature rises or falls from the normal level.

How is body temperature controlled?

The body has hot zones and cooler zones. The central core of the body never falls below about 36°C but hands and feet can get much cooler in cold environments with little or no damage. In fact, it is important that the body does lose heat to the environment. The many chemical reactions in the body produce a lot of heat and if this could not escape the body could become too hot.

The body has a powerful homeostatic mechanism to maintain the core temperature, even as it lets the skin temperature vary.

Figure 3.36: Impact of changes of body temperature on people (°C)

Temp (°C)	Result
45	Death
40	Unconsciousness
39	Person becomes delirious, often vomits
36.9	Normal body temperature
36	Person feels cold, an uncomfortable shivering begins
35	Uncontrollable shivering, clumsy movements and pain
33	Shivering slows or stops, people become confused and may not now realise they are cold, speech becomes slow, people can begin to go to sleep
25	Breathing and pulse very slow, heart attacks can occur
20	Death

Figure 3.37: Relationship between room temperature and body temperature (°C)

Room	Core	Skin (trunk)	Skin (hand)	Skin (foot)
21°	36.1°	32.5°	28°	21°
35°	36.5°	35.5°	35°	34.5°

Figure 3.38: Body temperature flow chart

External temperature falls so more heat is lost from the body and the skin begins to cool.	External temperature rises, so less heat is lost from the body and the temperature starts to rise.

Nerves in the skin detect this drop in temperature and send impulses to the temperature control centres in the hypothalamus and brain. Even a very slight drop in blood temperature can be detected by centres in the brain.	Nerves in the skin detect this rise in temperature and send impulses to the temperature control centres in the hypothalamus and brain. The slight rise in blood temperature is detected by centres in the brain.

Impulses sent out from the brain cause: • blood vessels near the skin to contract – this stops warm blood from the centre of the body flowing into cold skin and losing heat • sweat glands to become less active - this reduces evaporation from the skin • evaporation to cool the skin.	Impulses sent out from the brain cause: • blood vessels near the skin to dilate – this allows warm blood from the centre of the body to flow into top layer of skin where it can lose heat more easily • sweat glands to become more active – evaporation of sweat from the skin cools the skin.

Tiny muscles attached to hairs in the skin contract. This raises the skin and in humans gives us goosebumps. In animals with fur, the raised hair traps a layer of air near the body surface which insulates the animal against heat loss.	People tend to be more lethargic in warm conditions. They move around less and tend to rest – this reduces the production of heat by the body muscles.

Shivering is small twitches of the muscles. When muscles contract they produce heat which tends to warm the body. Shivering is an automatic response.

People may also start to move about and stamp their feet to get their muscles working and so produce heat. This is a conscious response – people have to choose to do this.

Figure 3.39: Skin and the regulation of body temperature

As body temperature rises...

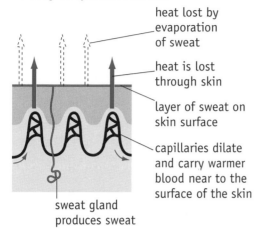

heat lost by evaporation of sweat

heat is lost through skin

layer of sweat on skin surface

capillaries dilate and carry warmer blood near to the surface of the skin

sweat gland produces sweat

As body temperature falls...

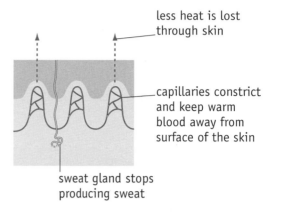

less heat is lost through skin

capillaries constrict and keep warm blood away from surface of the skin

sweat gland stops producing sweat

CASE STUDY

Dealing with hypothermia

Hypothermia occurs when the core body temperature falls below 35°C. In younger people the most common cause is an accident at sea or on cold mountains. In older people it is usually the result of poor housing and inadequate heating over the winter. In both groups the treatment is similar but particular care must be taken with frail, older people compared with fit, younger hill walkers.

Essentially, treatment involves reducing heat loss from the body to allow it to warm itself gradually. The best rate for warming is 0.5°C per hour. If possible, the victim should be fitted with a heart monitor to watch for any heart attacks. Blood pressure should be taken regularly during recovery. If it starts to drop this indicates that warming is too rapid and that the patient should be allowed to cool slightly. In some cases it may be necessary to supply external heat, but this should only be done under strict medical supervision. A person suffering from hypothermia will have diverted blood away from the skin (**vasoconstriction**) towards the core in an attempt to maintain core temperature. This means that the small amount of blood left in the skin is relatively cold. If the skin is heated, perhaps by sitting the victim near a fire, the blood vessels expand (**vasodilation**). Warm blood is drawn from the body core and the cooler blood returns to the core before it has had sufficient time to warm. This can deliver a temperature afterdrop to the core that can cause a sudden, catastrophic fall in core temperature.

Another common sense treatment to avoid is a drop of whisky or brandy to keep out the cold. Alcohol dilates the blood vessels in the skin and can produce a similar afterdrop. If the brandy is given on the hillside while the person is still in a cold environment the effect can be even worse! Warm blood is exposed to the cold skin and what little heat the body has managed to retain is lost.

ACTIVITY

Warming the body

A university lecturer volunteered to sit in a bath of iced water for over three hours while researchers studied his body's response to cooling and then rewarming. Not only did he volunteer for this work but he did it on three separate occasions so that they could look at three different methods of warming!

Method	Procedure
Bath	Subject was immersed in water at 20°C
Inhalation	Moistened air at 43°C was supplied through a face mask.
No extra heat	The subject was wrapped in a sleeping bag but no external heat was supplied.

1 How low did the core body temperature reach after 100 minutes in the bath?

2 What was the mean skin temperature at 50 minutes?

3 Mild hypothermia begins when core temperature drops below 36°C. When did this occur for the experimental subject?

4 Core and skin temperatures are very different for most of the experiment. Explain how this happens and how it helps to protect the body against hypothermia.

5 When the subject was warmed in a bath the core temperature dropped at first. Explain why this happened.

6 Which method of warming is most suitable? Give a reason for your answer.

▼ Position of temperature probes for hypothermia studies

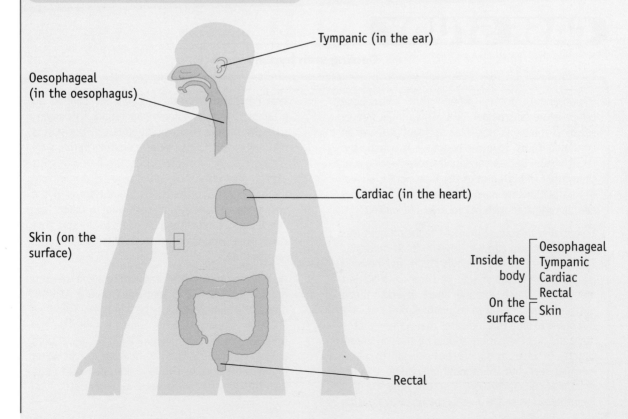

Tympanic (in the ear)

Oesophageal (in the oesophagus)

Cardiac (in the heart)

Skin (on the surface)

Rectal

Inside the body — Oesophageal, Tympanic, Cardiac, Rectal

On the surface — Skin

7 This experiment looked at hypothermia produced by immersion of a fit young man in cold water. Do you think the results are useful for planning care of an older person found in a freezing cold flat in winter? List any lessons we can learn from this research and apply to hypothermia in old people in Britain.

8 Would you repeat this sort of experiment with a frail, elderly person to get more relevant data? Give a reason for your decision.

▼ Temperature changes during cooling

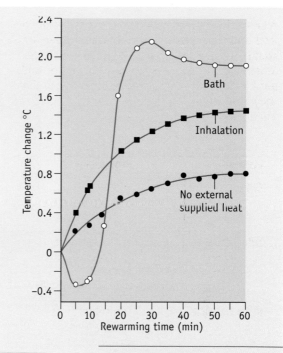

▲ Changes in cardiac temperature during rewarming

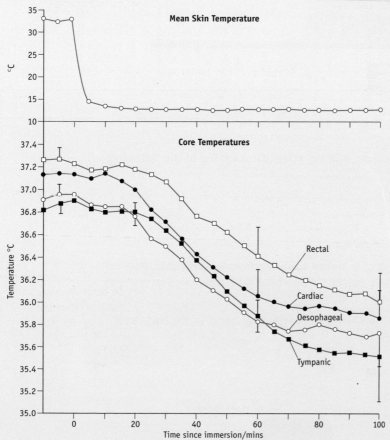

BUILD YOUR LEARNING

Keywords and phrases

You should know the meaning of the words and phrases listed below. If you are unsure about any of them, go back through the last five pages of the unit to refresh your understanding.

- Hypothermia
- Hypothalamus
- Vasoconstriction
- Vasodilation

Summary points

- Body temperature varies between the core (37°C) and the shell (30°C). Homeostatic mechanisms protect the core against changes in temperature.

- Temperature centres in the brain respond to a drop in temperature by constricting blood vessels in the skin, reducing sweat production and shivering to produce heat.

- Temperature centres in the brain respond to a rise in temperature by dilating blood vessels in the skin and increasing sweat production.

- Hypothermia occurs when body core temperature falls below 35°C. Death occurs when body core temperature falls below 20°C.

- Treatment for hypothermia involves gradual rewarming of the body, ideally using the body's own heat production systems rather than applying external heat.

QUESTIONS

1 Write a sentence to explain the scientific meaning of the following terms:

- vasoconstriction
- vasodilation
- normal body temperature.

2 List the symptoms of a person suffering from hypothermia. How would you treat this person? Why would it be dangerous to plunge him or her into a hot bath?

3 Draw a flow chart to show the changes that occur in the body as it starts to overheat.

Heart rate

How is the heart rate controlled?

EARLIER IN THIS UNIT WE described the structure and function of the heart (see pp. 140–5). But the heart has to be more than simply a muscular pump. It must beat at the correct rate for every possible body condition. During strenuous exercise, a rate of nearly 200 beats per minute (bpm) is essential to provide the muscles of the body with food and oxygen. At other times the same heart in someone sitting watching television might beat at a relaxed 70 bpm. How does the heart know how quickly to beat?

How is the heart rate controlled?

The muscle of the heart contracts and relaxes rhythmically even without nervous stimulation. Even a heart cut out of the body and kept alive in a suitable nutrient solution will beat at a stable rate for some time. This makes heart transplants possible. If surgeons had to reconnect nerves to the heart in transplant patients the chances of success would be very low. This is because nerves do not heal quickly enough to be useful, if they heal at all.

Organising the heart beat

The heart is made up of muscle. When the muscle contracts it squeezes the blood through the heart and into the arteries. However, if all of the muscle cells contracted and relaxed at the same time the heart would simply quiver like a nervous jelly! This quivering, disorganised contraction is called **fibrillation**. How does the heart organise the contraction and relaxation of the muscle cells in different parts of the heart to give a useful beat?

The contraction is started off by a small area in the left atrium called the **sinoatrial node**. This area of specialised cells produces a signal which causes muscle cells in the heart to contract. The signal passes across the top of the heart and makes the atria contract to force blood into the ventricles. Another specialised area called the **atrioventricular node** near the base of the atrium picks up the signal and sends it quickly down the **bundle of His** to the muscles of the ventricles. The signals then make the muscles of the ventricle wall contract, slightly after the atria have finished contracting. As the ventricles finish their contracting the sinoatrial node starts the whole process off again.

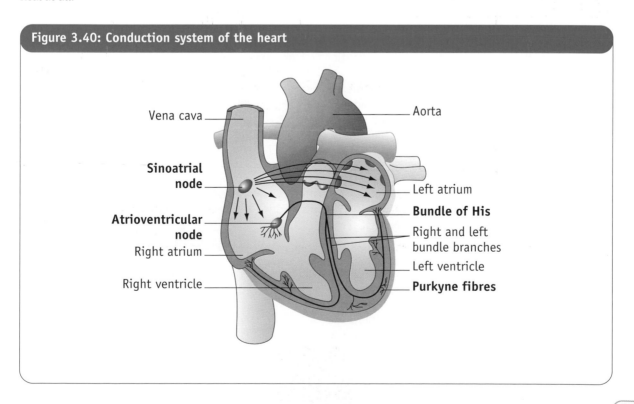

Figure 3.40: Conduction system of the heart

Vena cava

Aorta

Sinoatrial node

Left atrium

Bundle of His

Atrioventricular node

Right atrium

Right and left bundle branches

Left ventricle

Right ventricle

Purkyne fibres

The electrocardiogram

The electrocardiogram or ECG shows the signals passing across the heart very clearly. A skilled worker can tell from an ECG if any part of the heart's normal signalling and muscle system is not working properly. Damage to the muscle of the heart also shows up as an abnormal shape in the familiar ECG trace.

How is the heart rate changed?

The heart organises the contraction of the muscles itself but two groups of cells in the medulla at the base of the brain control the heart rate. These centres are the:

- **cardioacceleratory centre** which raises heart rate
- **cardioinhibitory centre** which lowers heart rate.

Both are connected to the sinoatrial node and the atrioventricular node in the heart by nerves from the autonomic nervous system. To lower the heartbeat, impulses from the cardioacceleratory system pass down the vagus nerve to the heart. At the sinoatrial and atrioventricular nodes the nerves secrete a chemical called acetylcholine. **Acetylcholine** is a chemical that acts on the nerve cells in the heart nodes. It inhibits the nodes so that fewer impulses are produced and the heart beats more slowly.

To raise the heartbeat, impulses from the cardioacceleratory system pass down a different autonomic nerve to the heart. At the sinoatrial and atrioventricular nodes the nerves secrete a chemical called noradrenaline. **Noradrenaline** is a chemical that acts on the nerve cells in the heart nodes. It increases the rate at which the nodes produce impulses. So, the heart rate rises.

But if the nerve centres in the medulla control the heart rate what controls the centres in the medulla? Specialised cells called chemoreceptors can measure the amount of a particular chemical in the blood. Chemoreceptors in the **carotid sinuses** in the neck measure the levels of carbon dioxide and oxygen. If carbon dioxide levels rise or oxygen levels fall, these cells send impulses along a nerve to the cardiovascular centres in the brain. Strangely, this seems to increase the breathing rate at first and this, in turn, raises the heart rate. The exact link between the two is not completely understood.

Pressure receptors in the aorta and the carotid sinuses also have an effect on the control centres. A rise in blood pressure detected by the pressure receptors stimulates the cardioinhibitory centre and inhibits the cardioacceleratory centres. This tends to reduce the heart rate.

Figure 3.41: The heart rate control systems

Impulses produced by the sinoatrial node stimulate the atrial muscles to contact

⇩

The impulses stimulate the atrioventricular node at the base of the atria.

⇩

Impulses from the atrioventricular node pass down fibres, collectively called the bundle of His.

⇩

The bundle of His divides into right and left branches, which spread through the walls at the base of the ventricles.

⇩

Purkyne fibres carry impulses up through the walls of the ventricles.

⇩

Impulses from the Purkyne fibres cause the ventricle muscles to contract from the base upwards, causing ventricular systole.

Adrenaline and heart rate

The hormone adrenaline also has a significant effect on heart rate and it can increase it dramatically. **Adrenaline** is released by the adrenal glands in times of stress and prepares the body for vigorous activity as part of the fight or flight response. Adrenaline acts directly on the muscles of the heart, making them more excitable and so making them contract more quickly. Adrenaline is used by doctors to treat people who have had a major heart attack. If the heart has stopped beating, an injection of adrenaline directly into the bloodstream can make it easier to start the heart beating again.

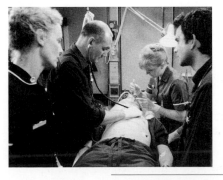

▲ Next time you watch Casualty listen carefully to the instructions the doctors give as they work on someone whose heart has stopped beating; you should hear them suggest a dose of adrenaline

ACTIVITY

The data in the tables show the changes in heart rate of two subjects using an identical exercise bicycle for ten minutes. At first the resistance of the bicycle is high and the subjects have to work hard to push the pedals. After five minutes pedalling the bicycle was switched to freewheel. This effectively reduced the amount of work the subjects had to do to zero.

	Subject A	Subject B
Weight/kg	87.9	79.5
Height/cms	179.0	183.0
Age/years	42.0	46.0
Gender	Male	Male

1 Draw a graph of the data for subject A and B on the same set of axes. Label each trace to identify each subject.

2 The value for 360 seconds has been lost due to a machine error. Estimate a suitable value for each subject.

3 Describe any differences you can see in the shape of the two traces.

4 What do these differences tell you about the level of fitness of each of the subjects?

5 Suggest another measure you could use to assess the fitness of each subject.

6 Explain the following observations:

■ the heart rate rises immediately exercise begins

■ the heart rate continues to rise even after exercise has stopped

■ the heart rate takes a long time to return to normal after exercise has stopped.

7 Draw a flow chart to show how the different parts of the body are involved in controlling the heart.

Time/secs	Subject A Heart rate /bpm	Subject B Heart rate /bpm
0	70	65
30	120	95
60	135	105
90	133	107
120	128	104
150	134	109
180	133	104
210	135	102
240	140	100
270	138	103
300	146	108
330	145	112
360	error	error
390	140	110
420	138	105
450	135	102
480	130	98
510	125	84
540	120	78
570	118	70
600	110	65

BUILD YOUR LEARNING

Keywords and phrases

You should know the meaning of the words and phrases listed below. If you are unsure about any of them, go back through the last three pages of the unit to refresh your understanding.

- Acetylcholine
- Adrenaline
- Atrioventricular node
- Bundle of His
- Cardioinhibitory
- Cardioacceleratory
- Carotid sinus
- Fibrillation
- Noradrenaline
- Sinoatrial node

Summary points

- The heart beats regularly without any stimulation from the brain. Centres in the brain are only needed to change the rate of the heart beat.

- The muscles of the heart need to contract and relax in an organised sequence. This sequence is started by the sinoatrial node near the top of the heart.

- The cardioacceleratory centre in the brain raises the heart rate by secreting noradrenaline from the nerves of the autonomic nervous system that end in the muscles of the heart.

- The cardioinhibitory centre in the brain lowers the heart rate by secreting acetylcholine.

- Chemoreceptors in the carotid sinuses in the neck measure levels of carbon dioxide and oxygen in the blood. These pass information to the cardiac control centres in the brain.

- Adrenaline increases heart rate as part of the fight or flight response.

- Exercise and activity tends to increase heart rate; resting, sleeping and a heavy meal tend to reduce heart rate.

QUESTIONS

1 Write a sentence to explain the scientific meaning of the following terms:
   - heart rate
   - fibrillation
   - sinoatrial node
   - carotid sinus
   - cardioacceleratory centre.

2 Which part of the brain controls the heart rate?

3 Which nerve increases the rate of the heart beat and which nerve decreases the rate of the heart beat?

4 Give two factors which tend to increase the heart rate.

5 What effect would an injection of adrenaline have on the heart rate?

Breathing

EVERY DAY AN AVERAGE ADULT human male breathes about 15,000 litres of air in and out of his lungs. That's the amount of air contained by a cube with sides of 2.46 metres, or just over 14 telephone boxes! Overnight the same person would get through a further 5,000 litres to bring his total for 24 hours to 20,000 litres. The rate of breathing changes throughout the day. Sometimes it will be as low as one shallow breath every six seconds while at other times it can rise to one frantic deep breath every second. This control over breathing is essential, because the body cannot store oxygen and even quite a small exertion, perhaps running for a bus, requires a good supply of energy. That means plenty of oxygen for respiration.

How is breathing controlled?

The amount of air that passes through the lungs every minute depends on how many breaths you take per minute (breathing rate) and the size of these breaths (the tidal volume).

Both the rate and depth of breathing are controlled automatically by part of the brain to make sure the level of carbon dioxide in the blood stays within acceptable limits. It is possible to override this control system with your conscious brain to some extent. If you hold your breath you can stop the muscles working but eventually your brain will be starved of oxygen and you will pass out. When this happens your automatic control systems will start the breathing movements again.

Chemoreceptors in the **medulla oblongata** at the base of the brain, the aortic body and the carotid body detect levels of carbon dioxide in the blood. During exercise the level of carbon dioxide in the blood rises. Chemoreceptors detect this rise and send impulses to the **inspiratory centre** in the medulla oblongata. The inspiratory centre sends impulses along autonomic nerves to stimulate the intercostal muscles of the ribs to work harder.

The inspiratory centre increases the rate and depth of breathing. This removes more carbon dioxide from the blood. The chemoreceptors detect the fall in carbon dioxide levels and inhibit the inspiratory centre. So breathing returns to normal.

CASE STUDY

Ventilation rates and exercise

A spirometer can record the volume of gases going into and out of the lungs by drawing a trace on a moving paper tape. If the volume of air is fixed at the start, then it is possible to measure the amount of oxygen used during the experimental session. The amount of oxygen used up by the subject is equal in volume to the amount of carbon dioxide produced. If the carbon dioxide in the equipment is absorbed in soda lime then the volume of gas in the equipment will drop. This drop in volume will be noticeable on the trace and will correspond exactly to the volume of oxygen used.

ACTIVITY

Ventilation rates and exercise

1 Why does the trace go up and down during the session?

2 What is the breathing rate in breaths per minute:

before exercise?

after exercise?

3 What is the average tidal volume before and after exercise?

4 Calculate the oxygen consumption of the subject at rest.

5 Calculate the oxygen consumption of the subject immediately after exercise.

6 Explain why these measures are different.

7 Even after exercise the breathing rate continues to remain above the resting rate for some time. Explain why this happens.

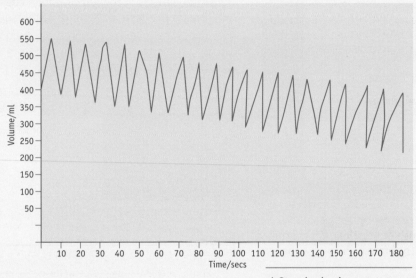

▲Standard spirometer trace

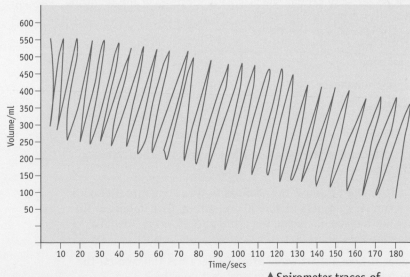

▲Spirometer traces of experimental subjects

BUILD YOUR LEARNING

Keywords and phrases

You should know the meaning of the words and phrases that are listed below. If you are unsure about any of them, go back through the last two pages of the unit to refresh your understanding.

- Chemoreceptors
- Inspiratory centre
- Intercostal
- Medulla oblongata
- Respiratory centre
- Spirometer
- Ventilation rate

Summary points

- Chemoreceptors in the carotid body and the medulla oblongata at the base of the brain monitor carbon dioxide and oxygen levels in the blood. When these levels move beyond acceptable limits impulses pass to the respiratory centres.

- The inspiratory centre stimulates the intercostal muscles of the ribs to work harder and increase the depth and rate of breathing.

- The increased breathing rate means the level of carbon dioxide in the blood falls and so the activity of the inspiratory centre is reduced.

QUESTIONS

1 Write a sentence to explain the scientific meaning of the following terms:
   - breathing
   - respiration
   - medulla oblongata
   - ventilation rate
   - chemoreceptor.

2 What two factors affect the amount of oxygen breathed in every minute?

3 Draw a flow chart to show the changes to breathing rate that occur when a runner competes in an 800 metre race. Give details of the control mechanism, including the chemoreceptors and medulla oblongata.

4 Why does it take a short while after the race has finished for the breathing rate to return to the normal resting value?

Osmoregulation

THE CHEMICAL REACTIONS IN our cells all work in solution and changes to the concentrations of these solutions can speed up or slow down these reactions. Even small changes to these concentrations can have very serious effects. The body needs water to:

- keep chemicals in solution so that they can react with each other
- move substances around the body dissolved in blood
- act as a heat store – water can absorb a lot of energy before its temperature changes
- produce sweat to cool the body
- carry waste out of the body dissolved in urine.

How is the level of water in the body controlled?

Control of the level of water in the body is called **osmoregulation**. Even quite small changes in water

levels in our cells can have very damaging effects on the body. (see Figure 3.42)

Water levels in the body are controlled by the **hypothalamus** and the pituitary gland in the brain and the kidneys see Figure 3.43). When water levels in the body fall, the hypothalamus signals to the pituitary gland to produce a hormone: **antidiuretic hormone (ADH)**. ADH makes the kidney secrete small amounts of concentrated urine so that water is conserved within the body. If water levels in the body are high the secretion of ADH is switched off and the kidneys produce lots of dilute urine to carry the excess water out of the body.

Osmoreceptors in the hypothalamus monitor the concentration of chemicals in the blood, particularly sodium ions, in order to decide when to switch on the pituitary. A hot day or extended periods without drinking can switch on these receptors. Blood volume is monitored by receptors in the aorta. If these detect a fall in blood volume they pass signals to the hypothalamus which, in turn, stimulates the pituitary to secrete ADH. These pressure receptors seem to come into play following a rapid loss of blood.

Figure 3.42: Percentage of normal water levels and symptoms

Percentage of normal water level	Symptoms
100	Happy and healthy
99	You will start to feel thirsty
98	You will feel very thirsty and uncomfortable, any activity will become more difficult
96	You feel tired, sick and moody
94	You start to look pale and ill. You become very irritable and aggressive
90	You stop sweating to save water, but this means your body temperature starts to rise
89	You need medical help now
80	You are now dead

Figure 3.43: Controlling water levels in the body level

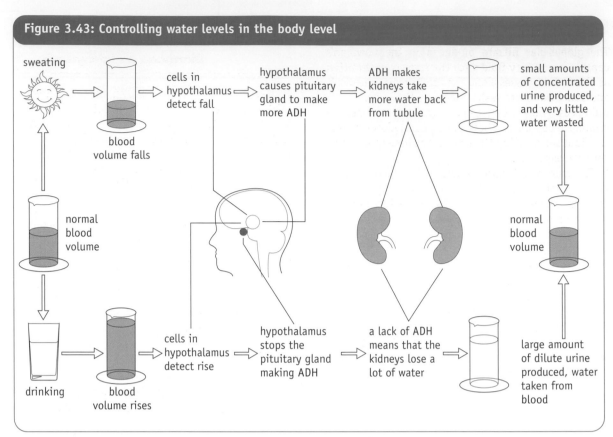

sweating → blood volume falls → cells in hypothalamus detect fall → hypothalamus causes pituitary gland to make more ADH → ADH makes kidneys take more water back from tubule → small amounts of concentrated urine produced, and very little water wasted → normal blood volume

normal blood volume

drinking → blood volume rises → cells in hypothalamus detect rise → hypothalamus stops the pituitary gland making ADH → a lack of ADH means that the kidneys lose a lot of water → large amount of dilute urine produced, water taken from blood → normal blood volume

Figure 3.44: Functions of kidney tubule

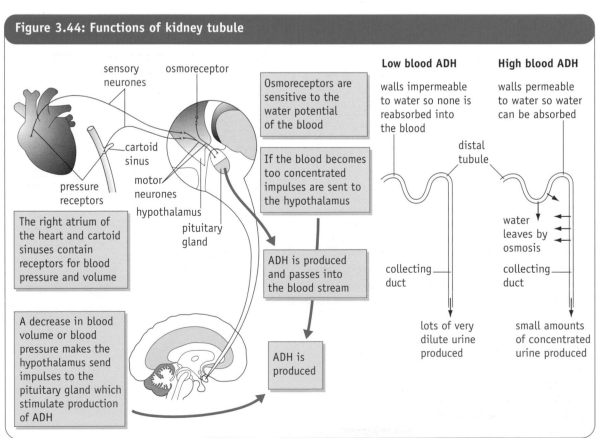

sensory neurones

osmoreceptor

cartoid sinus

pressure receptors

motor neurones

hypothalamus

pituitary gland

Osmoreceptors are sensitive to the water potential of the blood

If the blood becomes too concentrated impulses are sent to the hypothalamus

The right atrium of the heart and cartoid sinuses contain receptors for blood pressure and volume

A decrease in blood volume or blood pressure makes the hypothalamus send impulses to the pituitary gland which stimulate production of ADH

ADH is produced and passes into the blood stream

ADH is produced

Low blood ADH

walls impermeable to water so none is reabsorbed into the blood

distal tubule

collecting duct

lots of very dilute urine produced

High blood ADH

walls permeable to water so water can be absorbed

water leaves by osmosis

collecting duct

small amounts of concentrated urine produced

ADH and the kidney tubules

The glomerular filtrate produced in the Bowman's capsule is a watery fluid with the same concentration as blood. As it passes along the tubule many chemicals and some water are reabsorbed into the body. As the fluid passes down the **loop of Henle**, sodium chloride is pumped out of the tubule. The sodium chloride makes the fluid surrounding the cells at the base of the tube very concentrated.

The collecting ducts for urine run through this area of very concentrated cell fluids before they empty the urine into the middle of the kidney. The sodium chloride concentration is high enough to draw a great deal of water out through the walls of the collecting ducts. The hormone ADH controls the permeability of the wall of the collecting duct and so how much water can pass through.

When ADH is present, the wall of the tubule that comes after the loop of Henle and the whole of the collecting ducts are permeable to water. Water in the urine is reabsorbed and we produce small amounts of concentrated urine. However, if ADH levels are low the walls are almost impermeable, water cannot be drawn out of the urine and we produce large amounts of dilute urine.

CASE STUDY

Diarrhoea and dehydration

Every year diarrhoea kills four million children under the age of five across the world. The vast majority of these deaths are in poorer countries where dirty water and low general health combine to make what should be a normal, survivable childhood illness a life-threatening condition. Even in the USA, the richest country in the world, 500 children died from diarrhoea in 1999. These children, too, were typically from poorer areas and their mothers were on low incomes.

Diarrhoea causes damage by dehydrating the body. Fluids lost in diarrhoea mean the kidneys cannot retain enough water to keep the body's water levels up. If the illness also produces a fever and sickness the loss of water increases further. Small children can slip from being ill to being critically ill in a matter of hours.

Diarrhoea is a natural response to certain types of infection. The body is clearing material from the gut and to prevent this happening could make the situation worse. The best treatment for diarrhoea is to try to keep the water levels in the patient as near normal as possible and to let the body's defence systems deal with the disease.

ACTIVITY

Diarrhoea and dehydration

Oral rehydration therapy, or ORT, uses a simple mixture of salts and sugar to keep water levels up. The World Health Organisation (WHO) publishes a recipe for ORT which is used the world over. The mixture is dissolved and swallowed. The salt and sugar help the body to absorb the water.

WHO ORT recipe	
Sodium chloride	3.5 g
Trisodium citrate	2.9 g
Glucose	20.0 g
Potassium chloride	1.5 g

Mix with 100 mls of clean water. Use within 24 hours of making. Repeat dose three times per day.

1 Why do you think deaths from diarrhoea typically occur amongst the poorest families?

2 Give three ways water can leave the body.

3 Why is diarrhoea more dangerous if the patient is also suffering from a high temperature?

4 Why is diarrhoea so much more dangerous in small children than in adults?

5 You have been supplied with a 5 kg pack of each of the ingredients you need to make ORT.

■ How many packets of ORT mixture can you make using the standard WHO recipe?

■ Later you discover another pack containing 3 kg of glucose. How many more packets can you now manufacture?

■ If each child needs three packets per day and a typical bout of diarrhoea lasts for three days, how many children can you treat with your stock of ORT sachets?

BUILD YOUR LEARNING

Keywords and phrases

You should know the meaning of the words and phrases listed below. If you are unsure about any of them, go back through the last three pages of the unit to refresh your understanding.

- Osmoreceptors
- Osmoregulation
- Hypothalamus
- Antidiuretic hormone (ADH)
- Loop of Henle

Summary points

- Osmoreceptors in the hypothalamus monitor water levels in the blood. When these levels fall below acceptable limits impulses pass to the hypothalamus. The hypothalamus switches on ADH production by the pituitary gland.
- ADH controls the permeability of the parts of the kidney tubules and the collecting ducts. This allows water to be drawn back into the body and more concentrated urine is produced.
- When water levels in the blood are high the secretion of ADH is switched off and the kidneys produce large amounts of dilute urine which carries excess water out of the body.

QUESTIONS

1 Write a sentence to explain the scientific meaning of the following terms:

- osmoregulation
- diuretic
- diarrhoea
- dehydration
- osmoreceptor.

2 List the organs concerned with regulation of body water levels (you should be able to find three).

3 How does ADH affect:

a the permeability of the collecting duct in the kidney?

b the concentration of urine produced?

c the water level of the body?

4 Draw a flow chart to show how the body responds to a rise in the water level in the blood.

Making physiological measurements

THE CHEMISTRY AND WORKING of the human body is predictable. Sudden or unexplained changes can signal that something is wrong or about to go wrong. Care staff take measurements of body functions to:

- find out what is happening to the body chemistry
- help make predictions about what might happen next
- suggest the best way to care for the client.

Of course, care staff cannot measure everything, so medics will pick tests that:

- are easy and cheap to carry out
- provide useful information
- pose no threat to the patient or health worker.

Some tests are so useful and so routine that they are offered referred to as standard observations or standard obs. In a hospital, standard obs typically include body temperature, pulse rate and possibly blood pressure, taken every 30 minutes.

What tests are available?

There are hundreds of tests available to medical staff. Some are very specialist and give information about only one condition, for example the HIV test. However, a blood test that shows a person is anaemic could suggest many things. Is the anaemia due to a poor diet, a lack of certain vitamins, pregnancy, a hereditary disease or even malaria? Usually a collection of tests are used to pinpoint the exact cause of a condition. This explains the sometimes frustrating wait for patients and relatives as doctors carry out more and more tests to confirm their diagnosis.

Figure 3.45: Tests and their risks

Test	What information could it provide?	Are there any dangers?
Pulse rate	Can warn of any damage to the heart.	None.
Body temperature	A rise in temperature is often a sign of infection. A fall may indicate hypothermia (exposure).	Minimal, but be careful that infections are not passed from person to person on dirty thermometers.
Respiratory rate	Can tell us if the lungs are damaged.	None.
Peak flow rate	Peak flow rate results can assess damage to the lungs and monitor the progress of a patient with asthma.	None, but be careful that each patient is given clean, sterilised equipment. Heavy breathing can make some people feel dizzy, so look out for fainting.
Lung capacity	A low lung capacity could indicate an obstruction or growth in the lung.	None, but be careful that each patient is given clean, sterilised equipment. Heavy breathing can make some people feel dizzy, so look out for fainting.
Sugar in urine	Sugar in the urine indicates diabetes.	None.
Protein in urine	In a pregnant woman protein in the urine may indicate pre-eclampsia. This is a serious condition that needs treatment, often rest and hospital treatment. In someone who is not pregnant protein may indicate the presence of an infection.	None.
Cervical smear	Abnormal cells in the cervix can be the first sign of cervical cancer.	The test must be carried out by a qualified doctor using appropriate sterile technique.

Invasive tests involve placing something in the body to monitor its activity, perhaps a catheter to measure blood pressure or a lumbar puncture which draws fluid from the spinal cord to check for meningitis. **Noninvasive** tests do not involve entering the body. Measuring blood pressure with a cuff or taking someone's pulse are both noninvasive tests. Invasive techniques are powerful and can give very exact measures. However, they carry significantly more risks than noninvasive techniques and should not be attempted by anyone without appropriate medical qualifications and experience.

Measurement techniques

The result from any test depends on the accuracy of the equipment used and the skill of the person using it. In this section we look at common techniques used to take standard measurements. Skills develop over life and equipment changes as new pieces of kit are designed. Be aware that you must always get advice on good techniques from an experienced worker before carrying out any tests.

Measuring the pulse

The pulse can be taken from a range of pulse points across the body. Usually the wrist is used, although the neck is common in patients who are lying down. Beats are counted over 15 seconds and then multiplied by four to give the beats per minute.

Good technique means taking the following factors into account.

- Nervousness or tension in the patient tend to raise the pulse rate, as does exercise. If someone has rushed to a check-up and then has a high pulse rate this may be due to the exertion of getting to the appointment.

- Allow people to relax before taking the pulse, or take it twice during the session to see if it has dropped as the person relaxes.

Measuring body temperature

Body temperature is usually taken by placing a thermometer in the mouth.

- Make sure the thermometer is clean and has been kept in disinfecting solution.

- Shake the mercury below the pinch point.

- Place the thermometer in the patient's mouth below the tongue.

- Wait for 30 seconds.

- Remove the thermometer and read the temperature as quickly as possible.

Readings should be to the nearest 0.1 degrees Celsius.

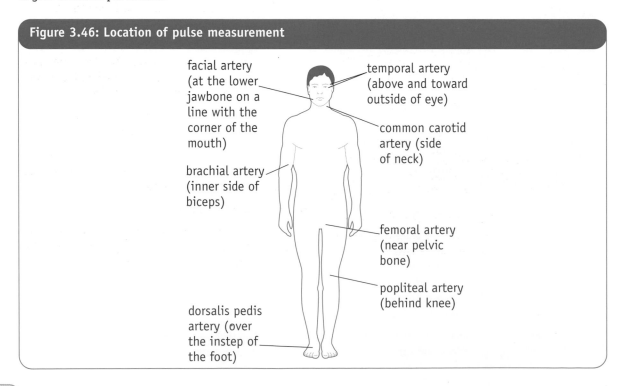

Figure 3.46: Location of pulse measurement

facial artery (at the lower jawbone on a line with the corner of the mouth)

temporal artery (above and toward outside of eye)

common carotid artery (side of neck)

brachial artery (inner side of biceps)

femoral artery (near pelvic bone)

popliteal artery (behind knee)

dorsalis pedis artery (over the instep of the foot)

Good technique means taking the following factors into account.

- Do not encourage patients to talk with a thermometer in their mouth. If it breaks they could swallow highly poisonous mercury!

- Recent heavy activity could raise body temperature.

- Hot food or drink can raise the temperature of the mouth artificially, while a few spoonfuls of ice cream could lower it!

Measuring blood pressure

Blood pressure can be measured electronically or with a mercury column **sphygmomanometer.** Both methods use an inflatable cuff, which must be positioned carefully to ensure accurate, reliable results. The use of mercury column sphygmomanometers is being phased out, as the mercury is a safety hazard and the electronic version is easier for non-medical staff to use.

When using the electronic pressure meter you should:

- wrap the uninflated cuff around the upper arm just above the elbow level with the heart

- make sure the cuff is secure and then inflate it

- record the blood pressure figure read out on the digital meter.

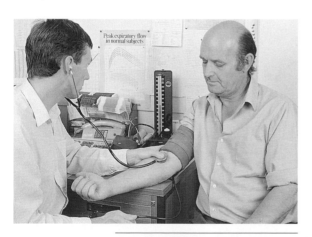

▲ A GP taking a blood pressure reading using a mercury column sphygmomanometer

When using the mercury column sphygmomanometer you should:

- wrap the uninflated cuff around the upper arm just above the elbow level with the heart

- find the artery running along the inner side of the arm

- place a stethoscope over the artery

- inflate the cuff – at a certain point the cuff will press on the arm so tightly that the artery collapses

- deflate the cuff slowly – at a certain point you will begin to hear blood flowing along the artery

- the first sounds will be intermittent as blood is squeezed through the artery with every heart beat – note the reading at this point (it is called the **systolic blood pressure**)

- continue to deflate the cuff – the next change in sound occurs when the blood swirls through the artery all the time – note the reading at this point (it is called the **diastolic blood pressure**)

- completely deflate the cuff so that the sound disappears as the artery opens to its original size and the blood flows normally.

Good technique means taking the following factors into account.

- Both methods of blood pressure measurement are prone to errors if the cuff is wrongly fitted.

- Children often need a smaller cuff than adults.

- Tension, nervousness or excitement raise the blood pressure and give an artificially high reading. Some people seem to be able to lower their blood pressure at the point of measurement by relaxing. This is rare but may give an unreliably low reading.

- If patients moves their arm so that the cuff is not level with the heart the reading is unreliable.

- Tightly fitting sleeves pushed up above the cuff can interfere with the reading. Blood pressure readings cannot be taken through clothes.

- Various medicines affect blood pressure.

- It is a good idea to repeat the measurements if you are at all unsure of the result, particularly if the result is surprisingly high or low.

Measuring the forced vital capacity

The maximum volume of air that can be breathed out of our lungs is called the forced vital capacity (FVC). It is one useful measure of the health of lungs. A **spirometer** is used to measure this volume.

- Prepare the spirometer, being careful to disinfect any parts that clients put into their mouth.

- Instruct the client to take a deep breath and blow into the spirometer. A long, gentle blow is just as effective as a short, stressed blow. The idea is to get the maximum volume not the fastest delivery.

Good technique means taking the following factors into account.

- Repeat the measurement three times to get the best reading. Use the highest value, not the average, as your result.

- Watch the patient carefully. People can pass out if they breathe very deeply for any length of time.

The forced expiratory volume

The volume of air blown out in the first second is called the forced expiratory volume (FEV1.)

- Prepare the **peak flow meter**, being careful to disinfect any parts that clients put into their mouth.

- Instruct the client to take a deep breath and blow into the peak flow meter. Encourage them to puff as quickly as possible, rather than taking a long, gentle breath out.

Good technique means taking the following factors into account.

- Repeat the measurement three times to get the best reading. Use the highest value, not the average, as your result.

- Watch the patient carefully. People can pass out if they breathe very deeply for any length of time.

BUILD YOUR LEARNING

Keywords and phrases

You should know the meaning of the words and phrases listed below. If you are unsure about any of them, go back through the last four pages of the unit to refresh your understanding.

- Diastolic blood pressure
- Invasive
- Noninvasive
- Peak flow meter
- Sphygmomanometer
- Stethoscope
- Spirometer
- Systolic blood pressure
- Thermometer

Summary points

- Sudden or unexpected changes in body chemistry can warn care staff of potential dangers to their clients. Tests can be used to measure any of these changes in the body.

- Chosen tests must be relevant and pose no threat to the client or worker. Ideally they should also be cheap and easy to carry out.

- Invasive tests require placing something inside the body to carry out the measurement. Invasive tests are generally more hazardous than noninvasive tests.

- Good technique must be observed for even the simplest tests if the results are to be reliable.

QUESTIONS

1 Give three characteristics of useful medical tests.

2 What do standard obs usually involve?

3 Which tests would you use to check the health of the following people? Explain what you would be looking for in each case and how your chosen test would help you.

- A child suffering from asthma.
- A middle-aged man complaining of pains in the chest.
- An older woman feeling faint.

4 Give three pieces of good advice to someone who is about to carry out the following tests:

- take a temperature
- measure blood pressure
- test the peak flow rate in a five-year-old child.

Reliability and safety

MANY OF THE PEOPLE YOU MAY work with will be ill or frail. Many of the tests and procedures you will need to use may be frightening, uncomfortable or messy. The results of the tests may have life-changing implications for your clients. For all of these reasons you will have to be aware of the safety and comfort of your clients. Of course, you will also need to be aware of any risks to yourself created by the tests or equipment. For example, radiologists have to be particularly careful of radiation given that they spend every working day of their lives around sources of radiation, whereas the clients they see may only come in for an X-ray once every few years.

The results of your tests will be a major factor in deciding what to do for the people in your care. If your results are unreliable you may end up making the wrong decision and possibly harming the people you are supposed to be caring for. **Reliability** depends on two issues: accuracy and validity.

Accuracy is a measure of the precision of a measurement. How sure are you that the reading you have noted down is correct? For example, a clinical thermometer that is only accurate to within 5°C is completely useless! If your thermometer is reading only 2.5°C below the correct value a temperature of 36.5°C on your thermometer could really be a life-threatening temperature of 39°C. Equally, if your thermometer was reading only 2.5°C above the real value, its 36.5°C could be masking a case of hypothermia at 34°C!

Test results need to be accurate enough to allow decisions to be made. Clinical thermometers are accurate to within 0.1°C. So, a temperature of 36.5°C on the thermometer could be anything from 36.45°C to 36.55°C. This is accurate enough for medical and care purposes. A thermometer accurate to 0.01°C would not provide any more useful information, since treatment decisions are made on temperature changes of 0.5°C.

Imagine you are caring for an older person with a fever. You have been asked to keep a close watch over her progress and so are measuring the level of sugar in her urine every half an hour. Your results could be accurate but they are irrelevant and so not valid! Measuring body temperature would have been much more useful. **Valid** measurements also need to be collected using the correct technique. Blood pressure measures taken through clothing or using the wrong-sized cuff will not be valid. They may appear to be accurate, but will be an accurate measure of the wrong thing!

To improve the reliability of your measurements you need to understand the limitations of the equipment and the test you are using. No piece of equipment is 100 per cent accurate. No test can be guaranteed to produce a useful result every time. So, keep your wits about you at all times. Reliable results depend on:

- understanding the test to make sure you are collecting the right information

- accurate equipment

- good technique.

Issues which affect the reliability of your results are set out in Figure 3.47.

Figure 3.47: Issues affecting the reliability of test results

Is the client ready?	Are they nervous or worried? Have they eaten something that will affect the test results? Are they taking any medicines that will affect the results?	Try to calm the client down by talking to them. Ask about any medicines they may be taking or whether they have eaten recently. Find out as much as you can before you even start the test.
Is the equipment ready?	Does it need to be cleaned out? Does it need to warm up before it can be used? Are all the bits here?	Check any equipment you need before you start. Look out for anything that is broken or missing – and leave the equipment so that people who come after you can use it!
Are you ready?	Do you know how to use the equipment or perform the test? Is this a new piece of kit that you have not used before? Has it been modified since you last used it?	Make sure you know what you are doing before you start. Do not be afraid to ask for help. It is better to do it beforehand than when you have a client with you.

BUILD YOUR LEARNING

Keywords and phrases

You should know the meaning of the words and phrases listed below. If you are unsure about any of them, look at page 199 to refresh your understanding.

- Accuracy
- Reliability
- Validity

Summary points

- Treatment decisions depend on reliable measurements. To be reliable a measurement must be valid, collected using proper technique and accurate enough. Measurements must be relevant to a decision to be valid.

- Poor technique will lead to errors in measurement or measurement of the wrong factor. Accuracy is a measure of the precision of a measurement. A measurement of 35.55°C is more precise than a measurement of 35.5°C.

- There is no point in increasing the precision of clinical thermometers beyond 0.1 degrees Celsius because the extra precision does not affect decisions. A measurement is accurate enough when a treatment decision can be based on it.

QUESTIONS

1 Write a sentence to show you understand the scientific meaning of these words:

- reliable
- accurate
- valid.

2 Explain how an accurate thermometer can still produce unreliable data.

3 Why is a clinical thermometer that can read to 0.001 degrees Celsius no more useful than one that can read to 0.1 degrees Celsius?

4 Give three pieces of good advice to someone who has to make sure the measurements they are about to take with a peak flow meter will be reliable.

Interpreting results

RESULTS FROM TESTS MEAN nothing until they have been interpreted. To interpret results properly you need to understand the significance of the test (what were you looking for?) and the circumstances in which the tests were carried out (was the subject resting after a heavy meal?).

To help with the interpretation of results you will usually consult tables of normal values, to see if your results match healthy ones. This usually means that the results have to be prepared in some way, to make them match the standard way of displaying the sort of data. Modern medical equipment will do a great deal of data preparation for you, so that you need to be able to read information in standard formats like tables, charts and graphs.

A word about data

Data is the information from tests. Data can be:

- a number - for example, temperature of 36.8°C, a lung volume of 5.7 l

- presence/absence - for example, sugar is absent in the urine, pulse is present

- a class label - for example, eye colours are blue, the pulse is strong.

Sometimes the data must be processed before it can be used, for example, the forced expiratory volume (FEV_1), sometimes called the peak flow rate, must be calculated from raw data supplied by a spirometer.

Figure 3.48: Standard units of measurement and conversion methods

Factor	Most commonly used units	Conversion methods
Body temperature	Celsius (also known as centigrade) or Fahrenheit	Almost everyone now uses Celsius. To convert Celsius to Fahrenheit: divide by 5, multiply by 9 and add 32. To convert Fahrenheit to Celsius: take away 32, divide by 9 and multiply by 5.
Body mass	Kilograms or stones and pounds	Almost everyone now uses kilograms.
Height	Usually measured in centimetres or metres, sometimes quoted in feet and inches	To go from centimetres to inches multiply by 0.394. To convert inches to centimetres multiply by 2.54.
Any lung volumes	Litres	You may see measures in millilitres (ml) or cubic centimetres (cm^3). To convert ml to l divide by 1,000. To convert litres to ml multiply by 1,000.
Forced Expiratory Volume (FEV_1)	Litres per second	You may see ml per second – the figure will be 1,000 times the figure in l/sec
Blood pressure	Almost always quoted as millimetres of mercury (mmHg), sometimes as bars.	
Pulse rate	Always quoted as beats per minute (bpm)	
Heart rate	As pulse rate	

Data is used, along with our theoretical understanding, to make treatment decisions. The data needs to be clear, easily understood and in the easiest format possible to read in a hurry. Data can be displayed in tables, as graphs and charts, or reduced to a single, representative value such as an average which will include information from perhaps 100 separate data points.

Standard units

Medical and care staff use a wide range of different units to measure body functions. The same value in two different sets of units can look very different, so it is important always to quote the units for every measurement you make, otherwise the data could be useless or even dangerous.

Concentrations are more complicated because they contain two units in one. To understand the concentration of X in Y you need to know the units for X and the units for Y. So, for blood sugar the normal range is 70–110 mg/100 ml. Look at all the possible ways of quoting this figure.

- 0.007–0.011 g/100 ml (by converting the mg to g)
- 0.07–0.11 g/l (by expressing the concentration in a litre of blood)
- 7,000–11,000 mg/l (and converting g back to mg)
- 70–110 mg/100 ml = 38 mmol – 61 mmol/100 ml

Some sources also quote the value for blood sugar in mmol/100 ml of blood. To convert mg to mmol divide by 180.

Which units are more correct? It's impossible to say – different people choose different units and you will need to be able to understand what they mean. The most common units for concentrations of substances in blood are mg/100 ml but you may come across some others.

Remember the following conversion factors for mass and volume.

- 1 kg = 1,000 g
- 1 g = 1,000 mg = 1000,000 µg
- 1 litre =10 dl = 1,000 ml

Tables, graphs and charts

Data can be displayed in tables, graphs and charts (see examples in Figures 3.49, 3.50 and 3.51 in the following pages). Tables are a useful way of organising data. They make looking up a particular value easy.

In some simple tables the results are shown as icons, in effect, a score for each value. More complex tables may need a key to explain some of the symbols used. The headings at the top of the column and the labels on the rows identify each individual item of data. Be careful when looking down columns or across rows that your eyes do not slip out of line and derive information from the wrong cell in the table.

Table headings often contain information about the units used to take the measurements or notes about the source of the information. The source reference allows you to find the full article it was taken from more easily and may alert you to unreliable data if the source seems suspect in any way.

Bar charts are used to display results where at least one of the axes shows categoric data. Categoric data is data that fits into a class. For example eye colour is a categoric variable because the values fit into classes like blue, brown or hazel.

The key issue with both tables and bar charts is to carefully read the axes. These should tell you what is being measured, what units are used and the scale of the axis.

Graphs are a way of displaying numerical data where both axes carry continuous data. Continuous data is data that shows a continuous range of possible results and is quoted as a numerical value. For example height and weight are continuous variables. Graphs usually make this data easier to interpret but there are other advantages to drawing graphs, as they show very quickly if one result looks unusual.

Figure 3.49: An example of a table

Nutrient	Benton and Roberts (1988)	Crombie and others (1990)	Benton and Buts (1990)	Naismith and others (1990)	Schoenthaller and others (1991)
Vitamin A, µg	375.0	1500.0	1000.0	1500.0	
Vitamin D, µg	3.0	3.0	10.0	15.0	10.0
Vitamin E, µg	70.0	15.0	15.0	70.0	30.0
Vitamin K, µg	100.0	100.0	100.0	0.0	50.0
Vitamin B1, mg	3.9	3.9	1.5	2.2	1.5
Vitamin B6, mg	12.0	12.0	2.0	6.0	6.0
Nacin, mg	50.0	50.0	20.0	24.0	40.0
Riboflavin, mg	5.0	5.0	1.7	2.8	3.4
Vitamin C, mg	500.0	500.0	60.0	50.0	120.0
Calcium, mg	9.0	9.0	1.6	100.0	95.0
Iodine, µg	50.0	50.0	0.0	100.0	300.0
Flouride, mg	0.0	0.0	0.0	0.0	2.5
Iron, mg	1.3	1.3	18.0	15.0	36.0
Magnesium, mg	7.6	7.6	25.0	15.0	80.0
Zinc, mg	10.0	10.0	10.0	15.0	30.0
Duration of supplementation	8 months	7 months	5 months	4 weeks	10–13 months
Age of children	12–13	11–13	13	7–12	13–15
CAT	◊	◊			
AH4 Part I		◊		◊	
AH4 Part II		◊		◊	
Calvert	+	◊	+		
WISC–R				+	
MAT				◊	
RM		◊			
Cattells culture-fair	◊				

Figure 3.50: Bar charts

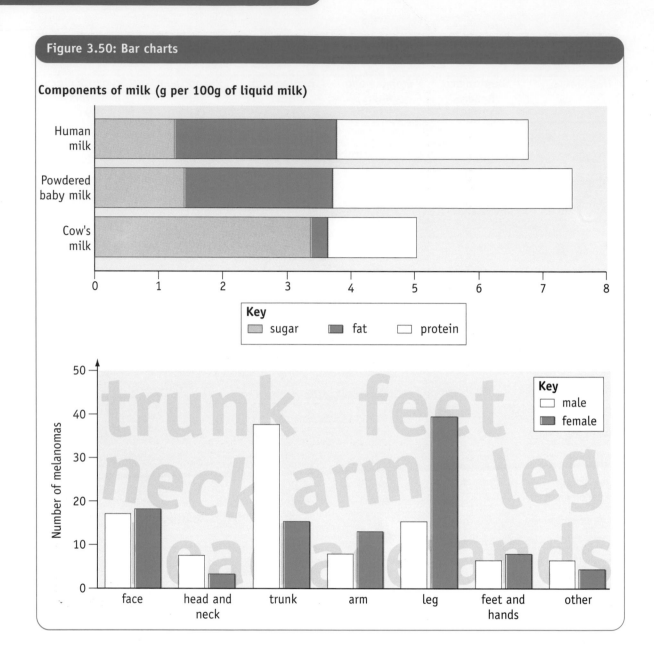

Components of milk (g per 100g of liquid milk)

Be very wary of graphs that simply show a line or bar charts that just show blocks of different sizes with no numbers or references on the axes – the graph will be, at best, a simplification of the real situation and may be misleading.

It is possible to use a single set of axes for more than one graph, provided you label the trace (the line of the graph) carefully. It can make comparisons easier between two groups (say male and female) if you put both traces on the same set of axes.

In biological and health care situations it is almost always better to draw a line of best fit rather than trying to draw a line through every point. Sometimes it is impossible to draw a line at all. Scatter graphs can then be used to display a likely connection between two factors, such as cholesterol intake and deaths from heart disease.

Sometimes graphs have more than two axes. In this case you need to decide which axis is relevant to each trace. The shape and colour of the points are often used to show this.

Figure 3.51: Graphs

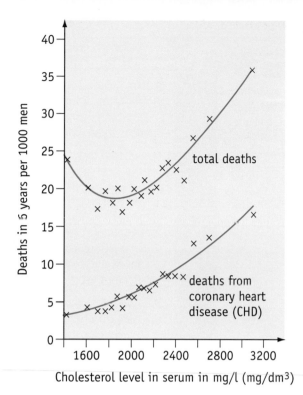

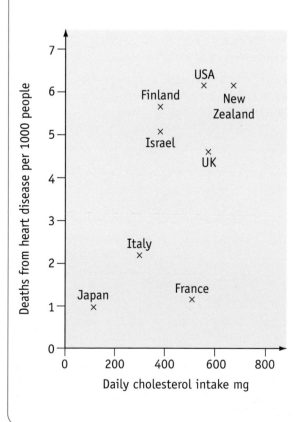

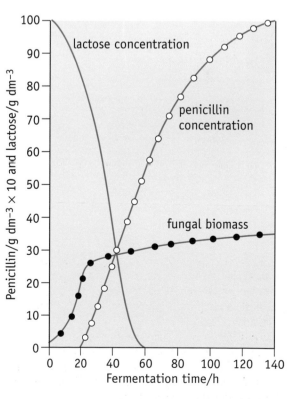

BUILD YOUR LEARNING

Keywords and phrases

You should know the meaning of the words and phrases listed below. If you are unsure about any of them, look back at the last five pages to refresh your understanding.

- Data
- Units
- Concentration
- Axis (plural axes)
- Trace
- Bar charts
- Line graphs
- Scatter graphs

Summary points

- Data includes simple observations, results from tests or information from other sources (e.g. tables of normal values). Data usually needs to be processed before it is useful.

- Care staff use a variety of units and these need to be quoted in all results. Some of these units have been adopted by almost all workers (for example, Celsius for temperature) but you should not make assumptions. Where different workers are using different units the results must be converted into common units before they can be compared.

- Tables can organise data to make access easier. Rows and columns should be labelled and all units stated either in the table or caption.

- Bar charts or histograms are useful for showing differences between two or more distinct classes, e.g. deaths from heart attacks in males and females.

- Line graphs are useful to show relationships between two continuous variables.

- Scatter graphs are useful to show trends where there is no direct connection between the variables.

QUESTIONS

1 A group of doctors in Helsinki looked for evidence of a fall in male fertility. They studied the testes of middle-aged men who had died suddenly. They chose sudden death males because they could carry out investigations that would not be possible on living males. The data shows a comparison of the two groups, from 1981 and 1991.

- How many men were there in each year group?

- How many deaths in the 1981 group were due to violence?

- What percentage of the 1991 group died of heart disease?

- Which year group had a larger death rate due to alcohol?

- Do you think it is fair to compare the two groups? Give reasons for your answer.

- Draw a bar chart of the causes of death for the 1991 group.

2 Do you think the evidence in these tables supports the idea that the quality of sperm is falling? Give reasons for your answer.

Sperm-producing status		1981 group	1991 group
Sperm-producing cells present	Sperm-producing cells active		
Yes	Yes	149	71
Yes	Some	83	128
Yes	No	21	53
No	No	11	12

Comparison of year groups	1981	1991
Age / years	54.0	52.2
Body mass index (kg/m²)	24.1	25.8
Cause of death		
Heart disease	138	126
Other disease	40	39
Intoxication	23	31
Violence	61	63
Unknown	2	5
Time from death to test /days	3.5	3.8

Year	Sperm density/ millions per ml ejaculate	Seminal volume per ejaculation
1940	113	3.40 ml
1990	66	2.75 ml

This unit enables you to develop your knowledge and understanding of human growth and development. This is an essential knowledge base area for health, social care and early years workers. It enables them to understand the needs and problems of the people with whom they work. Whilst human growth and development is a vast and potentially complicated topic, this unit introduces some of the key concepts and features of human growth and development across the life span.

The unit begins with an introduction to some of the key terms and concepts used by the academics and care practitioners who investigate, write about and work in the field of human growth and development.

The main body of the unit provides a description of the physical, social, emotional and intellectual changes that occur duringthe five life stages of the overall human life span. We focus on the developments and changes that

occur throughout infancy, childhood, adolescence, early and middle adulthood and later adulthood or old age, as it is often called. We also outline the range of skills that people acquire, develop and use at each stage.

The first half of the unit is largely descriptive. The second half of the unit is more explanatory. It includes a review of the so-called nature-nurture debate, in which we consider the key points and arguments put forward to explain the patterns and processes of human development. We also consider some of the social factors that affect human growth and development and then go on to look at some examples of theories that aim to explain how, and why, human beings develop in the ways that they do. In particular, we look at the ways in which the learning aspects of human development are explained by theorists using biological, behavioural, cognitive and psychoanalytic approaches.

Factors affecting human growth and development

Contents

Concepts in human development

AS A FIELD OF STUDY, HUMAN growth and development uses a number of important concepts and key terms that need to be defined at the beginning of the unit.

The terms growth and development are often used synonymously. That is, people use them to refer to the same thing. In fact, the two words have different meanings. Human beings experience **growth** when they increase their physical size or mass. Essentially, growth refers to the step-by-step process of getting bigger, which includes height and weight gain. Growth is a feature of a number of stages in the human life span. The extent to which people grow is thought to be influenced by a range of biological and social factors.

growth is often necessary for the initial acquisition of skills to occur (see case study) and is thus incorporated within the concept of development. However, human beings have a continuous experience of physical, social, psychological and emotional development throughout the life span. Whilst older people do not generally grow in the way that we have defined growth, they do experience physical changes that they need to adapt to and so develop skills that enable them to do so. For example, when you can no longer see well enough to do detailed embroidery or read a newspaper, developing the skill of using a magnifying glass is a good way of adapting to, and coping with, the changes.

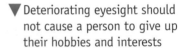
▼ Deteriorating eyesight should not cause a person to give up their hobbies and interests

▲ It is easy to see the physical growth that occurs from infancy to adulthood. It is less easy to see psychological, social and emotional development

Development is a term that is used to refer to changes in the complexity, sophistication and use of human capabilities. Physical, intellectual, emotional and social changes that occur over time which result in the person acquiring new and better skills, abilities and ways of living, are part of human development. Physical

Human development, like growth, is thought to result from the interaction of a variety of biological and social influences. These are discussed in detail later in the unit.

CASE STUDY

Human growth and development

In the early years of life children get taller and heavier very rapidly. Their brains also grow very quickly at this stage. Brain growth is necessary for a variety of other features of human development to occur. For example, as children's brains grow, they become capable, provided they are healthy and able to interact with other people, of speak. Most children aged between one and three years of age have grown brains that enable them to speak. The growth of the brain provides the physical conditions necessary for intellectual and language development to occur. This example shows that the processes of human growth and development are very much interrelated.

Influences on development

Many books on human growth and development distinguish between **nature** (biological) and **nurture** (environmental and social) influences on human growth and development. We need to look at both. We will look at the whole nature-nurture debate later in the unit, but at this stage it is important to outline a few of the ideas that explain how biological and social factors influence human growth and development.

Biological maturation

Arnold Gesell (1925) first used the term maturation to describe a genetically programmed sequence of changes in the human body. This term is still widely used today and is, in fact, a key concept in the field of human growth and development. **Maturation** is the process through which certain physical changes inevitably occur in a predictable sequence because we are biologically programmed (through our genes) for these to unfold. For example, during puberty girls are biologically programmed to change body shape, grow breasts and experience the onset of menstruation. Similarly, maturation in boys results in the growth of facial hair during puberty. Maturation also means that we will all develop wrinkles when we reach late adulthood. These physical changes unfold in a predictable sequence, though their timing may be different for different individuals. It is from the concept of maturation that we get the idea of a **biological clock**.

When we look at patterns of human growth that occur in different life stages in the next section of the unit, we will return to the concept of maturation. This is because maturational changes begin at birth and continue until a person's death.

Bee (1997) identifies three qualities that define a maturational change. It is:

■ universal – it appears in all children, in all cultures

■ sequential – it involves a predictable pattern of unfolding skills or characteristics

■ biological – it does not require environmental influence to make it happen.

Many maturational changes require some basic environmental support to help them to occur. For example, walking is a maturational change that children experience provided they have an adequate diet and the opportunity to move about. Diet and space to move in help children to develop walking skills as they mature but do not trigger its initial occurrence.

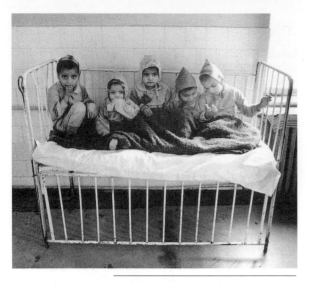

▲ Poor environments can delay areas of development

Shared experiences

Human development does not just unfold biologically from inside of the person in a programmed way. It occurs, and should be understood, within a wider cultural and social context. The norms, values, practices and institutions of the society into which people are born and live have a profound effect on the way in which they develop. External social influences are a very important feature of the complex human growth and development equation. There is an on-going debate (see p. 211) about whether the experience of social factors, such as culture, the family, and education are as powerful as biological factors in influencing human development. Nevertheless, people belong to, and their development is influenced by, the social groups,

▲ People expect certain events to happen at particular points in their life

institutions and processes of the society in which they grow up and live.

In the same way that we think of maturation as like a biological clock, there is also a **social calendar** to be followed in the developmental background. Within western, British culture we progress through sequences of social events and transitions that occur at typical ages or stages of development. For example, children in the United Kingdom typically begin school when they reach the age of four or five, leave school between the ages of sixteen and nineteen, and begin families of their own when they are young adults. Retirement from work is an event that most people don't expect to see in their social calendar before they reach later adulthood. This social calendar and the process of **social maturation** is not as universal or precise as that of biological maturation. However it is a useful concept when thinking about the influences on, and processes of, human development.

Interpretations of experience

Psychological and emotional, or inner, development results from the way that we respond as individuals to the developmental pressures of our biological clocks and social calendars, and the experiences that these lead to. How does this occur? An important idea in the human development field is that as individuals we possess an **internal model of experience**. The effect that an event or experience has on our development will to some extent depend on how, using our internal model of experience, we interpret it and give it meaning. Some people have insecure, negative models and hear criticisms implied when others give them compliments. 'You look cheerful today', is heard as 'You're not as glum looking as usual'! Researchers and practitioners in the human development field argue that as children we all create a set of internal models about the world, ourselves and relationships with others that we subsequently use to interpret our experiences.

Unique and unexpected life events

A life event is a critical incident or change that marks a turning point or transition in a person's life and development. Life events have also been defined as 'events likely to arouse strong negative or positive emotions and that involve change in an activity, role, relationship or idea', (Brown and Harris, 1978). Life events may occur unexpectedly and have a defining effect on one or more aspect of the person's development. For example, an unexpected accident that results in a disability could have an effect on the person's future physical development, relationships with others, self-image and self-esteem. Expected life events, such as starting and leaving school, becoming a parent and retirement are also influences on development, but are more likely to be part of the shared social calendar that we discussed earlier. Nevertheless, each person's development is shaped by a unique combination of specific life events whether they are expected or not.

Stages or sequences of growth and development

So far, we've used the terms stages and sequences to suggest that human growth and development follows a predictable pattern. This is commonplace in the field of human growth and development, but is it true? Your own experience will probably tell you that it is not so easy to distinguish between childhood and adolescence or between being an adolescent and an adult. In fact, at some point you've probably had arguments with your parents or friends about which life stage you are in. The idea of **sequences** of growth and development suggests that human beings gain more abilities or gain in size and that the gains are sequential. The idea of **stages** suggests that development involves a qualitative change, with people reorganising their skills and abilities at a new, qualitatively better or higher level. It may be the case that human development involves both stages and sequences of development, as we experience changes that give us both more (quantitative) and better (qualitative) physical, social, emotional and intellectual skills and abilities during our life span.

Continuity and change

The subject of human growth and development tends to conjure up images of change. For example, babies quickly grow and develop into toddlers and then into children who show changes in their physical appearance as well as their intellectual, emotional and social capabilities. However, whilst it is relatively easy to notice the changes, human growth and development also depends on continuity features. Many aspects of growth and development result from processes, like maturation and the influence of social environment, that continue to exert a developmental influence throughout life. The genes that we inherit from our parents, the patterns of behaviour and the ways of learning that we continually use when faced by new situations, are all continuing influences on our ongoing development. When you are trying to understand why people develop in the ways that they do, don't just think about the things that change. Remember that the things that stay the same are equally important.

Life terms

Life is an often repeated word in any book on human growth and development. It also comes with a number of other words attached to it. These each have different meanings and should not be used synonymously (to mean the same thing).

Life stage has already been defined as an age-band which is distinctive in terms of the pattern of growth and development that occurs within it. The classic human life stages that we will be referring to in this unit are **infancy**, **childhood**, **adolescence**, **early adulthood**, **middle adulthood** and **later adulthood**. There are potentially lots of ways of breaking these life stages into sub-stages, such as early and late childhood or early, middle and late old age. You may come across these in other books and in the ways that care organisations structure their services for people. The age stages referred to in this unit are as follows.

- Infancy   0 to 2 years
- Childhood   2 to 8 years
- Adolescence   9 to 18 years
- Early adulthood   19 to 45 years
- Middle adulthood   46 to 65 years
- Late adulthood/old age 65+ years

▲ How many different age groups do you think there are in this family?

The age-related stages are not precise transitional points in everyone's life span. Human growth and development are continuous processes that begin before birth and, biologically speaking, end at death. It is not possible to identify exactly when qualitative and quantitative growth and developmental change will occur for everyone. The age stages offer approximate periods that research and experience indicate as being times when transitions typically occur.

The term **life cycle** is commonly used to describe successive stages of life between birth and death. Life stages occur within the life cycle.

The term **life span** refers to the length of time between a person's birth and his or her death. It is also sometimes used to refer to the maximum human life span. As far as we know, the maximum human life span is about 120 years. This is the longest that anyone has ever been shown to have lived, but it is still unusual for people to survive to such an age.

The term **life expectancy** is sometimes confused with life span. Life expectancy refers to the number of years that a person can expect to live at a given point in time. It is expressed as an average for people of each sex in a particular country and depends on death rates in the population to which the individual belongs. The life expectancy at birth of people born in the United Kingdom in 1999 was 74 for males and 79 for females. Whilst life expectancy at birth has changed significantly over time (see Figure 4.1), the human life span has not been extended. In the future, it is likely that more people will survive for more of the potential human life span, but it is unlikely (barring a scientific miracle) that the life span will be extended.

The key features of human growth and development can be organised under the headings of physical, intellectual, emotional and social development. In the sections that follow we explore each of these areas of development in terms of changes and key features that occur at each of stage of the human life span.

Figure 4.1: Changing patterns of life expectation

United Kingdom	Years							
	1901	1931	1961	1991	1993	1996	2001	2021
Males								
At birth	45.5	57.7	67.8	73.2	73.6	74.4	75.4	77.6
At age 1 year	54.6	62.4	69.5	73.8	74.1	74.8	75.7	77.9
10 years	60.4	65.2	69.9	73.9	74.2	75.0	75.9	78.0
20 years	61.7	66.3	70.3	74.2	74.5	75.3	76.1	78.2
40 years	66.1	69.3	71.4	75.1	75.4	76.3	77.2	79.3
60 years	73.3	74.3	74.9	77.7	77.8	78.6	79.5	81.4
80 years	84.9	84.7	85.2	86.4	86.4	86.8	87.2	88.2
Females								
At birth	49.0	61.6	73.6	78.7	78.9	79.7	80.6	82.6
At age 1 year	56.8	65.3	75.1	79.2	79.3	80.1	80.9	82.8
10 years	62.7	67.9	75.4	79.4	79.5	80.3	81.1	83.0
20 years	64.1	69.0	75.6	79.5	79.6	80.4	81.2	83.1
40 years	68.3	71.9	76.3	80.0	80.1	80.9	81.7	83.5
60 years	74.6	76.1	78.8	81.9	81.9	82.6	83.3	84.9
80 years	85.3	85.4	86.3	88.3	88.3	88.8	89.1	90.0

Source: *Social Trends 26*, © Crown copyright 1996

BUILD YOUR LEARNING

Keywords and phrases

You should know the meaning of the words and phrases listed below. If you are unsure about any of them, go back through the last five pages of the unit to refresh your understanding.

- Biological clock
- Development
- Growth
- Internal model of experience
- Life cycle
- Life event
- Life expectancy
- Life span
- Life stage
- Maturation
- Nature
- Nurture
- Sequence
- Social calendar
- Social maturation

Summary points

- Growth refers to an increase in physical size or mass. Development refers to changes in the complexity and sophistication of physical, intellectual, emotional and social skills and capabilities.

- Human growth and development are continuous, life-long experiences that are influenced by a variety of nature and nurture factors.

- The key nature influence on human growth and development is the process of maturation. This is a biological process in which a genetically programmed sequence of changes unfold in a predictable age-related order.

- Nurture influences on human growth and development include the socialising effects of culture, the family and educational institutions.

- Life events are significant social experiences that have a powerful effect on people's development. Life events can be expected social transitions, such as leaving school or getting married, or unexpected events such as the occurrence of a serious disabling accident.

- Human growth and development is often described in terms of life stages. This idea suggests that people experience qualitative improvements in their skills and abilities as they progress through age-linked periods of change.

- Human growth and developmental changes occur in six age-related life stages. These are infancy, childhood, adolescence, and early, middle and later adulthood. Change occurs in areas of physical, intellectual, emotional and social functioning and ability in each stage.

- The human life span is the period of time between birth and death. Life expectancy is a term used to describe the average number of years that a person born at a particular time can expect to live.

QUESTIONS

1 Explain the difference between the terms physical growth and physical development.

2 What is maturation? In your answer give some examples of maturational changes experienced by girls and women.

3 Identify three sociocultural influences on human development. Explain briefly the effect that each can have on a person's development.

4 What is a life event? Explain the different types and their significance for human development.

5 Explain the difference between the terms life span and life expectancy.

Physical growth and development

IT IS IMPORTANT TO NOTE THAT the key features of human growth and development being described separately here do not, in fact, occur separately! In reality, human growth and development is **holistic** and complex, and its processes and events are interdependent and interlinked. They are only separated here to make them easier to explain.

Physical growth and development can be directly observed over relatively short periods of time. This is particularly the case in the early years of life and during adolescence, when physical changes are pronounced and occur rapidly. Physical change during adulthood and old age involves less growth but should not be thought of as simply involving physical decline. The key features of physical growth and development in each life stage are described below.

Infancy

Physical growth and development is rapid during the first phase of the life span. Between birth and 18 months of age, a child will grow to be three times its birth weight. Rapid growth occurs in all the major body systems, so that by the age of 18 months the child is very different in appearance and physical capability to when he or she was born.

Some of the key physical changes that affect both the physical appearance and capability of a child in the first 18 months of life are those that occur in bone and muscles. A newborn baby has very soft bones with a high water content. **Ossification**, or hardening, of the bones is a gradual process that occurs sufficiently quickly in the first 18 months of life to change a baby from a floppy, helpless state to one in which it can move and sit up independently. Two terms are used to

describe the overall pattern in which human physical growth occurs. These are **cephalocaudal** (from the head downwards) and **proximodistal** (from the trunk outwards).

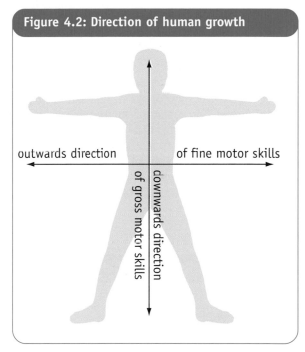

Figure 4.2: Direction of human growth

outwards direction of fine motor skills

downwards direction of gross motor skills

The first 18 months of life involve a spurt in the developing complexity of organs such as the brain and the nervous system, as well as the changes in body size and shape that can clearly be seen. By the time that

▼Between birth and 18 months of age, a child will grow to be three times its birth weight

the child has reached 18 months of age, the physical changes that have happened will have provided the basis on which **motor** (movement) **skills** can develop.

Motor development refers to the movement skills and abilities that human beings develop. Early motor development includes the emergence of:

- **locomotor skills**   pulling, crawling, walking, holding on

- **non-locomotor skills**   holding head up, pushing, bending body

- **manipulative skills**   reaching, grasping, stacking blocks.

The movement skills that develop first during infancy are the **gross motor skills**. These are the basic, unsophisticated but important abilities that allow the infant to control movement of its limbs, trunk and head. They give it the ability to reach out, hold its head up independently and roll over without help. These skills are gradually added to during infancy, adolescence and adulthood as the person develops **fine motor skills**. These are the sophisticated, highly skilled and controlled minor movements that many everyday activities (eating with cutlery, and getting dressed, for example) depend upon.

The expected pattern of physical growth during infancy is sometimes referred to as **normal development**. Whilst children grow (put on weight and get taller) at different rates during infancy, large-scale, long-term studies of patterns of growth have provided care practitioners with data on average and normal rates of growth. These data have been used to produce centile charts of height and weight for both male and female infants.

The bold line on the chart in Figure 4.3 represents the average measure of growth in weight expected in female babies over the first twelve months of their life. This means that if a five-month-old girl weighs 7 kg, on average 50 per cent of girls of the same age will weigh less than her and 50 per cent of girls of the same age will weigh more than her. If a girl weighs 12 kg at 12 months then the graph says that 97 per cent of girls of the same age will weigh less than she does and three per cent will, on average, weigh more.

By recording children's growth on centile charts, care workers such as health visitors and GPs can monitor their progress and note whether growth is proceeding in an expected pattern.

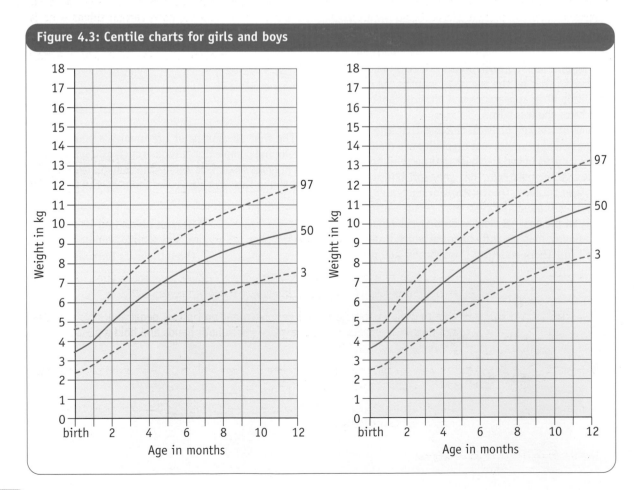

Figure 4.3: Centile charts for girls and boys

Assessing normal development

Jo Mills is a health visitor. She has been called to a case conference to discuss Laura Roberts, a nine-month-old girl. When Jo visited the family recently, Laura weighed 6.5 kg (14.33 lbs). She has put on 0.5 kg (1.1 lbs) over the last three months.

- Use the weight centile chart for girls to explain Laura's pattern of growth.

- Would you be concerned by these figures? Give reasons.

- What factors might account for Laura's weight at this point in her life?

Childhood (2–8 years of age)

At this stage, the person moves from being a dependent infant with very limited motor skills to being a more physically competent child. Physical changes are fewer and less rapid than in infancy. The child's growth in size is slower, at 5–7.5 cm (2–3 inches) per year and at about 2.7 kg (6 lbs) in weight per year, during this stage. Motor development extends further and consolidates to make the child more physically capable, skilled and robust. The child is also able to move more confidently and competently, and develops better hand and eye coordination.

During later childhood (six to nine years) there is a continuing pattern of gradual, steady physical growth and development. Qualitative improvements in motor skills allow children to move and complete tasks faster, and with better coordination, than they were able to in the previous phase. Girls tend to have more body fat and less muscle tissue than boys at this age but have very similar abilities in speed and strength. Hormonal changes begin to occur towards the end of this stage, but their effects are not really evident until a few years later.

Understanding motor development

Jim Thorne and Tracey Callaghan are both 17 years old. They met when they were at school together. Tracey has just had a baby. The level of family support is limited as neither set of grandparents lives close enough to help Jim and Tracey out. You are a health visitor working with Tracey and Jim to provide them with help and support. You need to stress how important it is to make the house safe for when the baby becomes mobile. Jim asks you to say when their child will be able to reach certain things – he is worried about the video and his stereo!

Write down in detail what you would say in answer to Jim's question.

Figure 4.4: Motor skill development in early childhood

Age	Motor skill development
18–24 months	Runs at about 20 months. Able to walk well at 24 months, able to push and pull boxes or toys on wheels, to stack blocks and to pick things up without overbalancing.
2–3 years	Can run easily, climb up and get off furniture without help, move large toys around obstacles, pick up small items and throw a ball forward.
3–4 years	Able to walk up stairs one foot per step, walk on tip toe, pedal and steer tricycles and toys with wheels, catch a large ball with both hands and hold a pencil between thumb and forefinger.
4–5 years	Can walk up and down the stairs one foot per step, hit a ball with a bat, kick and catch a ball and hold a pencil with ease.
5–6 years	Can play ball games well, skip on alternate feet and has fine control to thread a needle and sew stitches.

Source: adapted from Bee H (1994) *Lifespan development*.

Adolescence (9 to 18 years)

In contrast to the relative lack, and slow pace of, physical change in late childhood, adolescence is a period of rapid, major physical growth and development. **Puberty** is the term used to describe the period in adolescence when the onset of sexual maturity occurs and the reproductive organs become functional. The physical changes that occur during adolescence are mainly the result of hormonal activity. **Hormones** are the secretions of the endocrine glands. The human body produces a number of hormones from several different endocrine glands.

Males and females secrete both **oestrogen** and **testosterone** as a natural part of their physical functioning. Males secrete more testosterone than females whilst females secrete more oestrogen than males. The differences in levels of hormonal secretions largely account for differences in physical growth and development during this phase. At the end of puberty, hormonal activity slows down and the rate of physical change reduces dramatically as a result.

ACTIVITY

Explaining puberty

A group of primary school children, aged about 10, are to be given simple and straightforward leaflets to help them understand puberty and the physical changes that they are facing over the next few years.

Using language that year five children can understand, design a leaflet on a maximum of two sides of A4 that conveys the basic details about puberty to both girls and boys. Use charts, drawings and cartoons as appropriate. Try not to be too biological, mind boggling or frightening!

Figure 4.5: Action of the hormones at puberty

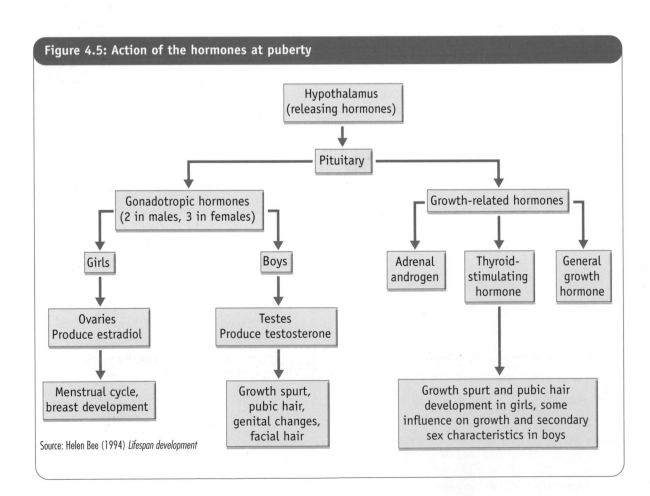

Source: Helen Bee (1994) *Lifespan development*

Early adulthood (19 to 45 years)

In the years leading up to adulthood, physical growth and development has occurred largely through a maturational process that results in increases in the person's size, ability and functioning. The **ageing process** affects human physical, cognitive and psychological functioning from early adulthood onwards. Part of this process involves the biological clock heralding a series of maturational changes, but unexpected life events, especially the experience of illness and disease, and lifestyle factors also have a major effect in adulthood.

Young adults are at their physical peak. They have more muscle tissue, stronger bones, better eyesight, hearing and smell, greater oxygen capacity and a more efficient immune system than at any other point in their lives.

Human physical development does not stop in early adulthood however, and cannot be sustained at this physical peak. There are a number of age-related changes to come which begin in early adulthood but which are experienced in middle and later adulthood.

▲ Race while you are young – young adults have more muscle tissue, stronger bones and greater oxygen capacity

Figure 4.6: Change of physical function by age

Physical function	Age of change	Nature of change
Vision	40–45	Thickening of the lens of the eye leads to poorer near vision and more sensitivity to glare.
Hearing	Approx 50	Loss of ability to hear very high and very low sounds.
Muscles	Approx 50	Loss of muscle tissue especially the fibres used for bursts of strength and speed.
Bones	After menopause in women, later in men	Loss of calcium in the bones and wear and tear on the joints.
Heart and lungs	35–40	Decline in most aspects of function when measured during or after exercise but not at rest.
Reproductive system	Mid-30s for women	Increased risk of reproductive problems and lowered fertility
Skin elasticity	Approximately 40	Increase in wrinkles due to loss of elasticity of skin and sweat and oil secreting glands become less efficient.

Source: Bee H (1994) *Lifespan development*

Middle adulthood (46 to 65 years)

From middle adulthood onward, physical maturation is concerned with the gradual loss of function and with decline. People who are aged 40 are at about the midpoint of their life expectancy and will be aware of some loss of physical ability. The pace of this decline is notably quicker, however, from the mid-60s to the 70s.

One of the major physical changes that happen to women during later adulthood is the onset of the menopause. The **menopause** occurs when the normal menstrual cycle ceases. It occurs because the ovaries no longer produce the hormones necessary for ovulation and menstruation. The average age of onset of the menopause is 49 to 50, though it can happen earlier.

During middle and later adulthood, vision and hearing become less acute, bones become more brittle and porous, and people become more susceptible to chronic health problems and disability.

ACTIVITY

Explaining the menopause

You have been asked to write an article of about 300 words for a teenage magazine. Use appropriate language and format to explain what the menopause is and how it can affect women physically and psychologically. You should highlight ways it may affect other family members and conclude by offering advice to teenagers on how to support women who are experiencing these physical changes.

You are advised to carry out some background research using sources of information such as human biology books, magazines and interviews with women who have experienced the menopause.

Later adulthood (65+)

The rate of physical decline for men and women accelerates between the ages of 75 and 80. Changes occur in the physical structure of the brain as well as in the body. For example, there is a reduction in brain weight and a loss of the brain's grey matter. There is evidence that people in late adulthood and old age have slower physical and cognitive (thinking) responses as a result of this physical decline. It is usual for older people to experience a reduction in the quality of their senses. Sleep patterns also appear to change and many older people adopting an early to bed, early to rise pattern, regardless of any experience of disease or illness that may also affect their need for rest and sleep.

▼ Despite the increasing physical decline of body systems, many older people lead a happy and healthy life

BUILD YOUR LEARNING

Keywords and phrases

You should know the meaning of the words and phrases listed below. If you are unsure about any of them, go back through the last six pages of the unit to refresh your understanding.

- Ageing process
- Centile charts
- Cephalocaudal
- Fine motor skills
- Gross motor skills
- Holistic
- Hormones
- Locomotor skills
- Manipulative skills
- Menopause
- Motor development
- Motor skills
- Non-locomotor skills
- Normal development
- Oestrogen
- Ossification
- Proximodistal
- Puberty
- Testosterone

Summary points

- During infancy, rapid physical growth occurs. This follows a head downwards (cephalocaudal) and trunk outwards (proximodistal) pattern.

- Physical growth during infancy provides the platform or basis on which skill development occurs.

- The expected, or normal, patterns and rates of physical growth and development are monitored and measured through the use of developmental checks and tools such as centile charts.

- The rate of physical growth slows down as childhood progresses. Children continue to gain in size but also develop a range of physical skills and abilities as they learn to control and use their bodies.

- A physical growth spurt is experienced during adolescence. This is largely driven by biologically programmed hormonal release. Puberty is the term used to refer to the onset of sexual maturity during adolescence.

- Human beings reach their physical peak during early adulthood. During this period the body is physically mature and able to function at its maximum level of efficiency.

- Ongoing growth in size as a result of maturation is not a feature of physical change during adulthood. Physical changes that are part of the ageing process begin in early adulthood but become more obvious and have more impact in middle and late adulthood.

- The rate of physical change speeds up in later adulthood as human beings typically experience a decline in the functioning and performance of their body systems and sensory abilities.

QUESTIONS

1   What do care practitioners and researchers mean when they say that human growth and development is holistic?

2   Describe the general process of physical growth and development during infancy. Use the terms cephalocaudal, proximodistal and motor skills somewhere in your answer.

3   What do centile charts tell health, social care and early years practitioners about children's growth and development?

4   Identify the biological factors that trigger and maintain physical growth and development during puberty.

5   Describe the key characteristics of the physical ageing process that people experience from early to later adulthood.

Social and personality development

CHANGES IN THE SOCIAL and personality aspects of developing human beings are less obvious than either physical growth or intellectual development. Our social skills, knowledge and personality are all influenced by innate, biological factors and external, environmental factors. However, whilst there are maturational aspects of both personality and social development, the social calendar of the person's culture and society is a more powerful influence on development in these areas.

We describe social and personality development here in terms of the age stages used previously. However, you should try to bear in mind the fact that the process of development in these areas does not follow the age stages as closely as as physical growth.

Infancy

To be able to understand human social development we need to look at people's earliest relationships. The foundations of social behaviour are established through relationships that are formed during infancy. The significance of the child's first relationship with its carer(s) is the subject of John Bowlby's theory of attachment. Bowlby (1969), argued that human beings have an **innate**, or natural, tendency to create strong emotional, affectional bonds with care givers. He termed this process **attachment**. This occurs when children feel a special sense of security and comfort in the presence of a particular individual, usually their parent. Bowlby was especially concerned with mother-child attachment. He claimed that 'mother love in

▲ It is important for a baby and its carer to form strong emotional bonds

infancy and childhood is as important to mental health as vitamins and proteins for physical health'. Bowlby, and others who have followed and developed his ideas, see the child's first relationship as the critical one. It is seen as providing a blueprint for all other relationships.

Attachment in children develops through three phases in the first eighteen months of life.

During infancy, the development of affectional bonds and attachment can't be directly seen, unlike growth in physical size. The degree to which a child has formed a successful attachment is assessed through judgement about its behaviour. Health and social care

Figure 4.7: Phases in the development of attachment in children

Stage of attachment	Approximate age	Characteristics
Indiscriminate	Up to six months	Anyone can hold the baby. The baby smiles at anyone. The baby protests when put down by whoever holds it.
Specific	Seven months to one year	The child is usually bonded to its mother, shows fear of strangers and separation anxiety. Intense for three to four months.
Multiple	One year and upwards	Begins three months after start of specific stage. Broadens to a wider circle of people.

workers, such as child psychologists and health visitors, who are interested in a child's attachment assess it by looking at:

- **fear of strangers** in the presence or absence of the mother

- **separation anxiety** – the amount of distress shown by the child when separated from the mother and the degree of comfort and happiness on reunion.

Evidence of strong attachment would be a major, negative reaction to a stranger and great distress followed by relief when separated from, and then reunited with, the mother. Psychologists are divided over the importance of the mother's role in forming an attachment with the child in the early stages of its social and emotional life. Most psychologists agree that it is important that the child forms a strong attachment with somebody who acts as a care giver and that this needs to happen in the child's first three years to enable successful emotional development to occur.

Research studies have suggested that the main factors involved in promoting strong attachments are:

- the intensity of interaction between the child and care giver in its early life – the quality of time spent with the child is more important than the quantity of time given

- the sensitivity and responsiveness of the child's care giver to its verbal and non-verbal signals

- consistency in care giving by the same individual or small group of individuals.

If a child fails to make a successful attachment to its parent or caregiver, it may experience emotional and relationship difficulties in later life. Whilst secure attachments provide the basis for social behaviour to develop, the later years of childhood are also an important time for social and personality development.

Childhood

If you can, think of a child of about eight years old whom you have known since he or she was a baby. Try to remember what he or she was like at the age of three and then at the age of eight. If you are able to remember, you will probably be able to identify a big difference in social development and capabilities. The social behaviour and skills of human beings change a great deal in the period between three and eight years. Some of the key features of social development during this stage include:

- an increase in **social skills** (language, communication and relationship-building) and the ability to relate to others

- a greater degree of independence from parents

- a wider set of social relationships, often including peers and other non-family adults

- episodes of conflict with others

- the beginning of the development of ideas about the self

- basic learning about social norms and relationships with others

- changes in the nature of behaviour towards others.

The person's **gender concept**, that is, his or her ideas about being male or female, is partly developed at this stage. A child is able to identify its own sex correctly by the age of two years, but is not aware that its gender will be a relatively permanent feature of its identity. **Gender constancy**, as this is known, is not fully established until the age of five or six years.

Children's attachment behaviours are less obvious during childhood than they were in infancy. Pre-school children, for example, are increasingly able to understand that even when an attachment figure, such as their mother, is not present, the relationship continues to exist and the person is likely to return. The children are able to understand this because of the development that has occurred in their cognitive functioning (pp. 217–19). This is not to say that the strength of the attachment bond diminishes. Anybody who has witnessed a group of five year olds beginning their first day at primary school will have observed the ways in which separation anxiety affects children of this age!

▲ Separation anxiety affects children as they begin primary school

Behaviour towards others

Children's friendships become increasingly stable as they progress through this stage. A noticeable feature of early childhood friendships is that they tend to be same-sex. By primary school age, and for most of the primary school years, children's friendships are almost exclusively other children of the same sex.

Aggression is a feature of children's social behaviour that seems to follow a developmental pattern. A child aged two to four years tends to be relatively physically aggressive. This type of aggression declines between the ages of four to eight years. Between these ages, verbal aggression and challenge is more likely to occur. One common form of this is the name-calling and taunting that children of this age become involved in. **Pro-social behaviour**, also known as **altruism**, is also evident and also increases throughout this age-stage. Studies have shown that while younger children are more likely to comfort another child, older children are more likely to donate something to another child who is described as being in need. The amount of altruistic behaviour that a child exhibits is related to familial patterns and norms.

Ideas about the self

During the early childhood years, a child's sense of self tends to be concrete. This means that it does not really involve any evaluation or idea of its global self-worth. However, children do have the ability to identify their own visible characteristics and make statements on their perception of how competent they are in physical, intellectual and social tasks. For example, they might say 'I'm no good at counting, but I am good at running'.

Socialisation is a term used to refer to the process by which people learn the culture of the society in which they live. In early childhood, up to about six years, children are said to experience **primary socialisation**. This involves learning the language and basic patterns of social behaviour in the family setting. Parents are the main socialising influence here. **Norms** are social rules or expectations that govern our behaviour in certain situations. Parents teach children a set of social norms by responding to the child's various behaviours with approval or disapproval, and by modelling, or demonstrating, social behaviours that the child copies. These norms then become a feature of the child's social behaviours inside and outside the family. Children also learn basic attitudes and values during primary socialisation. Again the child learns, or absorbs, a set of attitudes and values from its parents through what it hears the parents say, the ways in which the parents react and behave, and through the explicit teaching that it is given on particular topics.

While primary socialisation mainly takes place within the family during early childhood, socialisation is a lifelong process that doesn't really end. People continue to learn the rules and expectations of the society in which they live as they, and their society, develop over the course of their life. As people spend more time outside of the family, in the company and subject to the influence of other people, they are said to experience **secondary socialisation**. This will be discussed in more detail later.

ACTIVITY

Establishing social norms

As part of the primary socialisation process, children learn the social norms or expectations of the society in which they live. Examples of social norms might include 'don't push in front of someone in a queue' or 'don't pry into other people's belongings'. The way people dress is often a consequence of social norms. Breaking or disregarding social norms usually elicits different forms of disapproval to ensure conformity.

1 Write a list of all the ways people express their disapproval of what they regard as unacceptable or deviant behaviour by children:

■ in the home and family

■ at primary school

■ amongst a group of friends.

2 Would you say that there were any noticeable differences between the ways people express their disapproval at home, with friends and at school or work? What are they?

Parenting style

During childhood a balance needs to be achieved between the child's emerging skills and need for autonomy, and the parents' need to protect the child and to control its behaviour. A child's parents have a major role to play in socialising the child. Their approach to the way in which the child is brought up, or parented, is seen as having a major effect on its child's social and personality development. Psychologists have categorised parenting styles in a number of different ways. One method identifies four categories of parenting style (see Figure 4.8).

Critics of parenting style models like the one in Figure 4.8 argue that parents are not always, or even at any point in time, one or other type of parent. They may use more than one parenting style and if there are two parents in a family, they may each use different parenting styles.

Figure 4.8: Categories of parenting style

Parenting style	What happens?	Consequences
Authoritative	Parents combine control with acceptance and child-centred involvement. Their control of and demands on the child to behave in particular ways is combined with warmth, nurture and two-way communication. Authoritative parents take their children's opinions and feelings into account, and give explanations and reasons for punishing them where this occurs.	The children of authoritative parents tend to be friendly, independent, assertive and cooperative with their parents. They seem to grow up enjoying life and have a strong motivation to succeed.
Authoritarian	Parents try to control and assert their power over their children. In contrast to authoritative parenting, however, this happens without communicating warmth and nurture to the children. Authoritarian parents attempt to set absolute standards, make obedience an important issue, and place a high regard on respect for authority, work, tradition and orderliness.	The consequences of authoritarian parenting tend to be that children are moderately competent and responsible but are also socially withdrawn and lack spontaneity. Girls can be more dependent on their parents and lack achievement motivation. Boys tend to be more aggressive than usual. There is also a link between low self-esteem and authoritarian parenting.
Indulgent	Indulgent parents adopt a parenting style that is accepting, responsive and child-centred. They tend to place few demands on their children and exercise little control over their behaviour.	Children who have indulgent parents tend to show more happiness and vitality than other children but lack social assurance, self-reliance and impulse control.
Neglectful	Neglectful parents are concerned with their own interests and are relatively uninvolved with the concerns and activities of their children. Neglectful parents have fewer conversations with their children, are less aware of their school progress or social life and do not take their children's opinions into account when making decisions.	The children of neglectful parents tend to be moody, impulsive and aggressive. They are more likely to develop delinquent behaviour.

ACTIVITY

Explaining childhood behaviour

A three-year-old child new to a nursery displays the following behaviours:

- pulls the hair of other children
- throws food at meal time
- uses swear words
- pulls off other children's clothes.

Write an explanation for the nursery workers which explains how:

- some of the behaviour could be a problem of socialisation
- some of the behaviour could be a normal feature of development
- some of the behaviour could be the result of the parenting style the child has experienced
- the nursery workers might respond to ensure that the child's behaviour becomes acceptable
- other children are likely to react to this child.

Development of the self-concept

People's self-image combines with their self-esteem to make up their self-concept. An individual's **self-concept** is a central part of his or her identity. Having a clear, positive picture of who you are (**self-image**) and how you feel about yourself (**self-esteem**) helps to give you a sense of psychological security and affects the way that you relate to other people.

The self-concept becomes more sophisticated as we progress through childhood. Children move from being able to give surface, external descriptions of themselves to being able to describe their own internal qualities, beliefs and personality traits. They also become able to make **global judgements** about their self-worth and self-esteem.

Global judgement means that children form and express ideas about themselves and others using broad, internal terms (feelings and abilities) and evaluative terms (how good or bad they are in relation to others). Children are able to make global judgements independently from around seven or eight years old. This ability becomes more sophisticated through childhood and the child gradually develops an enduring sense of self-worth and personality.

Ideas about relationships, especially friendships, change during the middle years of childhood. It is common for children in early childhood to refer to playing together and to identify friends as those other children with whom they spend time and physically share their space. During middle childhood this idea of friendship changes to include the idea of **reciprocal trust**. That is, a friend is now someone whom you help and trust, and who does these things for you. Reciprocal trust is seen as the defining feature of friendship in the middle years of childhood.

Relationships with parents are also changing during childhood. Attachment behaviours are only visible in situations that are very stressful to the child. This is not evidence of a weakening of attachment. Children are still very attached to their parents but have extended their relationships to include other adults, such as teachers, and their peers.

▲ Sharing favourite toys is a sign of reciprocal trust

Relationships with peers increase in importance and are preferred to relationships with parents. In the middle years of childhood children seem to prefer to do things together, but even though children have a greater number of friends, their relationships tend to be very sex-segregated. There also seem to be differences between boys' and girls' friendships (see Figure 4.9).

Children's experience of relationships is an important influence on their early and on-going social development. Hartup (1989) suggests that social development occurs as a result of experiencing two types of relationship. **Vertical relationships** involve an attachment to a person with greater power or knowledge, such as a parent or teacher, for example. **Horizontal relationships** on the other hand refer to those with same-age peers. These two types of relationship serve different functions for the child. Vertical relationships are needed for protection and security. They also provide the child with opportunities to develop its basic social skills and relationship models. Horizontal relationships are needed to try out basic skills. It is only through horizontal relationships that children can develop the skills needed for cooperation, competition and intimacy with others.

Figure 4.9: Different characteristics of friendships between boys and between girls

Boys' friendships	Girls' friendships
Large groups	Small groups/pairs
Extensive friendships	Intensive friendships
More playing outdoors	More playing indoors
Competition/dominance focus	Agreement/compliance self-disclosure focus

Adolescence

There are significant age-linked changes in self-esteem during adolescence. At the beginning of adolescence, self-esteem typically drops. It rises steadily from then onwards. Self-definition becomes more abstract and ideological, and traits develop that are more enduring. There is some blurring of sex-role identity to include opposite sex characteristics.

Erik Erikson (1960) proposes that the main challenge, or crisis, of this stage is based on establishing a coherent sense of self. The adolescent has a need to form a new identity separate to that of his or her parents. Relationships with parents pose a contradictory dilemma. The adolescent needs to establish autonomy from parents but also to maintain a sense of relatedness. The autonomy need can lead to conflict, whilst the relatedness need leads to the maintenance of attachments.

Relationships with peers are very important during adolescence. Most of adolescents' time is spent with their peers. Stable friendships are more common than in childhood and are likely to be more complex and psychologically richer. There is more sharing of inner feelings. The peer group becomes the vehicle for transition from family to adult life. There is also a shift to preferring opposite sex relationships during adolescence.

Early and middle adulthood

The social calendar is bursting with developmental engagements during early adulthood. For most people there are three new roles to be undertaken, or at least begun, during the early part of adulthood: worker, partner and parent.

▲ Getting married is an important event in most young adults' social calender

ACTIVITY

Adolsecence and peer group pressure

Dear Jane,

I'm in a real dilemma. I'm 16 years old. My three main friends are absolutely boy mad and have started sleeping with their boyfriends. I'm a virgin and intend to be until I settle down with the right partner. I don't think they mean to be nasty but my friends drive me mad by calling me names like 'Miss Innocent' and 'Spinster'. They are making me feel like I'm some sort of weirdo.

When school finishes we're planning to go off on a week's holiday to Ibiza. I want to go because I like their company and it will be a good laugh. However, I know that if we meet any boys it could well turn into a difficult situation for me. I'm beginning to think that I'd be better off not going on holiday. What should I do?

Yours sincerely,
Kirsty

1 Write a sympathetic and practical response to Kirsty's letter to the problem page.

2 What does this sort of situation tell us about the power and role of peer groups in the socialisation process, particularly for adolescents?

Leaving home is a major social transition that takes place during this age stage. It involves separation from parents and family, the transfer of attachment from parents to peers and then to an intimate partner. Attachment to family and peers continues to some degree, though by their early twenties most individuals have become emancipated from their family.

Erikson (1960) sees the major task of early adulthood as that of finding a partner. Finding a partner enables the individual to create an intimate, secure attachment. When choosing a partner, people tend to seek a match in terms of similarities in:

- external characteristics, for example, quality of appearance and apparent social class

- attitudes and beliefs, for example, about sex, religion and politics

- role fit, for example, ideas about sex roles and sexual compatibility.

▲ During earlier adulthood people spend a lot of time looking for a partner

The individual's **internal working model of attachment** is also important in the search for and selection of a partner. Our expectations of a partner and of his or her behaviour tend to repeat, or recreate, the type of attachment we experienced in our first relationship with an adult. People tend to pick others with similar internal models of attachment. For example, adults with secure attachments are inclined to trust others and are not jealous, and seek similar partners. Adults with anxious attachments tend to be anxious in their relationships, are more likely to be jealous because they are unsure whether their feelings are reciprocated, and are drawn to partners who share this internal model of attachment. To a large extent we are drawn to people who are like ourselves and our parents!

New parenthood is also a feature of early adulthood. For most people it appears to be an experience that brings profound satisfaction, a greater sense of purpose and increased self-worth. It also introduces a number of role changes. Sex roles and spouse relationships tend to change because of the introduction of children. The birth of children appears to result in a drop in partners' relationship satisfaction and an increase in role strain. The roles of partner and spouse are at least partly incompatible.

The role of worker can also add to role strain in early adulthood. However, beginning work and a career also increases life satisfaction for both male and female workers.

The middle years of adulthood contain fewer developmental events in the social calendar. The three types of role (partner, parent and worker) continue to be important but have usually changed. Children leaving home usually affects the role of parent. Work tends to be less demanding and there are usually fewer potential promotion opportunities by middle age. Relationships, especially partnerships, are likely to be given more time and assume a new significance. Whilst individual experiences clearly vary, this tends to be the optimum time of life for many people. Partnership satisfaction tends to rise in mid-life, possibly due to the reduction in role strain that also occurs. Partners have more time to spend together in mid-adulthood and poor marriages tend to have ended by this point.

People in this age stage are very likely to have at least one parent (usually mother) still living. This pattern will become stronger as life expectancy increases. This has an impact on roles. The generation of people in middle adulthood tends to end up giving more help to others than they receive. They provide help and support to older and younger relatives. Caring for an ageing parent can become a new role for a daughter or daughter-in-law. At the same time, the role of parent doesn't necessarily cease when a child leaves home, it simply changes. Women seem to view the departure of the last child as a positive transition in their own life, except where their self-identity has been heavily invested in the role of mother.

Late adulthood and early old age is a time when considerable changes in roles and relationships are experienced. Many long-standing roles are shed. The role of worker is largely lost as people retire. The role of spouse is lost when a partner dies. The role of son or daughter is lost when parents die. The roles that remain are less complex and usually involve fewer duties. There is less structure to life as a result.

▲ The roles that remain in late adulthood are less complex and usually involve fewer duties

ACTIVITY

The effects of retirement from work

June and Bert have been married for 38 years. June is 62 and Bert 64 years old. They have three grown-up children. They live in a three-bedroom house. Bert is in his last year of working for a printing company. He has worked for them for the last 29 years. June works for seven hours a week as a dinner lady.

- Make a list of the issues and changes that may await June and Bert in retirement.

- Having made a list, write down what could be done to help them deal successfully with the changes that will occur in their lives.

- Think of someone whom you know personally who has retired. Without revealing personal details, describe the ways in which the retirement has been a positive or negative experience in his or her life.

Partner relationships in later life tend to be based on loyalty, familiarity and mutual investment in the relationship. Partners tend to spend more time with each other. Older women often expect to be widowed and to live on their own for a time. Older people tend to see their children regularly for purposes of practical help and emotional support. Continuity and adaptation are the themes of later adulthood relationships. Friendships remain important for companionship, but there is a reduction in the number of friends as they die and are not replaced with new friendships.

Bee (1994) refers to the creation of a convoy of relationships throughout life. This is 'a protective layer of family and friends who surround the individual and help in the successful negotiation of life's challenges'. This convoy seems to be relatively stable over time once established. People tend to choose friends who have similar social and psychological characteristics and who are at the same life-stage.

BUILD YOUR LEARNING

Keywords and phrases

You should know the meaning of the words and phrases listed below. If you are unsure about any of them, go back through the last eight pages of the unit to refresh your understanding.

- Altruism
- Attachment
- Authoritarian parenting
- Authoritative parenting
- Gender concept
- Gender constancy
- Horizontal relationships
- Indulgent parenting
- Innate
- Internal working model of attachment
- Neglectful parenting
- Norms
- Primary socialisation
- Pro-social behaviour
- Reciprocal trust
- Secondary socialisation
- Self-concept
- Self-esteem
- Self-image
- Socialisation
- Social skills
- Vertical relationships

Summary points

- Human beings have a continuous, lifelong experience of social and personality development. This is influenced by both nature and nurture factors throughout life.

- An infant's earliest relationships provide a blueprint for its subsequent relationships. A successful emotional attachment to a carer is particularly important for these future relationships to be emotionally successful.

- Social and personality development is a significant feature of childhood. Contact with an increasing range of peers and adults and socialisation within the family are important influences on development during childhood.

- People gradually develop their self-concept during childhood, though this is also a life-long process. During childhood, self-concept moves from being a concrete, descriptive sense of identity to one that involves sophisticated judgements about self-worth and self-image.

- Social skills and relationships develop greatly during adolescence. Adolescents are faced with the difficult task of establishing autonomy and a personal identity that is separate from their parents, whilst retaining emotional attachments to them.

- People typically take on a number of new social roles during early adulthood. Many life transitions occur which result in a move away from the family to form new attachments and relationships with other people.

- Finding a partner with whom an intimate, secure attachment can be formed is a key task of early adulthood.

- Middle adulthood often involves role changes as children leave home, work life takes on a different significance and people have more time to spend with their partner.

- Later adulthood can involve further social and emotional adaptation as roles and relationships are lost, and opportunities to develop new ones diminish.

QUESTIONS

1 Identify and describe the key features of emotional development during infancy.

2 What is gender constancy? Explain when this develops as part of your answer.

3 Explain how parenting style may affect a person's social and personality development.

4 How does a person's internal model of attachment affect his or her relationships in adulthood?

5 Is social and personality development complete by the time a person reaches later adulthood? Explain why or why not.

Cognitive and intellectual development

WE ARE OFTEN UNAWARE OF the thinking, or mental activity, that lies behind the decisions that we make as we go about our daily tasks. These mental activities are part of **cognitive functioning**, which is the consequence of **intellectual development**. One theorist who has contributed significantly to our understanding of how intelligence develops is Jean Piaget. Piaget developed an age-stage theory of intellectual development which we are going to introduce here. (We explore it in more detail on p. 267.)

Infancy

Piaget argued that during their first 18 months of life, children only have a basic form of intelligence. They respond to immediate physical stimuli only. There is no planning for, or memory of, events or experiences. This gradually changes over the first 18 months, as physical and intellectual developments occur. The child develops the concept of **object permanence**, ideas and memories of people and actions, over this time.

Figure 4.11: The three mountains task

This task is a test of the child's ability to imagine what the cat can see

Object permanence is the conceptual understanding that objects (including people) continue to exist when they move out of sight. Infants do not understand this, but gradually acquire the concept from the age of eight to ten months.

Figure 4.10: Object permanence

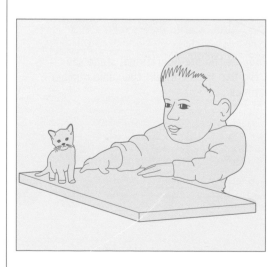

Young babies think that objects they can't see no longer exist and so rapidly lose interest in them

Childhood

Piaget argued that as the infant enters childhood, it develops the ability to use symbols, in the form of images and words. Children can manipulate these symbols intellectually and express them in their play. For example, a broom can become 'a horse', or a doll can be used to portray 'mummy'. Children tend to be **egocentric.** This means that they assume that everyone else sees the world in the same way that they do. The child starts to understand **identity constancy** and the ability to classify objects improves throughout early childhood. Identity constancy is the conceptual understanding that the child is a lasting object with enduring properties, such as gender and size.

Research suggests that young children have some ability to see things from other people's perspectives. They are able to adapt their speech and behaviour to the needs of a companion, for example. Again perspective-taking ability gets more sophisticated with age.

▲ Imaginative play is a feature of cognitive development

There is a significant change in cognitive development during later childhood. Children discover that there are general rules or strategies for examining and interacting with the world. Piaget refers to these as concrete operations. An **operation** is a set of powerful, abstract, internal **schemes** (ways of thinking) such as reversibility, addition, subtraction and serial ordering, which can be used to understand objects and their relationships. For example, children understand that adding something makes it more, whilst subtracting something makes it less.

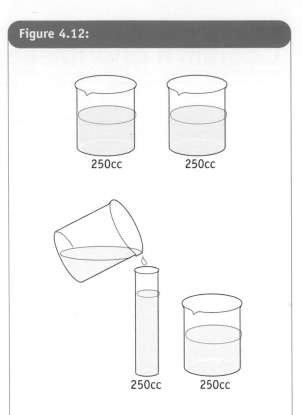

Children at the pre-operational stage believe that the volume of water is greater after it has been transferred to the taller glass.

Children at the pre-operational stage say that the two rows contain the same number of pennies...

...but also that there are more pennies in the more spread-out, second row.

Adolescence

During adolescence, a person's ability to think in concrete ways is extended, so that they are able to think about objects and situations that they have not directly experienced themselves. Teenagers develop **formal operational** thinking, that allows them to think abstractly about options and possibilities. This means that they don't have to actually experience these things to make decisions and judgements about them. Some theorists, including Piaget, suggest that not all adolescents reach an abstract thinking level of development. Indeed, others, such as Bee (1994), suggest that most people don't need to use abstract thinking very often in their personal or working lives and only do so when they have occupations which demand this type of thinking.

Early and middle adulthood

Patterns of cognitive and physical growth and development show a lot of similarities in this period of life. Intellectual and cognitive processes are at their peak from early to middle adulthood. They begin to decline in certain ways towards the end of this age stage,

however. Memory becomes less effective as we age. Nancy Denney (1982) proposed that cognitive and physical change and decline in adulthood could be understood using a single model of change (see Figure 4.13).

Denney (1982) suggests that there is a common curve of rising and then falling skills on nearly any physical or cognitive measure over the duration of this age-stage. She explains the variation in performance level between people, and between one person's actual and possible level of achievement, as the result of the extent to which they use both their physical and cognitive skills.

In the middle years of adulthood, cognitive ability gets better where tasks are based on highly practised skills or specific learning. Where tasks place demands on under-used or under-practised skills, or demand speed, a decline in the cognitive ability of the person at this stage can be observed. The amount of decline is quite small. Between the ages of 60 and 70 there is a much more significant loss of cognitive abilities. Memory ability and functioning show the same pattern.

Middle-aged adults retain their ability to do high level, productive work and problem solving, despite the gradual process of decline in certain intellectual abilities and processes.

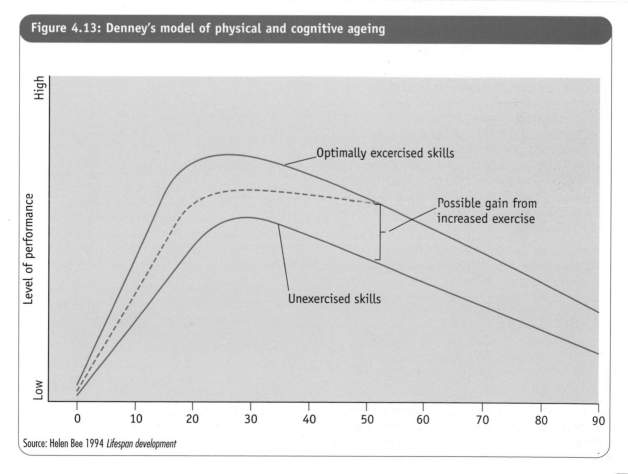

Figure 4.13: Denney's model of physical and cognitive ageing

Source: Helen Bee 1994 *Lifespan development*

Late adulthood

In later adulthood and old age, there is a much more noticeable decline in cognitive ability and functioning. Between the ages of 65 and 75 the changes are relatively small. From the age of 75 onwards the changes are much more noticeable. Most older people do not experience dementia, but although there is little change in the quality of short-term memory, many older people do experience some loss of function and slowness with recalling information from the long-term memory. Research studies show that people of this age are also less effective at problem solving.

ACTIVITY

The effects of neglect and abuse on child development

We have seen that the physical, social and emotional development of children and young people is dependent upon a supportive, nurturing and stimulating environment. People who experience neglect and abuse as children and young people may require the intervention and support of care workers at some point in their lives to deal with the difficulties that this causes. The following extract refers to a true story, in which a child suffered long-term neglect and abuse that dramatically affected her development. Read the extract and complete the tasks at the end.

Genie's early months of life were relatively normal. She grew normally and seemed alert and interested to the paediatricians who saw her. From that point on, things went downhill. Her father didn't want her and refused to allow her mother to spend much time with her. She became very sick when she was 14 months old, and the paediatrician who saw her said she was retarded. That was all the father needed. He used this diagnosis to justify the neglect and abuse that followed.

From the time she was about two, Genie spent nearly all of her time in a single bedroom of the house, tied to an infant potty seat. Except for the harness that she wore, she was naked. She apparently spent years in this way. When she was taken off the potty seat at night, she was put into a kind of straightjacket and left to sleep in a crib with wire mesh sides and top. No one talked to her and she couldn't hear other people talking to each other, since her room was in the back of the house.

When Genie tried to attract attention by making a noise, to get food for example, her father often beat her. He never spoke to her, even when he was beating her. He growled or barked at her like a dog. Genie's parents did feed her. But mostly she ate baby food and soft foods. This incredible treatment continued until Genie was 13 and a half years old, when her mother finally did something, and Genie's maternal grandmother found and rescued her.

Adapted from Curtis S (1977) *Genie – A psycho-linguistic study of a modern day 'wild child'*, Academic Press.

1 Describe how you think Genie's development would have been affected in the following areas:

- physical
- cognitive
- emotional.

2 Discuss what a case like Genie's tells us about the relative importance of inherited and environmental factors on human development. Does it show that human development is determined by either genetics or environment alone?

3 If such a case were to be discovered today, it would almost certainly require the work of a multidisciplinary team (child psychiatrist, psychiatric nurses, social workers and so on) to help to rehabilitate the child. If you were a member of such a team, how hopeful would you be that, in the long term, the child could lead a normal life? Give reasons.

BUILD YOUR LEARNING

Keywords and phrases

You should know the meaning of the words and phrases listed below. If you are unsure about any of them, go back through the last four pages of the unit to regresh your understanding.

- Cognitive functioning
- Egocentric
- Formal operation
- Identity constancy
- Intellectual development
- Object permanence
- Operation
- Scheme

Summary points

- Intellectual development involves various aspects of mental activity and ability. Thinking, intelligence and memory are important features of intellectual development.

- Jean Piaget is a key theorist in the area of intellectual development. He produced an age-stage theory in which he described how people progress from one form of thinking to another as they progress from infancy to childhood and then to adulthood.

- Intellectual development is an ongoing process. People reach the peak of their intellectual ability, and are able to function at this level, during early and middle adulthood.

- During the latter part of middle adulthood and in late adulthood, memory becomes less efficient and thinking speed slows down slightly. Despite this, cognitive (thinking) skills and ability levels are maintained by most people well into late adulthood.

- From about 75 years onwards, intellectual ability and functioning does decline, even though most people do not lose their cognitive abilities through dementia-related brain disease.

QUESTIONS

1 Cognitive functioning is dependent on intellectual development. Explain what this means, concentrating on the terms at the beginning and end of the statement

2 How does Jean Piaget explain the fact that an infant generally won't keep looking for a toy or object that disappears from sight when a young child will?

3 What are cognitive operations?

4 What type of thinking is typically developed in later adolescence or adulthood?

5 To what extent does intellectual ability decline with age?

Factors affecting development

SO FAR, WE HAVE DESCRIBED the general patterns and sequences of human growth and development that occur throughout the life span. At times we have touched on some of the factors and influences that are thought to stimulate and promote growth and development in each life stage. Next, we are going to review more explicitly the nature-nurture theories that seek to explain the reasons for, and processes of, human growth and development.

The nature-nurture debate

What is the nature-nurture debate? **Nature** influences on human growth and development are those things that we are born with. They include our biological heritage, transferred to us from our biological parents in the genes that we're born with. **Nurture** influences on human growth and development are the non-biological, external factors that affect what we do with, and how we express, our biological inheritance. Why have we put debate on the end? Because scientists still aren't sure how much of what we ultimately are and do is determined by the genes we are born with and how much is shaped by the environment we grow up in.

Some human development theorists and care practitioners argue, from a more extreme nature viewpoint, that genes programme human behaviour. From this position, one might, for example, suggest that men are genetically programmed, or destined, to dominate women, and that psychological and social factors play next to no role in bringing this situation about. Other theorists and care practitioners argue, from a more extreme nurture viewpoint, that psychological and social factors, working alongside geographic and economic influences, play a greater role and, in fact, mould human behaviour. It might be proposed, for example, that deeply ingrained social values and powerful socialisation influences nurture in men and women the expectation and belief that men should, naturally, be more dominant than women in personal relationships.

Extreme views in areas of uncertainty are not particularly helpful. It's better and more accurate to talk about possibilities. It is possible, for example, that certain personality traits are 50 per cent inborn and 50 per cent acquired (see p. 254). However, weightings like this can only be approximate, and need to be revised in individual cases.

Some books on this subject use titles like *Nature versus Nurture*. We prefer nature *and* nurture to *versus*, as human beings are biological, psychological and social animals all at the same time. The debate is not, therefore, about nature or nurture but about the extent to which human growth, development and behaviour are both:

- fashioned by nature (that is, **genetically innate**)
- shaped by nurture (that is, influenced by psychological, socioeconomic and geographical environments).

The interplay of nature and nurture in our human make-up is captured by the sociologist Runciman in his book, *The Social Animal* (1998) when he says that:

You... are at the same time three things. First, you are an organism – that is, a living creature born... of one male and one female parent from both of whom you have inherited your genes. Second, you are an organism with a brain, and therefore a mind.... Third, you are an organism with a complex mind living in regular contact with other organisms with complex minds, and therefore you have a social life in which you have relationships with other people to which you and they attach a meaning.

Being human, according to Runciman, must therefore be understood in terms of nature (our biological inheritance and development) and nurture (the sociological experiences we encounter in life). He might have added that geography and economics play a part too, as where you are born and live, and the extent to which you have access to money and other material resources, affects your growth and development.

Steve Jones, professor of genetics at London University, cannot understand all 'the endless fuss about genes and environment'. He believes that inheritance involves more than DNA. After all, he says, fat people usually have fat cats who get none of their owners' genes but all of their food!

The same point is true of humans, says Professor Jones. Drinking, he says, destroys lots of families. The fate of some drinkers and their offspring is linked to the inheritance of a variation in the body's ability to deal with alcohol, but the main influences that explain the link between drink and family breakdown are environmental: 'the family that drinks together sinks together'.

The relative weightings that researchers and practitioners in the field of human growth and development attach to genes and environment – more nature here, less nurture there – reflect their differing views, each of which, in their own way, has something to offer. This is what the nature-nurture debate is all about.

Some researchers and care practitioners believe that environmental factors only fine-tune a programme of growth and development that we inherit from our parents which is, fundamentally, genetically determined. Based on this view, we become good at remembering things, like telephone numbers or lists of names for example, because of genetically-based growth processes in our brains. Hearing a number and practising it (by repeating it in our heads) nurtures memory, but a person has to have inherited the brain capacity and ability which makes him or her good at remembering in the first place. If you agree with this view, you might argue that individual differences in memory ability are mainly due to genetic factors. You are either born with it or you are not.

An alternative view is that the environment plays a bigger role in our development. According to this perspective, people do better at intellectual tasks and learn more because they attend good schools and have good teachers. Being taught well and practising new reading, writing and thinking skills doesn't just make use of existing brain power, but stretches it to new limits. If you accept this opinion, you might believe that individual differences in learning are mainly due to environmental factors like parental encouragement, the quality of teaching and the amount of learning opportunities that children receive.

A third position is held by researchers and practitioners who argue that biological influences (nature) are more important for universal forms of development (for example, learning to walk), whilst environmental influences (nurture) are more prominent in particular forms of development (for example, learning to speak with a Liverpool accent). If you agree with this position, you might contend that our genes enable most of us to learn to walk, but only a Liverpool upbringing leads to the development of a genuine Liverpudlian accent.

Finally, other researchers and care practitioners say that it's impossible to separate or assign weights to genetic and environmental influences and say which are the most important because the two bounce off and affect each other. People who adopt this approach refer to **developmental transactions** (mutual influences) occurring between biology and the environment. For example, a violent boy might have been born with a genetic tendency towards aggression and this tendency might be environmentally reinforced if his parents don't try to check it. If you share this last outlook, you might think that a genetic tendency to be violent in a young child could be strengthened or inhibited by different styles of parenting (see p. 228).

ACTIVITY

Ways of shaping behaviour

How might effective parenting inhibit a child's aggressive disposition? Identify how parents might use environment to influence their child's innate, or natural, temperament and behaviour.

You might want to refer to the section on parenting style on p. 228 to help you to answer this question.

It can sometimes be frustrating to admit that there are no final definitive answers to the questions raised by the nature-nurture debate. However, it is important to accept that human growth and development is a very complex area and that nature-nurture debates will go on unresolved for a long time as researchers and practitioners develop and refine their understanding of growth and development processes. Next, we examine some of the current knowledge about the effects of nature (genes) and nurture (environment) on human development, starting with genes.

The influence of inherited genetic factors

When you next hold a baby, don't be taken in by its helpless demeanour, lolling head and milky mouth. Behind the cherubic face is a sophisticated data processor capable of understanding complex rules and structures.
Lusia Dillner, *The Observer*, 3 January 1999

The reference to a sophisticated data processor is, of course, to the baby's brain. A baby's brain is unique, but everyone's brain cells contain genes that have been inherited from their biological parents. All living matter is composed of cells, each of which is a microscopic compartment. Cell compartments, or nuclei, house a chemical ribbon, known as DNA.

▲ Underlying a baby's apparently simple behaviour are complex biological and brain processes

DNA, or **deoxyribonucleic acid**, is a chemical ribbon that instructs cells how to function. The human body is very complicated, so DNA imparts lots of instructions to enable it to work well. While every cell actually contains all the genetic information for the whole body, DNA tells each cell to only use the genetic information it needs. It tells brain cells to behave like brain cells, liver cells to behave like liver cells, skin cells to behave like skin cells, and so on.

DNA is packaged into long strands known as **chromosomes**. Chromosomes, in turn, contain shorter stretches of the DNA ribbon and these are called genes. With the exception of egg and sperm cells, each cell of the human body contains 46 chromosomes arranged in 23 pairs. This full complement of chromosomes in a cell is called the **genotype**.

Genes are units of **heredity** information. That is, they pass on information that affects biological characteristics like our eye colour and our susceptibility to diseases such as Huntingdon's chorea. We know this from scientific research that has identified and isolated the specific genes responsible for eye colour and Huntingdon's chorea. More recent (and currently speculative) research claims that there are also specific genes for aspects of intelligence, depression, alcoholism, crime, and sexual orientation.

Figure 4.14: The structure of DNA

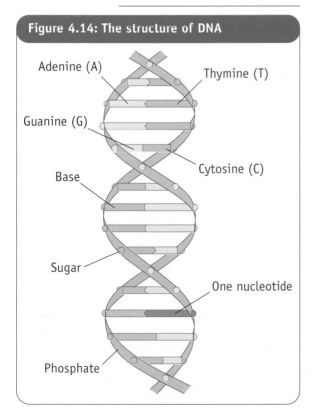

Adenine (A)

Thymine (T)

Guanine (G)

Cytosine (C)

Base

Sugar

One nucleotide

Phosphate

▲ Genes pass on information that affects biological characteristics including aspects of our appearance

The biology of genetic transmission

As we have seen, your parents give you your unique **genotype**. This happens at the moment of conception, when a sperm from your father fertilises an ovum, or egg, in your mother's fallopian tube. The sperm cell and the egg cell each contain their own distinctive genes, spun on a DNA ribbon, containing the instructions for the life of a new human being. Conception unites these two sets of DNA, one from the father and one from the mother. This genetic material from the two parents is then mixed into a new, unique and individual combination, that becomes the genetic blueprint or genotype.

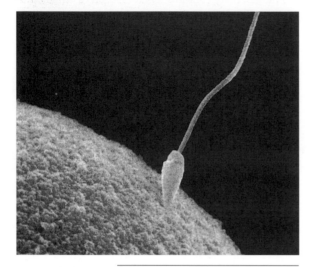

▲ A single sperm fertilising a human egg

Sperm cells and egg cells are made from so-called germ cells or **gametes** that are found in the male's testes and the female's ovaries. Sperm and egg cells are unlike other cells in the body, in that they do not contain all 46 chromosomes in 23 pairs. Each gamete has only 23 chromosomes instead of 23 pairs of chromosomes. When conception occurs, the egg cell's 23 chromosomes and the sperm cell's 23 chromosomes combine to form the 23 pairs that will be part of each cell in the new, developing body of the fetus.

Because you have pairs of chromosomes (23 from your mother and 23 from your father), you also have matching pairs of genes for nearly every biological trait. Twenty-two of the pairs, known as **autosomes**, look alike and can be matched. For these 22 genes, the instructions of the **dominant gene** are followed rather than those of the other, so-called **recessive gene**. A recessive gene's instructions are only followed if neither in its pair are dominant. The features and characteristics that a person inherits are therefore, generally those that are genetically dominant.

Suppose, for example, you inherit the gene for type A blood from one parent and the gene for type 0 blood from your other parent. In this particular case, the type A gene is dominant over the type 0 gene and means that you will have type A blood. Because the type 0 gene is recessive, you will inherit type 0 blood only if you inherit two type 0 genes, one from each parent. But what about people who have type AB blood? A person with type AB blood has inherited one type A gene from one parent and one type B gene from the other parent. Neither of these genes dominates the other, so the instructions of both come into play.

What about the twenty-third pair of chromosomes? These are the **sex chromosomes** and are different to the autosomes as they can be one of two types: X or Y chromosomes. Egg cells only carry **X chromosomes**. The sperm cells from the father can carry an X or a **Y chromosome**. It is therefore the father's sperm cells that determine whether the child will be male or female. If the sperm that fertilises the egg cell carries an X chromosome, the child will have an XX combination of sex chromosomes and will be female. If the sperm that fertilises the egg carries a Y chromosome, the child will have an XY combination of sex chromosomes and will be male.

After conception, the single cell, formed by the fusion of the two parental cells, multiplies. Before long, there are hundreds of different cells that are able to make about 50,000 proteins to control the work of all our cells. Soon, the cells gather into layers, then into organs, slotting into the right place at the right time to form a brain, an eye, a kidney, a blood vessel and so on. The sequence of pre-natal (pre-birth) development is precise, with, for example, nerves and veins arriving just in time to support the organs that will soon need them. In just nine months, around twenty-five trillion living cells will emerge as a human baby from the mother's womb. The baby will grow into an adult human being of some 100 trillion cells.

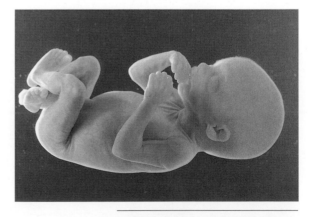

▲ Human fetus at approximately five months

In our description about how blood type is inherited, we explained heredity in a relatively simple way. It may have appeared that a person's physical traits or characteristics result from the influence of single dominant genes. This isn't quite true. Many human characteristics are the result of a combination of genes. Hair colour, eye colour and temperament, for example, are all affected by lots of pairs of genes working together. Advances in genetic research are continually revealing how complex combinations work. Nevertheless, scientific understanding of the processes of genetic inheritance and the significance of biological factors in human development is far from complete.

On a biological, or physical, level it is fair to say that genes do exert a powerful influence on human growth and development. In other areas of human development, notably, psychological and social development, we need to take account of lots of other factors alongside the influence of genes. We should also be careful about the idea that genes always have the last say on the biological level. For example, while we might inherit a genetic predisposition to cancer or heart disease, our lifestyle can increase or diminish the risk of disease occurring. So, while genes play an important role in who we are and what we become, the circumstances of our lives and the decisions we make are also very influential. We take a look next at some of the many non-biological social and economic factors that affect human development.

Socioeconomic factors

Health and social care practitioners are very interested in how human lives are affected by **life chances**. The term life chances refers to opportunities for enjoying a good standard of living, and is strongly linked to socioeconomic position, or, to call it by another name, to social class. A person's **social class** refers to his or her social and economic standing in society. People who

Figure 4.15: Two official models of social class

The Registrar General Scale	The Standard Occupational Classification
Middle class	Class 1: Managers and administrators Managers and administrators in government and large companies
Class 1: Professional and managerial, e.g. architects, doctors, solicitors	
	Class 2: Professional Teachers, solicitors, architects, social workers, librarians
Class II: Intermediate, e.g.teachers, nurses, pilots, farmers	
	Class 3: Associate professional and technical Computer programmers, nurses, journalists, surveyors
Class III: (non-manual): Skilled occupations non-manual, e.g. clerical workers, secretaries, shop assistants	
	Class 4: Clerical and secretarial Clerical workers, secretaries, typists, receptionists
Working class	
Class III (manual): Skilled occupations manual, e.g. bus drivers, electricians, cooks	Class 5: Craft and related Bricklayers, electricians, car mechanics, bakers
	Class 6: Personal and protective services Traffic wardens, police officers (sergeant and below), hairdressers, waiters/waitresses
Class IV: Semi-skilled occupations, e.g. bartenders, postal workers	
	Class 7: Sales Sales reps, supermarket checkout operators
Class V: Unskilled occupations, e.g. road sweepers, labourers, refuse collectors	
	Class 8: Plant and machine operators Assembly line workers, bus conductors, lorry/taxi/bus drivers
	Class 9: Other occupations Coal miners, refuse collectors, cleaners, postal workers

belong to the same social class tend to share similar life chances. They might, for example, drive the same kind of car, live in the same kind of house, earn similar pay, have comparable occupations, and, on average, live to the same age.

The UK Office of National Statistics places each of us within a social class based on jobs, earning potential and prospects. For example, teachers are at the top of the ladder in Class 1, whereas the long-term unemployed are in Class 8. Traditionally, the ladder was a short three-runged one, with an upper, a middle and a lower (working) class. But that model isn't thought to convey enough information about the subtlety of today's multirunged society. Even so, the three-class model is still popular among social scientists, and provides health and social care practitioners with a helpful general way of categorising the main income groups in society.

Income

Income (cash) and **wealth** (property) are the bedrock of social class, and both are very unevenly distributed in the United Kingdom, as the figures in Figure 4.16 indicate. More recent data from the United Nations' *Human Development Report* (1999) reveal that, compared with some of the other highly developed countries, the UK has relatively high levels of economic inequality and poverty.

Wages and salaries from paid employment are the largest source of income. Earnings between jobs vary hugely. In 1996, for example, solicitors got more than three times the pay of cleaners. Here we have an example of a social class difference in economic life

chances, solicitors being middle to upper class and cleaners working class. Cleaners are often women too, and **gender** plays an important role in income differentials. The gap between average female and average male earnings (more than £140 per week when in one's forties) hasn't changed much in real terms since the early 1970s. One of the reasons for this is that women do more unpaid work at home, rearing children and caring for relatives.

Ethnicity and age are also connected to income. Here are a couple of findings from a study by the Joseph Rowntree Foundation (1998) on income levels in the UK. By 1994–95:

- two-thirds of the Bangladeshi and Pakistani population were located in the poorest fifth of the general population of the United Kingdom, as were 25 per cent of the Indian population

- pensioners were disproportionately represented in the poorest half of the population.

By contrast, belonging to a different ethnic group (particularly, being white British) or having a job (particularly a managerial or professional one) are generally associated with higher incomes. Able-bodied people are also more likely to be better off financially than disabled people.

Whatever the reasons for income inequality, from the late 1970s to the late 1990s, income inequalities have generally increased. What are the consequences of income inequalities on people's lives? Put simply, the financially better off enjoy better health, better nutrition, better housing and better education than the less well off. We address some of these inequalities next.

Figure 4.16: Distribution of marketable wealth in the UK, 1976–93

Distribution of marketable wealth in the UK, 1976–93

Marketable wealth	Percentages				
	1976	1981	1986	1991	1993
Percentage of wealth owned by:					
most wealthy 1%	21	18	18	17	17
most wealthy 5%	38	36	36	35	36
most wealthy 10%	50	50	50	47	48
most wealthy 25%	71	73	73	71	72
most wealthy 50%	92	92	90	92	93
Total marketable wealth (£ billion)	**280**	**565**	**955**	**1,711**	**1,746**

Source: *Social Trends, 27* © Crown copyright 1997

Health

Health chances (how well or how unwell people are) are profoundly affected by socioeconomic inequality. For example, the **infant mortality rate** (the proportion of children dying during infancy) is twice as high for children born to unskilled manual workers as it is for those born to professionals. Research in the United Kingdom consistently shows that people's social position in society strongly affects their health and life expectancy (see Figure 4.17).

As far back as the 1840s, it was found that London gentlemen lived, on average, twice as long as labourers. From 1911, British death certificates have been coded for social class based on occupation. This has enabled researchers to study the links between social class position and mortality rates. One of the more important studies in this area was prompted by Richard Wilkinson, who, in 1976, wrote a letter to a social science journal called New Society urging the then Labour government to set up an urgent inquiry into the causes of different mortality rates between the social classes.

What subsequently became known as the **Black Report** appeared in 1980, when Sir Douglas Black, then President of the Royal College of Surgeons, produced evidence of marked social class-related inequalities in health chances. People in unskilled jobs had a two-and-a-half times greater chance of dying before retirement than professional people. The Black Report disclosed that the gap in mortality rates between rich and poor had actually increased between 1930 and 1970. In 1930, unskilled workers were 23 per cent more likely to die prematurely than professional workers. By 1970, the likelihood was 61 per cent.

The Conservative government in office at the time of its publication didn't seriously act upon the Black Report. However, evidence from later research has shown that the health divide increased even further during the 1980s. The Black Report was re-published in the 1990s, signalling a renewed interest in the links between health and social inequality. This is appropriate, given that, as we enter the twenty-first century, people at the bottom of the social ladder still experience much worse health than those at the top.

Nutrition

One of the areas explored by Sir Donald Acheson in his *Independent Inquiry into Inequalities in Health* (1998) was the effect of nutrition on life chances. He found that people in lower socioeconomic groups tended to eat fewer fruit and vegetables and other foods rich in dietary fibre. Low intake of fruit and vegetables has been linked to certain cancers and heart disease, and these diseases are more likely to strike lower socioeconomic groups.

This finding was of particular concern in relation to child development and growth, Acheson noted that the long-term health of babies is related to the nutrition and physique of the mother. A mother's healthy diet in pregnancy may, for example, reduce a baby's later risk of heart disease. Mothers who rely on State benefits or low incomes find it hard to afford a healthy diet. They may even go short of food to feed their children. This is bad for both the mother and her baby.

Breast feeding reduces the incidence and severity of many infant infections, and may protect children from later bad health. Yet here again, Acheson's report found that babies born into lower social classes come off worse. Babies born into higher social classes are more likely to be breast fed than babies born into lower social class families, and continued breast feeding is a lot less common in lower social classes.

Interestingly, food preferences seem to have pre-natal biological origins. If you crave curries, love pickles or adore fish and chips, blame your mother! Research indicates that fetuses can distinguish between distinctive flavours. Following birth, fetal taste might be reinforced through breast feeding because breast milk holds many of the flavours of the mother's food.

Education

Access to State education from the age of five to 16 is guaranteed for all children in England and Wales. More than 90 per cent of pupils attend publicly funded State schools. These schools make no charge to parents. In most areas, pupils aged five to 10 go to primary school, and transfer to secondary school at 11 for education up to the age of 16 or beyond. More and more young people are now entering further education (sixth forms and further education colleges) and university-level higher education.

Although access to State schooling is open to all pupils, access to the best educational institutions in British society is strongly affected by social class, gender and ethnicity. Sociological research provides compelling evidence here. Children from middle and upper class families have relatively better access to the best State schools and to private schools than children from working class families.

Access to education was another issue covered by Sir Donald Acheson in his comprehensive report on health inequalities. The report notes that those living in disadvantaged circumstances – the very people most in need of the benefits of education – may be least able to get access to them. Schools in poor neighbourhoods are more likely to be cramped, and children who come to school hungry are unable to take full advantage of learning opportunities. The capacity of schools to help poorer children has been compromised by measures such as the reduced entitlement to free school meals.

Figure 4.17: Social class and death rates in men and married women aged 20–64, 1970–1993

All causes
rates per 100,000

Social class	Year		
	1970–72	1979–83	1991–93
I – Professional	500	373	280
II – Managerial and technical	526	425	300
III(N) – Skilled (non-manual)	637	522	426
III(M) – Skilled (manual)	683	580	493
IV – Partly skilled	721	639	492
V – Unskilled	897	910	806
England and Wales	624	549	419

Lung cancer
rates per 100,000

Social class	Year		
	1970–72	1979–83	1991–93
I – Professional	41	26	17
II – Managerial and Technical	52	39	24
III(N) – Skilled (non-manual)	63	47	34
III(M) – Skilled (manual)	90	72	54
IV – Partly skilled	93	76	52
V – Unskilled	109	108	82
England and Wales	73	60	39

Coronary heart disease
rates per 100,000

Social class	Year		
	1970–72	1979–83	1991–93
I – Professional	195	144	81
II – Managerial and technical	197	168	92
III(N) – Skilled (non-manual)	245	208	136
III(M) – Skilled (manual)	232	218	159
IV – Partly skilled	232	227	156
V – Unskilled	243	287	235
England and Wales	209	201	127

Stroke
rates per 100,000

Social class	Year		
	1970–72	1979–83	1991–93
I – Professional	35	20	14
II – Managerial and technical	37	23	13
III(N) – Skilled (non-manual)	41	28	19
III(M) – Skilled (manual)	45	34	24
IV – Partly skilled	46	37	25
V – Unskilled	59	55	45
England and Wales	40	30	20

Accidents, poisoning, violence
rates per 100,000

Social class	Year		
	1970–72	1979–83	1991–93
I – Professional	23	17	13
II – Managerial and technical	25	20	13
III(N) – Skilled (non-manual)	25	21	17
III(M) – Skilled (manual)	34	27	24
IV – Partly skilled	39	35	24
V – Unskilled	67	63	62
England and Wales	34	28	22

Suicide and undetermined injury
rates per 100,000

Social class	Year		
	1970–72	1979–83	1991–93
I – Professional	16	16	13
II – Managerial and technical	13	15	14
III(N) – Skilled (non-manual)	17	18	20
III(M) – Skilled (manual)	12	16	21
IV – Partly skilled	18	23	23
V – Unskilled	32	44	47
England and Wales	15	20	22

Source: Independent Inquiry into Inequalities in Health Report, 1998

Figure 4.18: Social class and degree-level educational attainment

Great Britain								Percentages
	1991/92	1992/93	1993/94	1994/95	1995/96	1996/97	1997/98	1998/99
Professional	55	71	73	78	79	82	79	72
Intermediate	36	39	42	45	45	47	48	45
Skilled non-manual	22	27	29	31	31	32	31	29
Skilled manual	11	15	17	18	18	18	19	18
Partly skilled	12	14	16	17	17	17	18	17
Unskilled	6	9	11	11	12	13	14	13
All social classes	23	28	30	32	32	33	33	31

1 The number of home domiciled initial entrants aged under 21 to full-time and sandwich undergraduate courses of higher education in further education and higher education institutions expressed as a proportion of the average 18 to 19 year old population. The 1991 census provided the population distribution by social class for all years.

Source: Department for Education and Employment; Office for National Statistics; Universities and College Admission

In educational life chance terms, children born into higher social class families generally do better than children from lower social class families. Girls tend to outperform boys, and children from white and Indian backgrounds usually obtain better results than children of African-Caribbean, Bangladeshi and Pakistani origins.

In relation to social class, for example, local education authorities with a high percentage of pupils who are entitled to free school meals (a general indicator of lower social class) have a lower percentage of pupils achieving five or more GCSEs levels A*– C.

While it is probably true that we inherit some of our intelligence then, socioeconomic factors are also implicated in IQ scores and other measures of achievement. If things were otherwise, middle class parents with very intelligent children would not be so concerned about getting their children into good schools! Effective schools and committed teachers (environmental factors!) do make a difference to children's educational achievements.

Housing

The number of dwellings in the United Kingdom doubled in the past 60 years, from 10.6 million in 1938 to 20.7 million in 1997. During the same period, the proportion of owner-occupied dwellings has doubled, and the proportion of privately rented dwellings has fallen dramatically.

Since 1989, public subsidy for social housing (mainly council homes) has steadily fallen. Alongside a decline in council house construction programmes, there has been a big rise in the number of homeless people. Despite the growing popularity of owner occupation, it is often difficult for prospective first-time buyers to afford a property.

▲ Around 10,000 people sleep rough over the course of a year in England

People who own their homes report fewer neighbourhood problems (for example, crime and noise) than people who live in the private rented sector and in social housing. A report published by the Joseph Rowntree Foundation in 1998 revealed that amongst all homeowners in England, 7 per cent were dissatisfied with their neighbourhood. Amongst those in the private rented sector, 10 per cent were dissatisfied. Of those living in social housing, 18 per cent were dissatisfied. Here we see that life chances, as measured by neighbourhood dissatisfaction, are linked to different housing tenures. The worst off are, of course, homeless rough sleepers, which is why Tony Blair declared in Rough Sleeping (1998), a report by the social exclusion unit:

It is a source of shame for all of us that there are still about 2,000 people out on the streets around England every night, and that 10,000 sleep rough over the course of a year.

The physical environment

Physical, or natural, environmental factors play a significant role in influencing life chances. All of us, rich and poor, suffer the consequences of global pollution for example. Noxious emissions from cars and factories cross regional and national boundaries.

Closer to home, in local environments, industrial pollution hits the poor hardest. A report produced by the environmental charity called Pollution Injustice (1999) reveals that the poorest families in England and Wales (those on household incomes below £5,000), are twice as likely to live in a neighbourhood with a polluting factory close by than those with household incomes over £60,000. In some parts of the world, the burden of pollution turns disadvantaged groups into environmental refugees, moving from one shoddy neighbourhood to the next. However, in the United Kingdom, low income often makes it difficult for families living in heavily polluted areas to move out.

Socioeconomic issues aside, when environmental hazards strike, children are more vulnerable than adults. They receive greater exposures per unit of body weight than adults and are more susceptible to the ill effects of pollution because of their immature and developing bodies. Environmentally-linked health problems that are now on the rise among children and young adults include asthma, allergies, cancers, reproductive disorders and the damaging effects of tobacco smoke.

In 1999, the World Health Organisation (WHO) noted that the health of half of the world's children is endangered by the tobacco smoke they are exposed to from parents and others who smoke cigarettes around them. The WHO estimates that about 700 million children breath air polluted by tobacco smoke. Among the health problems that children exposed to tobacco smoke suffer are asthma and other respiratory illnesses, middle ear disease, sudden infant death syndrome (cot death) and childhood cancers. Research also shows that children whose parents smoke perform more poorly at school and have more behavioural problems than the children of non-smokers.

Worryingly, tobacco pollution, like lots of other pollution, is a worldwide problem. Researchers from poorer countries are finding the same things as countries like the UK, the US and Canada. In poorer parts of the world, tobacco smoke is exacerbating the ill effects of other forms of pollution.

Another major pollution problem is lead exposure. It is estimated that one out of every six children in the United States has levels of lead in the blood that are in the toxic range. Children are vulnerable because their growing bodies are particularly sensitive to the effects of lead. Common sources of lead include petrol, paint and even soil and water. When exposed to even small amounts of lead, children can become hyperactive, inattentive and irritable. Children with higher lead levels may also experience learning problems, delayed growth and hearing loss. At high levels, lead can cause permanent brain damage and even death.

BUILD YOUR LEARNING

You should know the meaning of the words and phrases listed below. If you are unsure about any of them, go back through the last 11 pages of the unit to refresh your understanding.

- Autosomes
- Black Report
- Chromosomes
- Deoxyribonucleic acid (DNA)
- Developmental transactions
- Dominant gene
- Gamete
- Gender
- Genes
- Genetically innate
- Genotype
- Health chances
- Heredity
- Income
- Infant mortality rate
- Life chances
- Nature
- Nurture
- Recessive gene
- Sex chromosome
- Social class
- Social housing
- Traits
- Wealth
- X chromosome
- Y chromosome

Summary points

- Human growth and development is influenced by a variety of nature and nurture factors. The relative importance of particular nature and nurture influences is the subject of ongoing debate by researchers and health and social care practitioners.

- An extreme nature viewpoint is that human growth and development is programmed and determined by genes. A contrasting but equally extreme nurture position is that psychological, social and economic factors play a definitive role in shaping human growth and development.

- A more widely held consensus viewpoint is that both nature and nurture factors are important influences on growth and development.

- Genetic inheritance is a powerful biological influence on aspects of growth and development. People inherit a range of physical characteristics and capabilities from the information contained in their biological parents' genes.

- At conception, two sets of chromosomes combine to form 23 pairs that contain the person's genetic blueprint or genotype.

- Socioeconomic factors, including social class, income, nutrition and access to educational opportunities affect human growth and development because of their influence on health and life chances.

- The physical environment, particularly the health effects of pollution, access to good quality housing and exposure to substances such as tobacco smoke and lead, plays a significant role in influencing life chances.

QUESTIONS

1 What, in essence, is the nature-nurture debate about?

2 Identify and describe two contrasting viewpoints on the nature-nurture controversy.

3 Summarise the process of genetic inheritance. Use the terms genes, genotype, heredity, dominant and recessive gene somewhere in your answer.

4 Explain why human growth and development can't be wholly or completely explained by genetics.

5 Define the term social class and explain how a person's life chances may be influenced by his or her social class position.

Biological theories of development

SO FAR, WE HAVE investigated factors affecting development without going into detail about particular theories. A theory is a set of ideas that explains something. Theories of human growth and development are sets or patterns of often speculative ideas, that seek to explain the nature of growth and development. We are going to look next at the ways in which biological, behavioural, cognitive, and psychoanalytic theories in turn approach key questions about human development.

We are beginning here by looking at biological theories of human development. In so doing, we build on some of the issues already examined in our discussion of the ways inherited genetic factors influence human growth and development (pp. 242–5). You might find it helpful to read that section again, because we assume a basic understanding of their importance here.

Biological theories aim to explain the processes and influences that are responsible for the shared, global patterns and features of human growth and development and also the reasons why human development results in individual differences between people. Key elements of any biological theory of development are genes and maturational processes (see pp. 244–5).

A few biologists see the child, and the adult that he or she becomes, like a robot, programmed at conception, fine-tuned during pregnancy and launched into the world as a sophisticated genetic machine without a mind of its own. The suggestion is that the individual grows, develops and behaves in accordance with the instructions contained in the genetic material that he or she has inherited. Most other biologists argue that genes don't have it all their own way, and that they work alongside the psychosocial and geographical environments in which we live to influence, rather than determine, how individuals grow and develop.

Whether they adopt the first or the second view, biological theorists do recognise that some forms of human behaviour are universal. They note, for example, common facial expressions such as anger, disgust, fear, happiness, sadness, and surprise among human beings. Given that these gestures don't vary much in different parts of the world, the evidence of a common biological influence on this area of development is fairly strong.

Recent developments in a field of study known as behaviour genetics has provided a lot of knowledge about how the genes that we inherit from our parents can affect our social, emotional and intellectual development. Behaviour genetics extends the biological theory of development from an explanation of how genetic inheritance determines growth features, such as height and weight, to claims that we also inherit tendencies towards specific behavioural characteristics, such as whether we are anxious and shy (neurotic) or outgoing (extrovert), and also whether we inherit particular styles of thinking or intellectual abilities. In this way, biological theories explain why we all have individual differences.

Evidence for biological theories

▲ Identical twins share exactly the same genetic inheritance

The key sources of evidence used by behaviour geneticists to support their biological theories of human development are studies of twins and adopted children. Identical twins share exactly the same genetic inheritance. Non-identical, or fraternal, twins develop from separate eggs that are separately fertilised and so have slightly different genetic inheritance. They are similar in the way that non-twin siblings are similar. Fraternal twins share the same pre-natal environment however, and probably grow up in the same family environment.

Behaviour geneticists study the behaviour traits of identical and non-identical twins. If identical twins turn out to be more like each other on any given trait than non-identical twins, the likely explanation is that this is caused by their shared genes. The conclusion then is that heredity plays a more important role than environment in shaping the particular feature of behavioural development that is being studied.

A review of 30 studies comparing the intelligence and abilities of identical and fraternal same-sex twins found that the IQ scores of the identical twins were more highly correlated (similar) than those of the non-identical twins (Mussen, 1990). This may be because they inherited the same IQ in their shared genes. However, several studies, also reported by Mussen (1990), have found that, compared to fraternal twins, identical twins spend more time with each other, are more likely to be in the same classrooms, and, in many other ways, share an almost identical physical and social environment. So it may be that their IQs are so similar because they experience a shared learning environment.

One way to control for, or reduce the possible influences of such environmental factors is to look at identical twins who have been reared apart. You have probably heard of studies of twins, who are remarkably similar in personality, intelligence and attitudes, even down to tastes in music and clothes, but who grew up in separate families, areas and even countries. The strong similarities that such identical twins show suggests that the DNA they got from their biological parents has left its mark, even though they were raised in different households. Evidence for this comes from a study by Pedersen et al (1988) of the personality of identical twins reared separately (see case study).

If heredity is more important than upbringing, we would expect to find identical twins with similar personalities, despite being reared differently. On the other hand, they would have little in common if their upbringing (environment) was more important than their heredity.

CASE STUDY

Heredity and upbringing in twins

Pedersen and his colleagues conducted a study of **extroversion** (high sociability) and **neuroticism** (high anxiety) using twins. Their study sample included 95 identical twin pairs brought up apart (190 individuals altogether), 150 identical twin pairs brought up together, 220 non-identical twin pairs brought up apart, and 204 non-identical twins brought up together. Of the twin pairs brought up apart, 48 per cent were separated before their first birthday. In total, 82 per cent of the twin pairs reared apart were separated by the age of five.

Pedersen's team concluded that 31 per cent of individual differences in neuroticism were the result of heredity and that 41 per cent of individual differences in extroversion were due to heredity. This suggests that our genes play a fairly significant part in aspects of our personalities that influence whether we have neurotic or extrovert tendencies.

Based on the results of earlier studies, Eysenck (1967) thought that, in general, around 50 per cent or so of individual differences in neuroticism and extroversion were due to hereditary influences. But even if Eysenck's calculations and those of the Pedersen study are right, this does not mean that genes contain fixed personality blueprints. If they did, our personalities (whether extrovert, neurotic or anything else) would faithfully follow a predetermined plan. This does not happen.

Wear your genes to work

Bernard Shapiro is an amiable, bespectacled 64 year old, and the principal of McGill University, Canada's Oxbridge. Harold Shapiro is Bernard's identical (and identically bespectacled) twin. He is president of Ivy League Princeton University in New Jersey. Even Bernard seems a little taken aback by the turn of events: 'It never occurred to me or, I believe, to my twin, to deliberately plan a parallel career development.'

The Shapiro brothers are just one of many pairs of twins to feature in a major new study by Professor Nancy Segal that provides the most compelling evidence so far that career choice, working style and job satisfaction could be significantly influenced by our genes. The headline finding in the study is that at least 30 per cent of the factors that propel an individual on their eventual career path could be genetic.

Professor Segal is anxious to side-step the charges of genetic determinism that traditionally ensue when geneticists try to argue that characteristics from musical taste to cross-word-solving ability are laid down before birth: social class, parental influence and educational environment all figure prominently too. But the thrust of her conclusions is clear.

Segal argues, 'We're not in the occupations we have by accident; I'm a teacher and researcher, and I could probably have been a clinical psychologist. But I couldn't have been an investment banker or a ditch digger. You choose to follow the job you take at least partially because you're pre-disposed to it.'

The Guardian, 3 November 1999

The environment in biological theories

Despite the claims, and the scientific evidence, for a strong biological influence on human growth and development, no academics or practitioners in the human development field believe that genetic inheritance is the only cause of growth or development. Environmental factors are very important and are often incorporated into biological theories of development. For example, although pre-natal (pre-birth) development is essentially an unfolding of programmed biological events, most biological theorists accept that the external environment in which the mother lives affects the internal environment that she provides for her unborn baby.

Figure 4.19 Cross section of a pregnant woman

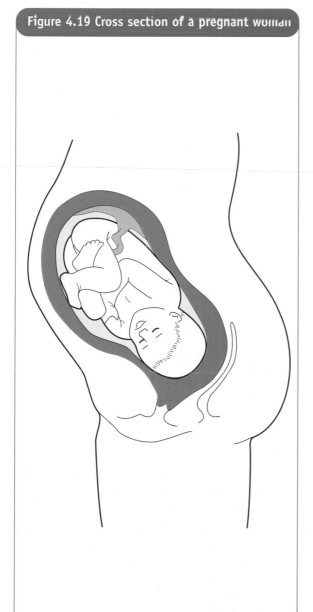

What the mother eats, for example, is very important for the well-being of the growing fetus. Babies born to mothers whose own diets are nutritionally poor are likely to be less resistant to diseases like bronchitis and pneumonia than babies whose mothers had an adequate, healthy diet.

pregnancy, folic acid, and you.

Reducing the risk of spina bifida.

▲ A Department of Health leaflet offering pregnant women dietary advice

Robert Plomin (1995) suggests that a person's environment itself is affected by heredity in two ways. First, a child's parents (from whom the child inherits its genes) use their own genetically acquired abilities to create the environment in which the child develops. Bee (1994) gives the example of parents with higher IQs being likely to create a richer, more stimulating environment for their child. Second, children's genetic inheritance, expressed through their appearance, behaviour and temperament are likely to lead other people to react to them in ways that affect how they experience the world and develop. Children with a cheerful disposition are likely to have a different experience of the world and other people than children who have a more negative disposition.

Steven Pinker, an American professor of brain science, is a biological theorist who believes that genes play a very important role in human development and behaviour. However, he also believes that genes don't determine who we become and how we behave. Pinker believes that people's capacity to shape their development is within their own control.

Like many other researchers, Pinker wants to find out what it is about our minds that allows us to control our own lives and shape our own development. The answer, he believes, lies in brain biology. The mind is what the brain does. The case study (on p. 256) sets out the example Pinker uses to illustrate his argument.

CASE STUDY

Why did Bill get on the bus?

To answer this question, we don't need to test Bill's DNA to find a specific behaviour gene. Our best bet would be to ask Bill himself why he got on the bus. Bill might reply, 'I was visiting my grandmother and the bus stops right outside her house'. That's what he believes and his belief explains his behaviour. 'I believe this bus will get me where I want to go, so I step on board'. This cause and effect relationship is as powerful as one snooker ball striking another and making the second ball move along the snooker table.

However, Bill's belief also has a biological basis. His belief is represented as a piece of information inside his brain and, in this sense, it is tied ultimately to the physical, biological level. At this level, Bill's belief is what his brain is doing. All mental activity – every emotion, every thought – gives off electrical, magnetic or chemical signals that can be recorded by scientific techniques such as functional magnetic resonance imaging scans and other long-worded gadgetry.

Bill's conviction that the bus will take him to his grandmother's house when he wants to visit is all that is necessary for him to get on the bus. He doesn't need to understand the electro-magnetic, chemical stuff. Past experience, encoded as memory in his brain circuitry, explains his belief and accounts for his action. He doesn't have to have a specific behaviour gene that makes him a bus passenger rather than a car driver or a walker.

So you see, Bill is exercising some control over his biology, rather than behaving like a programmed robot. His beliefs (mind) are produced by his biological brain, which has absorbed values from the people he grew up with, assesses situations on the basis of past and new information, and does many other things. All the things that we call socialisation – the learning and acting on society's values – are utterly real phenomena, but they have to be filtered through biological tissues. In this sense, who we are and what we do is based on biological potential rather than biological determinism. Bill's biology and genetic inheritance is seen to affect him, but doesn't make him think and behave in particular ways.

Acquiring skills

Reaching, walking and talking are universal skills acquired by all human beings who aren't impaired in some way. In that sense, they seem to be part of a genetic blueprint that unfolds in its own good time, assisted or unassisted by adult interventions. Or do they? Are some abilities innate, or do all abilities have to be learned?

▲ A baby stretching for a toy placed just beyond her reach

There are no easy answers here, though researchers lean towards one type of explanation or another. Some researchers (called **nativist theorists**) lean towards the argument that innate capacities unfold, driven by a genetic, biological clock. Others called behavioural learning theorists (see pp. 261–4) lean towards the view that genetic predispositions are much less important than environmental influences.

One of the leading proponents of the nativist view is the American psychologist Noam Chomsky. He believes that humans have an inborn brain mechanism that helps them to learn language. Evidence to support this theory includes the fact that all children, regardless of the language they are learning, progress through the same step-by-step stages: babbling, saying their first word around the age of one, using two-word combinations from around two-and-a-half to three years, and generally accomplishing grammatical rules by four or five years.

Chomsky believes that learning a language is essentially a natural rather than a taught process. He believes that the baby's brain contains a genetic package that's triggered by environmental exposure to speech sounds. Once the trigger has been pulled, children go on and eventually start talking by themselves. Provided they are exposed to the right environmental triggers, language acquisition and other skills develop along genetically programmed lines.

Most nativists probably don't believe that biology explains all skills acquisition, even if they think it accounts for a lot of it. As soon as an infant enters the world at birth, its brain begins to interact with the new psychological and social world. Instincts are what we are born with and they are initially expressed in the raw. However, instincts become tutored and policed over time as children become psychologically and socially adjusted to the world in which they grows up.

Explaining gender differences

We all know that boys and girls frequently behave differently. Pre-school age boys often play games in which they challenge each other and boast about winning. Little girls tend to prefer less competitive games, like dressing up. Are these and other sex-specific behaviours in our genes, or are they linked to our environments? The best way to answer is probably to say that nature and nurture work together.

Sometimes biology is strongly implicated. Before culture has had much chance to influence behaviour, boy fetuses are more active and restless than girl fetuses. Moreover, in the first year outside the womb, preferences for toys seem a bit too distinct to be explained by gendered norms. Boys rapidly gravitate towards mechanical toys and girls prefer cuddly toys with faces. Play, of course, soon develops gendered aspects, especially if parents insist on giving muscle-bound warrior figures to boys and cuddly baby dolls to girls. It turns out, in fact, that lots of little boys ask for dolls and other girl toys, but their parents quite often balk at the idea. In one study of almost 300 children, when boys asked for an armed and warlike soldier toy for their birthday, they got it about 70 per cent of the time. If they asked for a girl's doll, the success rate was 40 per cent or less.

But maybe there's some biological influence here too. During the first trimester (three months) of pregnancy, the embryo's sex-related genes go to work.

A gene on the male Y chromosome sets off a flood of sex hormones from the embryo's developing testes. These sex hormones eliminate potential femaleness, ensuring that an XY baby is born anatomically male. Female embryos, which also secrete sex hormones, but in smaller doses, are sensitive to and develop as a result of the secretion of oestrogen.

By the end of the ninth week, the female embryo's ovaries have tucked into place. In the late 1970s, a

▲ For various reasons, boys and girls gravitate towards different types of toys

psychologist at the University of Wisconsin called Robert Goy found that if testosterone levels were manipulated in monkeys – raised in females and reduced in males – the females exhibited a greater amount of typically male, rough and tumble activity, whereas the males in the experiment became more placid.

Monkeys are not humans, of course. There is, however, a condition called **congenital adrenal hyperplasia**, in which baby girls' adrenal glands boost testosterone levels. Research has shown that, when this happens, these girls generally prefer aggressive play and toy cars and trucks. They will play girl games with friends, but if left to their own devices, choose rough and tumble games.

Testosterone might define the essence of maleness, but masculinities come in different shapes and sizes. Tough guy swagger is just one version. Nor are women prisoners of their oestrogen. Thanks to the feminist struggle against sexist stereotypes, the category of woman has expanded to include top managers, fire fighters, astronauts and heads of state. Gender empowerment is a potent antidote to any gene.

We turn our attention next to psychological theories of development which, while taking account of our genetic inheritance, consider the effects of experience and learning on human development. In this respect, the theories of behaviourist, cognitive and psychoanalytic theorists are particularly important. We will explore each in turn.

BUILD YOUR LEARNING

Keywords and phrases

You should know the meaning of the words and phrases listed below. If you are unsure about any of them, go back through the last six pages of the unit to refresh your understanding.

- Behaviour genetics
- Congenital adrenal hyperplasia
- Extroversion
- Fraternal twins
- Genes
- Maturational processes
- Neuroticism
- Theory
- Twin studies

Summary points

- Theories of development are sets of ideas that set out and claim to explain how and why human growth and development occurs.

- There are a number of prominent theories of development. They can be classified according to the areas of development they focus on and attach most significance to.

- Theories of development can be classified as biological, behavioural, cognitive and psychoanalytic.

- Biological theories of growth and development claim to explain why people develop both broad similarities and individual differences. Genetics and maturation are key concepts in all biological theories of development.

- Behaviour genetics is an area of development research that aims to identify and explain how behavioural, intellectual and emotional characteristics develop as a result of genetic inheritance.

- The key research technique of behaviour genetics is the study of identical and non-identical twins. Research with twins suggests that genetic inheritance plays a significant part in the development of these characteristics.

- Behavioural geneticists tend to accept that environmental (nurture) factors play a significant part in supporting biological processes of growth and development, though they disagree over the extent to which genes determine development.

QUESTIONS

1 Why do behaviour geneticists use twins to develop their theories of human growth and development?

2 To what extent does research evidence support the view that genetics determines human growth and development?

3 Explain why biological theorists don't completely rule out the influence of environment on human growth and development.

4 What is a nativist viewpoint on the role of biology in human growth and development?

5 Summarise the research evidence which suggests that differences in the behaviour of boys and girls has a biological basis.

Behavioural theories of development

LEARNING AND DEVELOPMENT are two terms that need defining before we can proceed further.

- **Learning** is a process by which behaviour is changed or modified through experience or teaching.

- **Development** is physical and psychological change over time that usually leads to new and improved ways of living.

Change is the operative word in both cases. You end up being different to how you started when you learn and develop. Which comes first? This is a chicken and egg problem, so there are no easy answers. Sometimes, development has to happen before learning can take place. For example, children have to acquire a brain that's sufficiently developed before they can learn to speak. At other times, learning can trigger development. For example, new brain connections called synapses develop as new things are learned.

Behavioural learning theorists argue that development has more to do with nurture than nature. Behavioural learning theory does not make a clear distinction between learning and development. Rather, it proceeds from the view that learning is development (Vygotsky, 1978). Rewarding **desired responses**, the behaviours that you want to happen, lies at the heart of behavioural learning theory. According to the behavioural psychologist John Watson, humans are born with only a few reflexes and the emotional reactions of fear, love and rage. All other behaviour is learnt through **stimulus** and **response**.

According to behavioural learning theory, babies' ability to speak develops from making babbling sounds to saying words because their parents and others **reward** them for imitating the word-based speech. After children hit upon the correct **response** to a given **stimulus**, they receive a reward and repeat the response if they anticipate that they will get another reward. For example, if a baby's mother says, 'Say Mamma' (the stimulus) and this elicits something that sounds like 'Mamma', (the response), the mother is likely to reward this with a cuddle or a smile (the **reinforcement**). When the mother asks her baby to say, 'Mamma' again, the baby readily does so because it wants another cuddle. In this way, the child's behaviour is developing through **stimulus-response learning**. These kinds of finding about how human behaviours develop go back a long way, and were probably common sense until psychologists started studying, recording and refining them as theories.

Classical conditioning

One of the first psychologists to study and record the development of behaviour was the Russian physiologist and psychologist, Ivan Pavlov (1849–1936). During the 1920s, he discovered a learning phenomenon whilst working with dogs in his laboratory.

Pavlov discovered that if a bell was sounded a few seconds before a hungry dog was fed, then, after several trials in which the food and the bell were presented together, the dog would start salivating simply at the sound of the bell when there was no food. Before being introduced to the sound of the bell, the dog had only made what Pavlov called an **unconditioned response** (salivating) to an **unconditioned stimulus** (seeing food). In other words, salivating at the sight of food wasn't learned but was purely biological. All dogs salivate at the sight of food because they are genetically programmed to do so.

When the food was removed, the sound of the bell alone could make the dog salivate because it had become linked in the dog's brain with feeding time. Pavlov called the sound of the bell a **conditioned stimulus** and the dog's salivation a **conditioned response**. The dog had become conditioned to (that is, used to) associating the bell with the food. This kind of simple learning, whereby an unconditioned stimulus (for example, seeing food) is replaced by a conditioned stimulus (for example, hearing a bell) is known as **classical conditioning**.

▲ Ivan Pavlov (centre) demonstrating conditioned reflexes

To sum up:

- an unconditioned stimulus is one that naturally elicits a particular response, such as the sight of food

- an unconditioned response is an unlearned, biological reaction to an unconditioned stimulus, such as salivation at the sight of food

- a conditioned stimulus is one that doesn't initially elicit a response, but, through its pairing with an unconditional stimulus, elicits the same response, such as the sounding of a bell just before the serving of food

- a conditioned response is one that is elicited by a conditioned stimulus, such as salivation at the sound of a bell.

John B Watson (1878–1958) was the first psychologist in the United States to produce a learning theory from Pavlov's research. While studying for a PhD, Watson had looked after laboratory rats used in studies of learning tasks, such as navigating mazes. Although he became adept at training rats himself, Watson was also interested in human behaviour.

In a pioneering but controversial experiment, Watson conditioned an 11-month-old boy, little Albert, to fear a white rat that the boy had previously made friends with. Watson made a loud noise whenever the rat was shown to the boy. The noise frightened the boy. Before long, the boy became afraid (conditioned response) at the sight of the rat (conditioned stimulus). Watson also showed that the boy could unlearn his fear of the rat by repeatedly presenting the animal to him without making a loud noise. The unlearning of a conditioned response in this way is called **extinction**.

One of the most widespread applications of Watson's findings has been in the use of conditioning therapy in the treatment of phobias. The case of little Albert is often cited as the first scientific study in this field. It is also significant that Watson's work showed that conditioned responses occur in humans, not just in dogs and other animals.

Operant conditioning

It fell to another American psychologist, Burrhus Friederich Skinner (1904–1990), to develop behavioural learning theory beyond our understanding of simple associative learning. Skinner considered reward to be the most important element in learning. Actually, Skinner preferred the term reinforcement to reward, because reinforcement is a more neutral, less subjective concept.

▲ John B Watson

▲ B F Skinner

Initially experimenting with rats and pigeons, but later generalising his findings to human behaviour, Skinner identified two kinds of learning response.

- **Respondents** – responses triggered by a particular stimulus, such as Pavlov's bell.

- **Operants** – random responses in a particular situation, such as those that occur during conversation.

Operants are essentially hit and miss responses to things going on around the individual. For example, when a five-year-old child starts school, he or she exhibits a variety of responses without thinking about it: smiling at one pupil, pushing another, talking when the teacher takes the register, asking to play with other children, and so on. Gradually, the child's repertoire of responses gets whittled down as certain behaviours become reinforced and therefore repeated. When, for example, the pupil pays attention to the teacher, he or she is more likely to earn an approving smile that reinforces the behaviour of paying attention. The child likes this outcome and repeats the response.

The teacher's smile is an example of reinforcement. **Operant conditioning** is the reinforcement of a random response. Through operant conditioning, some responses, out of any number of responses arising in a given situation, become more dominant than others. As for the reinforcers that influenced his own development and behaviour, Skinner noted:

I have been powerfully reinforced by many things: food, sex, music, art and literature – and my scientific results, adding, *I freely change my plans when richer reinforcements beckon.*

Comparing Pavlov and Skinner

In Pavlov's classical conditioning, the consequence of a behaviour does not influence the learning of that behaviour. The conditioned stimulus is all that is needed to elicit the learned response. However, in Skinner's operant conditioning, the consequence of a behaviour does affect the learning of that behaviour. The reinforcement of the behaviour (the consequence) increases the likelihood that it will be learned and repeated. It is important to recognise that neither one of these behavioural theories is better than the other. Both explain different ways in which human learning (development) can happen and neither attaches any significance to age stages or biological influences on development.

Behavioural learning theory today

Although behavioural learning theory has moved on since the original works of Pavlov, Watson and Skinner, the basic ideas, as originally formulated, still explain a lot about how we learn and develop. In the 1960s, psychologists began using operant principles in schools, hospitals, prisons and other institutions. The aim was to influence human development by shaping or modifying behaviour through the use of selective reinforcers. Desired behaviours (including school learning) were suitably rewarded.

Under the broad umbrella term of learning theory, pupils in schools and patients in psychiatric and learning disability institutions underwent both classical and operant conditioning to get them to behave in particular, desirable ways. Right up to the 1980s, Skinner and other behavioural psychologists were insisting that the key to learning and development lay in schedules of reinforcement that shaped behaviour.

ACTIVITY

Using operant conditioning principles

An example of operant conditioning is cited by Myron H Dembo (1994). He refers to a high school teacher who wanted her pupils to tidy up the classroom without being told. The teacher began her experiment by noting how many times during each period she saw pupils picking up paper from the floor. After two weeks, she placed different signs around the classroom encouraging pupils to take pride in their room by keeping it clean. She continued checking to see how often the pupils picked up litter. The teacher found that paper was picked up more frequently. She then removed the signs and discovered that, in a week, the pick-up rate fell back close to the level it had been before she put the signs up in the first place. After two weeks, the teacher put the signs up again and, sure enough, the pick-up rate increased.

How does the teacher's experiment illustrate the use of operant conditioning?

Teachers often use behavioural theory to promote learning and shape the behaviour of their students. Here are some examples of everyday teacher actions that, in one way or another, are based on behavioural learning principles.

- Marking, returning and discussing homework promptly.

- Questioning pupils often and reinforcing correct answers.

- Praising pupil behaviours that are conducive to the development of good attitudes.

In our discussion of how behavioural theories explain human learning and development, we have concentrated on the influence of positive rewards and reinforcements in making people behave in particular ways. But what about the influence of punishment? Isn't punishment, or at least its deterrent effect, used to influence how people (especially children) behave and develop? In practice, of course, this is true. Teachers and parents, amongst others, do employ **punishment** – the use of an unpleasant stimulus or the removal of a pleasant stimulus – in order to suppress misbehaviour, but it doesn't actually help people either to learn or to develop. Some disruptive school pupils, for example, actually like being punished because they think it toughens their image, in which case punishment reinforces their rule-breaking behaviour! Naturally, this isn't true of most pupils. Nevertheless, reward of desirable responses is a much more effective (and, arguably, a more ethical) way of shaping behaviour than punishment.

▼ Teachers use a variety of social reinforcements to promote learning

BUILD YOUR LEARNING

Keywords and phrases

You should know the meaning of the words and phrases listed below. If you are unsure about any of them, go back through the last four pages of the unit to refresh your understanding.

- Classical conditioning
- Conditioned response
- Conditioned stimulus
- Desired response
- Development
- Extinction
- Learning
- Operant conditioning
- Operants
- Punishment
- Reinforcement
- Respondents
- Response
- Reward
- Stimulus
- Stimulus and response learning
- Unconditioned response
- Unconditioned stimulus

Summary points

- Psychological theories focus on human intellectual development and the learning of behaviour.

- Behavioural learning theories do not recognise age stages or the role of genetics. Behaviourists believe that people learn and behave in particular ways because the rewards they receive reinforce and make it more likely that the behaviour will be repeated.

- Behavioural theory has been accepted by health and social care professionals and educationalists as a useful way of explaining and promoting some forms of learning and behaviour development.

- Behaviourism has been criticised for not taking into account learning that is driven by simple, unrewarded human curiosity and interest alone.

QUESTIONS

1 Draw a flow diagram to show how Pavlov paired the food with the bell and then withdrew the food to get the dog to salivate at the sound of the bell only. Try to use the terms unconditioned stimulus, unconditioned response, conditioned stimulus and conditioned response in your flow chart.

2 Pavlov's stimulus-response approach and Skinner's operant conditioning approach to learning are sometimes also called associative learning. Explain why this might be.

3 What does the term reinforcement mean in operant conditioning theory? Use an example to illustrate your answer.

4 How might a knowledge of behavioural theories help parents to bring up their children?

5 Why do behaviourists believe that punishment is an ineffective way of helping people to learn or develop?

Cognitive theory

THE TERM **COGNITION** COMES from the Greek word for knowing. Cognitive psychologists believe that behaviour is based on knowing about the situation in which the behaviour occurs. As a result, cognitive theories of development encourage parents and teachers to help children think about what they are doing, thereby appealing to curiosity and interest.

Cognitive theories of development arose in part to explain that learning involved more than just reinforcement. Research into how monkeys learn suggested that motivation to learn is not only induced by the anticipation of a reward but also by enjoyment of the learning process itself. In one study reported by David Wood (1998), a monkey was being conditioned to pull a lever that sometimes delivered a reinforcer in the form of a peanut. However, when the peanut arrived, the monkey often stored it in its food pouch inside the mouth. As the experiment proceeded, the monkey's food pouch bulged to capacity. But despite being unlikely to gain from further reinforcement, the monkey continued operating the lever. It seemed that the monkey wasn't carrying on with the lever operations to win a reward, but because it found the task interesting! Cognitive theories, as we shall see, place a lot of emphasis on the learner's interest.

The work of Jean Piaget

The work of the Swiss psychologist, Jean Piaget (1895–1980), has been important in the development of cognitive psychology and in areas of care work such as early years, special needs and education. His research, much of it based on detailed observation of his own and other children, led him to conclude that the development of intelligence proceeds in four successive psychological stages.

- During the **sensorimotor stage** (0–2 years) infants experience the outside environment mainly through their senses and motor (physical) activity. The infant begins life with innate biological reflexes, some of which are modified through trial and error. The infant begins to think about its world, initially in terms of what it can actually see, but, at eight, nine or ten months, it starts looking for hidden objects

- The **pre-operational stage** (2–7 years) is characterised by the gradual development of language and the ability to think in symbols. For example, the word ball (a symbol) is understood to represent a real ball that isn't in view.

- The **concrete operational stage** (7–11) marks the beginning of operational (that is, logical) thinking that can be applied to concrete problems as long as they are related to personal experience. A child in this period can, for example, rank play objects like dolls in order of size, but needs to see and handle them in order to do so.

- The **formal operational stage** (11 years and older) is a more advanced thinking period in which the child, and later the adult, gradually progresses from concrete to abstract problem solving. People at this stage still think concretely, but can also use quite complex mathematical and linguistic concepts.

According to Piaget, all children proceed through these four learning stages one after the other. Even though the rates do differ somewhat (for example, a ten-year-old might be at the formal operational stage), the sequence of development is the same for all children.

In Piaget's model, ways of thinking belonging to earlier stages become incorporated into the stages that follow, so that one builds upon the other. Because Piaget's theory is concerned with how humans construct and reconstruct their knowledge and understanding of the world through different developmental stages, he is called a **constructivist** and his theory often goes by the name of constructivism

In some cases, of course, earlier forms of reasoning (such as 'Father Christmas gives us presents') are replaced, rather than built on, by more logical forms. These ways of thinking, or **schemes**, are inner representations of outer realities. They are what children and all humans construct in their minds in order to understand what's going on around them. Constructions are not, of course, exact copies of our outside world, just estimates. Nor are they simply right or wrong. For example, 'Father Christmas gives me presents', is an appropriate construction for a young child. It explains the presents in the stocking from the child's point of view. It is right, given the child's level of development. But we wouldd expect a more advanced explanation from an older child, such as 'Mum and Dad put them there'.

▲ Jean Piaget

deserves a bit more attention. All living things are born with a tendency to adapt to their environment. In humans, adaptation often involves learning new things. For example, a child might learn to push a door open by copying its parents' actions. It **assimilates** (takes in) what the parents do, and then does the same, using the assimilated knowledge that has now becomes a scheme (a construction).

But if the child encounters a door that opens by sliding, it is perplexed. The existing scheme can deal with doors that open when pushed but not with doors that require sliding. A state of disequilibrium exists. To open the sliding door, the child has to **accommodate** (adjust) to the new environment. Once the child is able to open the sliding door by itself, it will have assimilated a new scheme, in which case accommodation will have occurred. Another word for accommodation is learning. Through the process of accommodation, existing schemes are modified and new ones emerge.

Piaget's theory today

Although recent research has shown that Piaget underestimated the intelligence of children and overestimated the intelligence of adults, educational practice is still influenced by his broader findings. A number of important principles derive from Piaget's work. These include the following.

- When the gap between what a child understands and what is being taught is too wide, the child will not learn.

- The child's thinking must be sufficiently developed before learning can take place.

- When the gap between what a child understands and what is being taught is only slightly greater than the level of understanding, the child is likely to learn.

Getting the match right between the complexity of the subject matter and what the child is able to understand is crucial. A good way of creating a realistic and achievable learning dilemma is to set a task that, with perhaps a little adult guidance, a child will solve on its own.

What causes a child's development to move from one stage to another, from simple to more elaborate constructions of the world? Piaget attributes these transitions to:

- **maturation**, for example, the development of the brain that enables the child to walk and thereby explore its world more fully

- **physical experience**, for example, experimenting with objects, which promotes problem solving

- **social transmission**, for example, playing with adults and learning a language in the process

- **equilibration**, in which the child regains intellectual balance after finding out that Father Christmas does not exist.

This last factor, equilibration, is particularly important in the learning process and therefore

The theories of Vygotsky

The Russian psychologist, Lev Vygotsky (1896–1934) was a notable contemporary of Piaget's. His work on learning and development was also based on cognitive principles. Vygotsky knew of Piaget's research and held him in high esteem, even though he did not agree with every aspect of Piaget's theories.

▲ Lev Vygotsky

What he meant by this was that a child's current intellectual performance must be distinguished from its aptitude to learn with help from skilful others.

Vygotsky also focused on the social dimension of learning – the social chemistry that arises when children and adults interact – to a greater extent than Piaget. This is why Vygotsky is known as a **social constructionist** and his theory as **social constructionism**. Children develop their own constructions, as new schemes slot into place, but these constructions are often socialised by adult mediation. Interactions between children and adults are developmentally valuable. Human learning, says Vygotsky, is a social thing that helps children understand their culture and develop their language and thought.

At times adult culture perplexes and distresses the young child, for example, when it is told to eat with a spoon instead of playing with it. But gradually, children incorporate adult values into their own ways of thinking and behaving. In this way, the child's mind becomes socialised and it becomes better adapted to the society in which it grows up.

Vygotsky, like Piaget, accepted that children's intellectual schemes are age-rated and that they gradually give way to new schemes as children learn and develop. However, Vygotsky departed from Piaget's approach to intellectual development by saying that learning can come before, and even cause, development. Piaget, as we have seen, believed that children had to develop physically and socially to a certain point in order to be ready to learn in particular ways. Vygotsky, in contrast, believed that children's learning actually promoted their development. Central to this claim is Vygotsky's most important idea about learning and development. This is known as the **zone of proximal development**. Vygotsky (1978) explained the idea like this:

[T]he zone of proximal development...is the distance between the actual developmental level as determined by independent problem solving and the level of potential development as determined through problem solving under adult guidance or in collaboration with more capable peers.

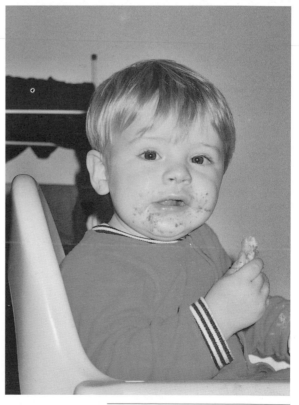

▲ Young children are gradually socialised into acceptable ways of eating

Vygotsky's theory today

Among the lessons that health, social care and early years workers can learn from Vygotsky's findings today are that:

- all children, including those with special educational needs, have potential and should be pushed to achieve their personal best

- instruction of the child by skilful others (notably, teachers and more able pupils) fosters mental development

- the teacher's assessment of a pupil's readiness to learn must take account of what the child can do now and what it is capable of doing with help.

The key message from Vygotsky for teachers and care practitioners who work with children is that they do important developmental work by promoting and supporting learning. Children learn some things by themselves, but they learn more when they receive instruction from a skilled adult. Defining intelligence as the ability to learn though instruction, Vygotsky adds weight to the dictum, 'Nobody forgets a good teacher'.

Piaget and Vygotsky – a comparison

Piaget and Vygotsky were both born in 1896. Piaget lived to old age. Vygotsky died young, from tuberculosis. Both were giants in the field of cognitive psychology. Vygotsky often praised Piaget, and they shared ideas in some areas and thought differently about other things. Both, for example, believed that development involves learning dilemmas whose mastery leads to learning, and both emphasised the importance of constructions of the world that people carry in their heads.

But, more than Piaget, Vygotsky focused on the social dimensions of learning, especially, the role of the pupil-teacher relationship. At times, Piaget's child seems like a lone warrior struggling single-handedly to come to terms with an adult world that sees things differently. Vygotsky's child, by contrast, stretches an open hand to the adult guide, not only needing help, but asking for it.

To be fair, Piaget did take account of social factors in the learning process. However, for him, social experience, while perhaps necessary, was not sufficient for development. To go forward, the individual child needs to readjust on its own terms and by means of its own mental resources.

In summary, Piaget believed that development tends to come before learning, whereas Vygotsky believed that learning often comes before development.

BUILD YOUR LEARNING

Keywords and phrases

You should know the meaning of the words and phrases listed below. If you are unsure about any of them, go back through the last four pages of the unit to refresh your understanding.

- Accommodation
- Assimilation
- Cognition
- Concrete operational stage
- Constructivism
- Equilibration
- Formal operational stage
- Maturation
- Pre-operational stage
- Schemes
- Sensorimotor stage
- Social constructionism
- Social transmission
- Zone of proximal development

Summary points

- Cognitive theory focuses on intellectual development. It explains how learning and development can be driven by curiosity and interest.

- Jean Piaget developed an important age stage theory of cognitive development. He identified four stages of intellectual development in which thinking ability gets qualitatively better as progress is made.

- Piaget believed that people construct their intellectual understanding from their explanations, knowledge and experience of the world.

- Vygotsky developed a social constructionist theory based on age stages. He focused more on the social influences that prompt and support people's learning as they try to bridge the gap between their actual and potential level of development.

QUESTIONS

1 Name the four age stages of cognitive development identified by Piaget.

2 Why is Piaget's theory sometimes referred to as a constructivist theory?

3 What happens when a child assimilates a new scheme? Explain these terms of Piaget's in your own words.

4 What, according to Vygotsky, is the zone of proximal development? Explain this in your own words.

5 What is the key difference in emphasis between Vygotsky's and Piaget's theories of cognitive development?

Psychoanalytic theories of development

PSYCHOANALYTIC PSYCHOLOGISTS focus on the emotional and personality aspects of human development rather than on the learning or intellectual areas that cognitive theorists explore. The psychoanalytic approach to development began with the work of Sigmund Freud (1856–1939). Freud was an Austrian physician who set up a private medical practice for the treatment of nervous diseases in Vienna in 1886. Freud learned a lot about human development from the patients he treated. He would sit and listen as his patients talked about their anxieties and fears.

▲ Sigmund Freud

Freud's therapy sessions would often centre on childhood memories and traumas. This led Freud to focus on early parent-child interactions, an area that is still important in modern psychoanalytic theory. Freud gradually developed theories to explain behaviour and personality formation.

Personality structure and formation

The word personality comes from the Latin word *persona*. This describes the mask worn during theatrical dramas. It refers to the relatively stable and enduring aspects of individuals that distinguish them from other people. Effectively, every human being develops a unique personality and identity. The development of personality is a dynamic and evolving process. Things are always changing and developing, even though the qualities of a person's personality remains relatively consistent over time.

Freud was interested in, and proposed a theory to explain how human personality is structured and develops. Freud believed that the mind consisted of three territories. These are the conscious, the pre-conscious and the unconscious parts of the mind. The **conscious mind** is aware of the here and now, functioning when the person is awake so that the person behaves in a rational, thoughtful way. The **pre-conscious mind** contains partially forgotten ideas and feelings. It also prevents disturbing unconscious memories from surfacing. The **unconscious mind** is the biggest part and acts as a store of all the memories, feelings and ideas that the individual experiences throughout life. The things that lurk deep in the unconscious are seen to play a powerful, ongoing role in influencing the person's emotions, behaviour and personality.

Freud also believed that the development and expression of a person's emotions and behaviour is driven by the operation of what he called the id, the ego and the superego. The **id** is a raw mass of powerful, unruly energies that are pleasure-seeking and that demand satisfaction. The operation of the id is unconscious but is continually seeking outlets. The id is most powerful and is least checked when we are in our infancy. Newborn babies are completely dependent on others to satisfy their needs. The powerful, demanding id causes the baby to kick and scream and react angrily when its needs are not immediately met. The simple pleasure-seeking of the id has to be controlled if the child is to adjust to a society in which he or she is not the centre of the universe.

The development of the **ego** begins when the child becomes aware that it will have to adjust its demands to fit in with the world around it. The **superego**

Figure 4.20: Freud's model of the human mind

The conscious level

The 'tip' of the iceberg consists of what we are aware of at any moment in time. For example, right now your conscious mind includes the words you are reading on this page. This level handles all the information which you receive from the outside world through your eyes and other senses.

The pre-conscious level

This level lies just below the surface of consciousness. It can we compared to a filing cabinet where we store everything we need to remember. The material in the preconscious level can easily be brought into conscious awareness. For example, at the moment you are probably not thinking about the taste in your mouth – but you are now!

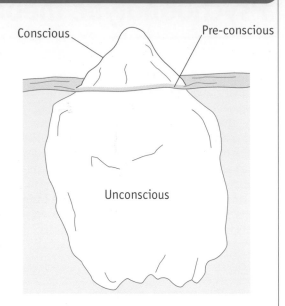

The unconscious level

According to Freud, the largest part of the iceberg is the unconscious, which contains all our instinctual drives and repressed memories, thoughts and experiences. The unconscious consists of material which we keep from conscious awareness because it may cause us psychological distress. Although we are not aware of these repressed memories, they are able to influence our behaviour. The unconscious contains our 'secret files' which are beyond the direct reach of memory. As a result, Freud believed that the real study of the mind involved probing beneath the surface of consciousness.

---

develops later, when the child incorporates the standards of behaviour of people whose approval it values. The superego is like the child's conscience, as it acts as an internal control on impulsive behaviour.

Psychosexual development

Freud's theories suggest that human development evolves as people progress through stages in which the basic instinctual sexual energy (called the **libido**) seeks expression in ways that are progressively more sophisticated. When Freud used the term **sexual energy**, he meant it in the broad sense of any pleasurable bodily sensation. This obviously includes the current, everyday use of the phrase but also refers to other sensual acts and experiences, such as eating.

According to Freud, the greatest source of pleasure for an infant is being fed. During feeding, particularly breast feeding, the child's attention becomes focused on the person providing the nourishment. In most cases, this is the mother. Freud referred to early infancy (from birth to age one) as the **oral stage** of the child's development. This is when the baby's oral organs – lips, mouth and tongue – are its main means of obtaining the pleasure of feeding. Freudian theory claims that a

happy, balanced oral stage can tilt a child towards a happy adulthood. On the other hand, insufficient or excessive gratification during the oral stage can lead to psychological problems in later life. For example, overindulgence can spoil a child, resulting in an overdependent adult.

During the second year of life, the anus and defecation become important sources of sensory pleasure for the child. Interactions between child and parents concerning toilet training take on special significance. It is from the age of one to three years – **the anal stage** – that other adult predispositions are formed. For example, refusing to defecate when it is appropriate to do so, can lead to obsessive cleanliness in adulthood. Toilet training routines cause the child to experience restrictions of the id impulses, but it also learns that it can challenge parental authority by rebelling against the training routine.

At around the age of three years, the child enters the **phallic stage**, which lasts until age six. In this period, the child's genital organs provide the main source of sensory pleasure.

During the phallic stage, children develop sexual desire for the opposite sex parent and hostility towards the same-sex parent, who is seen as a sexual rival. Boys fall in love with their mother and resent their father,

Figure 4.21: Freud's stages of psychosexual development

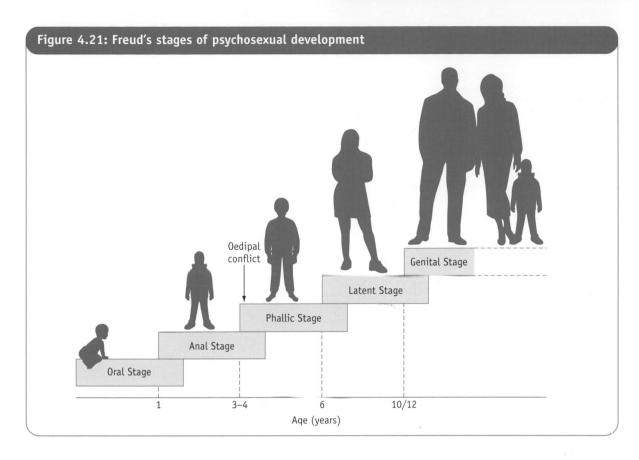

and girls long for their father and are jealous of their mother. This sexual attachment to opposite sex parents and hostility towards same sex parents is known, in the case of the boy, as the **Oedipus complex**, and, in the case of the girl, as the **Electra complex**. Faced with these powerful sexual urges, the child's mind does battle with its body's instincts. During the struggle, the id (the impulsive, instinct-driven part of the mind), is refereed by the ego (the growing self-awareness of the mind). Out of the tug-of-war, the child, fearful yet loving of the opposite sex parent, develops a superego (the conscience of the mind).

The phallic stage is followed by the **latency stage**, lasting from around age six to puberty. During this time, child sexuality seems to lie dormant and children concentrate on same-sex friendships. The **genital stage** comes next, beginning at puberty and lasting, more or less, for the rest of a person's life. Sexual interest is reawakened, and, for most people, the pursuit of opposite sex partners is the norm. Freud viewed adolescence as the final stage of personality development that lasts for the rest of our lives, but he also believed that the child within never completely disappears, as some of the drives from our oral, anal and phallic stages remain repressed in the unconscious, and are occasionally expressed.

Freud believed that people who have difficulty in passing through any particular stage of psychosexual development will find this reflected in their adult behaviour and personality. Unresolved oedipal conflicts may produce a person who has difficulty with authority figures and a poor sense of sexual identity. Anal personality types may show stubbornness, independence and possessiveness.

A number of theories stemming from Freud's psychoanalytic psychology keep faith with his assumption that the quality of parent-child relations have a bearing on later psychological well-being. On the first page of his mould-breaking book, *Child Care and the Growth of Love*, (1976) the British psychiatrist, Dr John Bowlby confidently declares:

Among the most significant developments of psychiatry during the past quarter of a century has been the steady growth of evidence that the quality of the parental care which a child receives in his earliest years is of vital importance for his future mental health.

The evidence that supports Bowlby's assertion comes from many sources. These include studies of the development and mental health of children in institutions (such as foster homes), case studies of the early histories of adults who have become mentally ill, and follow-up studies of children who have suffered maternal deprivation in their early years.

Attachment theory

In their work together at the Tavistock Clinic in London, Mary Ainsworth and John Bowlby found evidence that a child's early attachment to its mother played a crucial role in the child's later development, hence the term attachment theory. According to attachment theory, deprivation of mother love in early childhood can have far-reaching detrimental effects on the development of personality. These adverse effects, though not inevitable, include a lack of the capacity to form deep and lasting emotional ties with other people in later life.

'Engaging in parenthood,' said Bowlby, 'is playing for high stakes' (1980). The prospect of happy, healthy, self-reliant adolescents and young adults depends on the quality of the attachment of the child to its parents. Good parents are seen to provide children with a secure base: a place from which children can make forays into the outside world and return to a comforting home. Children whose parents respond sensitively to their needs, offering them comfort and affection, become adults who respond in a caring manner to the needs of others. The child who has an attachment figure in its parent to whom it can turn when frightened or distressed gains a strong sense of security. And, when the time comes to leave home, it is more likely to do so with confidence and eagerness to make occasional returns.

Erikson's psychosocial theory of development

Erik Erikson developed a theory of psychosocial development that used and extended many of Freud's psychoanalytic ideas. Erikson placed less emphasis on the developmental role of sexual drive than Freud and more on the emergence of, and search for, a sense of identity throughout the life cycle. Erikson believed that individuals progressed through psychosocial rather than psychosexual stages of development throughout life. Erikson identified eight stages of development (see Figure 4.22 on p. 278). Each stage centres on a psychosocial developmental crisis or dilemma involving two conflicting personality characteristics. Health, social care and early years practitioners have used Erikson's theory of development as a way of understanding service users' needs and difficulties at different life stages.

Erikson theorised that people have to take on and resolve a particular psychological crisis or dilemma in each age stage. Each of these developmental tasks is linked to the changing social demands made upon people at different points in their life. If a dilemma is not resolved during the appropriate stage, psychological and developmental problems are carried into the subsequent stages. This makes resolution of the next development dilemma more difficult. The early stages of Erikson's psychosocial theory are seen to be particularly important in providing the basis for social and personality development.

Psychoanalytic theory and development

As we have seen, psychoanalytic theory is more concerned with emotional and personality development than physical, intellectual or social development. Freud believed that human beings developed through psychosexual stages during which they learn to control id impulses and form a superego by internalising social values and ideals. Erikson, in contrast, believed that people need to resolve psychosocial dilemmas in order to develop the qualities and skills needed for successful identity development throughout life.

Freud and Erikson recognised that many of the emotional problems of adult life stem from an insecure and unhappy childhood. A good way of preventing these problems, according to psychoanalytical psychologists like John Bowlby, is for society to ensure that future generations become sensitive, caring and supportive parents. That is a very difficult but a very important task.

ACTIVITY

Applying theories of personality

Knowledge of the various theories of personality development is useful in helping care workers to understand the motivations, feelings and behaviour of patients and clients. This role play scenario asks you to express an understanding of how theories of personality may be applied to care work.

Role play

Lee Jones is 14 years old. He has been known to the education welfare service, social services and the police for some time. His parents cannot control him. Even though he is bright, Lee often truants from school. He recently set light to a shed in the school grounds. He is a loner with few real friends. He goes off on his own glue sniffing. He also has a history of self-harm, particularly cutting his arms.

Lee's parents have not got on well together for a long time. They are abusive to each other. Lee's father, who was in trouble with the police when he was younger himself, says that he has tried to beat some sense into Lee, arguing that his own father had controlled him in that way.

Lee's mother says that he has always been a difficult child and that he was always crying as a baby. Unlike his younger sister, Lee has never been easy to like. He was often left in the care of friends or relatives when he was younger. No one got on particularly well with looking after him. Recently Lee's mum has been depressed and has been given a police caution for shoplifting.

Because of concern about Lee's antisocial and destructive behaviour, he has been referred to an adolescent psychiatric unit. As part of the effort to understand what makes Lee the way he is, the help of three psychologists has been enlisted. Each tends to favour a particular approach to understanding personality and behaviour. They are :

- Brenda Malakowski, who takes a mainly psychoanalytic approach

- George McGeechan, who is much more influenced by behaviourist theory

- Doug Letterman, who favours a nativist biological approach.

1 Split into three small groups and elect a spokesperson for each group to play a particular psychologist in the role play discussion. All the group members must research their psychologist's particular theory of personality, so that they clearly understand its main points and features.

2 Each group should write a script for the spokesperson to use in the discussion amongst the three psychologists. The script should aim to explain Lee's development from the particular approach to personality adopted by its psychologist. They must also formulate a plan of action in trying to help Lee change on the basis of their particular theory.

3 After the role play, all participants should discuss together:

- which view was felt to be the most persuasive

- whether any other explanations could have been put forward.

Figure 4.22: Erikson's eight stages of psychosocial development

Approximate age	Dilemma to resolve	Key quality developed by resolution	Key relationship affecting development
0-1 year Basic trust *versus* mistrust	Establishment of trust in relationships with others and the outside world. A baby who experiences its carers as dependable, loving and helpful is likely to accept new experiences and tolerate the unknown in later life. A baby who has a negative early experience will not establish a sense of basic trust in others and will move on in life with this dilemma unresolved.	Hope	Main carer or mother
1–3 years Autonomy *versus* shame and doubt	Self-determination and independence. The child is becoming more physically and cognitively capable and has access to a wider range of experiences. The challenge for the child is to establish a sense of autonomy. Failure to do so will leave feelings of doubt and shame about its capability to act independently and competently.	Willpower	Parents or main carers
3–6 years Initiative *versus* guilt	Developing physical, intellectual and social skills to achieve new goals. Those children who successfully do so develop a sense of initiative and achievement. Those who fail to resolve this crisis are left with a greater sense of guilt at their lack of successful achievement and expression.	Purpose	Family members
7–12 years Industry *versus* inferiority	Industry refers to the child's concern with how things work, how they are made and their own efforts to make things work. Success at resolving this crisis enables a child to assess its own achievement positively. This is an important feature of self-esteem. Lack of success at this stage may lead to a sense of failure and low self-esteem.	Competence	Other adults, such as teachers and neighbours, and peers at school

Approximate age	Dilemma to resolve	Key quality developed by resolution	Key relationship affecting development
13–18 years Identity *versus* role confusion	The person makes attempts to establish his or her own sense of identity, questioning and challenging given values, separate to those of the parents. Those who successfully resolve this crisis are said to achieve an integrated psychosocial identity. Those who do not experience an identity crisis, feel that they do not fit in social situations and are dissatisfied with the direction of their life.	Fidelity	Peer group, role models and outgroups
19–25 years Intimacy *versus* isolation	Erikson argues that we have an essential need to relate our deepest feelings, hopes and fears to another person and to accept another person's need for intimacy in turn. Our personal identity only becomes fully consolidated through sharing ourselves with another. The result of not doing so is sense of isolation.	Love	Partners in friendship, sex, competition and cooperation
26–40 years Generativity *versus* stagnation	Generativity refers to a person's concern with others beyond the immediate family. This includes future generations, the nature of society and the world in which those generations will live. Failure to establish this leads to a sense of stagnation and a preoccupation with one's own needs and situation. Some commentators feel that most adults never reach this stage. Most men get stuck at the industry stage, concerned with their own achievements and competence. Women tend to get stuck in the identity stage, concerned with establishing their sense of self.	Care	Partners, friends and family
40+ years Ego integrity *versus* despair	The main task at this stage is one of reflection on one's life and assessment of how worthwhile and fulfilling it has been. If, as a result of this reflection, the positive outweighs the negative, the person will end their life with greater ego integrity than despair.	Wisdom	Humankind

BUILD YOUR LEARNING

Keywords and phrases

You should understand the meaning of the key words and phrases listed below. If you are unsure about any of them, go back through the last seven pages of the unit to refresh your understanding.

- Anal stage
- Attachment theory
- Conscious mind
- Ego
- Electra complex
- Genital stage
- Id
- Identity
- Latency stage
- Libido
- Oedipus complex
- Oral stage
- Phallic stage
- Pre-conscious mind
- Psychosocial development
- Secure base
- Sexual energy
- Superego
- Unconscious mind

Summary points

- Psychoanalytic theory focuses on emotional and personality development. Key theorists include Sigmund Freud, Erik Erikson and John Bowlby.

- Freud believed that the unconscious part of the mind plays a powerful role in shaping and determining human emotions, behaviour and personality.

- Freud proposed that early experiences and the expression of sexual energy play a key role in personality and emotional development. The importance of attachment in an early relationship is a significant feature of a subsequent psychoanalytic theory developed by John Bowlby and Mary Ainsworth.

- Erik Erikson developed a psychosocial theory based on many of Freud's principles in which he proposed that people develop through eight psychosocial stages.

- Erikson proposed that there are particular psychological dilemmas that have to be resolved at each stage for development to progress smoothly.

QUESTIONS

1 According to Freud's psychoanalytic theory, which part of the mind plays the most important role in emotional and personality development?

2 Use Freud's ideas to explain why infancy is seen as a key stage in life for emotional and personality development.

3 What is the key difference in focus between the psychological theories of Sigmund Freud and of Erik Erikson?

4 Use examples to explain the significance of psychological dilemmas in Erikson's developmental theory.

5 What, according to Erikson, is the key developmental task of adolescence? Based on your personal experience of adolescence, do you agree with Erikson?

References

Acheson, Sir Donald, (1998) *Independent Inquiry into Inequalities in Health*, HMSO

Bee, E (1997) *The developing child*, Eight edition, New York, Longman

Bowlby, J, (1969) *Attachment and Loss: Volume 1 Attachment*, New York, Basic Books

Bowlby, J (1976) *Child Care and the Growth of Love*, Second edition, Penguin

Bowlby, John (1980) 'Lecture 1 Caring for children', In Bowlby, J (1989) *A Secure Base*, Routledge

Brown, G and Harris, T (1978) *The social origins of depression*, Routledge

Dembo, M (1994) *Applying Educational Psychology*, Fifth Edition, New York, Longman

Denney, N (1982) 'Ageing and cognitive changes', in Wolman, B (ed) (1982) *Handbook of Developmental Psychology*, New Jersey, Prentice Hall

Denney, N and Pearce, K (1989) 'A developmental study of practical problem solving in adults', *Psychology and Ageing*, 4, pp. 432–442, 17

Dillner, L (1999) *The Observer*, 3 January, p.11

Erikson, E (1980) *Identity and the Life Cycle*, New York, Norton

Eysenck, H (1967) *The Biological Basis of Personality*, Springfield, IL: C C Thomas

Eysenck, M (ed) (1998) *Psychology: an integrated approach*, Longman

Friends of the Earth (1999) Pollution Injustice, www.for.co.uk

Hartup, W (1989) 'Social relationships and their developmental Significance', *American Journal of Psychology*, 44, pp. 120–126, 8

Gesell A (1925) *The Mental Growth of the Pre-school Child*, New York, Macmillan

Hills, J (1998) *Income and Wealth: The latest evidence*, Joseph Rowntree Foundation

Mussen, P, Conger, J, Kagan, J and Huston, A (1990) *Child Development and Personality*, Seventh Edition, New York, HarperCollins

Piaget, J, (1980) *Conversations with Jean Piaget*, Chicago, University of Chicago Press

Runciman, W (1998) *The Social Animal*, HarperCollins

Social Exclusion Unit (1998) *Rough Sleeping*, Social Exclusion Unit, HMSO

Townsend, P, Davidson, N and Whitehead, M (eds) (1988) *Inequalities in Health: The Black Report and the health divide*, Penguin

United Nations (1999) *Human Development Report*, New York, Oxford University Press

Pedersen, NL, Plomin R, McClearn, GE and Friberg, L (1988) Neuroticism, extraversion, and related traits in adult twins reared apart and reared together, *Journal of Personality and Social Psychology* 55: pp. 950–57

Vygotsky, L (1934) 'The development of academic concepts in school-aged children', in Van Der Veer, R and V (eds) (1994) *The Vygotsky Reader*, Blackwell

Vygotsky, L (1978) *Mind in Society*, Cambridge Massachusetts, Harvard University Press

Wood, David (1998) *How Children Think and Learn*, Second Edition, Blackwell

Woolf, M (1998) *The Observer*, 11 January, p.1

This unit helps you to develop your knowledge and understanding of health, social care and early years care services in the United Kingdom. The unit focuses on how various organisations and care sectors have developed, on how the care system is currently organised and on the kinds of care services that are now provided by different types of care organisation.

We begin the chapter by looking at the origins and development of the 'welfare state' in Britain from the end of the Second World War onwards. The emergence of the welfare state in 1948 was a defining moment in the evolution of care services in the United Kingdom. This saw the birth of the National Health Service (NHS) and the early development of Local Authority social care provision. The first part of the chapter provides a review of the main issues and developments that occurred in these service areas.

The second part of the chapter outlines how health, social care and early years services are organised in the United Kingdom. To make this easier to understand we've described health, social care and early years organisations separately and sub-divided each of these areas into statutory and independent sectors. This is a little artificial as, in reality, there are overlaps in what is a relatively complicated care system. Additionally, a lot of care is also provided by non-paid or informal carers who are not part of any organisation and usually provide care out of necessity and a sense of duty to a relative or friend. We will briefly consider the needs of informal carers and look at their role in the care system before going on to describe methods of accessing health, social care and early years services and the issues that relate to this.

The funding of care services is a very important and politically sensitive topic. We outline the main approaches to and patterns of funding and look at some of the current issues in this area. Issues such as private sector finance and public-private partnerships are having a profound affect on how care services are developing and will be provided in the future.

The chapter ends with a review and discussion of the range and effects of government policies on health, social care and early years organisations and service provision. The NHS and Local Authority Social Services Departments are always politically important as people who vote are also service users. People always want to access to the highest quality services and politicians are under a lot of pressure to provide them. In the final section of the chapter we will look at how the present New Labour government aims to modernise health and social services in order to meet the publics demand for quality care within a limited spending budget.

Health, social care and early years services

Origins and development of services

HEALTH, SOCIAL AND EARLY years services are provided and run by a variety of different organisations. Some operate nationally, others locally, some are large, some are small. Each health, social care and early years organisation has its own history, its own funding arrangements and its own ways of doing things.

Put together, the many different organisations in the statutory, voluntary and private sectors make up the formal care system. However, despite the best efforts of all those who work within the system, these cannot cover everybody's care needs. It is therefore necessary to be aware of the vital contribution made by informal carers, that is to say, the efforts of millions of ordinary, unpaid, family members, friends and neighbours. (How the formal and informal care systems support and relate to each other is discussed later on pp. 315–17.)

The system of health, social and early years services can be seen as a sort of patchwork made up of national organisations, smaller local organisations and ordinary people combining in many different ways that are constantly changing. We begin by charting the origins of many of the services we know today.

The welfare state

The modern welfare state in Britain was created just after the end of the Second World War. Most people agree that its principal architect was the civil servant and former Liberal MP, Sir William Beveridge. In 1942, in the middle of the Second World War, Beveridge produced his *Report on Social Insurance and Allied Services*. In it he outlined what he described as five evils, or giants, which were in the way on Britain's road to reconstruction and social progress.

Beveridge's five giants were:

- want, that is to say, poverty

- disease

- ignorance, by which Beveridge meant lack of proper education

- squalor, which referred to poor housing

- idleness, which was the term Beveridge used for unemployment.

Beveridge's remedy to these social problems was a set of proposals that were greeted enthusiastically by the British people. Among them were the proposals to set up a National Health Service and a wide-ranging scheme of social security.

The proposals set out in the Beveridge Report formed the basis of an extensive programme of social legislation. Four key pieces of legislation helped form the basis of the welfare state in Britain.

- The Family Allowance Act 1945 recognised that having children was a drain on the family economy and therefore provided an allowance to families for all children except the first. Today we have child benefit, which is based on the same idea.

- The National Insurance Act 1946 introduced a comprehensive contributory scheme designed to help cover people's loss of earnings because of unemployment, retirement, sickness, disability or widowhood. People made their own National Insurance contributions, employers also contributed and so did the government. Today we still have National Insurance contributions and the main benefits that Beveridge proposed are still with us, although some have different names and different terms and conditions.

- The National Health Service Act 1946 established a free health service that everyone was entitled to use. The idea was that as the health of the British people improved, less money would need to be paid out for sickness and disability, thus saving the country money in the long run.

- The National Assistance Act 1948 was designed as a safety net for those who were destitute (in total poverty) and not covered by the National Insurance scheme. It also required local authorities to provide care services and other facilities. Much of what social services departments do today is still guided by the National Assistance Act 1948.

The founding principles

The welfare state was originally founded on three main principles. It was to be free, comprehensive and universally available. The overall effect of the legislation was that, regardless of their ability to pay, every British citizen was entitled to services, such as health care and education, which were to be made available in every part of the country. Before this, most services were provided on a selective basis. The range of government-funded health, education and welfare

ACTIVITY

Tackling the five giants

Read this article reproduced from the Daily Mirror of 1942.

What do you think is meant by cradle to grave benefits?

Who is going to run and provide all the services outlined in the article?

Beveridge tells how to banish want

SIR WILLIAM BEVERIDGE'S Report, aimed at abolishing Want in Britain, is published today.

He calls his Plan for Social Security a revolution under which every citizen willing to serve according to his powers has at all times an income sufficient to meet his responsibilities.

Here are his chief proposals: all social insurance – unemployment, health, pensions, lumped into one weekly contribution for all citizens without income limit – from duke to dustman.

These payments, in the case of employees, would be:

Men 4s. 3d. Employer 3s. 3d.

Women 3s. 6d. Employer 2s. 6d.

Cradle to the grave benefits for all, including:

Free medical, dental, eyesight and hospital treatment.

Children's allowances of 8s. a week each, after the first child.

Increases in unemployment benefit (40s. for a couple) and abolition of the means test; industrial pension in place of workmen's compensation.

A charter for housewives, including marriage grant up to £10; maternity grant of £4 (and 36s. for 13 weeks for a paid worker); widow's benefit, separation and divorce provision; free domestic help in time of sickness.

Old age pensions rising to 40s. for a married couple on retirement.

Funeral grants up to £20.

To work the scheme a new Ministry of Social Security would open Security Offices within reach of every Citizen.

The 1d.-a-week-collected-at-the-door insurance schemes of the big companies would be taken over by the State.

Sir William says the Plan depends on a prosperous Britain, but claims that it can begin by 1 July, 1944, if planning begins at once.

Daily Mirror, 2 December 1942

▼ This cartoon from 1942 sets out the choice facing Parliament at the time

RIGHT TURN

services available before the welfare state was developed were not only less generous, but access to them was limited to certain groups who had to prove that they were very poor.

The costs of the welfare state were almost all paid for by the government out of taxation and the new National Insurance scheme.

ACTIVITY

- Name six new benefits that people could expect to receive from 5 July 1948.

- What do you think is meant by: 'All this, and the heaven too of being free from the spectre of want, is YOURS BY RIGHT.'

- Do you think after reading the article that the media is in favour of the welfare state or not? Explain your answer.

World's biggest health army yours today

Today the greatest army ever assembled to fight sickness and want goes into action in Britain. It is the army raised by the government to operate the new Social Insurance and Health Service.

Nobody in this world before has had such a powerful force ranged on his side as YOU have now.

Your army's ranks include:

Nearly 19,000 family doctors;

Thousands of specialists – experts on everything from childbirth to brain disease; and

Thirty-two thousand trained men and women in nearly 1,000 local offices under the Ministry of National Insurance – all there to help and advise you with the social security scheme.

Your army's equipment:

533,000 hospital beds;

4,000 infant welfare centres;

The best drugs, medicines and instruments know to science; and

On the insurance side, a vast £2,000,000 "town" of office buildings, specially built and equipped throughout, to arrange the vast number of payments every week.

All this – and the heaven, too, of being free from the spectre of want – is YOURS BY RIGHT.

Almost anything you can need you will be able to get from these new services.

For instance, a year from now, say the Ministry of Health, the health battalions of your army will have:

Issued 140,000 million prescriptions;

Fitted four and a half million people with glasses;

Given four million people free dental treatment; and

Fitted many thousands of deaf people with the best hearing aid yet made.

So vast is the campaign planned for the insurance battalions of your army that the new town had to be built for headquarters.

"Insurance Town" at Longbenton, new Newcastle-on-Tyne, spreads over nearly 100 acres and houses 8,000 Civil Servants.

From here the greatest national insurance scheme ever conceived will be operated.

Opponents have tried to get the scheme delayed because all the facilities are not yet ready.

But on the health side, most doctors have entered the scheme wholeheartedly since the BMA gave its approval – and if the rich man has to put up with a little less personal attention, the poor man will get more than ever before.

All the same, the Health Service will only give of its best if we all cooperate.

Your first step – if you have not yet taken it – is to enrol. DO IT TODAY.

Daily Mirror, 5 July 1948

By 1948, the State had accepted responsibility for the welfare of individual citizens. Having been through the ordeal of the war and seen how people working together under government control could succeed, the majority of the British people, the press and politicians in the post-war period were less concerned about individual freedom and choice or about private arrangements. They were much more in favour of massive State provision as the means of dealing with the social problems facing Britain.

Key developments in the NHS

We have seen that the NHS was originally set up as a universal, comprehensive and free service to be funded by the government. However, as the newspaper articles in the activities show, this cost a lot of money. The principle of free services was soon challenged.

The 1950s

With the bulk of the government's funding derived from taxation, it did not take long for the NHS to run into financial difficulties. The Labour government had to face some hard choices at the beginning of the 1950s. The costs of the NHS were proving to be high and there were many other big programmes, such as housing and roads, which the government needed to spend money on. The choices facing the government were to:

- cut back the National Health Service in some way

- raise taxes higher

- introduce charges.

After a lot of fierce debate, the government decided to abandon the principle of completely free services and to introduce charges in certain areas. Dental charges, prescription charges and a contribution towards the costs of glasses were introduced.

Within a few years of creating the NHS, the government set up the Guillebaud committee to look at the problems of maintaining the NHS as an essentially universal and free service, and of keeping the costs from becoming too high.

The findings of the **Guillebaud committee** were outlined in a report called *The Costs of the NHS* (1956). This concluded that, for all its problems, the NHS was doing the best job in the circumstances and should continue to be run on the same basis. However, as we shall see, the NHS has been reorganised and restructured several times since its creation.

The 1970s

The idea of a universal National Health Service is based on the notion that everyone should enjoy unrestricted access to the same range of health care services, and receive the same quality of service, wherever they live in the country. In reality this has not been the case at any time since the NHS was set up. There have always been regional variations and inequalities in health care provision across the country.

In an attempt to address this problem the Labour government set up the **resource allocation working party**, (RAWP) in 1977. This working party created a funding formula that aimed to redistribute resources more fairly. This meant taking resources from comparatively well-off regions with fewer health problems and giving more to those areas that suffered poor health but which had insufficient resources to deal with them properly.

Decisions made under the RAWP formula depended heavily on demographic data. The word demographic comes from the Greek word demos meaning people. **Demography** is about studying distributions of people. In particular, health care planners need to know about the numbers of people in a particular area, where they are, how old they are and what illnesses and impairments they have. They also seek data on other demographic characteristics, such as ethnicity, gender and fertility rates, that have an impact on the need and demand for health care provision.

ACTIVITY

Demographics and resource allocation

Region A	Region B
Total population 50,000	Total population 70,000
People 65+ 10,000	People 65 + 7,000
Children under 5 5,000	Children under 5 3,000
Location mainly scattered in small villages	Location one town accounting for 60,000 people

Look at the demographic characteristics of the two regions in the table above. If you had £1 million to spend on funding the health care of both Region A and Region B, would you split it down the middle on the basis of equal shares? Or would you apportion it differently? What factors would you be taking into account when allocating the money?

The 1980s

The next change that we will look at here, and arguably the one that has had the biggest impact, is the introduction of the **internal market** into the NHS in 1991. This idea is generally attributed to an American health economist called Alain Enthoven and is a good example of how reforms can be inspired by **political ideology**. A political ideology is a set of beliefs and views that are held about how something – such as health care – ought to be run.

During the 1980s, a combination of demographic factors (more people living longer), the rising cost of medical technology (as more new treatments were developed), and rising public expectations, left the Conservative government with the problem of how to maintain the NHS, which was still very popular with the public, whilst keeping costs down to affordable levels.

The Conservative government was opposed to raising taxes to obtain more funding for the NHS. It did not like the idea of channelling more and more public money into a large bureaucratic organisation which it thought was inefficient and a drain on the economy. Alain Enthoven's idea was to bring market forces into the NHS to solve this problem.

So what are **market forces** and how do they work? Markets are all about the buying and selling of goods and services. To have a market you need more than one seller. This means that the buyer has a choice of who to buy from. Think about your behaviour when you want to buy something like shoes or clothes. Do you always go to the same shop or provider, regardless of the cost or the quality of their products? How do you ensure that you get exactly what you want and also get value for money? The answer is that you shop around for the best combination of quality and value for money.

How does this work in relation to the buying and selling of health care services? The internal market solution split parts of the NHS into separate **purchasers** and **providers** of health care. So, for example, district health authorities and GP fundholders became purchasers and self-governing health care trusts, such as hospitals, became providers. Health care purchasers shopped around for the best value health care for their patients from a range of competing providers. Before this, GPs and their patients mainly had to use the services contracted for them by their local health authority.

The internal market idea had great appeal to Margaret Thatcher, the Prime Minister at the time. Margaret Thatcher's governments believed that markets or market-like mechanisms were the best way of delivering public services because they:

- create competition between providers
- create choice for purchasers
- cut costs as providers try to win contracts
- reduce inefficiency and save money.

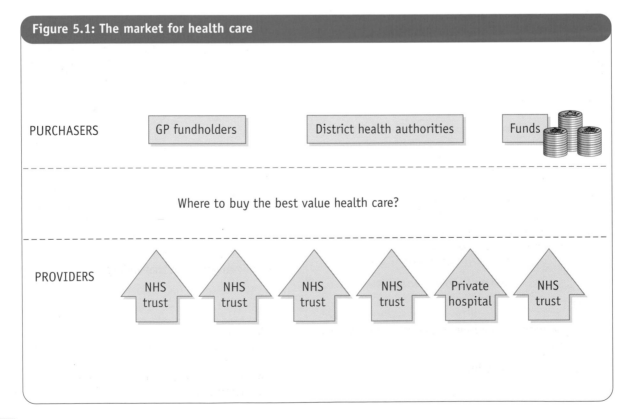

Figure 5.1: The market for health care

PURCHASERS | GP fundholders | District health authorities | Funds

Where to buy the best value health care?

PROVIDERS | NHS trust | NHS trust | NHS trust | NHS trust | Private hospital | NHS trust

The decision to split up the NHS into an internal market was one of the biggest and most radical in its history. The decision to do this was set out in the **NHS and Community Care Act 1990** and the scheme first came into operation in 1991.

The 1990s

In 1997, the new Labour government published a White Paper called *The New NHS: Modern, Dependable*, which introduced reforms to the NHS internal market. The government accepted that competition for contracts between health care providers in the internal market had distorted what should have been a needs-based health care system. A return to the old-style centralised system was also ruled out, though a comprehensive solution was pursued.

It was also felt that the general principle of giving GPs greater choice and power through budget-holding had considerable merit, but that a division, and inequality, had developed between budget-holding GPs and non-budget-holders. The answer, according to the Labour government, was to abolish fundholding GPs, and to create primary care groups in their place.

The new NHS, as the Labour government calls it, has a number of key organisational elements. Some of these are new, while others have been retained from the previous internal market structure. The way many of the retained elements, such as NHS trusts, function has been modified to reduce competition and encourage cooperation and integration within the NHS. The structure of the new NHS is outlined on pp. 296–9.

Key developments in social care services

The history of social care services is different from that of the NHS in that there was no one single body, like the NHS, set up to coordinate the provision of social care. To some extent this reflects uncertainty about what social care is or should be. Social care services have mainly been the responsibility of **local authorities** (county councils and borough councils) and have been developed for particular groups of people.

The main groups of social care service users are:

- children and families
- older people
- people with disabilities (physical, sensory and learning)
- people with mental illness.

Services for children and families

In 1945, a boy called Dennis O'Neill died as a result of child abuse. This caused a great outcry among the public and professionals alike. As a consequence, a committee of enquiry was set up and headed up by Myra Curtis. The **Curtis Report**, *The Care of Children*, was published in 1946 and formed the basis of the **Children Act 1948**. The 1948 Act made local authorities responsible for childcare. **Children's departments** were established, employing specialised children's officers whose job it was to promote children's welfare. Greater professionalism was encouraged and, over the next 15 to 20, the work of the children's departments expanded from accommodating homeless children and receiving children into care, to dealing with child abuse and undertaking preventive work with families. Before the children's departments were set up, a lot of the work with vulnerable and deprived children was carried out by voluntary groups, such as Dr Barnados and the NSPCC (both set up in the nineteenth century), although local authorities also had responsibility for child welfare. The work of the children's officers formed the basis of today's social work with children and families.

Services for people with disabilities

The National Assistance Act 1948 made local authorities responsible for people with disabilities. It laid down a range of powers and duties for people defined as:

> *aged 18 or over who are blind, deaf or dumb, or who suffer from mental disorder of any description and other persons aged 18 or over who are substantially and permanently handicapped by illness, injury or congenital deformity or such disabilities as may be prescribed.*

Local authorities set up **welfare departments** to cater for the needs of people with disabilities. The kinds of services provided ranged from giving advice and support to practical assistance with holidays, travel and housing. Payment of money was prohibited, however.

Section 29 of the National Assistance Act 1948 also gave local authorities the power to make charges for services. So, at the outset, unlike the NHS, the principle of charging for social care services was accepted even if at first charging was not that widespread.

Services for older people

In 1948, services for older people (those over the age of 65) also became the responsibility of the newly created welfare departments. The main emphasis at the time was on residential care. The provision of residential care, whether it was in converted workhouses or in new custom-built accommodation, expanded greatly. In subsequent years services such as home helps and meals on wheels were introduced, as the idea of looking after older people in their own homes took hold.

ACTIVITY

Researching into workhouses

Workhouses were usually harsh places that people used only very reluctantly, however desperate they were. Most areas still have old workhouses that are now converted for different uses. Go to your local library's local history section and gather information about the old workhouses in your area. Finding out what workhouses were like should help you understand why people were so enthusiastic about the coming of the welfare state!

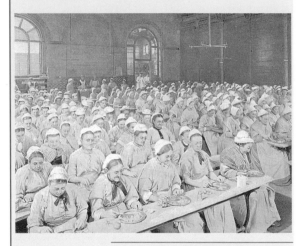

▲ Women in the refectory of St. Pancras workhouse, London 1895

Services for people with mental illness

The establishment of the NHS in 1948 meant that provision of many of the services for mentally ill people, such as hospitals, was taken away from local authorities. However, local health departments continued to employ mental welfare officers and operate community services.

The 1960s

As we have seen, social services developed in a way that was fragmented and uncoordinated. For example, a family experiencing problems might be visited by three separate workers and get services from different departments working independently. This often led to duplication of effort and time wasting, and it could be confusing and unsatisfactory for family members and workers alike.

In 1965 the Labour government set up the **Seebohm committee** to review the way welfare services were organised. The committee produced its report, *Local Authority and Allied Social Services*, in 1968 and suggested that new, unified and expanded social services departments should be set up by each local authority. The report started off by saying:

> *We recommend a new local authority department providing a community-based and family oriented service which will be available to all.*

These new, unified social services departments were to be developed throughout the United Kingdom. They were given more powers and more responsibilities. Social workers were to be trained to work **generically**. This meant that social workers would no longer specialise in one narrow area of work, such as childcare or mental health, but would have the skills and knowledge to work professionally with all sorts of social work problems. Working with families and doing preventive work acquired a much higher profile in the new social work training.

Two years after the Seebohm report was published, the **Local Authority and Social Services Act 1970** became law. Each local authority had to set up its own social services committee, and the Seebohm recommendations were put into operation. This resulted in the establishment of modern day social services departments (see Figure 5.2).

Social services departments have continued to change and develop. A range of factors have influenced this, including:

- demographic changes
- changes in social and political attitudes
- costs
- changes in the law
- changes in professional thinking about how social work should be practised.

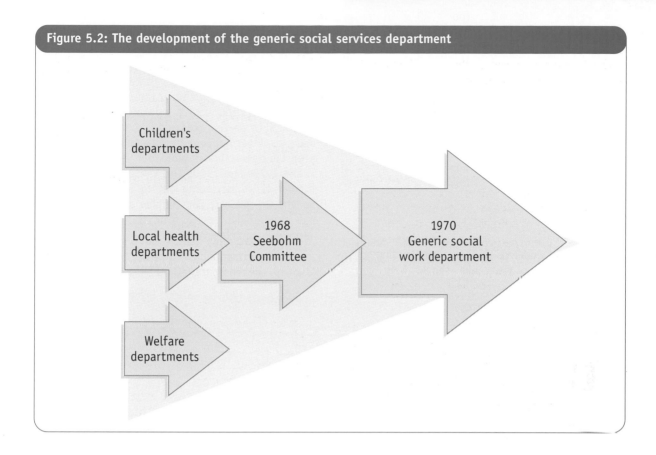

Figure 5.2: The development of the generic social services department

The 1980s

Following the publication of the **Barclay Report** in 1982, social services departments became more community focused and localised. Big centralised offices were broken up so that smaller, more local offices could be placed nearer to where people actually lived. The emphasis was on networking and working in partnership with local communities.

The 1990s

One of the biggest changes in social care was the formal introduction of community care with the passing of the **NHS and Community Care Act 1990**. This is discussed in more detail on pp. 306–7.

Key developments in early years services

There are different types of early years service. Some are exclusively day care, but in other services education plays a more important role. They have always been fragmented and there has never been just one provider, at either national or local levels.

The 1940s

Early years childcare provision has mostly been privately funded. The extent to which the State has become involved has invariably been linked to shifts in attitudes towards working mothers. Before the Second World War, home was generally considered to be the best place for the pre-school child. However, during the Second World War, the Ministry of Health ordered nursery provision to be expanded from 14 nurseries in 1940 to 1,345 in 1943. The reason for this was that most of the men had been called up for military duties and the women were needed to replace them in the factories and on the land in order to keep industry working.

The **1944 Education Act** placed a duty on local authorities to provide nursery education. Despite this, nursery education has had a low profile and, over the years, not much has been provided. In 1945, when the Second World War was over, the responsibility for running day nurseries was transferred from central government to local authorities. However, they were only given 50 per cent of the funding. This, together with a growing view backed by many experts that mothers of young children should not go out to work, meant that nursery provision was significantly cut back again.

The 1950s and 1960s

During the 1950s and 1960s, research was carried out which showed that nursery education was beneficial for both parents and children alike, particularly in areas of social deprivation and where there were children from ethnic minority families who did not speak English as their first language. The government was slow to respond and it was left mainly to voluntarily groups to help set up playgroups in different neighbourhoods to provide the social benefits of childcare and education.

The 1970s

The **Plowden Report** was published in 1967. Amongst many other points, it stressed the importance to children and to society as a whole of early childhood education. This point was accepted by subsequent governments. In 1972 Margaret Thatcher, the then Conservative Secretary of State for Education, recommended that, within a ten-year period, some form of nursery education should be provided for 50 per cent of all three-year-olds and 90 per cent of all four-year-olds. What happened in practice was that school reception classes took in more four-year-olds.

The 1970s and 1980s also saw an ever increasing number of women going out to work and growing demand for childcare. The number of private nurseries and childminders grew over this period, as did voluntarily-run playgroups.

BUILD YOUR LEARNING

Keywords and phrases

You should know the meaning of the words and phrases listed below. If you are unsure about any of them, go back through the last nine pages of the unit to refresh your understanding.

- Barclay Report 1982
- Beveridge, William
- Children's departments
- Curtis Report 1946
- Demographic characteristics
- Demography
- Early years service
- Five giants
- Formal care system
- Generic
- Guillebaud committee
- Informal care system
- Internal market
- Local authority
- Market forces
- Plowden Report 1967
- Provider of care
- Purchaser of care
- Resource Allocation Working Party (RAWP)
- Seebohm Committee
- Selective services
- Universalism
- Welfare departments
- Welfare state
- Workhouses

Summary points

- The modern welfare state was created after the Second World War, to great public acclaim, following the recommendations of the Beveridge Report.

- The NHS was originally set up to be universal, comprehensive, free at the point of delivery and available to all in need.

- Welfare state proposals envisaged health and welfare services being provided and paid for by the government out of tax revenue.

- The high costs of the NHS led to charges being introduced very soon after it was created.

- Demographic factors have an important impact on provision of services and allocation of resources.

- Demographic data are used by the NHS to ensure that health care is distributed where it is most needed.

- Because of demographic factors, rising costs, and political ideology, the Conservative government decided to introduce an internal market into the NHS in 1990.

- The provision of social care has always been the responsibility of local authorities and not of a national body.

- Unified social services departments were set up in 1970. There were previously separate children's, welfare and health departments.

- The next biggest shake-up of social care for adults was when community care was formally introduced in the early 1990s.

- The demand for early years services is linked to women's participation in the labour market.

- Early years services have always been run by a range of providers and have traditionally had the least national or local coordination.

- The Plowden Report recommended that pre-school education should be taken more seriously and the 1960s–80s saw a growth of all kinds of early years provision.

QUESTIONS

1 What were Beveridge's five giants? Identify them using his terms and explain how we would describe them today.

2 Identify four major pieces of post-war legislation that followed the Beveridge Report.

3 What was it about the welfare state that made it a universal service? In your answer, explain why the welfare situation before the creation of the welfare state could not be described as universal.

4 Why were charges introduced into the NHS?

5 Briefly explain how social services were organised before the Seebohm Report and explain how the report changed this. As part of your answer use the word generic.

6 Give two reasons why the number of early years services have increased over the last 40 years.

The organisation of health care services

To understand the basic structure and responsibilities of the various agencies and individuals in health, social and early years services it makes sense to separate them out and take each type of service provider in turn. This is because, as we have seen, each service has its own distinct origins and has developed in its own way.

However, it makes sense at the outset to make sure that some key terms are fully understood in the context of health, social and early years services.

The statutory sector

Health care services are mainly dominated by one large statutory organisation, the NHS. The word **statutory** comes from the word statute, meaning law. **Statutory organisations** are those that have been set up by law and whose responsibilities are laid down in law. We have seen how the NHS was set up when a law – the National Health Service Act 1948 – was passed. Local authority social services departments are also statutory organisations. They were created by the Social Services Act 1970. Laws also set out how a service should operate in terms of duties and powers. A duty means that an organisation must carry out certain specified activities, whereas a power gives an organisation the choice of carrying out an activity if it decides to.

Types of care

Statutory health services provide three main types of care. These are primary health care, secondary health care and tertiary health care.

The term **primary health care** describes health care that is provided by professionals who work in the community and who can be contacted directly by the public. They include GPs, health visitors, district nurses, chiropodists and others. They are called primary health care workers because they are most people's first, or primary, port of call when they are concerned about some aspect of their health. For a lot of people, seeing someone in the primary health sector is sufficient.

The term **secondary health care** refers to hospital services. This includes treatments provided for inpatients, day cases, outpatients and patients who attend wards for treatment such as dialysis. Hospital services are usually the second, or secondary, port of call, once people have seen their GP. Accident and emergency cases are the obvious exception to this.

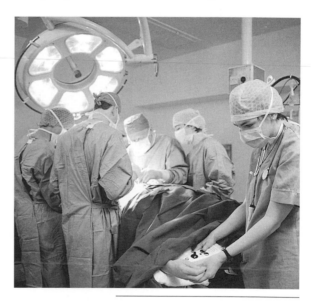

▲ Secondary health care includes treatment for inpatients

"Quick, let me through! I'm a Primary Health Care Provider"

The term **tertiary health care** is used to describe even more specialised services such as the Hospital for Sick Children at Great Ormond Street, Moorfields Eye Hospital, and the National Hospital for Neurology and Neurosurgery, all in London. These services are centres of excellence in their fields of medicine. Patients are referred to these services when highly-specialised treatments are required which are not necessarily available in the local general hospital.

The structure of the NHS

The Department of Health

The **Department of Health** is the central government department that has general responsibility for promoting the health of the people. The **Secretary of State for Health** is the minister in central government with overall responsibility for health in England. He or she also has overall responsibility for the National Health Service in England. (For information about health services in Northern Ireland, Wales and Scotland, see pp. 298–9.)

Like all departments in the government, the Department of Health gets its money from the Treasury, which is the central government department responsible for balancing the country's finances. Every year, negotiations take place to decide how much this figure will be. The Department of Health competes for money with all the other central government departments, such as education, defence, environment and the Home Office. It never gets as much money as it wants, so one of its functions is to set priorities for expenditure.

In 1990, the gross sum given to the Department of Health by the Treasury was around £29 billion. By the late 1990s this figure was closer to £40 billion. These figures should give you an idea of the sheer scale of health-related activity in the UK. The National Health Service is one of the single biggest organisations in Europe.

The Department of Health is the first point of entry in the health care system for government funds. These funds are then channelled throughout the various parts of the NHS. The Department of Health decides how health in general will be promoted and how the NHS in particular will operate. Through official documents such as Department of Health circulars and other regulatory guidance, the Department of Health tells other departments within the field of health and social care what to do.

The Department of Health has a broad range of responsibilities including public health, social care, nursing and the NHS Executive. As far as the NHS is concerned the Department of Health's role is one of strategic decision making and of setting out the overall direction of the NHS. The Chief Medical Officer is a doctor and provides medical advice to the whole department. However, final policy decisions are made by government ministers.

NHS Executive

The NHS Executive is part of the Department of Health. It is based in Leeds and has eight regional offices in England. It was first set up in the 1980s by a Conservative government under Margaret Thatcher. It was part of a widespread introduction of managers at all levels of the NHS at the time. The aim of this strategy was to improve financial performance and efficiency. Before this, the NHS was mainly run by the medical profession and by health administrators. One of the effects of setting up an NHS Executive under a chief executive (top manager) was to diminish some of the powers of the doctors. The idea was that specialist managers would have better expertise in managing resources, setting and meeting targets and negotiating contracts, thereby leaving doctors to concentrate more on what they are expert at – their clinical practice.

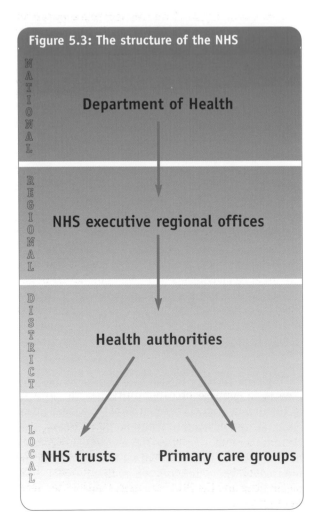

Figure 5.3: The structure of the NHS

NATIONAL — Department of Health

REGIONAL — NHS executive regional offices

DISTRICT — Health authorities

LOCAL — NHS trusts   Primary care groups

The main functions of the NHS Executive are to:

- secure resources from the Treasury and make allocations of money to health authorities, in order that they can arrange the provision of health care

- set up priorities for service agreements between health authorities and providers

- develop national policies on human resources

- develop the national research and development and information technology strategies

- make allocations of money to providers organisations such as hospital trusts, for capital building and equipment programmes.

NHS Executive regional offices

Regional offices are required to ensure that NHS trusts, primary care groups, local authorities and health authorities all work together efficiently and in partnership. There are eight NHS Executive regional offices covering England, with one each for Scotland, Wales and Northern Ireland.

Health authorities

The role of health authorities in England and Wales is to assess the health needs of the local population and make arrangements for services to be provided by NHS trusts and other agencies. Since 1997, health authorities have been required to:

- work in partnership with other local agencies and organisations

- support and oversee primary care groups

- commission health care for their area over and above that commissioned by primary care groups

- establish local health targets and standards in the light of national priorities

- work with local authorities to produce annual community care and children's services plans.

NHS trusts

NHS trusts are providers of health services within the NHS. They need not just be hospitals. Community health services, ambulance services and mental health services are all examples of health services that can be delivered by NHS trusts.

NHS trusts were created by the NHS and Community Care Act 1990. They were part of the plan to create an internal market in the NHS. By March 1994 there were 419 trusts competing for contracts from health care purchasers. The reform of the internal market introduced by the Labour government since 1997 has reduced competition between NHS trusts.

NHS trusts are the key providers of secondary-level health care through hospitals and via community-based services. However, NHS trusts now have to establish formal, cooperative links with primary care groups through long-term service agreements. These three-year agreements set out what services will be provided at what cost, and have to incorporate national and local health targets and standards.

Primary care groups

Primary care groups (PCGs) are now a key feature of the primary care-led NHS. Each PCG typically covers a population of about 100,000 and their functions include.

- the management and planning of primary health care services in their area

- ensuring cooperation and joint working with other agencies in the area such as local authority social services departments

- commissioning health care services that they cannot deliver themselves, such as specialist treatments from NHS trusts.

Primary care groups then, are made up of all the GPs, health visitors and community nurses in an area and are responsible for commissioning services for the local community. They also have a close working relationship with social services departments. Ultimately, primary care groups may become free-standing primary care trusts, with responsibility for running community hospitals and community health services. GPs will remain as independent contractors to the NHS.

These arrangements have modified the system that existed under the internal market. Instead of having thousands of commissioner and fundholding groups, the new system of primary care groups means that there are fewer commissioners with more purchasing power. They have the freedom to make decisions about how they use resources. They control a single unified budget that gives maximum choice to GPs and community nurses about how best to meet individual patient needs.

Community health councils

The main purpose of community health councils (CHCs) is to represent the interests of the general public in local areas. Although CHCs are statutory bodies, they are independent of the NHS management structure. Community health council members are volunteers who are appointed by voluntary organisations, local authorities and the NHS Executive. Usually they serve for four years.

The role of community health councils is to monitor the quality of local health services and assist with any complaints people may have. They are a means by which people can make their views about the NHS known. Community health councils also have a statutory right to be consulted about major changes in the way local services are delivered. For example, they would need to be consulted if a NHS trust planned to cut back the number of health visitors and redeploy them.

Community health councils can only be truly effective and representative if people are aware of them and understand their functions and purpose. In reality, very few ordinary people know what they are and what they do. This somewhat weakens their role as the voice of the ordinary patient.

The structure of the NHS in Northern Ireland

The Department of Health and Social Services (DHSS) is the central government department in Northern Ireland which is required by law to secure the provision of an integrated service that promotes the health and social welfare of the population. Health Services in Northern Ireland are managed by the Health and Social Services Executive (HSSE).

Health and Social Services Executive

The Health and Social Services Executive is the Northern Ireland counterpart to the NHS Executive in England. It is headed by a chief executive who is supported by six directors. Its primary purpose is to secure improvements to the health and social well-being of people in Northern Ireland.

Health and social services boards

There are four health and social services boards in Northern Ireland (Northern, Southern, Eastern and Western). They act as agents of the DHSS in planning, commissioning and purchasing health and social services for residents in their areas. They function in a similar way to health authorities in England.

As commissioners and purchasers, boards are required to plan, secure and pay for the services needed to meet the health and social care needs of their population. In deciding which services are needed, the boards assess the population's health and social care needs by collecting information about patterns of death, illness and community care needs and by consulting local people. They also liaise with GPs and statutory and voluntary agencies to build up a picture of the health and social care needs of their residents.

Health and social services trusts

The health and social services trusts are the providers of health and social services. They are responsible for the management of staff and services at hospitals and other establishments. The trusts control their own budgets and, although managerially independent of boards, are accountable to the HSSE.

There are 20 trusts in Northern Ireland. It is the only part of the UK that, because of the integration of health and social services, has trusts based solely on the delivery of community health and social services.

GP fundholding arrangements are due to disappear in Northern Ireland in 2000 and to be replaced by health and social care partnerships. These will be made up of primary care cooperatives, whose role will be to assess the health and social care needs of their area (consisting of between 50,000 and 100,000 people) and to commission the appropriate services.

The structure of the NHS in Wales

From 1999, the National Assembly for Wales, whilst not having the power to make laws, was given the power to develop and implement policy in the field of health and social services. The National Assembly for Wales has a nine-member health and social services committee drawn from all the main political parties in Wales. Below regional level, the structure of the NHS in Wales is similar to that of England. Instead of primary care groups, however, Wales has local health group boards.

The structure of the NHS in Scotland

The Scottish Executive health department is responsible for health policy and the administration of the NHS in Scotland. This was set up as a consequence of devolution in Scotland in 1999.

The chief executive of the Scottish Executive health department heads a management executive which oversees the 15 area health boards responsible for the planning of health services and the 28 NHS trusts. The public health policy unit of the health department is responsible for promoting the health of the people of Scotland.

The independent health care sector

Not all health services are provided by statutory organisations. Voluntary and private organisations also deliver health services. Together these two types of organisation are said to make up the **independent sector**

The independent sector has grown noticeably over the last 30 years. The main reasons for this are that:

- recent governments have deliberately encouraged the participation of the independent sector

- demographic factors such as the rising numbers of elderly people have created growing demand for health and social care

- growing numbers of working mothers have created a strong demand for early years services

- there is a lack of adequate public services in some areas.

Voluntary health care organisations

A large number of care organisations are run on a **voluntary** basis. This does not necessarily mean that they are run only by volunteers, rather, it means that they have come into being because an individual or a group of people has voluntarily decided to set up an organisation for a particular purpose. No law was required to create it. Many voluntary organisations are also charities, but not all. For example, registered social landlords, or housing associations as they are also known, have been a growing form of voluntary organisation since changes in housing law in 1988. Like all voluntary organisations they are run on a not-for-profit basis.

Voluntary organisations, even big national ones, do not necessarily cover all localities. This is one obvious difference between statutory and voluntary organisations. Very few voluntary organisations are involved in the direct provision of heath care services. Those that do operate in the health field tend to provide information, advice and support services rather than direct treatment. However, there are voluntary organisations, in the mental health field for example, that provide forms of direct care, such as counselling and psychotherapy, that are also provided by NHS statutory providers. These services, and much of the work of the voluntary sector, could also be said to have a strong social care element to them.

Private health care organisations

Private organisations are run on a commercial basis. This means that they operate to make a profit. There are different types of private organisations and it is important to understand some basic distinctions. People who set up in business on their own (such as a person who decides to open his or her own nursery) are known as sole traders. Bigger private organisations are usually one of either two kinds of company:

- private limited companies – you will often see Ltd after their company name

- public limited companies – you will see the letters plc after their name.

Ownership and management of a private organisation is not necessarily the same thing. For example, the manager or head of care of a private home is responsible for the day-to-day running of the home. However, he or she will almost certainly not be the owner. The owner could well be a sole trader, or a company. Large care companies often own and operate chains of private homes, each with its own manager.

▲ BUPA provides a range of independent health and care services

It is estimated that around 14 million people in Britain use private health care of one kind or another. The reasons for this vary, but many people use it because they do not want to wait for NHS treatment. About 850,000 people have private operations each year, accounting for 20 per cent of all routine surgery. Almost a third of all hip replacements are carried out privately and almost half of all abortions.

Research shows that over the course of the 1990s there has been a general increase in the use of private health services, particularly for dental and eye care. The proportion of people receiving private inpatient care, on the other hand, has remained low and fairly constant.

Many health professionals such as medical consultants, physiotherapists, opticians, dentists and those working in the field of complementary medicine practice privately and many people buy low-cost treatments, non-prescription drugs and therapies directly from private suppliers, such as chemists.

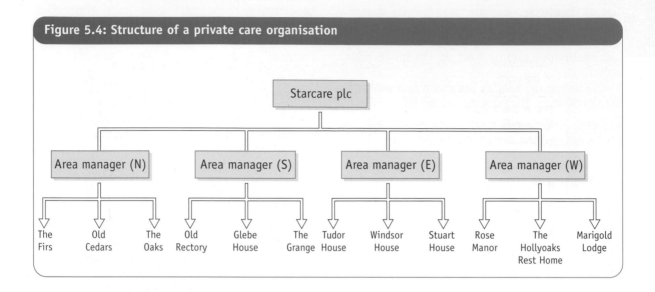

Figure 5.4: Structure of a private care organisation

BUILD YOUR LEARNING

Keywords and phrases

You should know the meaning of the words and phrases listed below. If you are unsure about any of them, go back through the last six pages of the unit to refresh your understanding.

- Department of Health
- Health authorities
- Regional health authorities
- GP fundholders
- Internal market
- NHS Executive
- NHS trust
- Secretary of State for Health
- Two-tier system
- Statutory sector
- Voluntary sector
- Private sector
- Independent care sector
- Primary health care
- Secondary health care
- Tertiary health care

Summary points

- Health care organisations operate in the statutory and independent sectors in the UK.

- The key statutory health care organisation is the National Health Service. This a complex organisation that operates throughout the United Kingdom.

- Statutory health services tend to specialise in the provision of either primary, secondary or tertiary health care.

- The Department of Health has overall responsibility for health and health care in the United Kingdom. Policy is developed and implemented through the NHS Executive, which has regional offices throughout the UK.

- Health care is actually delivered by NHS trusts and primary health care services at a local level.

- Wales, Scotland and Northern Ireland have a slightly different NHS structure to England.

- There are far more private health care providers (organisations and individuals) than voluntary health care providers in the UK.

- Private health care providers tend to offer a narrower range of specialist services compared to the NHS.

QUESTIONS

1 What are the two main statutory organisations in health and social care?

2 Statutory organisations are given powers and duties. What are the differences between these two terms?

3 Health care can be classified in three sectors. What are these sectors called? Give examples of each.

4 Which government department has overall responsibility for the NHS?

5 What are the main four functions of the NHS executive?

6 Give three examples of how people in Britain use private health care.

The organisation of social care services

UNLIKE HEALTH CARE WHERE THE NHS is dominant, social care is organised and provided by a **mixed economy**. This means that apart from statutory organisations, voluntary and private agencies play a significant part, as does the informal sector.

The Department of Health is the central government department with overall responsibility for social care. The social care group leads the department's policy work on the personal social services. Its objective is to secure 'responsive social care and child protection for those who lack the support they need'.

The Social Services Inspectorate (SSI) is located

Figure 5.5: Structure of a typical social services department

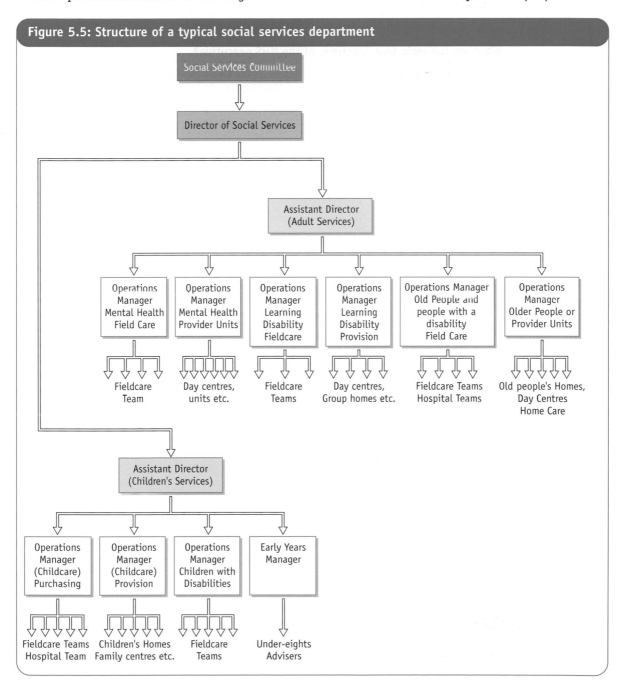

within the social care group of the Department of Health and has four main functions. These are to:

- provide professional advice to ministers and central government departments on all matters relating to the personal social services

- assist local government, voluntary organisations and private agencies in the planning and delivery of effective and efficient social care services

- run a national programme of inspection, evaluating the quality of services experienced by users and carers

- monitor the implementation of government policy for the personal social services.

Local authority social services departments are the principal statutory organisations responsible for planning, purchasing and providing social care at local level. Each local authority, by law, must have a social services committee and appoint a director of social services. The role of the committee, which is made up of local councillors, is to:

- supervise the work of the social services department

- provide local personal services

- make recommendations about social services

- provide a community care plan for the local authority.

We can see that the department in Figure 5.5 is split organisationally into children's services and adults' services. This is very common and represents a clear move away from generic social work to separate, specialised departments. Figure 5.5 also shows us that

Figure 5.6: Roles and responsibilities in children's services

The team manager
Responsible for the overall running of the children and families team. Liaises with senior management, manages the team's budget and supervises the practice of the social workers.

Social workers
Work in a variety of settings, in the community (field social workers), in residential settings, in family centres or attached to health units such as hospitals or child guidance clinics.

Child protection manager
Convenes and chairs conferences, records meetings and administers the child protection register.

Early years team
Regulates all the facilities for children under eight years of age in the area. In 1999, the government decided to transfer this function to the Office for Standards in Education (Ofsted).

Leaving care team
Team workers offer practical help with finances, employment and accommodation to young people leaving care. They also provide emotional support, advice and counselling where necessary. The main objective of this work is to help the young person successfully achieve independence.

Residential social workers
Work in children's homes and, unlike field social workers, spend much contact time with the children in their care. Their main role is to ensure that the needs of the children and young people in their care are met.

Fostering
These teams are often called family placement teams or homefinders. They are responsible for the recruitment, vetting, support and training of foster carers, matching foster carers with children and liaising with field social workers.

Adoption
Known as adoption officers, these social workers recruit and vet adopters, help match adopters with children, provide after-care if necessary and undertake section 51 counselling for people who have been adopted and who wish to trace their family of origin.

Children with disability teams
Social workers in this area carry out a variety of tasks, typically supporting families, arranging holidays, respite care and other practical help, and helping to plan for the future with health and education plans.

departments are usually divided between those units with a responsibility for purchasing services and those that have a responsibility to provide care.

Children's services

Children's services cover a range of activities that are often very complex. The work takes place within strict guidelines that are laid down either in legislation such as the Children Act 1989 or in other official guidance. Social services departments are under a statutory duty to look after and protect children who are suffering from, or are at risk of, harm. Different forms of child protection work are a very significant part of the work of children section within a social services department. Other areas of work include the provision of residential care, adoption and fostering services and social work contributions to child health teams.

ACTIVITY
The under-eights adviser

- How does Sandra help to promote good child care practices?

- If you were appointing an under-eights adviser, what skills and qualities would you consider to be important?

- If, in the course of her job, Sandra suspected that child abuse was happening, which other professionals should she report to?

Adult services

In social services departments, adult services include services for:

- older people (over 65 years old)

- adults with mental health problems

- adults with physical disabilities

- adults with sensory impairments

- adults with learning disabilities

- adults who misuse alcohol, drugs or other substances

- Adults with HIV/AIDS.

CASE STUDY
A day in the life of an under-eights adviser

Sandra Doyle is an under-eights adviser working for the local authority social services department early years team. Her job is mainly to inspect and register early years services provided for children under eight, as laid down in the Children Act 1989. This includes nurseries, playgroups, childminders, after-school clubs, playschemes and creches. The Children Act regulations lay down clear rules on staff ratios and space requirements, as well as health and safety and childcare practice.

Sandra's first job of the day is to call a woman who wants to become a childminder. Sandra explains the registration procedures and arranges to send her an information pack. She answers the woman's initial enquiries.

Later, Sandra makes an unannounced visit to the Rocking Horse playgroup. Every playgroup must be visited at least twice a year; once announced and once unannounced. The purpose of this visit is to ensure that the playgroup is keeping to the regulations laid down by the Children Act and that there are no problems. This is a lengthy visit and takes over four hours.

Sandra returns to the office to start completing the necessary paperwork and to answer her many telephone calls. In her job many calls are from members of the public wanting to find child care.

After a short break, Sandra makes an announced visit to the Daisy Day Nursery. As with her earlier visit, this is an annual inspection to ensure that the nursery is running according to regulations. All is well with the nursery and Sandra returns to the office to begin writing her report. To complete the report fully will require nearly 10 hours of work altogether.

Towards the end of the day Sandra receives an anonymous call from someone alleging that a childminder is not treating the children in her care particularly well. The fact that the call is anonymous makes it difficult for Sandra to deal with, but she records the call and decides that tomorrow she will make further enquiries.

Each local authority decides how to organise its department in order to provide these services. Figure 5.7 shows the key workers in the provision of adult services.

Figure 5.7: Roles in adult care services

Care manager
Assesses people's care needs. Works using eligibility criteria (see p. 323) to assess whether people are eligible for services and, if so, formulates a care plan.

Occupational therapist
Ensures that people can be as independent as possible in the activities of daily living (getting up, getting dressed, washing and preparing food).

Psychiatric social workers
Work with people suffering from mental illness, usually work in a multidisciplinary team made up of nurses, occupational therapists, psychologists, and psychiatrists. They can be based in hospitals, clinics or in the community.

Approved social workers (ASWs)
ASWs are psychiatric social workers who have completed special training under the Mental Health Act 1983. They make assessments in cases where compulsory admission to hospital (sectioning) is the issue.

Home care team
Home care assistants are domiciliary workers. Formerly known as home helps, they carry out a range of tasks for people in their own homes.

Day care
Day centre workers perform a range of tasks according to the service user group. Their work in a day centre for adults with learning disabilities might emphasise the acquistion of skills necessary for independent living, whereas work in a day centre for elderly people might emphasise social contact and recreational activities.

Residential care
Workers in residential homes provide 24-hour care for people who can no longer manage looking after themselves in their own home.

Adult services work within the framework of community care. Since 1990, community care has changed the organisation and function of social services departments. So how did this come about?

Community care

The same NHS and Community Care Act 1990 that ushered the internal market into the NHS also radically changed adult social care services and created the current era of community care.

In the 1970s and 1980s the fact that many more people in Britain were living longer led to a great expansion in the use of residential and nursing care for elderly people. This was largely funded from social security and the costs soared.

At the same time it was common for adults with learning disabilities to live out their lives in special hospitals or in large homes. Many people suffering from chronic mental illness would also spend many years of their lives on long-stay wards in psychiatric hospitals

However, since the 1960s academics, politicians and those working in social care had been advocating care in the community as the way forward. The idea of community care is that people who would normally have no option but to live their lives in institutions such as hospitals, residential and nursing homes are able to get sufficient support to live in their own homes or at least in homely settings.

In addition to these ideas, the Conservative governments that were in power in the 1980s were strong believers in the idea that families should take responsibility for their members and not automatically rely on State help. They were also keen to keep a tight rein on public spending. They commissioned studies to be carried out on how best to deliver social care and, in 1991, the NHS and Community Care Act 1990 was implemented.

Community care therefore came about for several reasons:

- demographic reasons, such as people living longer

- changes in attitudes towards care practice

- concern over the costs of the existing system which favoured residential care

- political views about family responsibilities

- the ideological desire to create a 'mixed economy' of care.

Rather then being major providers of care as they were before, social services departments are now principally planners and purchasers of care. Care managers and social workers whose job it is to assess and arrange care for people are on the purchasing side. Those services such as day centres or residential homes that actually perform the caring tasks are known as provider units.

Whether community care has been a success or not depends on the perspective from which it is judged. As far as the different user groups are concerned, adults

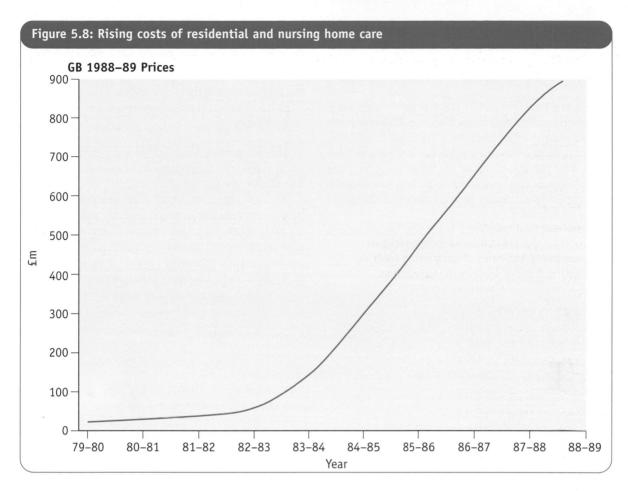

Figure 5.8: Rising costs of residential and nursing home care

GB 1988–89 Prices

with learning disabilities have probably gained the most. They are now more likely to live in the community than in long-term institutional care.

People with mental illness have had a more mixed experience. The closure of many big mental hospitals has not always gone hand in hand with the creation of adequate facilities in the community.

Older people have also gained in the sense that more old people have the opportunity to remain in their own homes for longer. However, older people can get lost between the health services and the social care services and research is under way to develop strategies for providing a seamless and more user-friendly service for older people.

The independent sector

The independent sector in social care is growing. Voluntary and private agencies have been deliberately encouraged by the implementation of the NHS and Community Care Act 1990.

■ Most residential care is now in the independent sector and many nursing homes are now run by private care groups. Many local authorities have transferred their own homes to independent providers. Social services departments block purchase beds for their clients. However, people can also pay privately if they can afford to.

■ Many home care agencies are run by voluntary or private agencies. They provide a range of services from shopping and laundry to live-in carers. Most of the time their services are commissioned by social services care coordinators on behalf of their clients. However, people can also access them directly.

■ Many meals on wheels services have also been run by voluntary organisations. The WRVS has been the main one. Social services departments commission meals from them on behalf of their clients. Some authorities are replacing meals on wheels with other forms of hot meals services. Private companies are entering the market to meet this demand.

■ Voluntary and private organisations run a number of different types of day centre. For example, a local church might run a day centre for elderly people or MENCAP might operate a day centre for people with learning disabilities. Places at day centres are usually purchased by social services.

It can be seen, then, that more and more care provision is run by the independent sector and that the role of social services departments is increasingly as an agency for assessing people's needs and for purchasing care.

Non-statutory, and particularly voluntary, organisations also have a long history of different kinds of involvement with children and families. The NSPCC, for example, is a voluntary organisation but has been given the statutory power to investigate in child protection cases and many children's homes are run by voluntary organisations such as National Children's Homes or Barnados.

Other national and local voluntary organisations provide help of a different kind. For example:

- Homestart helps support families

- Kidscape focuses on preventive polices, trying to stop abuse from taking place

- Childline was set up to give children the opportunity to talk about their experiences and worries in confidence.

These voluntary organisations are offering help in areas where statutory organisations are either weak or do not offer the service at all.

We can see, then, that the statutory and the independent sectors in social care are interdependent on each other. Statutory organisations work closely with voluntary and private organisations, whether it be on the basis of partnership, as purchaser and provider, as regulator or in a range of other ways.

BUILD YOUR LEARNING

You should know the meaning of the words and phrases listed below. If you are unsure about any of them, go back through the last six pages of the unit to refresh your understanding.

- Community care
- Day care
- Domiciliary care
- Mixed economy of care
- Multidisciplinary team
- OFSTED
- Purchasers and providers of care
- Residential care

- Social care is the overall responsibility of the Department of Health.

- The statutory organisations responsible for the organisation and provision of social care at local level are local authority social services departments.

- Many local authority social services departments are organised according to user group. There is usually a split between children's and adult services.

- Many local authority social services departments are also separated into those units within the organisation which purchase care and those which provide care.

- The duties placed upon local authority social services departments come from legislation and other official guidelines.

- The work of children's services is guided by the principles of the Children Act 1989.

- The independent sector plays a significant role in children's services.

- Adult services work within the framework of community care.

- Much of the work carried out by adult services is guided by disability legislation.

- The independent sector plays a large role in adult services as providers of domiciliary, day, residential and nursing care.

- The independent sector is inspected, regulated and registered by statutory bodies.

QUESTIONS

1 Which group within the Department of Health leads the department's policy work on the personal social services?

2 What is the role of the local authority Social Services Committee?

3 Along what two main lines would a local authority social services department be organised?

4 What piece of legislation mainly governs the work of children's services? Give two examples.

5 Which piece of legislation governs a large part of the work of adult services?

6 Give three reasons why the above piece of legislation was officially introduced.

The organisation of early years services

CENTRAL GOVERNMENT HAS not actively sought overall responsibility for the provision of services for pre-school children and the United Kingdom has a poor record on the public provision of childcare compared with the rest of the European Community. The responsibility for financing and organising services for young children has mainly been left to parents, voluntary groups and local authorities.

In June 1997, however, the UK adopted the European **social chapter**, which encourages member states to promote equal opportunities and to expand childcare facilities to allow greater participation by women in the workforce. A national childcare strategy which aims to remedy the situation and make affordable childcare more widely available began to be implemented in 1999.

Compared to the main heath and social care organisations, most early years services are small-scale operations without a complex organisational structure. It is estimated that there are around 6,000 day nurseries and 17,000 playgroups in Britain.

Social services are responsible for the inspection of the care side of early years services. The education side is the responsibility of the Office for Standards in Education (OFSTED), the government agency responsible for inspecting schools. Ofsted is due to take over both of these functions in 2001 and to administer a new register of childminders and nursery staff.

Local authority services

Nursery schools are run by local education authorities for children aged between three and four years. They are staffed by nursery teachers and nursery nurses. **Nursery classes** and **reception classes** in infant schools are for rising five year olds. Staffing is by infant school teachers and nursery nurses. Four year olds mixed in with children who are five years old perform activities laid down in the national curriculum.

If children are officially recognised as having learning disabilities they are entitled to start **special education** at the age of two. Most special schools are run by local education authorities, although some are run by independent organisations such as SCOPE. Staffing can vary, but usually consists of special needs teachers, nursery nurses and learning support assistants. Therapists may also be available, depending on the needs of the children.

Some local authority social services departments run **day nurseries** and contribute towards the costs.

Parents can be means tested to assess how much, if anything, they will pay. In many areas this sort of provision has been replaced with family centres, which provide more than just day care. They carry out assessments and work with both children and families where there are problems, for example with parenting.

Some areas operate **combined nursery centres** which are jointly funded by social services and education. Whether or not there is a charge depends on the authority responsible. The centres are staffed by education and care professionals, depending on their particular emphasis. They are often used for children under the age of five who have special needs, behavioural or emotional problems.

The independent sector

Early years provision, unlike health care, is largely provided by independent sector organisations. Organisations and individuals operate in this area on a private, commercial and voluntary not-for-profit basis. The services that are provided tend to be a mixture of early, pre-school education and child care provision.

Voluntary services

Most **playgroups** are supported by the **Pre-school Learning Alliance (PLA)**. The PLA has more than 430 local branches and is registered as an educational charity. Eighteen thousand pre-schools are members of the Alliance, about 80 per cent of all groups.

Playgroups are primarily for children between the age of two-and-a-half and five years. They charge a small fee. They are usually managed by a management committee with help from a PLA representative, and run by paid staff and volunteers (often parents) who have been trained by the PLA. Playgroups are inspected and registered by social services.

Parent and toddler groups are run by volunteers. Some of these groups are supported by the Pre-school Playgroup Alliance. Fees are low and charged as a contribution to cover costs.

Many **out of school** and **after school clubs** are run by the Kids Club Network and care for children over five years of age, as well as under-fives. They employ playleaders and nursery nurses and use other workers and volunteers depending on the focus of the scheme. They are inspected and registered by social services and parents pay for each session.

Private services

Childminders are self-employed people who use their own homes to look after other people's children for money. They are inspected and registered by social services if they are looking after children under eight. The National Childminding Association acts as an advisory body on such issues as insurance and account keeping. It also speaks on behalf of Britain's 100,000 childminders.

Nannies (and au pairs) have been up until now one of the least regulated forms of paid childcare. A nanny is someone who looks after children in the children's own house. Fees are paid by private arrangement between the nanny and the employer. Nannies do not have to be trained, but many have nursery nurse training. Nannies involved with three or more families must, under the Children Act 1989, be registered with social services. Apart from this provision, no statutory checks are made. Agencies which find nannies employment use their own vetting procedures. Several high-profile media stories involving nannies have heightened the debate about how this form of childcare should be regulated.

Along with childminders, private nurseries are the mainstay of Britain's childcare system. Nurseries have a manager and employ nursery nurses to staffing ratios laid down in the Children Act 1989. They are inspected and registered by social services, although as we have seen, this function is expected to pass to Ofsted in 2001.

Parents have to pay the full cost of having their children looked after. In certain cases of great need or risk, as with other early years services, social services may help with costs. If it is a workplace nursery, the company sometimes subsidises its own workers' childcare costs.

Creches are temporary child care arrangements. For example, the organisers of a wedding might organise a creche if there are going to be a lot of young children there. Creche facilities must also conform to Children Act 1989 standards.

▲ Day care for children is a large, and growing, area of provision in the UK

BUILD YOUR LEARNING

Keywords and phrases

You should know the meaning of the words and phrases listed below. If you are unsure about any of them, go back through the last two pages of the unit to refresh your understanding.

- After school club
- Childminder
- Combined nursery centre
- Creche
- Day nursery
- Nanny
- Out of hours club
- Parent and toddler group
- Preschool Learning Alliance
- Playgroup
- Private nursery
- Reception class
- Social chapters
- Special education

Summary points

- Central government does not ensure that there is sufficient childcare provision throughout the UK, despite a European social chapter commitment to improve services in this area.

- Under-fives provision can involve care, education or a combination of both.

- The majority of pre-school playgroups belong to the PLA.

- The Children Act 1989 requires early years provision of whatever kind to meet certain standards.

- Early years services mainly have small, simple organisational structures.

QUESTIONS

1 Give five examples of early years services provided by the independent sector?

2 When do nannies have to be registered with social services?

3 Name two independent sector organisations that provide child care services.

The provision of informal care

Informal care is the term used to describe the many care tasks performed by family members, friends or neighbours who do not do it as a paid job. Many people are wholly dependent on informal care. It is estimated that in the UK around seven million informal carers (mainly female) perform care tasks for others on a regular basis. Two-thirds of carers who are of working age combine caring and working. The Carers' National Association estimates that over 10,000 carers are young people aged 18 or under, generally caring for a parent.

According to the General Household Survey carried out in 1995, one in eight adults was providing informal care and one in six households contained a carer. Carers were defined as people who were looking after or providing some regular service for a sick, handicapped or elderly person living in their own or another private household.

Other key points found out about carers are as follows.

- Women were more likely to be carers than men, but the difference is quite small – 14 per cent compared with 11 per cent. However, since there are more women than men in the total adult population of Great Britain, the number of women caring (3.3 million) is considerably greater than the number of men (2.4 million).

- Ninety per cent of carers were looking after someone who was related to them; 40 per cent were caring for parents or parents-in-law and 20 per cent were looking after a spouse.

- The peak age for caring was 45–64. One-fifth of adults in this age group were providing informal care.

- Sixty per cent of carers had dependants with physical disabilities only; a further 15 per cent had dependants with mental and physical disabilities and 7 per cent had dependants with mental disabilities only. In almost all the remaining cases carers said that their dependant's disability was the result of ageing.

- Over a third of carers with a dependant in another household spent fewer than five hours a week caring, while nearly two-thirds of those who lived in the same household as their dependant spent more than 20 hours a week caring.

- Major care needs do not usually manifest themselves among those aged under 75.

- Over a third of carers reported that no one else helped them look after their dependant. A further 26 per cent did receive help, but spent more time looking after their dependant than anyone else, and just under 10 per cent shared the task of caring with another. Women were more likely than men to be caring unaided, while men were more likely not to be main carers.

ACTIVITY

Identifying informal carers

Think about the street where you live. Make a list of the people who, because of impairment, sickness or frailty, are receiving some form of informal care from others.

- Who provides informal care for these people?

- What would happen to these people if the various informal care tasks weren't undertaken?

Types of informal care

Many important care tasks are carried out informally. Some examples are:

- a relative helping with someone's personal care, washing and dressing

- a neighbour doing shopping or collecting prescriptions

- a relative helping with the cleaning

- a neighbour walking a housebound person's dog

- a friend calling in to give someone living alone some company

- a granddaughter calling round in the evening to sit with her disabled grandfather, allowing her grandmother to go out.

It is clear that if no informal care was available then there would be no way the formal care sectors could fill the gap.

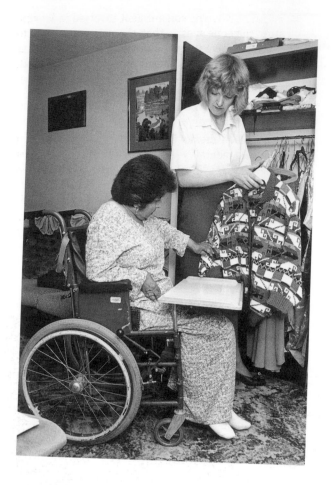

▲ Many important care tasks are carried out by informal carers

Support needs of informal carers

Although there is no such person as the typical carer, informal carers do have certain needs in common.

- **Physical needs**. Caring can be very physically tiring. This is because it might involve lifting, supporting and getting up and down many times during the day and night.

- **Emotional needs**. Caring can have a range of emotional effects. For example, it can make people tired, depressed and angry, and it can lead to a loss of identity. Generally speaking, continual informal caring is stressful.

- **Social needs**. The commitment involved in looking after someone means that the carer often has to restrict or give up going out socially. The effect is that carers can become socially isolated. Opportunities to socialise are limited and the carer may not feel like entertaining at home either, because of tiredness and stress.

Carers need breaks from caring or else their own physical and mental health will suffer. In order to have this, they need to be reassured that the person they are caring for is safe and well looked after in someone else's care. Caring can produce strong feelings of guilt and, despite the obvious need for a break, many carers are reluctant to give up their role. Care organised in order to give informal carers a break is known as **respite care**.

▶ Informal carers will need breaks from caring

BUILD YOUR LEARNING

Keywords and phrases

You should know the meaning of the words and phrases listed below. If you are unsure about any of them, go back through the last three pages of the unit to refresh your understanding.

- Informal care
- Respite care

Summary points

- There are over six million informal carers including a significant number of young carers providing a substantial amount of care for people who are sick, disabled or elderly.

- Of all the care sectors, the informal care sector is by far the biggest in terms of time spent caring.

- Over a third of carers claim that no one else helps them look after their dependants.

- The main reason why people become carers is that their dependant has either become physically disabled, or aged and infirm.

- Caring is stressful and carers need to be given a break or else face physical or mental ill health.

QUESTIONS

1 Roughly how many informal carers are there in the UK?

2 How did the 1995 General Household Survey define carers?

3 What is the peak age for caring? Give reasons why this should be so.

4 What is the difference in time spent caring between those who live in the same household as the person they care for and those who live elsewhere?

5 Informal care is unpaid, time consuming and often stressful. Why do so many informal carers, especially women, get involved?

6 Give three reasons why informal carers can become socially isolated.

Access to services

THERE ARE MANY DIFFERENT health, social and early years services and different ways in which the potential service user gains access to these services. We are going to look at these different ways of accessing the services. However, just because someone has a right, or entitlement, to a service, he or she may not receive it, for a variety of reasons. We therefore also discuss the barriers that exist to access to health, social care and early years services.

Referrals

Making an application for, or requesting, a service is known as a referral. Referrals are usually classified in three ways.

- **Self-referral** occurs when service users themselves apply for a service. This is usually done by calling in person, by telephone, by letter or by application form. An example of a self-referral is deciding you want to see your GP to discuss a health problem and telephoning the surgery to make an appointment.

- **Third-party referral** occurs when people apply for a care service on behalf of another person. For example, an elderly woman's daughter might telephone the social services department to refer her mother for a care service.

- A **professional referral** is similar to a third-party referral. However, the difference is that the person applying for a service on someone on else's behalf is a health or social care professional. An example of a professional referral occurs when your GP decides to refer you on to be seen by a specialist to conduct further investigations.

Access to health care

Access to statutory health services is covered by the Patient's Charter. This sets out what people can expect from the NHS in terms of waiting times and standards of service. There are separate Patient's Charters in Wales and Northern Ireland. The Patient's Charter is under review and is likely to be replaced by a NHS Charter in the future.

Access to primary health care

As we have seen, primary health care is the term used to describe those health services provided in the community that can be accessed directly by the public. Access to any of these services is by self-referral or third-party referral. The Patient's Charter says that everyone has a right to register with a GP. It also states that you can expect your local health authority to find you a GP within two working days. People also have the right to change their GP and vice versa.

Access to secondary health care

The term secondary health care is mainly used to describe more specialised services, usually hospital care. Accident and Emergency (A&E) services and certain specialist clinics such as those that specialise in genito-urinary medicine (GUM) can be accessed directly. However, in the vast majority of cases, secondary health care services are accessed via a GP's professional referral. This applies to both inpatient care (when the patient stays at least one night in a hospital bed) and to outpatient services (when the patient attends during the course of the day).

Having examined the patient, the GP writes to, or occasionally faxes or telephones, the relevant hospital consultant requesting an appointment or an admission. There is usually a waiting list. The GP indicates the urgency of the referral and, in emergency cases, the patient can be admitted on the same day. Because GPs undertake this role they are described as gatekeepers.

Out-patients

The Patient's Charter states that when your GP or dentist refers you to the hospital, nine out of ten people can expect to be seen within 13 weeks. Everyone can expect to be seen within 26 weeks.

A&E

According to the Patient's Charter, if you are admitted to hospital through an accident and emergency department, you can expect to be given a bed as soon as possible, and certainly within two hours.

Ambulance services

The Patient's Charter says that if you call an emergency ambulance (999 call), you can expect it to arrive within 14 minutes in urban areas, or 19 minutes in rural areas.

▲ Examples of the Charter standards

ACTIVITY

The Patient's Charter

Find out where your local Community Health Council is. Phone or visit it to obtain an up-to-date copy of the Patient's Charter and find out what patients can do if the standards set out in the charter are not being met for any reason.

NHS waiting lists and times are a favourite topic for debate between political parties, as they know that people are very concerned about how long they may have to wait for treatment.

Barriers to health care

Even when we have a right to a health care service, we do not always use it. There are several reasons for this. Some of the most common reasons are:

- attitudes
- cost
- disabled access
- lack of information (education)
- language
- location (transport)
- opening times
- waiting lists
- bed blocking.

We are going to look at each of these barriers in turn.

Attitudes

Health is a very personal thing, and not everyone takes the same attitude towards their own health. People do not like going to see doctors for a variety of reasons. This could involve embarrassment, indifference to one's own health and fear of the consequences. The Department of Health recognises the importance of people's attitudes towards seeking health care. It tries to target those groups and illnesses that create the biggest problem in this respect. For example, the Department of Health has been trying to reduce the incidence of testicular cancer amongst men by launching a campaign to raise awareness and to get men to examine themselves and seek help early if they find anything unusual. Traditionally, men have been very reluctant to do this.

Cost

Not all NHS services are free. Unless you fall into an exempt group you will have to pay for prescriptions, eye tests and dental charges. Free eye testing for people over 65 was withdrawn in 1989 and the result was a dramatic fall in the number of pensioners having the test. The British Medical Association claimed that this led to serious eye diseases and potential blindness going undetected. These free eye tests have recently been reintroduced. Needless to say, the additional costs involved are a major barrier to people wanting private health care.

Disabled access

The Disability Discrimination Act 1995 requires public buildings to be accessible to people with impairments and part III of the Act requires service providers such as banks, restaurants and shops to make 'reasonable adjustments' for disabled people. However, this legislation has yet to be implemented across the country and there are also problems in getting to the buildings in the first place.

Education and lack of information

Few people know about the complete range of health services available. For example, many GP practices offer help with stress management and tranquilliser addiction, and NHS trusts operate special sports injury clinics. These are not always well publicised.

Location and lack of transport

Health care facilities may not always be easy to get to because they may be several miles away from where people live. This is particularly true for those who live in rural areas. The problem is made worse again for those who rely on public transport. Sometimes people have to travel great distances for specialist treatments that are not available in their own health district.

Language

The Patient's Charter is published in 11 languages apart from English. This is recognition of the fact that Britain is a multiethnic society and that not everyone speaks English as their first language. It also acknowledges that sensory impairments can restrict access to information. The Patient's Charter is available in large print, audiocassette and Braille formats for visually impaired people, and on sign language video for people with hearing problems. However, not all health information is available in so many languages and formats in every locality.

Most people's first port of call to the health service is their local GP's practice or health centre, yet these facilities are sometimes limited in the access they provide to people from ethnic minorities or to people with sensory impairments. People can be deterred by communication problems. It is hard enough for people who speak English to talk about some health problems; having additional difficulties makes the barrier harder to overcome. In areas where there are large numbers of people from ethnic communities who may not have English as their first language, health authorities try to ensure that linguistic difficulties are overcome. However, smaller groups from ethnic minorities in predominantly white areas are often at a disadvantage.

Opening times

Opening times can restrict access. This is particularly true for people who have difficulty in getting time off work, those reliant on public transport and those living in rural areas where GPs may only operate a surgery once a week.

Waiting lists

It is not always possible to be seen by a GP on the day that you want. If yours is a non-urgent case you could wait some days. GPs are being asked to develop their own practice charters in order to help with this problem. Hospital capacity is limited and people referred by GPs can sometimes wait a long time. At certain times of the year, for example in winter, hospitals have to operate a one in–one out policy. Elderly patients have been the most likely to face this problem in the past.

Bed-blocking

Sometimes hospital patients no longer need health care but are not fit enough to be discharged without an appropriate care package. They might, for example, require a place in a residential home. If there are no places available, they have to stay in hospital until a place can be found. This situation is called bed-blocking and patients who find themselves in this situation are known as PAAFES (Patients Awaiting Alternative Facilities Elsewhere).

Access to social care

Access to social care and social work services for both children and adults can be by self, third-party or professional referral. In the first instance, the referral is taken up by a duty social worker whose job is to clarify the situation and to find out what is needed.

Children's services

Social services departments have clear procedures for dealing with child protection enquiries. In other children and families cases, for example, where there are family relationship problems, an assessment is made to establish whether the children involved are in need. If so, as with child protection cases, a care plan is formulated and services are arranged.

ACTIVITY

Caring for Darren

Darren is seven years old and has suffered intermittent physical abuse by his stepfather, especially when his stepfather has been drinking. Darren's mother and stepfather nonetheless have a stable relationship and Darren gets on well with his younger stepsiblings. Recently Darren's stepfather has agreed to attend Alcoholics Anonymous.

Use the welfare checklist to guide your thinking about whether Darren should be removed from the home. What factors would you take into account?

Welfare checklist

- The ascertainable wishes/feelings of the child considered in the light of age and understanding.

- The child's physical, emotional and educational needs.

- The likely effect of any change in her/his circumstances.

- The child's age, sex, background and any characteristics which the court considers relevant.

- Any harm s/he has suffered or is at risk of suffering.

- How capable each of the parents/relevant others are of meeting the child's needs.

- The court's available range of powers for the proceedings in question.

Adult services

The key to accessing adult services is an **assessment of need**. Social services departments work according to their various legal duties, such as the requirements of the NHS and Community Care Act 1990. They also work within eligibility criteria that they draw up themselves. People receive services if they meet the eligibility criteria that apply in the area where they live. The person carrying out the assessment, usually a care coordinator or social worker, is described as a gatekeeper to services.

Social services departments are covered by the **Citizen's Charter**, which sets out certain minimum service standards. For example, most social services departments would aim to start an assessment within two weeks of becoming aware that an adult has social care needs.

In the independent sector, much domiciliary, day and residential care is available directly from voluntary and private agencies. A self or third-party referral will gain access to services. Most agencies carry out their own assessments and there is less emphasis on eligibility criteria. Services are provided as long as the person is able to pay, and the agency has the staff to supply the service.

Barriers to social care

The barriers to accessing social care are in many ways similar to those that occur in health care, although three are perhaps most important.

- **Attitude.** Many people feel that there is a stigma (or sense of shame) attached to using social services, so they avoid doing so, even if there is a need.

- **Cost.** Adult services are means-tested. Service users have to undergo financial assessment. People can be put off by the costs involved or by having to disclose financial information.

- **Eligibility criteria.** As local authorities attempt to manage scarce resources they often raise the eligibility criteria for services. For example, in the past many local authorities would help someone who was reasonably independent but who needed a home help to do some cleaning and shopping. Today these services are not available in many areas and someone would have to require personal care on a daily basis before they became eligible.

Figure 5.9: Eligibility criteria for services

NEEDS	DEGREE OF RISK					
	1 Low or little immediate impact	2 Limited impact	3 Some concerns	4 Major concerns	5 Major risk of harm	6 Immediate or very high risk of harm
A Physical safety of individual			Some concerns about physical safety. Risk slight.	Daily support required in view of continuing risk of harm.	High risk to in physical safety.	Cannot be left alone.
B Physical health/ disability of individual and others		Some concerns about physical health. Reduced quality of life due to disability.	Possible risk of deterioration in health/quality of life without support.	Requires daily support to prevent deterioration in health/maintain quality of life.	Requires assistance several times a day. Carer under severe stress.	Requires continuous care from others Carer at risk of collapse.
C Mental health of individual and others		Some concerns about mental health.	Temporary or recurring depressive or anxiety state affecting ability to care for self or relate to others.	Severe depression or delusional condition affecting ability to care for self or relate to others.	Likelihood of self harm/neglect or harm to others, although not detainable under the Mental Health Act.	Likelihood of self harm/neglect or harm to others with history of detention under the Mental Health Act.
D Independent living skills	Unable to fulfil potential due to limited skills.	Reduced quality of life due to limited skills. Requires minimal help.	Requires support from others (several times a week) in order to remain at home.	High level of support required (daily) due to loss of skills.		
E Opportunities for social interaction	Limited opportunity for social contact.	No contact outside immediate family and neighbours.	Very isolated.	Rejected by neighbourhood or carer.	Rejected by neighbourhood or carer.	Rejected by professionals, neighbourhood and carer.

Most social services departments use eligibility criteria, such as in Figure 5.9. In most areas, to be eligible for services, a person would need to score at least four, five or six.

Access, and barriers to access, to early years services

For the most part, access to early years services is achieved by parents who apply directly to an independent service provider such as a private nursery or childminder. Children are usually offered places if there is space available, if the child is considered suitable and if the parents are able to afford the fees. Barriers to access occur because:

- there is a shortage of free, state-run nursery education and day nursery places

- although the overall level of early years provision is set to increase, parents will generally still be expected to pay for it

- not all areas are well covered for pre-school provision so, location and transport become problems

- parents from minority cultures struggle to find care which is able to meet their cultural needs, for religious observance and language, for example.

BUILD YOUR LEARNING

Keywords and phrases

You should know the meaning of the words and phrases listed below. If you are unsure about any of them, go back through the last five pages of the unit to refresh your understanding.

- Bed-blocking
- Citizen's Charter
- Gatekeeper
- inpatient services
- Outpatient services
- Patient's Charter
- Professional referral
- Self-referral
- Stigma
- Third-party referral

Summary points

- The three main means of referral to health, social care and early years services are self-referral, third-party referral and professional referral.
- In the NHS, the GP is the key professional gatekeeper in gaining access to services.
- Statutory social care is accessed through the process of referral followed by assessment.
- Social care is much more likely to carry a charge to the user than health care.
- Several barriers exist, often in combination, which restrict access to services.

QUESTIONS

1 Give one example each of a self-referral, a third-party referral and a professional referral.

2 What official document lays down standards for access to health care?

3 Identify two barriers to health care.

4 Identify two further barriers to social care.

5 Which piece of disability legislation is designed to improve access to buildings and services for people with disabilities?

6 What particular problems might someone from a minority culture face when trying to gain access to health, social and early years services?

The funding of services

THE FUNDING OF HEALTH, SOCIAL and early years services has become more complex since the welfare state was established. Because there is now a mixed economy of care and a greater interrelationship between the various care sectors, it is important that workers who work in health, social and early years services understand not only how their own organisations are funded but how other related organisations are funded as well. It is particularly valuable to know this when discussing care options with service users and when making decisions for yourself and your family.

Financing the NHS

Around 80 per cent of the cost of the NHS is paid for through general taxation. **General taxation** is the money the government raises from taxing the earnings and spending of people and businesses. The main forms of taxation are VAT, income tax and corporation tax. The remainder of NHS funding mainly comes from:

- National Insurance contributions

- charges, such prescription charges and dental charges

- other revenue from, for example, the sale of land.

In addition, health authorities can raise money from voluntary sources, by organising fundraising, for example and some hospital trusts increase their revenue by taking private patients who pay the full cost of their treatment.

The private finance initiative (PFI)

The private finance initiative was introduced by the Conservative government in 1992 in order to bring private money that does not come from taxation into public services. A major reason for this strategy was that it meant taxes would not have to be put up to increase public spending. In the NHS, PFI involves the use of private finance to fund the design and construction of building projects, such as new hospitals or laboratories. Instead of borrowing the money from the Treasury, NHS trusts are required to raise the funds from commercial institutions. Since Labour was elected to power in May 1997, 31 PFI developments worth £3 billion have been approved in the NHS.

This scheme is not without its critics. This is because the new hospitals are now owned by private companies which lease the facilities back to the NHS. The British Medical Association also thinks that the use of private finance means that the NHS is paying higher interest rates and charges than it did before.

PFI is a complex system. However, it looks as if it is here to stay, as it has been adopted by both Conservative and Labour governments. It is a good example of how attitudes to funding the NHS have changed since the days of William Beveridge, when it was envisaged that all welfare would be fully funded by general taxation.

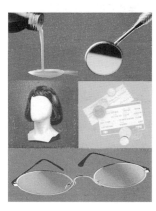

HC11 Help with health costs

Are you entitled to help with health costs?

- NHS prescriptions
- NHS dental treatment
- sight tests, glasses and contact lenses
- travel to hospital for NHS treatment
- NHS wigs and fabric supports

NHS

▲ To what extent do you think Beveridge's original vision of health care being free at the point of delivery has changed?

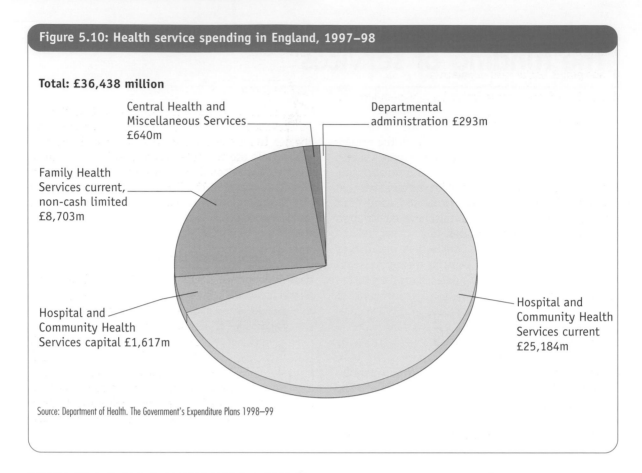

Figure 5.10: Health service spending in England, 1997–98

Total: £36,438 million

Central Health and Miscellaneous Services £640m

Departmental administration £293m

Family Health Services current, non-cash limited £8,703m

Hospital and Community Health Services capital £1,617m

Hospital and Community Health Services current £25,184m

Source: Department of Health. The Government's Expenditure Plans 1998–99

Financing the private health sector

Many NHS consultants do private work. The cost of their time is paid for by the private patient. Other private health care professionals such as physiotherapists, dentists or chiropodists are also paid directly by their patients for the work they do.

The growth in private health care has led to an increase in private health insurance schemes. According to the Consumer's Association, around 13 per cent of people in the UK are covered by private health insurance, many through employer schemes. Some people face a problem in obtaining private health care insurance, as not all health insurers are prepared to take on certain high risk (or potentially expensive) groups. People over 65 or those with a existing illness or disability are seen as high risk, for example.

Private hospital care is mainly provided by private companies. In Britain, there are three main providers of private health care; General Healthcare Group, BUPA Hospitals and Nuffield Hospitals. Many NHS trusts also operate private beds to boost their revenue. Whilst many private health treatments are paid for from health insurance, people can pay directly for their operation.

Private health providers are funded from charges to patients, health insurance schemes, and money borrowed from banks and other financial institutions.

Financing social services

In England and Wales, local authorities (which are responsible for social services departments) get their funds from three main sources:

■ grants from central government – the main source is the revenue support grant

■ money raised from local taxation, such as the council tax and business rates

■ charges for services.

Revenue support grants

Each year the government decides what it believes local authorities need to spend on the various services that they provide. This includes education, the police, highways and social services. This **revenue support grant** is distributed on the basis of a **standard spending allocation** (SSA) for each of the services.

As far as the money for social services is concerned, the SSA is based on measures of relative need in the area. Those areas with the highest indicators of social deprivation and social need should get more revenue support grant.

The calculation for each area takes into account, among other factors, the:

- age profile of the local population
- number of older people with a long-term illness
- number of children of lone parents.

Council tax

Local authorities in England and Wales raise about 20 per cent of their revenue from council tax. District councils in Northern Ireland raise money through domestic rates and business rates.

Charges

Social services departments are legally empowered to charge for nursing, residential, day and home care. Service users are **means-tested**. This means that the amount of income and savings that they have (their means) are assessed (or tested) to make sure that they are within certain limits. Broadly speaking, in the case of residential and nursing care, if the person going into care has over £16,000 in savings then he or she must pay the full cost of care. If he or she has less than £10,000 the costs will be fully subsidised. Between those figures, social services pay a contribution on a sliding scale.

Where the money goes

You can see from Figure 5.11 that nearly half of all social services spending in the period 1995-96 was on elderly people. The biggest single item of expenditure was residential care for older people, which made up a quarter of all spending. Following a comprehensive spending review in 1998, it was decided to invest nearly £3,000 million in local authority social services up until the year 2002.

The Independent Living (1993) Fund

The Independent Living (1993) Fund (ILF) is a trust set up to provide financial assistance to people with severe disabilities. It offers people with impairments the chance of living at home by helping with the cost of their domiciliary care. The ILF is used together with cash and or services from the local authority social services department. If, under community care arrangements, the social services department agrees to provide £200 per week in cash and services to a disabled person, then up to a further £300 per week can claimed from the fund.

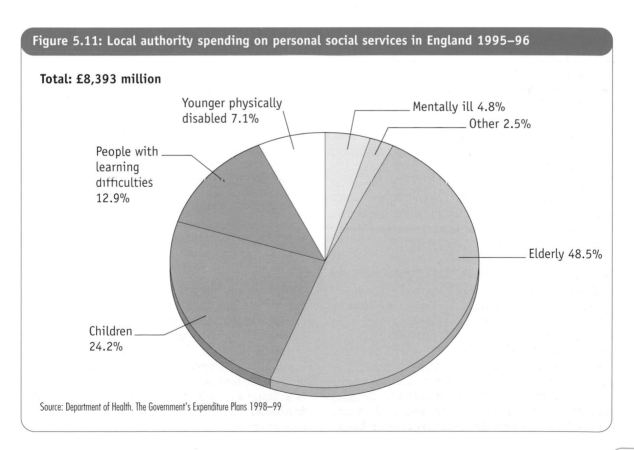

Figure 5.11: Local authority spending on personal social services in England 1995–96

Total: £8,393 million

- Younger physically disabled 7.1%
- Mentally ill 4.8%
- Other 2.5%
- People with learning difficulties 12.9%
- Elderly 48.5%
- Children 24.2%

Source: Department of Health. The Government's Expenditure Plans 1998–99

Figure 5.12: Top fund-raising charities in the field of health and social welfare 1996–97

Charity	Income from contributions*	Total income
Imperial Cancer Research Fund	£73.9 million	£84.5 million
Cancer Research Campaign	£69.2 million	£75.1 million
British Heart Foundation	£65.2 million	£72.9 million
The Salvation Army	£61.0 million	£107.1 million
Barnados	£52.5 million	£107.5 million
Help the Aged	£50.8 million	£60.7 million
SCOPE (Cerebral Palsy)	£41.3 million	£86.5 million
Marie Curie Cancer Care	£40.7 million	£ 51.4 million
British Red Cross Society	£38.7 million	£ 97.1 million
Macmillan Cancer Relief	£38.6 million	£ 43.3 million
Save the Children Fund	£36.6 million	£81.9 million
NSPCC	£36.2 million	£49.3 million
Royal National Institute for the Blind	£31.8 million	£67.1 million

Source: Charities Aid Foundation

*Includes donations, legacies, covenants and Gift Aid, and charity shop income.

Financing the voluntary sector

Voluntary organisations receive income from several sources, including:

- contributions from individuals, businesses and trusts (donations, legacies, covenants and Gift Aid)
- grants from central and local government
- earnings from commercial activities and investments such as charity shops and sales of merchandise
- fees from central and local government for contracted services for example, for providing home or residential care
- Lottery money via the National Lottery Charities Board.

Figure 5.12 illustrates that many national charitable organisations are multi-million pound enterprises. They play a significant part in health and social welfare provision and funding. It also shows that whilst some charities' income is mainly derived from contributions, others get a much greater percentage of their income from other sources, such as grants from the government. Those charities which actually provide health and social care services as a major part of their role, as opposed to funding research, get more of their income from fees charged to government organisations and private individuals for contracted services.

Registered social landlords

Registered social landlords (housing associations) in England get their money from three main sources:

- rent
- the Housing Corporation
- local authorities.

This means that the people who live in special housing schemes do not pay the full cost. They are subsidised. Many registered social landlords provide supported housing to meet the special needs of various groups, such as frail elderly people, young people at risk or those with learning disabilities, mental illness or drug and alcohol problems. They are non-profit making. In Britain, new housing schemes carried out by housing associations can qualify for social housing grants if they are one of more than 2,000 schemes registered with the

Housing Corporation (in England) or Tai Cymru (in Wales). Similar assistance is available to registered social landlords in Northern Ireland.

Financing the private sector

Private nursing and residential homes are funded by two main sources. In the first instance, residents pay the full cost of care directly to the home. Nursing home fees vary, but a typical weekly charge in 2000 would be around £400. Residential homes cost less; a typical weekly charge would be £300. Charges vary according to the area and the facilities on offer.

However, many nursing and residential homes have residents whose care is subsidised by local social services departments. This is the second source of funding. Once a person's savings fall below £16,000 they qualify for financial support from the social services. They also qualify for Income Support, a social security benefit available from the Department for Social Security. Social services will only pay up to a defined maximum amount per week. This is often called a benchmark figure. As a result, many private homes set their fees at this level but they could decide to charge their private residents more. So, private nursing and residential care is financed by:

- income support contributions
- charges paid by residents
- charges paid by local authority social services departments
- money borrowed from banks and other financial institutions.

There are many private home care agencies and they carry out a variety of services for their clients. These can range from nursing care, personal care, household cleaning, shopping or a sitting service. Many people pay for these services direct. The charge in 2000 is typically about £8.50 to £12 per hour, although this varies around the country. Local social services departments purchase care from these agencies on behalf of their clients. Private home care agencies are funded by:

- fees paid by private clients
- social services departments
- money borrowed from banks and other financial institutions.

ACTIVITY

Funding residential and nursing home care

Use Yellow Pages or a social services department's list of registered private nursing and residential homes to contact a local private nursing or residential home. Ask for their brochure (most homes have these). Use information from the brochure or from a follow-up telephone call to find out:

- whether the home accepts private and social services-funded residents
- what their fees are and whether there is any difference in the amount they charge the two types of resident.

Contact a social services adult services team and find out what its benchmark figure is for nursing and residential care.

Financing early years services

Day nurseries run by social services, or nursery schools run by local education authorities, are funded in the same way as other local authority services.

The independent sector

Playgroups that belong to the Pre-school Learning Alliance (PLA) can get grants from the PLA, especially if children have special needs. Otherwise, funding comes from privately-paid fees. Very little money comes from central or local government.

Other playgroups are usually financed by private fees and some grants given by local authorities. Private childcare provision, whether it be nursery school, nursery, childminder, nanny or creche is paid for by the people placing the child, usually the parents. The cost is calculated by the provider to enable it to make a profit.

BUILD YOUR LEARNING

Keywords and phrases

You should know the meaning of the words and phrases listed below. If you are unclear about any of them, go back through the last five pages of the unit to refresh your understanding.

- Benchmark figure
- Council tax
- General taxation
- Means test
- Private Finance Initiative
- Private health insurance scheme
- Standard spending allocation
- Registered social landlord
- Revenue Support Grant

Summary points

- The NHS is mostly paid for out of general taxation.
- Recent governments have introduced more private finance into the NHS.
- Social services are mainly funded by grants from central government, local taxation and charges.
- The voluntary sector gets its revenue from several sources. A significant percentage of this is grants or fees paid by central and local government.
- Much private health care is covered by insurance.
- Many of the residents of private and voluntary nursing homes have all or part of the costs of their care paid for by social services departments.
- Because much early years provision is private, much of the funding is provided by the users themselves.

QUESTIONS

Answer either true or false to each of the following statements.

1 The NHS is completely paid for out of taxation.

2 The large block of money local authorities receive each year from central government is called the Revenue Support Grant.

3 Social care is free to most users.

4 The national voluntary organisations get most of their money from street collections and sponsored events.

5 All voluntary organisations are charities.

6 The government subsidises most childcare in the UK.

7 All people who use private social care services pay privately themselves.

The effects of government policies

It is clear that the structure and delivery of health, social and early years services has not remained the same since the welfare state was created and that many developments have taken place which have affected how services are organised, funded and delivered. There are many reasons why changes have occurred, but one of the main ones is that government policies on welfare services frequently change. We examine next what government policies are, the factors that affect them, some of the more recent major policy changes and their effects on services.

What are government policies?

Government policy can most easily be understood as a course of action adopted and pursued by a particular government. So, for example, one government's health care policy might involve building lots of hospitals, while another government might stop building hospitals and expand care in the community instead. Policies are about what a government wants to achieve, or how it intends to tackle particular issues. The government is always developing policies and putting them into action across all areas of public life, whether it be the economy, the environment, transport, law and order or health, social care and early years services.

Factors affecting government policies

Government policy results from many different but interrelated factors. Key factors affecting the development of health and social care policy include ideologies, public opinion, pressure groups and a range of other factors such as the state of the economy.

Ideology

Ideologies are sets of political and economic ideas that influence government action. The Labour government under Tony Blair embraces an ideological view that it calls the 'Third Way'. This means that it is not in favour of market forces and the freedom of the individual as much as the Conservative governments that preceded it. Nor is it committed to State ownership of large

industries, like steel making or the railways, and a large public sector as previous Labour governments were. Instead, it has developed a new, 'Third Way'. The reforms of the NHS could be said to be part of the Third Way approach. The reforming Labour government is against the internal market but does not rule out using private finance to fund hospital building.

Public opinion

All governments have to take full account of **public opinion**. Failure to do so means unpopularity and the likelihood of losing power. Since it began, the NHS has always been very dear to the British public's heart. Thus, every government's health policy always involves a strongly stated commitment to the NHS.

Pressure groups

Pressure groups are non-governmental, usually single issue organisations that seek to influence public opinion and change government policy on issues that concern their members. Pressure groups are most effective if they can raise awareness and gather sizeable public support. For example, Age Concern and other campaigning groups ran a very well publicised and supported campaign and were able to influence the government's decision to set up a committee looking into long-term care.

Pressure groups also play an important part in providing the government with statistics and information upon which to base policies. The Carers National Association produced much relevant information and useful evidence which led to the passing of the 1995 Carers Act.

Disability rights pressure groups have been successful in bringing disability issues to the government's attention. They have used a variety of techniques such as petitions, letters to MPs, public demonstrations and media campaigns. All of these actions bring their views to both the public and the government's attention.

Other factors

A range of other factors come together to influence and shape government policies. As we have seen, demographic factors play an important role. Recent governments have had to give serious consideration to provision for the UK's ageing population. The UK is also increasingly influenced by European policy and it borrows ideas from other governments around the world. Finally, economics play an important part in any policy-making decision. Policies have to be affordable and not damaging to the economy. In reality, government policies are usually the outcome of a combination of a number of influences.

Policy developments in the NHS

The Health Act 1999

When the new Labour government was returned to power in May 1997 it pledged to reform the NHS. The Department of Health published its proposals in a White Paper called *The New NHS – Modern, Dependable*. A **White Paper** is a government report that sets out what its policies are in a particular area. This White Paper formed the basis of the Health Act 1999. It stated:

> *The NHS has stood the test of time of time for 50 years. But the government was elected to change the NHS for the better – to modernise it for the next 50 years. The new NHS sets out how the internal market will be replaced by a system of integrated care, based on partnership and driven by performance. Abolishing the internal market will cut £1 billion of red tape costs over the lifetime of the parliament for investment in patient care.*

A new organisational structure for the NHS was unveiled in this document (see Figure 5.13) and a number of new initiatives were launched including:

- integrated care
- primary care groups
- Commission for Health Improvement
- health improvement programmes
- health action zones
- NHS Direct
- NHSNet
- walk-in centres
- National Institute for Clinical Excellence
- *Our Healthier Nation*
- national service frameworks.

Integrated care

The New NHS – Modern, Dependable described a new system of integrated care to replace the internal market. **Integrated care** is about organisations working together and in partnership. It is about bringing health and social care closer together, getting the statutory and independent sectors working closer, and developing a more coordinated approach than was possible under the internal market. Some of the difference between the two approaches of integrated care and the internal market are set out in Figure 5.14.

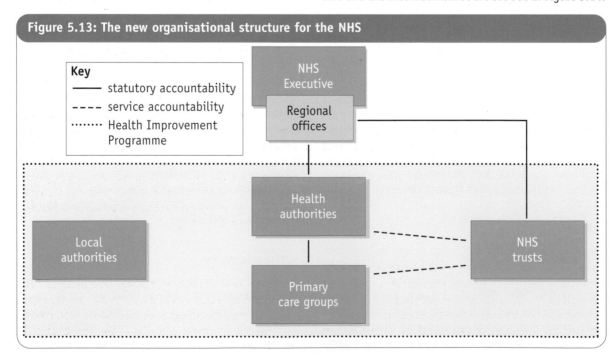

Figure 5.13: The new organisational structure for the NHS

Key
— statutory accountability
- - - service accountability
.... Health Improvement Programme

NHS Executive

Regional offices

Local authorities

Health authorities

Primary care groups

NHS trusts

Figure 5.14: Differences between the internal market and integrated care

Internal market	Integrated care
Competition between providers. Some GPs get better treatment for their patients at the expense of others. Managers have more power than health care professionals.	Patients treated according to need, not who their GP is, or where they live. Cooperation replaces competition. Health care professionals more involved.
Competition prevents sharing of best practice, to protect 'competitive advantage'. Variable quality of services.	New system to share best practice. New performance framework to tackle variable standards of quality.
Soaring administrative costs, diverting effort from improving patient services. High numbers of invoices and high transaction costs.	Management costs capped. Number of commissioning bodies (purchasers) cut from 3,600 to 500. Transaction costs cut.
Fragmented responsibility between 400 NHS bodies. Little strategic planning. Patients passed from pillar to post.	Health improvement programmes agreed by all who are charged with planning or providing health and social care.

Primary care groups

The current thrust of government policy is towards a primary care-led NHS. The concept of the primary care group builds on the GP's traditional role as the gatekeeper or the first port of call when someone is worried about their health. The government has also built to some extent on the achievements of fundholding GPs, who proved to be better than health authorities at commissioning health care and making the most of resources.

Primary care groups are a key feature of the government's organisation of the NHS and the likely long-term aim is for primary care groups to expand and take over the role of the health authorities completely. The thinking behind this is that primary care groups have a better understanding of the needs of their patients.

Primary care groups now agree long-term service agreements with NHS trusts. **Service agreements** are basically contracts setting out what services will be provided for what money. The new service agreements are for three years as opposed to the one-year contracts used in the old internal market. These agreements have to fit in with the framework of national and local targets and standards.

Our Healthier Nation

Our Healthier Nation was first published in 1998 as a **Green Paper** (a set of government proposals for consultation). It outlined the government's aims to improve the health of the population and to deal with inequalities in health, giving direction to the NHS in key areas. The document took the view that people should take responsibility for their own health and set the following specific national targets for health, with the expectation that real improvements would be seen by 2010.

- Cancer: to reduce deaths from cancer by at least a fifth in people under the age of 75 years.

- Heart disease and stroke: to reduce the death rate from heart disease, stroke and related illnesses by at least two-fifths in people under the age of 75 years.

- Accidents: to reduce the death rate from accidents by at least a fifth and the rate of serious injury by at least a tenth.

- Mental health: to reduce deaths caused by suicide and undetermined injury by at least a fifth.

By setting these targets, the government believes it can prevent up to 300,000 premature deaths over the 10-year period in question. The emphasis in *Our Healthier Nation* is on a three-way partnership between individuals, communities and the government. Each has an important role to play in improving health. Medical practitioners claim that many of the targets in *Our Healthier Nation* would have been met anyway, especially heart disease, as these diseases have been on a long, downward trend.

Commission for Health Improvement

This is an independent, statutory body that has been set up to ensure that medical and health care standards are being met. Launched in October 1999, it started its first full year of operation in 2000. The Commission for Health Improvement's (CHI) role is to review all hospitals, clinics and primary health trusts over a four-year period. It is also to ensure the quality of clinical governance, that is, how clinical standards are maintained. The CHI is therefore a quality assurance organisation or **watchdog**. The Secretary of State for Health has been given the power to act on its recommendations. For example, the boards of health authorities or NHS trusts can be removed if they are shown to be failing.

Health improvement programmes

Health improvement programmes are three-year strategic plans developed jointly by all partner organisations that have an interest in, or impact on, health related issues. One of their main purposes is to encourage the formation of partnerships within the community to achieve the targets laid down by *Our Healthier Nation*.

Another major function is to help address any inequalities in health in local communities and to ensure that effort goes into planning specific programmes to bring about improvements in their area. The health improvement programme for an area should involve the health authority, the community health council, primary care groups, the local authority, the district authority and the voluntary sector, all working in partnership.

Health action zones

The health action zone initiative was launched in 1997 with the aim of targeting a special effort on a number of areas where it was believed that the health of local people could be improved by better integrated arrangements for treatment and care.

The purpose of health action zones is to bring together all the local bodies that can affect health and to put into action an agreed, coordinated strategy for improving the health of the people in that area.

The first wave of 11 health action zones was announced in 1998 in areas thought to have the greatest need.

NHS Direct and NHS Direct Online

NHS Direct is a 24-hour confidential telephone advice line staffed by nurses and backed up by computer technology. It gives on-the-spot advice and help. Three pilot helplines began in 1998 and the whole country will be covered in 2000. The idea is to make health advice more accessible. Some argue that it is designed to take pressure off GPs, but that it is not an adequate substitute for a proper face-to-face consultation.

NHS Direct Online (www.nhsdirect.nhs.uk) was launched in December 1999. This is a health information and diagnostic website that the government hopes will become one of the most popular websites in the country, with more than 25 million hits a year. As well as helping users to diagnose illnesses, the site has a vast range of information on support groups and how to navigate round the NHS. Advice comes in several languages and can be played as audio. It is all part of Labour's strategy to modernise the NHS.

National Institute for Clinical Excellence

This recently established body is made up of health professionals, academics, health economists and those representing the interests of patients. Its role is to advise on best practice in the use of existing treatment options, to assess new treatments and technology, and to advise the NHS on how best to apply them.

NICE aims to look for treatments and technology that are not only the most clinically effective but also the most cost effective. It is hoped that by spreading information about best practice on a national basis this will also help with the problem of geographical variations in care.

ACTIVITY

The role of NICE

GPs told not to prescribe new flu drug

Relenza, the anti-flu drug, will not be made generally available on the NHS this winter after the Health Secretary, Frank Dobson, yesterday said that he has accepted his experts advice that there is not enough evidence of its benefits.

Mr Dobson has asked the National Institute for Clinical Excellence (NICE) to issue guidance to GPs that they should not give it to their patients. NICE's rapid assessment panel had advised Mr Dobson that there was not enough evidence that Relenza benefited those who are most at risk from flu – the elderly and people with conditions such as bronchitis and heart disease, for whom flu can be fatal.

Source: Adapted from an article by Sarah Boseley, *The Guardian*, 9 October, 1999

What do you understand to be the relationship between NICE and the Secretary of State for Health?

National service frameworks

National service frameworks set national standards in particular areas of health care. They also define the way in which the services for particular care groups should be delivered. The first two national service frameworks were for coronary heart disease and mental health. Another, for older people, is due in 2000 and one for diabetes in 2001. Like many of the other initiatives, national service frameworks are designed to improve quality and reduce variations in standards of care and treatment.

National service frameworks require partnerships with a wide range of organisations. These include primary care groups, NHS trusts and health authorities and also social care providers, local authorities, voluntary organisations, business and industry. Users and carers are to be involved as well.

Mental health

In 1998, the government announced that it intended to undertake a radical review of the Mental Health Act 1983. The Mental Health Act 1983 is the main piece of legislation that covers work with people suffering from mental illness. Among other points, it lays down the criteria under which people with mental disorders can be sectioned, or compulsorily admitted, to hospital.

The initial phase of the review was to be undertaken by a small group of experts in the field which reported to ministers in 1999. From this, the government will develop proposals for new legislation. Some of the more controversial points raised were to do with those people considered to be a danger to themselves and others. Proposals seemed to imply a weakening of mentally ill people's rights in this area.

Policy developments in social care

As with the NHS, there have been several recent major policy initiatives in the way social care is organised, funded and delivered, particularly since the Labour government came to power in 1997. This is an area in which changes will be happening for some time as the government implements its policies.

Joint working

Better Services for Vulnerable People (1997) is a major national policy initiative which both local authorities and health authorities are required to implement by working together. It is a good example of integrated care. *Better Services for Vulnerable People* expects social services departments, health authorities and other agencies to work together to improve services for all vulnerable adult groups. It brings together several of the key themes we have seen emerging in the late 1990s. For older people, for example, the policy has three main strands:

- improving the content and process of multidisciplinary assessments of older people in both hospital and community settings

- compiling joint investment plans for services to meet the continuing community care needs of the local population

- developing health and social care services for older people which focus on optimising independence.

Disability legislation

Over the latter part of the twentieth century disabled people have gained more rights. There are several reasons for this. One major reason is that disabled people themselves have become more organised and have formed themselves into pressure groups such as Disability Awareness in Action in order to campaign for more rights and recognition. At the same time, social care professionals have adopted the principle of **empowerment**; the idea that users of care services should not just passively receive care, but should participate fully in decision making and have control over their care.

The actions taken by disabled people's groups, and changing attitudes within social care itself, have, in turn, informed the policy making of governments. For example, the Labour government elected in 1997 promised to combat **social exclusion**, (by which social groups, including disabled people, are unable to participate fully in society) and to extend the rights of disabled people. There is still a long way to go in this area, particularly as, with all issues in social welfare, resources are at stake.

The Disability Discrimination Act 1995, which is designed to stop discrimination against disabled people in the provisions of goods and services, is being implemented in stages. Part III of the Act became law in 1999. The Act makes it unlawful for a provider of services to discriminate against a disabled person. In effect this means better access must be provided, better information about services must be available in a range of formats, and organisational policies, practices and procedures must be adjusted. One effect is that public buildings and other facilities such as road crossings and toilets must be made fully accessible for all users.

The Disability Discrimination Act 1995 also provides a right for disabled people not to be discriminated against in employment (employers of more than 20 staff have a duty to adjust their terms and conditions to make the employment of disabled people easier). The Disability Rights Commission was set up in 1999 in order to protect, enforce and promote the rights of disabled people.

Modernising Social Services

The White Paper *Modernising Social Services* is an important document as far as social services for adults are concerned. It sets out several reforms. Priorities for improvement are:

- promoting independence
- improving consistency
- providing convenient user-centred services.

The direct payments scheme which is available to people with disabilities under the age of 65 years and which allows them to buy the care they want is to be extended to people over 65 years, allowing them greater control over how their care needs are met.

There is to be a particular emphasis on improving rehabilitation services for adults and on improving hospital discharge arrangements. Money is promised to develop preventive strategies for people at risk of losing their independence. An example would be schemes that allow people a quick and safe return home following a hospital admission. The longer older people stay in hospital, the more likely they are to end up in residential or nursing care.

The government is anxious to see a greater level of consistency and fairness in social care. Their action programme includes:

- taking a greater role nationally in setting objectives and standards for social services
- the introduction of national service frameworks, in partnership with the NHS
- a *Fair Access to Care* initiative
- action to establish greater consistency and fairness in charging.

A long-term care charter is also being developed. This will set out more clearly what service users and informal carers can expect if they need support from health, housing and social services.

The White Paper says that authorities should make services easier and more convenient to use. The one-stop shop is seen as the best model. This would be a single point of access, not only to all council services, but also other partner agencies including community health services and the Benefits Agency. This is a good example of integrated care. All authorities will be required to carry out local user satisfaction surveys from 2000.

Social care inspection systems

The government considered that the arrangements for inspecting and regulating care services that existed throughout the 1990s were unsatisfactory for a number of reasons. The local authority-run inspection and registration units lacked independence, coherence and consistency. Accordingly, the registration and inspection functions are to be removed from local authorities and health authorities, and become the responsibility of newly established regional commissions for care standards. These commissions will regulate a wider range of care services, including domiciliary care, small children's homes and local authority-run homes. All the commissions will work to the same national standards, and registration requirements will be uniform, regardless of whether an organisation is private, voluntary or statutory.

A children's rights officer is to be appointed for each region, who will ensure that the views of children receiving care services regulated by the commissions are given proper weight.

Best value

In 1999 the government laid down a statutory duty for local authorities to demonstrate best value in all their services. The reasons for this are laid out in detail in the 1998 White Paper *Modern Local Government in Touch with Local People* but it is mainly to do with driving up the quality of services, encouraging innovation and generating efficiency savings. What this means in reality will be different in each local authority, but it will have an impact on how social services are purchased from the independent sector, which services are kept in-house (still run by social services departments themselves) and what goes into service agreements with voluntary and private providers.

Policy developments in services for children

Although the Children Act 1989 is currently the main piece of legislation in the field of child care, it is important to be aware of more recent developments governing work with children and families.

Quality protects

Quality protects is a three-year programme launched in 1998. It developed out of various official reports that were critical of how effectively social services departments looked after children, particularly those who were in care and who had been in care.

Quality Protects sets out clearly defined targets that local authorities must achieve in relation to looked-after children, as they are known, and children in need. These include:

- a high level of care and protection from harm for children

- minimising the number of moves between carers for looked-after children

- ensuring that referral and assessment processes reflect individual children's needs

- improving educational opportunities and outcomes

- improving opportunities to participate socially and economically in society as adults.

As a result of Quality Protects, local authority social services departments have had to change their practices to fit in with central government's requirements. For example, all local authorities have to submit a Quality Protects management action plan to the Department of Health. The programme has been backed up with £375 million of extra money from the Department of Health.

Modernising Social Services

Modernising Social Services: Promoting Independence, Improving Protection, Raising Standards, the government White Paper published by the Department of Health in 1998, set out the government's vision of how social services departments should operate across all the service user groups. For children's services, the White Paper's proposals are set out under the priority areas of:

- protection

- quality of care

- improving life chances.

Other reforms include the introduction of tough new inspection arrangements covering all children's homes including small homes, independent fostering agencies and residential family centres. The national register of people who are unsuitable for working with children is to be strengthened so that such people are effectively excluded from working with children.

Radical improvements in educational opportunities for children in care are planned also in the health services they get. New requirements will also be introduced for helping children make the transition from care to independent adult life. All local authorities are subject to social services inspectorate scrutiny to ensure that national objectives are being met.

The national childcare strategy

This policy was launched by the government in 1997–98. Its main aims were to provide high quality, affordable and accessible childcare provision. The strategy sought to make it possible for mothers to join or rejoin the workforce. The government pledged to double the proportion of three year olds in nurseries to 66 per cent, by creating 190,000 new places in England by the year 2002. The government also wants to make out-of-school childcare available in every community.

An obvious effect of this policy will be a big increase in the demand for trained childcare staff. The Early Years National Training Organisation is the main body responsible for coordinating training for all types of workers with 0–8 year-olds.

Policy developments affecting informal carers

In recognition of the stress of caring and the important role that informal carers play, the Conservative government introduced the Carers (Recognition & Services) Act 1995. This applies to people who provide a substantial amount of care on a regular basis. If the person they are caring for has had a community care assessment, then, as carers, they can request an assessment of their own needs. However, the Carers Act 1995 did not guarantee that services would be made available following the assessment.

Caring about Carers

In 1998 the Labour government launched *Caring about Carers*, which forms the basis of the national carers strategy. This strategy has three elements.

- Information. A new charter on long-term care services is to be launched. Initiatives such as NHS Direct and NHS net are examples of trying to get more helpful information to carers about services.

- Care. Carers are to be consulted and involved more in the planning and provision of services.

- Support. New powers are to be given to local authorities to provide services for carers, particularly in helping carers take a break (respite). Financial help is promised in order to help make this happen.

It is unrealistic and undesirable that formal care could ever replace informal care. The thrust of recent government policies has therefore been to care for the carer. Extending the amount of respite care available has therefore become a key strategy.

BUILD YOUR LEARNING

Keywords and phrases

You should know the meaning of the words and phrases listed below. If you are unsure about any of them, go back through the last seven pages of the unit to refresh your understanding.

- Carers National Association
- Commission for health improvement
- Community health councils
- Disability Rights Commission
- Green Paper
- Health action zone
- Health improvement programme
- Ideology
- Integrated care
- National carers strategy
- National childcare strategy
- National Institute for Clinical Excellence
- NHS Direct
- NHSnet
- National service frameworks
- *Our Healthier Nation*
- Pressure groups
- Public opinion
- Quality Protects
- Service agreements
- Walk-in centres
- White Paper

Summary points

- Government policies determine what health, social and early years services we have.

- Many factors – usually acting in combination with each other – affect government policy on health and social care.

- *The Health Act 1999* the desire to replace the internal market with a system of integrated care which involves agencies working together more closely.

- *Our Healthier Nation* sets out specific targets in the four key areas of cancer, heart disease and stroke, accidents and mental health.

- Health improvement programmes have been introduced to help coordinate the achievement of the targets set in *Our Healthier Nation* and to help deal with inequalities in health care.

- Since 1997, social services departments have been expected to work much more closely with health agencies and other local organisations (integrated care).

- The work of children's services is guided by the principles of the Children Act 1989.

- The national childcare strategy aims to provide places for all three and four-year-old children and to expand out-of-school provision.

- The government has recognised the importance of carers through the Carers Act 1995, *Caring about Carers* and the national carers strategy.

QUESTIONS

1 Identify five different factors that affect government policies towards health, social and early years services.

2 Identify three ways in which the new system of integrated care differs from the internal market.

3 Describe four instances in which there should be partnership between agencies in the planning and providing of health services.

4 Identify two initiatives that set targets for health.

5 Explain how and why the system of inspection of social care is set to change.

6 What is the national childcare strategy and what will its impact be on jobs in childcare?

References

Beveridge Report, Report of the Committee on Social Insurance and Allied Health, HMSO, Cmd. 6404, 1942

Curtis Report, Report of the Care of Children Committee, HMSO, Cmd. 6922, 1946

Guillebaud Report, Report of the Committee of Inquiry on the Cost of the National Health Service, HMSO, Cmd 9336, 1956

Plowden Report, Children and their Primary Schools: report of the Central Advisory Council for Education (England), HMS, Vol. 1, 1966, Vol. 2, 1967

Seebohm Report Report, of the Committee on Local Authority and Allied Social Services, HMSO, Cmd. 3703, 1968

Barclay Report, Barclay, P (1982) Social Workers: Their Roles and Tasks, HMSO, London

Department of Health (1998) *Our Healthier Nation*, HMSO, London.

Department of Health (1998) *The New NHS: Modern, Dependable*, HMSO, London.

Department of Health (1998) *Modernising Social Services: Promoting Independence, Improving Protection, raising Standards*, HMSO, London.

Department of Health (1999) *Caring about Carers: a national Strategy for Carers*, HMSO, London.

Modern Local Government in touch with local people, HMSO, London.

Office for National Statistics (1998) *General Household Survey*, HMSO, London

Useful addresses

National Statistics Public Enquiry Service
Zone DG/19
1 Drummond Gate
London SW1V 2QQ

Department of Health Publications
PO Box 777
London SE1 6XH

Pre-school Learning Alliance (National Centre)
69 King's Cross Road
London WC1X 9LL

Carers' National Association
20–25 Glasshouse Yard
London EC1A 4JT

Patient's Charter Unit
NHS Executive HQ
4N34B Quarry House
Quarry Hill
Leeds LS2 7UE

Disability Awareness in Action
11 Belgrave Road
London SW1V 1RB

Independent Living (1993) Fund
PO Box 183
Nottingham NG8 3RD

Kids Clubs Network information line
020 7512 2100

This unit enables you to develop your research skills by improving your knowledge of the research process. You are required to undertake a research project in the area of health, social or early years care.

Most advanced health and social care students want to become practising care workers. As health and social care practitioners, you need to be able to understand a variety of types of research. This has implications both for your practice and for your patients' and clients' health and well-being. This unit covers the background knowledge needed to enable you to develop the basic skills to understand and conduct research relevant to health and social care.

First, we provide an introduction to the purpose of research in health and social care. What does research mean in the context of health and social care? Why do care practitioners and specialist researchers carry out research? What kinds of research investigations are conducted in care settings? We explore these questions, illustrating the discussion with examples of research carried out in different health and social care settings.

Next, we take a closer look at the ideas and assumptions underpinning research. There are a number of different

methods (often referred to as methodologies) of carrying out research and collecting data. We look at how closed system methodologies, such as experiments and surveys, and open system methodologies, such as participant observation and interviews, are used in care-related research. We consider the value and weaknesses of each approach in relation to health and social care research.

We move on to examine the ethical issues and procedures that are part of any research in health and social care. Ethical issues are not simply academic and hypothetical matters. Anyone carrying out research must find practical ways of conducting their investigations ethically. This discussion forms an important link to the last part of the unit, which is practically focused.

We guide you through the process of planning research investigations and obtaining research data and cover the key topics taking a practical approach. The aim is that you will then be able to plan your own research project and collect valid data. Finally, we focus on how to analyse, or make sense of, research data. We work through examples of some of the main analysis techniques and end by considering how to write up your final research report.

Research perspectives in health and social care

The purpose of research

Health and social care practitioners work in a fast developing vocational area. They are often faced with reports produced by government organisations, professional bodies, voluntary groups and commercial organisations in which research and data on various aspects of health and well-being are quoted. As professionals, health and social care workers need to be able to understand and critically evaluate these sources of research. They may have important implications for care practice. On the other hand, they may be badly put together, flawed research investigations, resulting in findings that should be treated warily. It is important to be able to know which is which. Health and social care practitioners who have a good understanding of research methodology and data collection methods are in a better position to evaluate the research that they read and hear about. Ultimately, this will help to make them more informed and effective practitioners.

The place of research in health and social care work has become more critical over the last 10 years. Care interventions are increasingly sophisticated and organisations more complex. Purchasers and users of health and social care services expect a high level of clinical and cost-effectiveness from care practitioners and the organisations which employ them. They want to know that care interventions and processes are based on sound evidence. As a result, health and social care professionals are developing their practice in response to research findings.

What is research in health and social care?

Bowling (1997) defines research as 'the systematic and rigorous process of enquiry which aims to describe phenomena and to develop explanatory concepts and theories. Ultimately it aims to contribute to a scientific body of knowledge'. Although this definition makes research sound a little complicated, it is important that you see it as something more than simply asking people a few questions that you think up quickly, getting their opinions and then trying to make sense of the process.

You have probably heard people use the term research to refer to general forms of information-seeking enquiry, such as looking up information in books or on a CD-ROM. However, the types of research investigations that we are going to learn about involve more than simply collecting information from libraries, books or other sources and then summarising it. Perhaps one of the reasons for the widespread and varied use of the term research is that it has a high status. This in itself affects how people view any activity labelled as research and influences how people receive the outcomes of the activity.

The research enquiries that we are concerned with involve:

- putting forward ideas that can be tested

- collecting data to test these ideas in a systematic way

- analysing the collected data

- drawing conclusions based on the research evidence.

ACTIVITY

What is research?

Imagine that you are about to begin a work placement in a health and social care setting as part of your GNVQ course. At the interview your supervisor describes her work role and says, 'I'm also currently doing a research study on staff attitudes to GNVQ student placements'.

- What do you think that such a research study involves?

- How do you think that she might go about it?

- What might she produce in the end?

If you are doing this activity on your own, jot down a few ideas and then go back and review them when you have worked through the rest of this part of the unit. If you are working with class colleagues, discuss and share your ideas and, again, return to review your thoughts when you have finished working through this part of the unit.

Health and social care research studies are enquiries, or investigations, that are planned, organised, and systematic. The knowledge that results from them is generally valued more highly and can be contrasted with our common sense, or everyday, understanding of the world. The difference between research-based knowledge and common sense knowledge is that common sense is based on assumptions that are unquestioned.

In many health and social care situations it isn't enough to rely on common sense or intuition. Both of these qualities may be useful in certain circumstances but they can't be used to justify care interventions. 'It seemed like a good idea', or 'We've always done it this way', are not phrases that most health and social care service users, their lawyers or members of accident inquiries are likely to find convincing when a problem occurs. You should always be able to justify your care practice by reference to **research-based knowledge**.

This is superior to common-sense knowledge as it is based on **evidence**.

Evidence-based practice is now a very important feature of all health and social care practitioners' work. In order to develop evidence-based practice, care workers need to take a **systematic approach**, testing their ideas and practices by conducting their own, and reading about other people's, research. Health and social care professionals are now likely to be called upon to provide evidence to answer questions like the following.

- Are you providing a service that people want?

- How do service users benefit from what you do?

- Is what you do the most effective way of helping service users?

- Are the services you provide cost effective?

ACTIVITY

Research or common-sense knowledge?

Would you choose to receive treatment at a hospital where staff base their practice and intervention approaches on research evidence? Or would you be happy to use the services of a hospital where the health and social care staff rely on their common sense to make decisions about your condition and care? Take a minute to think about the pros and cons of each option.

Why carry out research in health and social care?

We have already partly answered this question through our discussion of the difference between research-based knowledge and common-sense knowledge. The objective of all research, whether it is about health and social care or not, is to produce knowledge. The point of doing research in the health and social care field is to produce knowledge that is useful to health and social care practitioners and service users. The results of research can, at one extreme, usefully lead to new theories and ideas that add to knowledge in disciplines related to health and social care, such as sociology, psychology or human biology, for example.

The findings of research investigations can also be used to influence and help policy makers and managers to make their decisions about which services should be provided, or can lead to changes in the care practices of health and social care workers. For example, if you were a health service manager and had enough money in your budget to fund one of three possible hip replacement treatments for older people, what would you want to know before you made your decision about which to spend the money on? Apart from the cost of each method, it would be important to know how effective the treatments were in restoring the mobility of older people. This information could only come from a research study that compared the effectiveness of the three treatments.

Health and social care workers frequently need to employ research skills and understanding on an immediate and practical level in their everyday working life. Here are some further examples of situations in which health or social care practitioners would need to use research skills and knowledge.

- A social worker begins a new job. She has a brief to find out what a local community thinks about the proposed opening of a refuge for women who are victims of domestic violence.

- A school nurse wants to know how many children eat breakfast before they come to school and whether boys are more likely to do so than girls.

- A youth worker wonders whether teenagers who are having problems at home would benefit from either regular individual counselling sessions at the youth club or a group holiday where they could get away, meet and talk to others in a similar position.

- A social work manager wants to know whether a new 'drop-in' centre for mental health service users is effective in reducing the rate of admission to the local psychiatric hospital.

- A GP is keen to find out why men seem to use the practice less frequently than women and whether they want any new services to be introduced to meet their particular health needs.

- A health visitor wonders what the main factors are behind a sudden rise in the number of 16-year-old girls who are becoming pregnant in the town where she works.

- A social worker in the child and families team has been asked to assess support service for children who care for a disabled parent. He wonders what life as a child carer is like and what kind of services, if any, they would like the local authority to make available.

- A nursing home manager wonders whether employing a specialist occupational therapist to develop appropriate activity and leisure opportunities for elderly residents would be an effective way of improving their sense of well-being and self-esteem.

These examples give some indication of the wide variety of phenomena relating to health and social care policy, practice and procedures that researchers study. It is also important to outline the various different types of research investigation, and we do this next

Types of research investigation in health and social care

An understanding of research principles and practices is important for all health and social care professionals. Evidence-based practice is a major area of health and social care work at present. The term evidence-based refers to research knowledge that positively supports the effectiveness of undertaking particular practices and procedures. Many of the practices of doctors, nurses and other health and social care practitioners that have been used in the past have been shown to be rituals based on common sense and tradition, rather than on rational, effective interventions. This is no longer acceptable. Increasingly, purchasers and users of health and social care services use research-based evidence to make their decisions about whether to use a care organisation. A failure to demonstrate that a service is effective, clinically and financially, will lead purchasers and service users to question why it is being provided.

Descriptive research

Descriptive research tends to look at a situation or set of circumstances in detail. The researchers simply describe what they observe. They will be able to answer the question 'What is happening?' but won't necessarily set out, or be able, to answer the subsequent question, 'Why does this happen in this way?' Descriptive research is not usually an end in itself. It is often the starting point in a bigger research study and leads on to further research to answer the why questions. Descriptive research might involve an observation of children's play. The aim might be to extend knowledge about the different forms of imaginative play which boys and girls engage in at a nursery.

Evaluative research

Evaluative research is concerned with whether something is being achieved. Action research is a form of evaluative research in which care practitioners become involved in actively, deliberately introducing some change in policy or practice. They then use their research knowledge and skills to monitor and evaluate its effect. Evaluative research might involve a survey of service users' satisfaction with the weekend opening hours of a day centre.

Predictive research

Predictive research might involve conducting an experiment into the effect of using a new drug to treat a particular illness. The aim is to predict the biological action and clinical effectiveness of the drug.

Explanatory research

Explanatory research might involve a study that examines why teenage pregnancy rates are relatively high in the United Kingdom compared to other European countries. This type of research aims to answer the question 'Why?' It seeks to find the answer to a particular problem, often looking for causes.

Because of the high priority that research skills now have for health and social care practitioners, a research module is a compulsory element in many basic professional health and social care training courses. As part of your GNVQ Health and Social Care course you will begin to develop your research knowledge and skills. You will carry out your own research project. This will be useful and valuable if you carry it out correctly and obtain valid data. You will then have become actively involved in the process of creating 'knowledge' and exploring research questions in the health and social care field.

BUILD YOUR LEARNING

Keywords and phrases

You should know the meaning of the words and phrases listed below. If you are unsure about any of them, go back through the last four pages of the unit to refresh your understanding.

- Data
- Descriptive research
- Evaluative research
- Evidence-based practice
- Explanatory research
- Prescriptive research
- Research-based knowledge
- Research methodology
- Systematic approach

Summary points

- Research-based knowledge is now given a high priority by health and social care practitioners, service users and purchasers. Research is highly valued because it is a means of evaluating the effectiveness of different care practices and interventions.

- Research into health and social care is characterised by a systematic and rigorous process of enquiry in which researchers collect data to test their ideas and hypotheses.

- Research-based knowledge is founded on empirical evidence. This is in contrast to common-sense knowledge, which is based on assumptions.

- Research provides health and social care workers with greater understanding of the people for whom they provide care and of the practices and interventions that they use. Research knowledge is also an important influence on policy making, as it assists policy makers in developing and purchasing effective care services.

- Health and social care practitioners carry out and use a number of different types of research. These include descriptive, evaluative, predictive and explanatory research. Each offers a particular type of insight and approach into health and social care issues.

QUESTIONS

1 Briefly describe some of the key characteristics of health and social care research investigations.

2 What is the main difference between research-based knowledge and common-sense knowledge?

3 Why is research an important feature of health and social care work?

4 Name three types of research investigation, briefly explaining the nature of each.

5 What is evidence-based practice in health and social care?

Research methods

▲ The cliché about researchers is that they are people with clipboards who ask questions; as with all clichés, it's only partly true

Research involves the planned, systematic collection and analysis of data. **Data** is simply items of information. Researchers often refer to the data that they collect as **empirical evidence**. The word empirical comes from the Greek word for experience. It is used by researchers to refer to evidence that is collected from the real world through observation. It is contrasted with the hunches, beliefs and traditions that inform common-sense knowledge. There are a variety of methods of generating and collecting empirical research data. You may already be aware of questionnaire, interview and participant observation methods.

We are going to look at two contrasting theoretical approaches to research. In effect, these two approaches offer different views on what counts as valid, that is soundly reasoned, research evidence. This will hopefully encourage you to review, question and further develop your thinking about how to approach your own research project at a later stage of your GNVQ Health and Social Care course.

Approaches to research

As well as choosing data collection methods, health and social care researchers also have to adopt a theoretical approach to their research investigations. The approach that they adopt links their ideas and beliefs about knowledge and the world to the practice of obtaining research data. The two key approaches that are outlined below are known as the positivist and the interpretive approaches.

The positivist approach

The **positivist approach** to research is the one that is commonly adopted in, and associated with, the natural sciences (physics, chemistry, biology). It is widely used within health and social care, particularly by researchers in fields such as medicine and psychology.

The intellectual tradition of positivism is based on a number of key assumptions. It is claimed that:

- researchers can discover and measure true facts

- only knowledge gained through observed experience is valid and scientific

- research that is carried out in a controlled and rigorous way enables scientific laws to be discovered

- researchers should avoid influencing the research process and findings by being objective and minimising the influence of their own values and culture on participants and the research situation.

Positivist researchers use data collection methods such as experiments, questionnaire surveys, structured interviews and observational checklists to collect facts about some aspect of the health and social care world. The facts tend to be recorded in a numerical form, or are reducible to numbers. These are known as **quantitative data**. Positivist researchers tend to set out to collect data that measures how many, how often, what percentage or proportion, or whether there is a connection between X and Y. When the data has been collected, statistical techniques are used to establish what patterns and relationships exist in the data. These patterns and relationships are then presented as facts, supported by hard, quantifiable empirical evidence.

Positivist researchers try to set up controlled situations where the relationships between variables can be tested and observed. Natural or physical

variables are the characteristics of entities that are physically manipulated, such as the heat or volume of a substance. For example, the volume of alcohol that people are able to consume before becoming unconscious is a variable that is related, in part, to their body mass. Larger, heavier people can consume more. Social variables are attributes which are fixed for each person but which occur in different levels, strengths or amounts within the population. For example, marital status is a social construct (idea) that varies in terms of whether a person is single, married or divorced.

Positivist researchers try to control the variables that they study so that they can look at possible cause and effect relationship between them. The classic controlled research situation is the laboratory experiment (see p. 361) in which researchers can control the physical environment and guard against external variables interfering with the laboratory tests. However, people who put together questionnaires, interviews with pre-arranged questions or observation checklists with pre-defined observation categories also try to control the research situation. They set limits and boundaries on the possible sources and nature of the data by deciding in advance what they will ask about, look for or test. Figure 6.1 gives some indication of how much control each data collection method allows the researcher to impose.

Positivist researchers who collect data through experiments want a high level of control so that they are able to say with certainty how the relationship between the variables works. They are looking for **scientific laws**. These are things that under specific conditions always happen or apply. Positivist researchers can then claim that the relationships and patterns that they find in their data are capable of generalisation. That is, their findings are facts that can be applied outside of the research setting to the world in general.

One factor that positivist researchers try to control against is the possibility that their own values or behaviour might influence their research findings. Positivist researchers try to remain separate from the research participants and outside of the events that they are studying. They feel that this is necessary to protect their objectivity and to avoid influencing, or being influenced by, the people or events they are studying.

The positivist approach is widely accepted as a scientific method of researching health and social care topics and situations. It is important, effective and valuable for investigating certain kinds of phenomena. Research into the action and effects of medicines, into the physical processes of disease and into the effectiveness of new treatments, can all be conducted by adopting a positivist approach. However, it is not the only approach to research in health and social care and

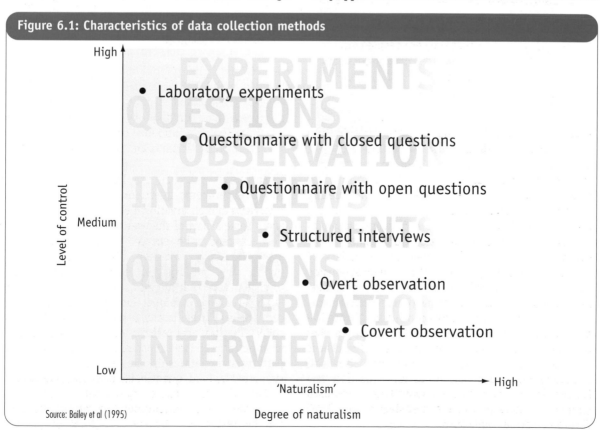

Figure 6.1: Characteristics of data collection methods

High →
- Laboratory experiments
- Questionnaire with closed questions
- Questionnaire with open questions

Medium
- Structured interviews
- Overt observation
- Covert observation

Low

Level of control

'Naturalism' → High

Source: Bailey et al (1995)

Degree of naturalism

it is not always the most appropriate. Research investigations in health and social care settings often involve the study and participation of people. Human beings behave in much less predictable and controllable ways than the chemical substances and other phenomena that positivist scientists study. The interpretive approach is an alternative that has developed out of criticism of some of the claims and weaknesses of positivist, quantitative research.

ACTIVITY

Is it a scientific law?

One scientific law that is at the forefront of the minds of health care staff in emergency situations is that a person must receive a supply of oxygen to live. It is always true, for everybody, anywhere in the world, that survival depends on receiving a continuous and sufficient volume of oxygen.

Can you think of any other health-related scientific laws? Remember you are trying to identify relationships between variables that always happen or apply.

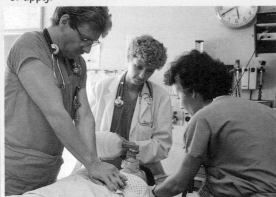

The interpretive approach

This approach to research is strongly associated with the disciplines of anthropology and sociology. In health and social care settings it is likely to be used by members of non-medical disciplines like social workers, nurses and occupational therapists who want to understand the experiences of the individuals and groups whom they study.

Interpretive researchers tend to look in detail at a specific group of people or a particular situation. They do not try to discover scientific laws or establish causal relationships. The interpretive approach is based on the idea that knowledge is continuously created by people and that no fixed, objective reality exists independently of peoples culture, values and experience.

Researchers adopting an **interpretive approach** base their data collection strategy on the assumption that their main task is to understand reality from the inside, from the perspective of the researched. Interpretive researchers are interested in the real meaning of human behaviour and relationships, and believe that this can only be discovered and understood in the natural setting where it occurs. As a result, interpretive researchers use data collection methods such as participant observation and unstructured in-depth interviews that allow them to gain access to and make use of a wide variety of non-numerical **qualitative data**. They might be interested in what people say and write, what they do in different situations and how they look and present themselves. All of this data is non-numerical but may help researchers to understand what is going on if they are able to appreciate their meaning and significance.

The interpretive approach suggests that whilst it is important for researchers to acknowledge their own values and position in relation to the research group or topic, they cannot avoid becoming involved in the research process. This does not mean that they should deliberately manipulate research participants or bias the findings, but that their existing social characteristics, experiences and culture will influence what it is possible for them to see, understand and experience. For example, the existing beliefs and values of the researcher are seen to play an important role in influencing their decisions about what is important, interesting and useful data.

While it is possible to distinguish between a positivist and an interpretive approach to research, you should be aware that researchers do not join sides as it

▲ It may be impossible for some researchers to fit easily into the group they wish to observe

were, and become a positivist or an interpretive researcher forever! In practice, health and social care researchers may use both approaches, either at different stages in a research investigation (see triangulation p. 364) or over a series of studies. Both positivist and interpretive approaches are useful and necessary for research in health and social care. Neither, in themselves are better than the other. Researchers will, however, make judgements about which is the best approach to use in the circumstances they are working in and take into account what they are trying to achieve.

Sources and characteristics of data

The term **data** refers to the items of information that are produced through research. For example, when using a questionnaire the data that researchers collect are the answers that each respondent gives to the questions asked. This is only one form of data. There are many others. Research data is often described in terms of whether it is quantitative (numerical) or qualitative (non-numerical) and whether it is obtained from primary data or secondary data sources.

Quantitative and qualitative data

▲ A source of primary data for waiting times

As we have seen, quantitative data is items of information that tell the researcher things like how many, how often or how much. If you were to research how long people have to wait to be seen in your local Accident and Emergency department, the data would be quantitative. The data would be measurable and quantifiable information. If you wanted to research the attitudes and opinions of people about Accident and Emergency department waiting times, you would be seeking non-numerical, or qualitative, data. You would want to know about their feelings, beliefs and opinions. These are items of information that are expressed in words not in numbers.

Primary and secondary data

▲ Finding secondary data

Imagine that you were asked to carry out research into Accident and Emergency department waiting times. Where could you get the data from? One strategy would be to go to one or more Accident and Emergency departments on one or more occasions and ask people how long they had been waiting to be seen (quantitative data) and what they felt about this (qualitative data). Just to ensure that people did not exaggerate or underestimate how long they had been waiting, you might also carry out your own observations and time their wait yourself. The data that you collected yourself is known as **primary data**. This kind of data is new, original research information.

An alternative kind of research information is secondary data. It may be appropriate in your research study of waiting times in Accident and Emergency departments to look at sources of data that already exist on this topic. The hospital Accident and Emergency department may have already produced some statistics or have already carried out some in-depth interviews to find out about patients' views on waiting times. The government also produces official statistics on waiting times in Accident and Emergency departments throughout the country. All of these existing sources are known as secondary data sources. The data that can be obtained from them is known as **secondary data**.

Researchers often use secondary data sources in their investigations. For example, they may use secondary sources to find out what has already been researched on the topic. This gives them background information. Alternatively, they might compare their own findings to existing (secondary) data on the same topic or issue. For example, the conclusion that waiting times have got longer could only be drawn by comparing two or more sets of data.

Populations and samples

Health and social care research usually involves a study or investigation in which a group of people take part. The group of people who become involved in a research investigation are known by terms such as subjects, participants and respondents. The total number, or set, of people who could potentially take part in a research study is known as the research population. All members of a **research population** must share specified characteristics or criteria. For example, David Farrington (1991) has produced reports of a longitudinal (long-term) study of the development of aggressive behaviour.

Farrington used a very specific population of subjects in his research; 400 boys who, at the beginning of his research, were eight years old, from working class backgrounds and who lived in England. The population criteria therefore excluded all girls, older and younger boys and any children not living in England or not from a working class background.

It is important to have precise population characteristics and only to select from the group of people who meet all of these characteristics.

The number of people in a research population is usually too large for a researcher, or even a group of researchers, to meet face to face or even to contact by post. To get around this problem, a sub-group from within the overall population is usually selected to participate in the study. This sub-group is known as a **sample**. A key quality or characteristic of the research sample is that it must be representative of the population. What is true of the research population must also be true of the research sample. That is, the sub-group must be an accurate reflection of the larger population. There are a number of different ways of selecting a **representative sample**. These are outlined on pp. 381–2.

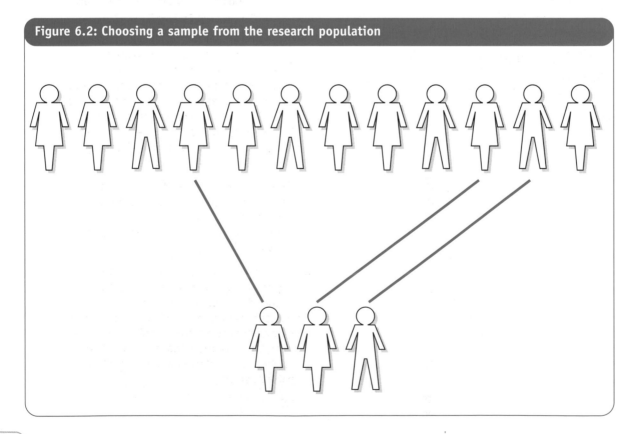

Figure 6.2: Choosing a sample from the research population

BUILD YOUR LEARNING

Keywords and phrases

You should know the meaning of the words and phrases listed below. If you are unsure about any of them, go back through the last five pages of the unit to refresh your understanding.

- Data collection methods
- Empirical evidence
- Interpretive approach
- Population
- Positivist approach
- Primary data
- Representative sample
- Research population
- Qualitative data
- Quantitative data
- Sample
- Secondary data
- Variables

Summary points

- Health and social care researchers aim to conduct their investigations in a planned, systematic manner. Two of the main theoretical approaches that they use to organise their ideas, and which influence their choice of data collection methods, are known as the positivist and the interpretive approaches.

- The positivist approach is associated with the natural sciences and tends to be used by researchers with a background and training in medicine or psychology. Positivist researchers aim to establish facts and scientific laws, and try to prevent their personal attitudes and values from influencing the research situation.

- Positivist researchers tend to use data collection methods such as experiments, questionnaire surveys and structured interviews in health and social care settings. These methods typically elicit, or draw out, quantitative (numerical) data.

- The interpretive approach is associated with the social sciences and tends to be used by researchers with nursing and social care backgrounds. Interpretive researchers aim to describe and understand a group of people or social situation from the insider's point of view. Interpretive researchers are interested in understanding the meanings that people give to their lives and actions.

- Interpretive researchers tend to use data collection methods such as participant observation and semi or unstructured interviews. These methods typically elicit qualitative (non-numerical) data.

- Research data can be thought of in terms of whether it is qualitative or quantitative and whether it is obtained from primary or secondary data sources. Primary data is new, original information that is collected by the researchers. Secondary data is information that has been collected and produced by another person.

QUESTIONS

1 What is empirical data?

2 What are the key characteristics of the positivist approach to research? Include the terms scientific, qualitative data, variables and control somewhere in your answer.

3 What is a scientific law? Give an example in your answer.

4 Identify four ways in which the interpretive approach differs from the positivist approach to research.

5 Why is the length of time a person waits to see his or her GP quantitative rather than qualitative data?

Judging the quality of research methods

People who read and use health and social care research, such as care practitioners, purchasers of care services and service managers, judge research investigations and their findings in terms of several important criteria. Researchers in any field of investigation are expected to be aware of the meaning and importance of:

- the reliability of data collection methods
- the validity of the data that is collected
- the representativeness of the research sample used
- the objectivity of the researcher
- the ethical standards of the research.

Reliability

Reliability is a key concept in research. The reliability of the data collection method used in a research investigation is one of the criteria against which the research conclusions are judged. McNeill (1990) says that 'if a method of collecting evidence is **reliable**, it means that anybody else using the method, or the same person using it at another time, would come up with the same results'. For example, a reliable thermometer will always give a reading of 100°C when placed in a bowl of boiling water, regardless of who places it there. A tape measure could also be regarded as reliable if it produced the same measurement each time it was used (correctly) to measure the same thing.

Some data collection methods in research are seen as more reliable than others. Data collection methods that involve researchers working on their own, in situations that cannot be replicated (repeated) and where the researchers use their beliefs, values or preconceptions to decide which data is important, tend to be less reliable than data collection methods that don't have these characteristics.

Using unreliable data collection methods or tools leads to validity problems with the data.

▲ Why would you doubt the reliability of the data gained from this thermometer?

Validity

Validity refers to the issue of whether the data collected is a true picture of what is being studied.

There are many reasons why the data that researchers collect can be invalid. For example, the data can be a product of the research instrument that is used, rather than a true picture, or indicator, of what it actually claims to be. This may sound odd if you think back to the thermometer and boiling water example above. We are fairly certain that thermometers only measure the temperature of natural phenomena such as water, or the human body. They are reliable in this respect, but they also produce valid results in that they do actually reveal the degree or level of heat. We can be much less certain that the tools we use to measure social variables, such as intelligence, are valid.

Intelligence tests have been shown to be quite reliable, in that if the same IQ test is used on repeated occasions with the same person, they are very likely to produce the same results each time. However, it is questionable whether the result is really a true, valid, measure of the person's intelligence quotient (IQ). The validity of IQ test results is often questioned on the grounds that what they really reveal is how good people are at doing IQ tests, not the true level of people's IQ.

Similarly, the validity of questionnaire and interview data can be questioned on the grounds that people may give answers that are not actually true because they deliberately lie or give answers that do not actually represent how they behave. For example, research subjects often portray themselves as non-sexist and non-racist, and may well believe this about themselves. While they may not be deliberately lying, their real behaviour at work and when they are with their friends, for example, may reveal something about their beliefs that they do not wish to acknowledge or admit. The validity of questionnaire and interview data should never be taken for granted or relied upon for both of the above reasons.

The reliability of data collection methods and the validity of the data that is obtained are always important issues to consider when evaluating your own research or the conclusions that others arrive at when they publish research findings. A third factor that must be taken into account when judging the quality of research conclusions is representativeness.

Representativeness

McNeill (1990) says that **representativeness** 'refers to the question of whether the group or situation being studied are typical of others'. If a group or situation is representative of others, then researchers can **generalise** their findings. That is, they can say that what is true for this group or situation is true of others. If we do not know whether the group or situation is representative, it is not safe, or correct, to claim that the research findings can be generalised outside of the group or situation that has been studied. Researchers use various sampling methods (see pp. 381–2) to try to ensure that their research is based on a representative group of people or a representative situation. There are also many situations where researchers do not use sampling methods and acknowledge that their findings cannot be generalised. For example, researchers who use participant observation (see p. 363) or case study (see p. 362) methods do not usually seek to study a representative group or situation and so do not use sampling techniques.

Objectivity

Researchers are expected to be objective, as opposed to biased or prejudiced, in the way that they carry out their research investigations. They must suspend their judgements and view research situations and problems from the viewpoint of a stranger. Researchers who are **objective** avoid letting their values, beliefs and existing ideas affect or influence the way that they develop their project, conduct the research or analyse the data.

In order to be objective, researchers must be open about the way that they conduct and explain their research. In the final research report and presentation it is important that they show clearly how the research was conducted, present the data in an accessible way and justify any conclusions that are reached. This allows other interested parties to check and question whether the research has been conducted in an acceptable way and whether the conclusions drawn are valid and reliable. Objectivity and openness reduce the risk that false conclusions will be deliberately or accidentally reached from a flawed piece of research. In part, this relates to the ethical issue of honesty. This and other ethical aspects of research investigations are discussed further on pp. 370–5.

BUILD YOUR LEARNING

Keywords and phrases

You should know the meaning of the words and phrases listed below. If you are unsure about any of them, go back through the last two pages of the unit to refresh your understanding.

- Ethical standards
- Generalise
- Objectivity
- Population
- Reliability
- Sample
- Representativeness
- Validity

Summary points

- The quality of research investigations and their findings are judged on the grounds of their reliability, validity, representativeness, objectivity and ethical acceptability.

- If a data collection method is reliable it enables researchers to produce the same results in given research circumstances. Data collection methods used in health and social research tend to be less reliable than those used in natural sciences research.

- Validity refers to the true nature of data. Valid data gives a true picture of what is being studied.

- Social research tools, such as questionnaire and interview methods, do not always produce valid data. For example, people can give false or misleading answers to questions that do not truly reveal what they believe or how they behave.

- Health and social care research often involves studying groups of people or social situations. The data and conclusions that are produced are often judged in terms of whether the sample of people or the chosen situation is representative of other people and situations, so that the findings can be generalised beyond the sample.

- Researchers are supposed to be objective in the way that they carry out their research and analyse their data. Objectivity is related to honesty, in that researchers must not deliberately bias or falsify their methods or data and must make all efforts to ensure that their values and beliefs do not cause this to happen accidentally.

QUESTIONS

1 When is a data collection method unreliable?

2 What is valid data?

3 Why do samples have to be representative of the research population?

4 Explain why health and social care researchers should conduct their investigations in an objective way.

Methods of data collection

We are concerned here with different methods of collecting primary data.

Questionnaire surveys

Surveys, using questionnaires as the data collection tool, are a popular method of collecting data in research investigations. Positivist researchers use questionnaires that include lots of closed questions, rating scales and forced choice items.

- Closed questions offer limited scope for response. They are usually of the yes or no variety. An example of a closed question is, 'Do you smoke cigarettes?'

- Rating scales require the respondent to indicate a degree of preference from a limited range of choices. An example of a rating scale is 'Choose the item nearest to your own view about the statement that students learn a lot from work placements:

  ☐ Strongly agree
  ☐ Agree
  ☐ Neither agree nor disagree
  ☐ Disagree
  ☐ Strongly disagree.'

- Forced choice items set out the possible range of responses and are generally used to obtain factual information. An example of a forced choice question is, 'Which of the following age groups do you currently fall into? 14–16, 17–19, 20–22, over 22'.

These kinds of response items allow researchers to collect large amounts of quantitative data that they can then analyse statistically. Positivist researchers try to survey a representative sample of the population they are interested in and then generalise their findings and conclusions to the wider population.

Researchers who adopt an interpretive approach use surveys and questionnaire methods much less frequently. Where they are used by interpretive researchers, questionnaires are likely to be less structured and less restrictive in the responses that they permit. Typically, interpretive researchers would include a lot of open questions that allow for a variety of individual responses. This would also help researchers to avoid accidentally introducing any of their own preconceptions and protect the validity of the data.

There are a number of ways of gathering data through questionnaires. These include postal, telephone and face-to-face personal methods. The general advantages and limitations of questionnaires are outlined in Figure 6.3.

Figure 6.3: Advantages and limitations of questionnaires as a data collection method

Advantages	Disadvantages
Can be a cheap and efficient way of collecting data.	Can be difficult to get people to complete. Response rate of postal questionnaires is particularly low.
Can collect a large amount of data relatively quickly.	Respondents often have limited choice of answers. They may not reveal their real views or attitudes if they do not match the forced choices.
Relatively reliable as a method of data collection.	Unless questionnaire is conducted face-to-face, cannot be sure of the true identity of the respondent.
Comparison of respondents answers possible.	Respondents tend to be people who have stronger attitudes on the subject being surveyed.
	Cannot be sure that respondents have understood the questions or use follow-up questions to explore unusual answers.

Interviews

How do you feel about an interview?

Interviews are a very widely used method of collecting data in health and social care research. They are similar to questionnaires in that they are organised around a series of questions and rely on interviewees' ability to answer and tell the truth as they see it.

However, interviews are more than long-winded alternatives to questionnaires. They can be used within either a positivist or an interpretive research approach, depending on the extent to which they are structured by the researchers. People who adopt a positivist approach to research tend to produce a more highly structured schedule of questions that they ask all interviewees in the same order. Sometimes researchers who use these structured interviews read from a questionnaire and give respondents a limited choice of possible answers.

Researchers who adopt a more interpretive approach use semi-structured or unstructured interviews. In these situations, researchers have fewer pre-determined questions and are more likely to let the interview develop as a guided conversation, according to the interests and wishes of the interviewee. The fact that the researcher is physically present during interview-based data collection can be both advantageous (people may be more likely to answer questions fully, the interviewer can ask for further explanation and give clarification) and a disadvantage (their presence may have an effect on responses) over questionnaires. The advantages and disadvantages of semi-structured interviews are outlined in Figure 6.4.

Health and social care researchers tend to use **triangulation** (see p. 364) in major research investigations. This means that they might use an unstructured interview at the beginning of the study to identify the key issues and terms and then use this information to develop a more structured set of interview questions or a questionnaire. The case study describes how this might happen in practice.

Figure 6.4: Advantages and limitations of semi-structured interviews as a data collection method

Advantages	Limitations
Avoids too much pre-judgement where the questions are not pre-determined. Can obtain the interviewees' real views and beliefs.	Validity of data is always suspect. It is never possible to be 100 per cent sure that interviewees are not either deliberately lying or that they recall the truth correctly.
Allow probing of what the respondent says. Researchers can discover and make use of unexpected and unforeseen information as it is revealed.	Recording information can be difficult. Writing down what people say is difficult and intrusive. It is hard to keep up and stopping interrupts the flow of the interview. Tape recording the interview is much better but introduces confidentiality issues and may cause respondents to limit what they say.
Depth of information is improved because the interviewer can explore what respondents really mean or really believe, as they talk more freely.	People give too much information in semi and unstructured interviews. Most of what they say is not usable and goes into too much depth.
Response rates can be very good as the interviewer is present to ensure completion of data collection.	Interviews take a long time to complete and even longer to transcribe into a written record of what was said.
Help and guidance can be provided to explain questions and give additional information where it is needed.	Reliability of data is poor. It is very difficult to generalise between respondents because they have usually not been asked exactly the same questions and as a result can give very different responses.

CASE STUDY

Triangulation

As part of her nurse training course, Louise undertook a study of the role of the health care assistant (HCA) in residential homes. She began by conducting two unstructured interviews with care assistants she knew. These highlighted some of the key features of the HCA role and enabled her to identify some important issues.

Louise then produced a structured questionnaire that focused in more detail on aspects of the HCA role and sought data on the overlap between the role of the HCA and the qualified nurse.

Louise used her questionnaire in structured interviews with 25 HCAs and 10 registered nurses. Louise carried out some visits to residential homes to provide a third source of data, making notes of her observations on the work of HCAs.

Experiments

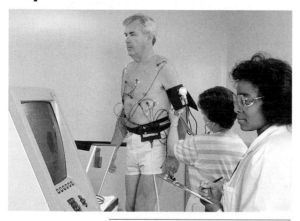

▲ Collecting data about the effect of exercise on the body

Experiments are a very common and important method of collecting data in health and social care research. They are usually the method of choice where biological, psychological or natural science phenomena are being investigated. The vast majority of experiments in health and social care are laboratory experiments or clinical trials where the effectiveness of medication and treatments for physical or psychiatric illnesses are investigated. **Single case experiments** involve only one individual. However, it is more common for an experiment to involve a large number of participants who have been selected as a representative sample of the research population being studied.

Experiments involve situations in which researchers identify two or more variables and then construct an experiment to manipulate, or change, one variable to see what effect, or consequence, this has on the other(s). These variables are called the dependent and independent variables. The **dependent variable** is the thing or behaviour that we want to explain. The **independent variables** are the things that we think might have an effect on the dependent variable and that the researchers manipulate. The case study explains the basic experimental process and the role of researchers in an experiment.

CASE STUDY

The experimental process

Gemma Jones, a health care researcher, was asked to research the effect of music on dental patients' levels of anxiety. She decided to do an experiment. She began collecting data after recruiting 60 people who described themselves as very anxious dental patients. She divided the volunteers into three groups, trying to match each group according to age, gender and the length of time that had gone by since their last check-up. All the participants were told that they would undergo a routine dental check-up but that they would not receive any follow-up treatment on the same day.

The participants sat alone in the dentist's waiting room for five minutes before and five minutes after their check-up. During this time they each filled in a short questionnaire in which they rated their level of anxiety and noted how they felt at each point.

The first set of participants, known as the experimental group, were played soothing classical music when they were in the waiting room. They were also given a placebo sugar pill, after being told that it was part of the procedure but that it would not harm them in any way. The second set, known as the placebo group, were not played any music but were given the placebo sugar pill and the same explanation about it. The third set, known as the control group, were not played any music and were not given the placebo sugar pill.

Gemma Jones's role involved planning and setting up the experiment, recruiting the participants, selecting the music, giving out the sugar pills, developing the questionnaire and then analysing the data. She did not conduct the dental check-ups, take part herself or observe the participants in the waiting room.

ACTIVITY

The experimental process

1 What was the dependent variable in the experiment in the case study?

2 What were the two independent variables that the researcher, Gemma Jones, experimented with?

3 Identify at least two other (extraneous) variables that could have influenced the results of the experiment.

4 Why do you think the researcher used a placebo and a control group in this experiment?

Researchers who use experiments typically wish to generate quantitative data and adopt a positivist approach to research. Experimental researchers place a lot of importance on objectivity and on excluding the influence of external variables. In health and social care situations, medical researchers use strategies like control groups, placebos, and blind and double-blind protocols to maximise the objectivity of their research.

A **control group** is a sub-group of research participants who are not experimented on. They are selected to be similar to the experimental, test or treatment group. Results obtained from the experimental group are compared to those obtained from the control group.

A **placebo** is an inert substance or phenomenon that has no known effect on the variable being tested. For example, instead of being given the real test medication in a clinical trial, some people may be given a placebo, or sugar pill, that looks the same but has no medication in it. Placebo tablets usually contain vitamin C. In clinical drug trial experiments it is usual for half of the participants, the treatment group, to be given the real drug (the independent variable), whilst the other half, the control group, receives the placebo. For the drug to be judged a success, the treatment group must experience significantly greater change in the dependent variable than the placebo group. This would show that the independent variable (the real drug) was the factor that had a significant effect on the dependent variable. That is, that the drug worked!

Most clinical trials use a **blind protocol**. This means that the participants do not know whether they are receiving the real drug or the placebo. Some people who think that they are receiving the real drug but who are actually receiving the placebo experience what is known as the **placebo effect**. That is, they experience some change or improvement that is not attributable to the drug!

In **double-blind** studies, the participants are allocated to the respective treatment and placebo groups by independent researchers who play no part in collecting the data on the drug's effects. The researchers who collect and analyse the data are unaware which of the participants are in the treatment group and which are receiving the placebo. When the data has been collected and fully analysed the independent researcher tells the other researchers which participants belong to which group. The aim of all of this is to minimise potential bias.

Case studies

In research, a **case study** is a systematic investigation into a single individual, event or situation. Case study research is often conducted over a long period of time, so that in-depth data is obtained. The case study is not a data collection method in itself. Researchers who conduct case studies make use of a variety of data collection methods including interviews, observations and analysis of documents. Case study research is widely

---

Figure 6.5: Advantages and limitations of experiments as a data collection method

Advantages	Limitations
The reliability of this data collection method is very high, as experiments can be duplicated in exactly the same circumstances.	Researchers can only collect data on a very specific and narrow topic – the relationship between two variables. There is no flexibility beyond this.
Quantitative data is produced, allowing statistical analysis and comparison between changes in experimental circumstances.	Validity of data can be suspect as experimenters cannot be certain that they have all non experimental variables under control.
The scientific status of the experimental method gives it credibility with potential participants and with health and social care practitioners.	The use of human beings in experimental situations raises many difficult ethical issues.

used in the health and social care field as it allows researchers to study individuals and small groups in clinical or natural settings in detail. For example, when mental health hospitals began to close down in the late 1980s, a number of case studies were made of long-stay wards to find out how the closure process affected long-stay residents and staff. The research findings from these studies gave managers and staff a better insight into the closure process and its impact on the various people involved.

Participant observation

In a **participant observation** study, researchers join the group or situation that they are studying. Participant observers try to enter the world of the group they intend to study and get to know them. They need to try to understand the motives and meanings of the people they are studying. The aim of this is for the researchers to gain a deeper insight into the real way of life, beliefs and activities of the group in the natural setting. It is believed that the researchers' own experience of the group gives them access to data that might not be elicited (drawn out) from a questionnaire or interview.

Participant observation is closely associated with the interpretive approach to research. It is a data collection method that most positivistic researchers reject, as participant researchers do not remain detached or

separate from the research participants or situation. Because of the danger that participant observation may not produce objective data, researchers also use other methods, such as interviews, alongside it, to provide complementary data.

▲ Observation should be unobtrusive

Observational methods in participation studies can be **overt**, where researchers identify themselves and their purpose to the people being studied, or **covert**, where they keep their identity and purpose a secret. The advantages and limitations of participant observation as a data collection method are outlined in Figure 6.6.

Figure 6.6: Advantages and limitations of participant observation

Advantages	Limitations
Validity of data can be very high, as observations of real life in natural setting gives access to valid data.	Researchers need to have a way of remaining objective and not becoming so involved in the group as to influence behaviour or events.
Produces data rich in meaning and gives access to otherwise hidden data.	May never really understand the group or setting, as unable to appreciate deep meaning and significance of behaviour from standpoint of a detached outsider.
Can achieve long-term, in-depth collection of data.	Participant observation studies tend to be small scale and the group studied may also not be representative of any other social group, so findings can't be generalised.
Covert participant observation may be the only way of accessing hidden data or hostile groups	Covert observation has serious ethical implications and problems.
Researchers do not have to decide what they are looking for in advance. They can make decisions about what is and is not significant behaviour as events occur and unfold naturally.	Reliability of data collection method is relatively low as observations are often personal and unrepeatable.

Action research

Action research is a relatively new research method that has gained a lot of popularity with health and social care practitioners. This is because it involves collaboration between researchers and care practitioners. In essence, **action research** is a method of investigating and solving practice problems and a way of introducing and evaluating change in health and social care settings. It gives health and social care practitioners the opportunity to identify real problems and then to participate in, and evaluate the effects of, implementing possible solutions.

Action research can be used within both a positivistic and an interpretive approach to research. Like case study research, the action researcher can use one or more of the data collection methods discussed above (questionnaires, interviews, participant observation).

Triangulation

In practice, researchers often use more than one data collection method and approach in their research investigation. This strategy is known as **triangulation**.

Triangulation enables researchers to explore different aspects of the same topic and to look at it from different sides. In terms we have used previously, researchers can collect both quantitative and qualitative data from primary and secondary sources. Research investigations that use triangulation tend to be based on one main data collection method that is supplemented by others.

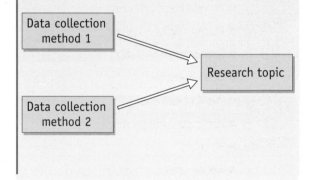

ACTIVITY
Research into eating habits

Imagine that you have to conduct a research study on the eating habits of primary school children. Suggest how you will make use of triangulation in your study. Produce a diagram identifying your data collection methods and research focus, and briefly explain what kind of data your triangulation approach would aim to produce.

RESEARCHING CAKES

Quantitative data   Qualitative data   Both types of data

BUILD YOUR LEARNING

Keywords and phrases

You should know the meaning of the words and phrases listed below. If you are unclear about any of them, go back through the last six pages to refresh your understanding.

- Action research
- Blind protocol
- Case study
- Closed question
- Control group
- Covert observation
- Dependent variable
- Double-blind protocol
- Forced choice question
- Independent variable
- Open question
- Overt observation
- Participant observation
- Placebo
- Rating scale
- Representative sample
- Response rate
- Semi-structured interview
- Single case experiment
- Structured interview
- Triangulation
- Unstructured interview
- Variable

Summary points

- Questionnaires contain open, closed and forced choice questions and rating scales to obtain data from a representative sample of a research population. They are cheap, efficient, relatively reliable and enable researchers to collect large amounts of data quickly. But response rates to questionnaires can be low and data can lack validity.

- Interviewing is a method based on asking a series of questions. Interviews can be structured, semi-structured or unstructured. They allow researchers to adopt a more flexible and responsive approach to data collection. Disadvantages include the relative weakness in validity of the data and the difficulties associated with recording data.

- Experiments are used to collect numerical forms of biological and psychological data. Experimental methods tend to be highly reliable if relatively inflexible, and present ethical problems when involving people.

- Case study research involves an in-depth analysis of an individual, or a specific group or situation. This may involve the use of a variety of data collection methods.

- Participant observation is an interpretive approach that involves entering the world of the group that the researchers intend to study. Participant observers aim to understand the motives and meanings of the people they are studying. The data obtained can be high in validity, though participant observation is a relatively unreliable method of data collection.

- Action research involves identifying and solving practice-related problems. It is a way of introducing and evaluating change in health and social care settings.

- Triangulation involves using more than one method of data collection to investigate a topic from several angles at once.

QUESTIONS

1 Write a forced choice question on ethnic origin that could be included in a questionnaire.

2 Identify and explain two advantages that questionnaires have over participant observation as a data collection method.

3 Explain how an experiment works as a method of collecting data. Use the terms dependent variable and independent variable and try to illustrate your answer with an example.

4 What is a double-blind research study? Include the terms placebo effect and control group somewhere in your answer.

5 What are the main strengths of participant observation as a data collection method? Try and give examples to illustrate your points.

6 What is triangulation and why do health and social care researchers use it?

Using secondary sources and data

Health and social care researchers often use data that has been produced and analysed by others. This is known as **secondary data**. It is distinct from primary data, which is collected by the researchers themselves, because it is obtained second hand. A variety of forms of secondary data are used in health and social care research. Some of these are described below.

Data from earlier research

Health and social care researchers generally review the existing literature on their chosen research topic at an early stage in their research project. Sometimes researchers make direct use of the data on their topic that others have already collected and analysed. For example, researchers might choose to re-analyse existing data, using new techniques or with a new hypothesis in mind. Alternatively, and more commonly, researchers refer to previous findings in literature reviews and may compare the findings of earlier studies to their own. In all of these situations, the researchers are making second-hand use of data from earlier research.

Statistics

Government bodies, commercial organisations and voluntary sector groups produce a vast range of **statistical data** that is of use to health and social care researchers. Government bodies, such as local authorities, NHS trusts and education authorities collect and produce statistical information on a broad range of health and welfare related topics. This information is used by the government for policy-making and service planning purposes but it is also made publicly available by the Office for National Statistics in publications such as *Social Trends* and the *General Household Survey*. Researchers often use these statistics as ready-made data in their research studies. This form of secondary data is commonly found in the introduction to research reports, where background information on the research topic is given.

Documentary sources

Health and social care researchers have used a variety of public and personal **documentary sources** in past research. Examples have included the diaries and letters of research participants but more commonly involve official medical and other case note records.

The official reports of public enquiries and government committees are also a source of documentary data. Again, these are most likely to be used in the early stages of research and may be cited as relevant background literature or in the discussion section of studies, where researchers' findings may be compared with earlier research and available data.

Problems with secondary data

The extent to which secondary data may be problematic depends on the source. The key issues that need to be considered when using secondary data are validity and reliability and the possibility of personal bias in documentary sources.

Validity and reliability

Official government data from large-scale, ongoing research, such as the Census, tends to be thought of as both valid and very reliable. This is in contrast to data obtained from personal letters or diaries for example, where validity is often questioned. However, many researchers remain wary of official data, on the grounds that the government is not a neutral body which is just collecting data. On the contrary, they argue, it is important to recognise that governments have their own policy agendas and may carry out research which produces data that suits that agenda.

One commonly cited example is data on hospital waiting lists and appointment waiting times. While the government claims that the data are valid and reliable, the government's critics often dispute this and counter claim that the way waiting time is defined and the data collected has a dramatic effect on the results.

Personal bias

Documentary sources such as letters and diaries may well not provide valid, unbiased data. This is particularly true if they were written with even the slightest hope that one day they might be published or examined by researchers. The **personal biases** of the writers of such documents are likely to an inherent part of the data. The biases and views of the people who produce the documents could become a valid research focus themselves, but the validity of the data itself should never be taken for granted.

Understanding statistical tables and graphics

Researchers present their statistical findings in a variety of ways. Frequency tables and bar and pie charts are very common formats. Researchers need to be able to understand how to read statistical tables and graphs to make sense of the data that they contain. Figure 6.7 shows a typical statistical table and is presented in a format that you are likely to come across when reading research studies or searching for secondary data.

In order to make sense of the data contained in Figure 6.7, you need to be able to dissect the various elements of the table and understand how they work together to appreciate what it is aiming to show. This can be done by following a few simple steps.

1 Read the title of the table or graph.

2 Check what area(s) or group(s) the data refers to.

3 Note what the figures represent in terms of numerical units.

4 Identify the period of time that the figures cover.

5 Put all the above together in a brief summary of the table. What does it represent?

6 Look for patterns and significant findings.

The same steps are useful in helping you to read and understand bar charts, pie charts and line graphs.

Figure 6.7: A typical statistical table

Time use (hours): by employment status and gender of men and women aged 16–45 in Great Britain, 1999

Weekly hours spent on:	In full-time employment		In part-time employment	
	Males	Females	Males	Females
Sleep	57	58	62	60
Free time	34	31	48	32
Work, study, travel	53	48	28	26
Housework, cooking	7	15	12	26
Shopping	1	6	4	10
Eating, personal hygiene	13	13	13	21
Free time per week day	4	4	6	4
Free time per weekend day	8	6	8	6

Note: all data in this table is hypothetical

Figure 6.8: Typical bar chart and pie chart

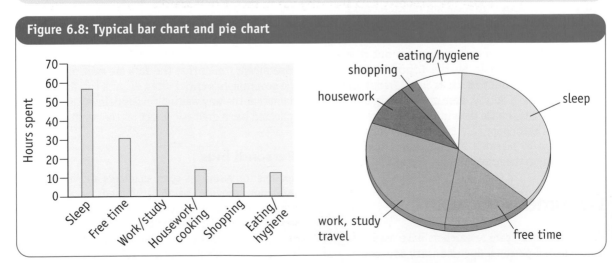

BUILD YOUR LEARNING

Keywords and phrases

You should know the meaning of the words and phrases listed below. If you are unsure about any of them, go back through the last two pages to refresh your understanding.

- Personal bias
- Documentary sources
- Statistical data
- Social Trends
- General Household Survey

Summary points

- Researchers often use secondary data in their own research studies. This is data that has been collected and analysed by another person.

- Data from earlier research, official statistics and documents are the main sources of secondary data used by health and social care researchers.

- The main weakness of secondary data is that its validity and reliability is not assured and researchers cannot guarantee that documentary sources are not inherently biased.

- The ability to read and understand statistical graphs and tables is an important skill that all researchers should develop. This is essential for making an assessment of the quality of secondary statistical data.

QUESTIONS

1 Describe two ways in which researchers may use secondary data in their own studies.

2 Explain, using examples, why researchers should always be wary about the secondary data that they use in their own research.

Ethical issues in research

Research activity in health and social care is generally presented as a good thing. It has a positive association with progress, discovery of new knowledge and improvement in our understanding of factors and issues relating to health and well-being. However, if your GP told you that he or she would be trying out a few new techniques, procedures and drugs on you as part of a research study, you may discover that you actually have a few reservations about research! How would you feel? What if he or she didn't tell you and you found out by chance after the research had begun? You might like to think briefly about the conditions that you would impose before you agreed to take part and about your likely reaction to finding out that you were an unwitting participant in research.

▲ An advert for volunteers to take part in a clinical trial

Research is a good thing providing it is carried out in an acceptable way and with certain safeguards in place. We look next at the ethical principles that must be met in order that research investigations are acceptable and justifiable.

The nature of ethics in research

Research ethics is about the practical standards of behaviour and procedures that researchers are expected to follow. It is not about identifying and discussing big and difficult philosophical issues that are somehow hidden in your research.

Homan (1991) makes a distinction between ethics as a philosophical discipline and the nature of ethics in research situations. In philosophy, ethics is seen as the science of morality. Questions of what is moral (right and wrong) are a part of the ethics of research. However, researchers do not usually have to become involved in deep philosophical thinking about the big moral issues that are a general feature of research. They simply need to find ways of applying a limited set of ethical principles to their own research investigation.

There is now some agreement about which ethical principles should be applied in research situations. Professional bodies such as the British Psychology Association and the United Kingdom Central Council for Nursing, Health Visiting and Midwifery, and health and social care organisations, such as NHS trusts, produce a number of codes of ethics which provide guidelines on how these key principles should be put into practice during research investigations.

Ethical principles in research practice

The ethical criteria that must be considered and met before research is considered ethically acceptable are:

- autonomy – the participants' rights and confidentiality should be protected

- non-maleficence – no harm should be done to others as a result of the research

- beneficence – some good or benefit to others should come out of the research, so that it provides a positive contribution to knowledge and human understanding

- honesty and integrity – researchers should act in an honest way and be truthful and open in their methods and behaviour.

Each of these principles is discussed in more detail below. Health and social care researchers put the principles into practice by following some basic practical guidelines and behaviour conventions when they actually carry out their research. These guidelines and conventions are discussed further on p. 390.

Autonomy

Autonomy means self-government or self-determination. In research situations it covers issues such as respecting people and their right to make a fully informed decision about whether or not to participate in a research investigation. In order to ensure that they protect the autonomy of potential participants, researchers must develop clear, practical ways of gaining their informed consent and of protecting the confidentiality of the data that they obtain.

Informed consent

Researchers must be able to demonstrate that participants have actively, freely given their **consent** to involvement in the research investigation and that they have a full understanding of what the research involves. They must be aware of the aims of the research and of any risks that they may face if they participate. They must also be fully aware of what they will be required to do or experience during the research investigation.

There are established and relatively straightforward procedures for obtaining informed consent. These involve explaining what will happen and asking whether the person will volunteer to take part in the research. It is an established principle that researchers should not trick people into unwittingly participating in research and that they should not lie to conceal the fact that they are doing research without the people whom they are studying knowing about it. The consequences of this for the participants, and the credibility of research generally, can be damaging.

In health and social care research there are some situations in which obtaining informed consent can be problematic. For example, if researchers wanted to carry out a study in which children or people with mental impairments were the intended research subjects they may well have difficulty in ensuring that the potential participants fully understood the nature, requirements and risks of the research. It would be unethical to unwittingly involve such people in a research investigation.

A related issue in health and social care research is the way in which the status and perceived power of health and social care professionals can influence and persuade service users to give their consent because they think the professional knows best. Service users can sometimes do this against their better judgement as the case study illustrates.

CASE STUDY
Informed consent

During the late 1980s a young psychiatrist became part of a research study investigating changes in the brain structure of people who had been diagnosed with schizophrenia. The research was undertaken at a large psychiatric hospital in the south-east of England. The investigation had already been running for 10 years and involved detailed examinations of cross-sections of brain tissue taken during post-mortems. The psychiatrist explained this to Arthur, who had been a resident at the hospital for over 30 years. Arthur signed a consent form agreeing to participate in the research investigation. The psychiatrist thought nothing more of it and filed the consent form with others that had been obtained.

A few days after the consent was obtained the charge nurse on the ward asked the psychiatrist to see Arthur again as he had become very upset and worried. When they met, Arthur wanted to talk about the research study. The psychiatrist explained that the study would involve taking a small piece of Arthur's brain to analyse. To check that he had fully understood what was involved the psychiatrist asked Arthur whether he had any questions. Looking nervous Arthur asked, 'Will it hurt me?' The psychiatrist reassured him that it would not, as it would occur only after he had died. With some relief Arthur said, 'Oh, after I'm dead! That's all right then'.

There are a number of other situations, apart from the issue of mental capacity, in which it is difficult or impractical to obtain the informed consent of all participants in a research investigation. For example, where researchers are carrying out an observational study of a crowd or other large group of people, it may not be possible to explain the study and ask them all for their individual consent to study them.

Where researchers wish to carry out an investigation into a subject that is very sensitive they may have to do so covertly. This means that the only way of gaining access to the data may be to secretly carry out the study without informing the people being studied. In most circumstances this would be unethical. However, there may be some circumstances in which a covert study is justifiable. If the benefits to others of conducting it could be shown to outweigh the rights of the people being studied it may be justified. For example, if researchers wished to investigate the incidence of drug dealing in a hospital or other care setting, they would probably have to use covert strategies to gain access to appropriate data. The key rights of the drug dealers that would be overridden in such a situation would be those of informed consent and privacy.

Confidentiality

All research participants have a right to privacy. This includes the right to withdraw from the research investigation at any point if they wish to, the right to refuse to answer any question asked, the right to remain anonymous and to have the confidentiality of their data protected.

In research situations, **confidentiality** is taken to mean that the information, or data, given by a participant is not revealed to others who are not part of the research team, except in an anonymous form when the results, or findings, of the study are reported. It also means that the data obtained in the research study should only be used for the purposes of the research study. No part of it should be sold to, or be reused by, people for other research or non-research purposes.

Non-maleficence and beneficence

The golden rule of research is that researchers should never do any harm to research participants or those who may be affected by the research. Researchers in health and social care need to clearly identify and document any, and all, of the risks that participants may face. Research that involved injuring, maiming or harming another person could never be ethically justifiable. Where a research study may have a negative impact on the physical or mental health of participants, they should be fully informed of this risk and researchers should take every possible step to minimise any harm coming to them.

Research involving animals is now a very controversial subject. Many research studies and clinical developments have, in the past, made use of animal subjects, typically in experiments where it was felt to be too dangerous to use human participants. Animals have died and have been deliberately maimed and killed for research purposes. Until recently the ethical principles and standards that are applied to research involving human beings were not applied in animal-based research. Sometimes this is impractical. For example, informed consent is not something that monkeys, dogs or rats can give. This is not to say that it is acceptable to disregard the welfare of animals in

research situations. Bailey et al (1995) suggest that because of this, researchers have a greater responsibility to protect the welfare of animals used in research situations.

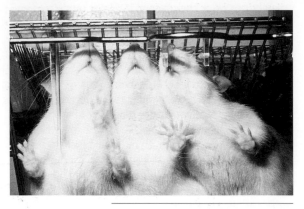

▲ Animal experiments are compulsory before some types of new products can be released

The key ethical questions seem to be first, whether animals have rights and, second, whether the benefit to human beings of overriding these rights outweighs the harm that the research might involve. The animal rights movement rejects vivisection (breeding and using animals for experimental purposes) and other uses of animals in research situations. Many medical and pharmaceutical researchers continue to defend the use of animals in research on the grounds of benefits to humans. The issues require a lot of thinking about and are not easy to resolve.

Ideally, a health or social care research study should do some good or at least be of benefit to participants. Some of the criticisms that were made of animal-based research in the past were that the findings were trivial, purely academic or resulted in little or no actual benefit to human beings. Health and social care research should not be carried out for the sake of it or simply to benefit the career or reputation of the researchers. There are many situations in which the findings will not be as expected or where they are less than earth shatteringly important. However, if the research began with a serious and legitimate intention and could potentially have a beneficial outcome, adding new knowledge to human understanding, it could be said to be ethically justifiable. It is not ethical if it is frivolous, involves illegal behaviour or unjustifiable suffering or has no beneficial intention or purpose.

Honesty and integrity

The final ethical principle is linked to the above point in that it is concerned with the standard of behaviour and integrity of researchers. There is a general expectation that researchers will be truthful and act with **integrity**. Data must be gathered carefully, results be reported honestly, and any problems, errors or distortions be acknowledged. Researchers must never falsify their data or make false claims that are not backed up by the data. Sadly, researchers do not always live up to the ethical standards and expectations that others have of them. Given the potential implications for people's health and well-being, a lack of honesty and integrity by health and social care researchers is completely ethically unacceptable.

ACTIVITY

Research fraud

1 Read the article below on a possible case of research fraud. If Dr Herrmann has, in fact, faked his research findings, what ethical criteria has he breached?

2 Identify some of the negative effects of faked research on other health care research and on care practice.

German scientist faked cancer research

Tony Paterson in Berlin

German university investigators are on the verge of exposing a 'scientific Chernobyl' involving scores of bogus scientific papers they claim were fraudulently published by a cancer research professor who duped the international medical community for 15 years.

The case centres on the German professor Friedhelm Herrmann, until two years ago a leading cancer research specialist at the universities of Mainz, Freiburg and Ulm, and the Max-Delbruck Institute for Molecular Medicine in Berlin.

A special task force at Wurzburg University, which has been examining Dr Herrmann's work for 18 months, says it has evidence that the results of at least 80 of his published cancer research tests were faked. The task force is due to publish its initial findings next month.

'The extent of the fraud is far greater than we expected,' said Roland Houben, a task force member. 'Initially we assumed that there were 47 doctored papers, but now we suspect at least 80 were faked.'

The task force leader, Professor Ulf

Rapp, said: 'They developed an aversion to using genuine data.'

Dr Herrmann, who gave up research in 1977 when suspicions were raised and now works as a general practitioner in Munich, has refused to talk to the Wurzburg team, and was not available for comment yesterday.

In an interview with the German magazine Focus earlier this year he said he was not aware that his published studies had been faked. He blamed the fraud on co-authors and said he should have intervened. 'It is a drama. My main calling is not research. I was and still am a doctor,' he said.

The German scientific press has dubbed the case 'the Chernobyl of science'.

Many of the dubious papers were published in respected US and European journals. Dr Houben said that although many had been withdrawn, it was impossible to gauge their impact on medical research.

Faking scientific research, however, is not a criminal offence under German law.

The Guardian, 8 November 1999

The rationale for research ethics

So far we have explained what ethics involve and how they are applied in research situations. However we have not explicitly looked at the reasons why people who become involved in research, both the researchers and the researched, attach such importance to ethics and the ethical standards of research practice. Homan (1991) suggests that the reasons are based on both an altruistic, or unselfish, concern for others and on the self-interest of researchers.

Researchers and the general public do have a strong concern with the rights and interests of people who take part in research investigations. Ethics and ethical standards of research practice are important because it would be morally wrong to put another human being in danger or do them any harm through research. This is very important in the health and social care field, as the participants in the research can be people who are particularly dependent and vulnerable because they are experiencing ill-health, developmental difficulties or social disadvantage. Written ethical guidelines set standards that aim to protect the participants and the public from reckless and harmful research.

At the same time, researchers who promote good ethical standards in research have their own self-interest in mind. They stand to gain from being ethical. The unethical treatment of research participants would probably result in researchers losing the trust and cooperation of the general public. Research as a practice would get a bad name. Research participants would be wary and reluctant to participate in studies. This might result in researchers having access to poorer or more limited data sources. It is clearly in the interest of researchers to maintain public trust and confidence in their methods and their findings. Promising, and being seen to maintain, high ethical standards of practice is central to this.

ACTIVITY
The effect of deception

Read the article about the alleged deceit used to get armed forces personnel to participate in medical research during the 1950s.

■ Would you voluntarily participate in any research studies being carried out at Porton Down?

■ How do stories like this affect public confidence in medical research?

Soldiers tricked into chemical tests

By Andrew Gilligan and Rob Evans

Dozens of servicemen say they were tricked into painful chemical experiments at the Government's Porton Down test centre by being told they were helping with research into the common cold.

The veterans volunteered for the experiments in the 1950s and 60s. 'I went to Porton after seeing a notice asking for volunteers for common cold research,' said Gordon Bell. 'I would never have set foot in Porton if I had known it was for chemical warfare. It was betrayal.'

Although the original misinformation came from unit-level notices, the volunteers say that at no stage after arrival in Porton were their misconceptions corrected – an apparent breach of the Nuremberg Code on human experiments, which prescribes that experiments must not be performed without the subject's 'informed consent'.

Mr Bell, who was experimented on at Porton in 1959, said: 'Nobody told us anything.' For one experiment he was ordered to stand in front of a stream of gas so acrid that he could bear it for less than a minute. 'My face was stinging, my eyes were running, my throat was red raw, my lungs were burning,' he said.

Douglas Shave was put into a gas chamber for periods of up to 45 minutes with no gas mask or other protection. To this day he has no idea what the gas was in the chamber. Both men now suffer from severe skin problems, including boils on the face, eczema and blotches.

Porton Down's spokesman confirmed that the establishment had never conducted research into the common cold. But any misinformation supplied by the volunteers' units was their doing, not Porton's, he said. 'We are certain that once they got to Porton they were given sufficient knowledge for informed consent,' he said. 'But what informed consent meant in the 1950s was less structured and detailed than it is now.'

Daily Telegraph, 2 November 1997

Who judges whether research is ethically acceptable?

You may have already wondered who judges and decides whether a proposed research investigation is ethical and acceptable. There are basically four different parties involved in what is an ongoing process of evaluation:

- the researchers themselves
- ethics committees
- the research participants
- users of the research report.

The ethical role of researchers

Researchers should be aware of the need to adopt ethical standards of practice and behaviour when conducting their research investigations. They should know about the main ethical principles that we discussed earlier (see pp. 370–3) and find ways of putting them into practice. There is a general expectation in the research and health and social care community that researchers will scrutinise, or check, their research proposals for any potential ethical problems before they begin their data collection. That is, they will look hard and critically at the research idea and the proposed methods and try to identify all possible ethical issues. Whilst there are ethical issues in every proposed research project there are also usually ways of resolving or minimising the ethical problems that are identified. The researcher plays an important self-regulatory role, both in the identification of possible problems and in proposing possible solutions.

The role of ethics committees

Universities, hospitals and welfare institutions generally have ethics committees that have a formal scrutiny and regulation role in respect of research. Their role is to review research proposals and scrutinise the ethical implications before permission is given to proceed with the research. Health and social welfare organisations usually have very strict, formal ethical guidelines and procedures that must be met before research can be carried out within any institution that they have responsibility for. Ethics committees are usually made up of senior practitioners, academics and some lay people (members of the general public) in order to gain a broad spectrum of expertise and opinion.

Researchers are usually required to complete large amounts of paperwork and provide a wide range of information and evidence about their proposed research. Some ethics committees require researchers to appear in front of them to answer questions and explain and justify their research proposal in person. Where a research investigation is going to be conducted within a number of institutions or places at the same time, the researchers may well have to complete paperwork for, and present themselves to, several different ethics committees before they can proceed with the research. This can seem, and actually be, a very time-consuming and bureaucratic process.

The role of the research participant

The people who participate in research studies also play a part in determining whether the research is ethically acceptable to them, but their role is more informal.

Potential research participants should be fully informed about the nature of the research, the procedures involved and any potential risks to themselves. They then have the opportunity to judge whether the proposed research meets their personal standards of ethical acceptability. Problems arise when potential participants are not fully informed about the research by the researchers and when they are not fully aware of the minimum standards of ethical practice. However, while many members of the public may not be able to make a judgement about the implications of a proposed research investigation on technical grounds, they are likely to appreciate, and be able to make a judgement about, basic issues such as confidentiality and personal risk. Should an unforeseen ethical problem arise during the research, the participant should be encouraged to withdraw from participating.

The role of the research report users

People who read and use research reports, such as other researchers, health and social care practitioners and care service purchasers, are likely to judge the quality of the research findings and the study in general partly in terms of whether it was conducted according to appropriate and acceptable ethical standards. Research findings that are obtained through investigations that breach acceptable ethical standards are likely to be treated with some scepticism or may even be disregarded. Members of the research and health and social care community are not likely to respect or accept unethical researchers or their findings and are likely to be overtly critical of such people and their practices. This prospect should be a deterrent to any researchers who are tempted unethically to cut corners where they face problems and difficulties.

BUILD YOUR LEARNING

Keywords and phrases

You should know the meaning of the words and phrases listed below. If you are unsure about any of them, go back through the last six pages to refresh your understanding.

- Autonomy
- Beneficence
- Confidentiality
- Ethics
- Ethics committee
- Honesty and integrity
- Informed consent

Summary points

- The practices and procedures that researchers use in their investigations are expected to meet certain ethical standards.

- Ethics is about what is right and wrong, and in research is concerned with the use of acceptable procedures and standards of behaviour.

- Key ethical principles include obtaining informed consent, protecting confidentiality, doing good and not harm, and being honest. Researchers need to find ways of incorporating these principles into their research practices.

- The ethical standards of research investigations are judged by the researchers themselves, by ethics committees, and by users of, and participants in, research studies. Failure to meet appropriate ethical standards will result in criticism and censure by professional bodies, and colleagues and the researchers' findings will be disregarded.

QUESTIONS

1 Explain why it is important for health and social care researchers to observe high ethical standards in their research investigations.

2 What is informed consent and why should health and social care researchers obtain it?

3 What should researchers do to ensure that their proposed research investigations are ethically acceptable?

4 What is an ethics committee?

5 Who might be affected by research that is carried out in an unethical way?

Planning and obtaining valid data

We have seen that there are contrasting approaches to research and that a range of data collection methods are available to health and social care researchers. This results in a broad variety of research studies in the health and social care field. These studies all generally involve working through a series of planning, data collection and analysis stages that are known collectively as the **research process**.

A version of the research process is outlined in Figure 6.9. The process shown is one general version of the research process which, in practice, researchers modify to cope with the situations that they face. Health and social care researchers benefit from conducting their research in a planned, systematic way. The first three planning stages are particularly important. If a research study is not planned well, problems are likely to occur later on when faults and weaknesses show themselves. We outline what happens in the different stages of the research process next.

Deduction or induction?

Health and social care researchers generally follow a version of the research process outlined in Figure 6.9. However, researchers who use a positivistic approach tend to begin their research differently to researchers who adopt an interpretive approach. Positivistic researchers tend to adopt a deductive approach, whereas interpretive researchers tend to adopt an inductive approach. The differences between these two ways of working are outlined in more detail below.

Deductive reasoning

Health and social care researchers who use a positivistic approach tend to begin their research with an idea or theory. They then carry out data collection to test it against the empirical evidence. They follow what is known as a **deductive approach** to research.

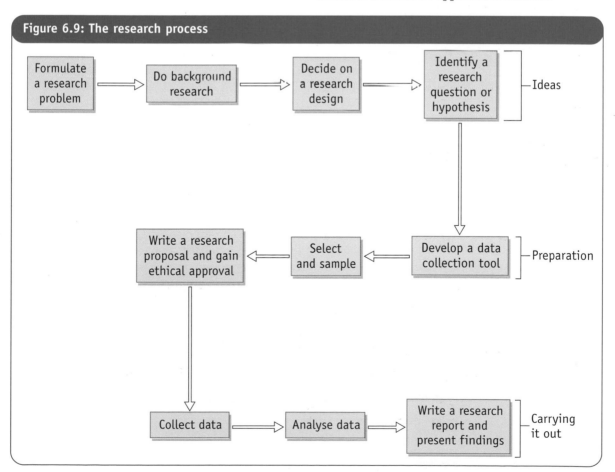

Figure 6.9: The research process

Figure 6.10: Deductive reasoning

Researchers' actions	Deductive thinking
Researchers wonder...	What is going on?
Researchers think they have an explanation and come up with a theory.	I think this is what is happening.
Researchers make a prediction to test their theory. This is an hypothesis.	In these circumstances, this will happen.
Researchers collect empirical evidence using one or more data collection methods.	Does the data support my hypothesis or not?
Researchers analyse the data to see whether to accept or reject the hypothesis.	The patterns in the data suggest 'X' is happening

Deductive research is sometimes referred to as theory-testing research. The research process outlined in Figure 6.9 expresses a deductive approach. It is also sometimes referred to as the hypothetico-deductive method. However, it is not the only way to begin and carry out research.

Inductive reasoning

Interpretive researchers tend to begin their research in the opposite way to positivistic researchers. They do not start with theories and hypotheses about aspects of the health and social care world. They claim to begin their research investigations with no preconceived ideas or theories about the topics or issues that they are interested in. They adopt an **inductive approach**, whereby they become very involved in the natural setting and social world of the research participants. They collect as much data as they can, from a wide variety of sources, and then develop their theories and hypotheses by analysing this data. They collect as much data as possible and then work out the sense in it. The idea is that the patterns and relationships in the data will emerge out of it and through repeated, careful

analysis will be built up into a coherent theory. Interpretive researchers say that they do 'grounded research' as their theories are grounded in the data.

In practice you may make use of both inductive and deductive approaches at different stages of your research investigation. In the early stages you may opt for an inductive pilot study to try and identify the key issues and questions. You can then test the theory that you arrive at in a deductive way. That is, you can collect empirical data to see whether your hypothesis is supported by the evidence.

However you decide to begin your research investigation, you will first need to come up with a research idea and should carry out some background research on your topic area.

The first idea

Researchers decide to carry out investigations for all sorts of reasons. It is important that you have a clear interest in researching a particular topic. In health and social care research, problems relating to treatment, policy and care practice often prompt research ideas.

Figure 6.11: Inductive reasoning

Researchers' actions	Inductive thinking
Researchers become involved in a setting or with a group they wish to study.	What is interesting here?
Researchers make observations and record them.	I have noticed this is happening.
Researchers begin to sort and order observations.	These things seem to be interesting.
Researchers build a theory that explains the observations.	My observations suggest that X is happening because of Y.

ACTIVITY

Brainstorming

When people are asked to conduct a piece of research, they can become overwhelmed by the endless possibilities and find it hard to reach a decision. New researchers often want to do too much at once. To avoid this, they go through a brainstorm and focusing down process.

- Brainstorm some big ideas as possible topics, for example smoking.

- Brainstorm sub-topics and reflect on your preferred approach (positivistic or interpretive) to the subject (smoking during pregnancy).

- Work out the topic boundaries (the attitudes of girls aged 16–19 studying at Denton College to women smoking whilst pregnant) so that you focus down on a clearly defined topic.

It is usually necessary to spend a bit of time on the brainstorm, thinking and focusing process. It is a good idea to initially explore a few different topics and see which one interests you most or offers the most possibilities as a research project. You will need to ensure that the topic is actually researchable, relevant and feasible in the time and with the resources you have available to you.

Background research

Check out what information and research is already available on your research idea or area. Libraries (books, magazines and journals), the internet, and health and social care organisations are all good sources of background information and research studies. Read as much as possible around the subject. Note the key points and findings. These should help you to refine your research idea. As you talk and read about your project your ideas develop and focus.

Identifying a research hypothesis

Research investigations are based on a process of asking questions and seeking evidence in answer to them. Earlier we looked at the different types of health and social care research (see p. 345). The research questions that you ask and seek answers to are affected by the type of research that you do.

An **hypothesis** is a prediction. Hypotheses are usually phrased as if-then statements. If A happens then B will result (or be true). For example, a researcher might conduct an experiment with the hypothesis: 'If

Figure 6.12: Different research questions

> ## Different kinds of research: different kinds of research question
>
> ### Exporatory and descriptive research
> Exploratory and descriptive research starts from questions about what is happening, designed so that you can give an adequate description: questions of who, what, when, how much and how many.
>
> ### Explanatory and theory-testing research
> Explanatory and theory-testing research starts from questions asking how far what is observed supports or undermines a particular explanation, usually framed as a hypothesis.
>
> ### Applied research
> Applied research starts from questions designed to produce information on which future decisions can be based: questions about how well things are being done (evaluation) or questions designed to establish what would be the consequences of new policies.

alcohol consumption affects physical coordination then the more alcohol that a person drinks the worse his or her physical coordination will become.' This is known as an **experimental hypothesis**, as it is predicting that something will actually occur. Researchers also usually state what is known as the **null hypothesis**. In our example this is: 'There will be no (statistically significant) relationship between the amount of alcohol consumption and physical coordination ability.'

You do not always need to have an hypothesis in a research investigation. Researchers who are conducting exploratory and descriptive research, for example, generally stick to simply asking research questions. A researcher may ask: 'How much alcohol is needed before physical coordination is affected?' This focuses the research, but does not make any sort of prediction.

If you adopt a deductive approach to your research investigation you will need to work out your research question or hypothesis before you start collecting data. If you adopt an inductive approach you will formulate research questions at the same time as you collect data. This makes the process a bit messier. In inductive situations you will have to gradually make decisions about which issues you want to concentrate on and focus your observations on these matters.

It is a good idea to use your project title to identify the background information and list the questions that need to be answered to complete the investigation. For example, if the project title is 'The attitudes of 16–19 year-old girls studying health and social care towards pregnant women who smoke', what questions should you investigate and what information would you need? We set these questions out in Figure 6.13.

Develop an overall plan

Coming up with a topic and developing research questions are important early parts of planning a research investigation. However, you must carry on from this point and plan out the whole of the investigation before you begin collecting any data. There is quite a lot of work involved in the planning stage. It ends when you complete a **research proposal**. This is a document that:

- clearly expresses your planned research idea

- says what the research question or hypothesis is

- explains what the research population is and how you will sample it

- describes how you will collect and analyse the data

- identifies the ethical issues involved in the project

- explains how you will deal with the ethical issues.

Choosing a source of data

One of the key decisions that you will have to make when planning your research investigation will be to decide where, or from whom, you are going to obtain your data. You need to think about and find ways of gaining access to the groups of people or situations that you are interested in studying.

Many students who are new to research begin with investigation ideas and expectations that are overambitious and unrealistic. It is highly unlikely that your GNVQ research investigation will shed light on a long-standing medical mystery or provide the data needed to solve pressing social problems. Being realistic about your investigation involves designing and developing a feasible and manageable project. One of the key aspects of this is selecting an appropriate sample or case study to investigate.

Selecting a sample

As we have seen, the research population is the whole data source (group of people, period of time, set of situations), or wider group, from which data could potentially be drawn in the research investigation. A sample is a section or proportion of that population. Ideally, a sample should be representative of the whole population, so that research conclusions can be generalised from it. In student research projects, however, the sample does not necessarily have to be precisely representative of the population but such a lack of representativeness should be acknowledged where it occurs. Case studies need not be representative at all.

The first step in successfully selecting a sample is to ensure that you identify the research population clearly and specifically. For example, an investigation of respiratory health knowledge could be carried out amongst (option 1) GNVQ students who smoke; (option 2) GNVQ students currently at your college who smoke;

Figure 6.13: Research project – Female students' attitudes to smoking during pregnancy	
Possible research questions	**Background information needed**
How much do 16–19 year-old students know about the physical health effects of smoking on women and developing children?	What are the effects of smoking on the physical health of pregnant women and on the health and development of the fetus?
What views do 16–19 year-old students have about why some women smoke during pregnancy?	How prevalent is smoking during pregnancy?
What are the thoughts and feelings of 16–19 year-old girls when they see a pregnant woman smoking a cigarette?	What advice does the Department of Health and the medical profession give about this issue?

(option 3) female GNVQ Health and Social Care students currently at your college who smoke.

The population is defined in ever more specific terms. In option 1, the population would be all GNVQ students throughout the world. It would be impossible to interview or survey a representative sample of such a large group. The second option is still fairly large. It would be practically impossible to contact and interview or survey all GNVQ students at your college. Option 3 is far more realistic. A list of female GNVQ health and social care students currently studying at your college should exist and a sample that is representative in terms of their age, ethnicity, social class and educational attainment for example, could be selected.

The generalisability of the findings will depend on whether GNVQ Health and Social Care students studying at your school or college are representative of GNVQ Health and Social Care students studying at other institutions. It is also important to be aware that the sample is only representative in terms of the particular characteristics that we are targeting (age, ethnicity, social class and educational attainment). The sample is not representative of GNVQ Health and Social Care students in other ways, such as gender, for example.

When you define your research population you should be very specific about the criteria needed for inclusion. As a GNVQ student researcher you will also need to ensure that you define a population to whom you can gain access relatively easily. Remember that you will need to be able to make contact with a number of these people in a relatively short space of time.

Sample size

Health and social care researchers use relatively complicated statistical techniques to work out how big a sample they need in order to make it representative of their research population. In GNVQ student research projects, size is less important. There are some general considerations to bear in mind.

- Smaller samples are less likely to allow you to truly represent the diverse characteristics of the individuals who make up the population.

- Samples of less than 20 individuals will not usually generate enough data to allow you to produce meaningful statistics.

- Larger samples mean that you will be able to find out less about each individual in the sample.

Practical considerations, such as how much time you have available, also affect decisions about sample size. You should discuss this issue with your tutor who will be able to take into account the circumstances and nature of your investigation. As a very rough guide, a GNVQ student's questionnaire survey that used a sample of between 30 and 60 individuals would generate enough data for analysis. Of course this depends on how many questions are asked. If you only ask two questions, you will not have enough data. Fifteen to twenty questions would provide a more adequate and appropriate amount of data.

Sampling methods

There are basically two approaches to sampling a research population. These are known as probability and purposive sampling. There are a number of specific methods of sampling within each of these basic approaches.

Probability sampling methods give each member of the research population an equal chance (or probability) of being chosen as a part of the sample. For example, in a study about knowledge of respiratory health, we might select every second female student nurse from a list provided by Manchester University. Every student nurse on the list has a 50 per cent chance of being chosen at random. Chance determines which particular members of the sample are selected. The purpose of **random sampling** is to reduce the potential for bias.

You will need to be able to obtain, or produce, a complete list of all of the members of the research population before you can use a probability sampling method. This list is known as the **sampling frame**.

Examples of sampling frames include:

- the telephone directory
- outpatient clinic lists
- sports club membership lists
- school and college enrolments and class registers
- lists of employees and pay rolls
- the electoral register
- the post office address file
- the community charge register.

Sometime lists don't exist (for example, students who smoke cannabis do not put their names on a list of cannabis users) or access may be refused (for example, to records of students who have made appointments with the college counsellor). In such circumstances researchers have to find a way of constructing their own sampling frame or choose another data collection method that does not involve sampling.

One way of selecting members of the population at random is to number their names in a list and then use a random number table to pick numbers from the list. Alternatively, if you have a relatively small number of names, cut the list up and pick them out at random from a hat. Another alternative is to randomly choose one item as a start point and then to select every name at a given point onwards. For example, begin at item four on the list and then select every eighth name.

Random samples may be unrepresentative. They can throw up, by chance, collections of people who are somehow untypical of the population as a whole. The risk of this happening can be overcome by using a form of probability sampling known as **stratified random sampling**. This involves identifying subgroups, or strata, within a population and then conducting a random sample of each of these to ensure that they are all represented in a sample. For example, in the respiratory health study it may be appropriate to divide the list of student nurses by age band or ethnic group and then to randomly select individuals from each stratum for the sample. This would arguably reduce the risk of obtaining an unrepresentative sample.

In **purposive sampling** methods, the chance of a member of the research population being chosen is not equal and is sometimes unknown. For example, we might select all student nurses in the second year of their course at Manchester University. In this scenario, the second year students have a 100 per cent chance of being chosen for the sample but the first and third years have a 0 per cent chance. Alternatively, we might select all student nurses who admit to smoking. We do not know how many there will be, so we do not know what the chance (probability) is of being selected for the sample.

The best known form of purposive sampling is **quota sampling**. Quota sampling allows researchers to control variables in their study without having a sampling frame. The researchers must identify the key criteria that all participants need to meet and then approach people randomly to ask if they meet these criteria and recruit a quota of this group for research purposes. Once the quota for a particular group has been filled, the researchers will not seek to include any more people from that group.

Quota sampling is useful when the overall proportions of particular groups in the population are known. For example, if you wanted to do a survey that compared the attitudes of men and women in your town or city to surrogacy, you would need to know the proportion of men and women in your area. You could then select a more representative sample. Quota sampling is not truly random, as not everyone in the population has an equal chance of being selected. Usually the researchers simply identify and ask people who fit the population criteria to participate. These people are selected on a convenient first come first served basis.

Quota sampling is very useful to GNVQ students carrying out relatively small research investigations in a short period of time. There is no need to have a definitive or complete sampling frame (unlike in stratified random sampling). GNVQ student researchers who have good knowledge of the population they seek to study can make an informed guess to select quotas of people who are roughly representative of their research population. In a GNVQ project, the quotas do not need to be in strict proportion to their incidence in the population, but should be roughly so.

The choice of sampling method is usually determined by the need to keep the sampling process as simple as possible, by the likelihood of there being a bias in the sample and by the practicalities of what is actually possible.

Selecting a case study

If you want to conduct a research investigation into an organisation or a particular situation or a type of person, you will not need to sample as such. You will, instead, have to select an appropriate case or example of the organisation, situation or type of person to study in detail. Case study research is quite common in health and social care research. One limitation of the case study method is that the findings and conclusions are not usually generalisable to wider populations of similar organisations, situations or individuals. That is, unless you consider and find ways of explaining why the case that you have chosen is typical of other similar cases. This is very difficult to do.

BUILD YOUR LEARNING

Keywords and phrases

You should know the meaning of the words and phrases listed below. If you are unclear about any of them, go back through the last six pages to refresh your understanding.

- Deductive reasoning
- Experimental hypothesis
- Hypothesis
- Inductive reasoning
- Null hypothesis
- Population
- Probability sampling
- Purposive sampling
- Quota sampling
- Random sampling
- Research process
- Research proposal
- Research question
- Sample
- Stratified random sampling

Summary points

- Researchers generally plan and carry out their investigations by working through a number of stages of the research process.

- Researchers begin their investigations in either a deductive or inductive way.

- Deductive researchers begin with an hypothesis or theory and test it out against the empirical evidence that they collect. Inductive researchers collect data and then build their explanatory theories out of this.

- Health and social care researchers get their initial ideas for research investigations from a variety of sources and often begin with a big topic idea.

- Before they can actually carry out practical investigations, researchers focus down on a very specific, precisely expressed research problem

- Before any data is actually collected health and social care researchers have to work through the planning stages of the investigation and produce a research proposal. This sets out the researchers' ideas and explains how they will carry out their research.

- In the planning stage, researchers must identify and evaluate background information on their topic; identify a clear and researchable question or hypothesis; identify and then sample their population; decide on their data collection methods; produce the data collection tools that they will need; and identify and deal with the ethical issues that arise from the research.

QUESTIONS

1 Explain how a piece of deductive research begins.

2 Why is focusing down on the research topic critical to the success of an investigation?

3 Explain what a hypothesis is and produce an example of your own to show how hypotheses work.

4 If researchers want to generalise their findings, what key characteristic must their sample have?

5 What is a probability sample? Use the term sampling frame somewhere in your answer.

Methods of collecting data

YOUR CHOICE OF DATA COLLECTION method will depend on a number of factors. These include the type of data you wish to collect (qualitative, quantitative or both), the time and resources available and whether or not your research population is easy to contact. The three main methods that are most suitable for small-scale research in a GNVQ course are questionnaire surveys, interviews and forms of short-term observational research. Let's look at each of these in turn.

Developing and using questionnaires

Questionnaires are a popular and practical way for GNVQ students to obtain data for their research projects. Developing questions is the most critical, and most difficult, part of questionnaire-based data collection. The quality and validity of the data that is collected depends on the formulation of good questions. Your questions must be clear, unambiguous, relevant and unbiased.

Writing questions

You need to be able to write both closed and open questions for your questionnaire. Closed questions have fixed or limited answer possibilities. They expect a short, factual answer. If you had a question, 'Have you ever had a broken leg?', it would probably result in a yes or no response. The information that you can obtain from closed questions is relatively predictable. In contrast, if you asked an **open question** you would phrase it so that there were a range of possible responses. For example, 'What were your feelings when you found out your GCSE results?' does not impose a restricted set of response choices or limit the kinds of answers that a respondent might give. The drawback to open questions is that they can produce responses that are harder to analyse and compare between respondents.

Your choice of whether to use an open or closed question will depend on the type of data that you require on a particular issue. If you want to know about the gender of respondents, simple closed questions ('Are you male or female?') are obviously better. If you want to know about thoughts, views and feelings, open questions are better.

You need to write questions in clear, simple and unambiguous language. They should mean the same thing to all respondents. None of the questions should be leading, or biased.

Structuring the questionnaire

The structuring of your questionnaire plays an important part in making it easy to use and understand. It is best to begin with relatively straightforward, easily answered closed questions and gradually work towards the open questions that require more thought. Try to incorporate some of the points below when structuring a questionnaire.

- Begin with a short, clear statement that explains what the research is about and that covers the important issue of confidentiality.

- Next, ask some straightforward, clear questions about the demographic attributes of the respondent (such as age, sex, ethnicity, for example).

- Ask a range of open and closed questions that explore issues relevant to your overall research question and topic area. The questions that you ask should ultimately provide sufficient data for you to address the overall question that you have set out to investigate.

- Make sure that questions are presented in a logical order, that you only ask about ONE specific thing in each question and that each question will lead to a distinct piece of useful information.

- Avoid loosely worded questions that allow the respondent to repeat a previous answer.

- All questions should be self-explanatory. You should not assume that respondents will have any prior knowledge of the subject(s) you are interested in.

- Make sure that the method of responding is clear and easy for each question and that you provide guidance on the order in which questions should be answered.

- Thank your respondents for completing the questions when they have finished.

Biased and leading questions

A **biased**, or leading, question leads a respondent to give a particular reply or type of reply. For example, both of the following questions are biased.

■ Do you agree that abortion is murder?

■ What do you think about the torture of animals by scientists for medical research?

You should avoid using any biased or leading questions in your questionnaire. It is easy to make a mistake and miss them when you are first drafting your questions, so make sure that you check them for bias before you print your final questionnaire. Failure to weed out biased and leading questions will mean that the objectivity of your research is weakened and the validity of the data undermined.

Recording replies

We said earlier that questionnaires need to include open and closed questions and we have briefly discussed how these can be written. However, as well as writing the questions you will also have to think about how you will record the responses to them.

Answers to closed questions are easy in this respect. You can provide clear, straightforward tick boxes to record responses to simple forced choice questions (see Figure 6.14).

Figure 6.14: Answer to a closed question

Have you ever fractured one of your bones?

Yes	☐
No	☐

Closed questions can also be written in such a way that respondents are given a number of forced choice options from which they choose their answer. You should always specify how many of these choices of answer the respondent is allowed to choose (see Figure 6.15).

Alternatively, you could use a **rating scale** to measure the response using a **Likert scale**. You are probably very familiar with these (see Figure 6.16).

Figure 6.15: Answer with forced choice options

What were your immediate feelings after experiencing the fracture? (Tick as many answers as applied.)

Severe pain

Nausea

Disorientation

Numbness

Discomfort

None/Other

Figure 6.16: Answer using a Likert scale

How painful was the fracture? (Choose the ONE that is nearest to your memory.)

Extremely painful

Very painful

Painful

Slightly painful

No pain

You can also provide a number of choices and ask respondents to **rank** them in a specific order. Ranking needs to be clearly explained in the question, as people frequently get confused between rating (choosing one or more responses without putting them in a particular order) and ranking (putting choices in an order of preference) (see Figure 6.17).

Figure 6.17: Answer using ranking

Which of the following bones are most likely to be fractured during sports activity? (Place them all in rank order, from 1 = most likely to be broken, to 5 = least likely to be broken.)

Femur (thigh)

Tibia (shin)

Radius (forearm)

Clavicle (collar bone)

Patella (Knee cap)

Answers to open questions are more difficult to record through a questionnaire. If the respondents are completing the questionnaire themselves you will need to leave enough space after the questions for them to write their responses in. People do not usually write very much in these spaces. It is best to include an instruction to encourage them to express themselves fully, but you should still not expect detailed and considered responses unless you are leaving the questionnaire with them or giving them plenty of time to complete it.

Data collection

Once you have put your questionnaire together and coded (see p. 393) all of the potential responses that you can in advance, you will need to carry out the actual data collection process. There are three basic ways of doing this with a questionnaire: face to face, by post, or by telephone. Each of these options has advantages and disadvantages (see Figure 6.18). You should choose the option that most suits your particular circumstances and that enables you to collect the data that you require.

Think through the practicalities of how you will collect your data and get your questionnaires completed and returned to you. It is sometimes a good idea to collect the data with a partner. This can give you more confidence, cut down the time it takes to get enough questionnaires completed and protect your personal safety. **You should never put your personal safety at risk by going unaccompanied to places you** are not familiar with to see people whom you do not really know. You should also not give respondents whom you do not know any personal details about yourself or where you live.

You will need to present yourself in a confident and friendly way, and should think about how you will explain your project and persuade people to complete the questionnaire. Even if you do all of these things well, it is likely that at least half of the people you ask to fill in the questionnaire will decline. Do not take this personally, go on to the next person.

Planning and carrying out interviews

Interviews play an important part in collecting data in health and social care research. They are also very popular with GNVQ students as a data collection strategy. One of the attractions that interviews have for GNVQ student researchers is that they provide an opportunity to explore topics in some depth with people such as care workers and service users. More impersonal methods like questionnaire surveys or experiments do not allow this.

In order to obtain research data through interviews, researchers have to identify potential interviewees, recruit them into the investigation, arrange the interview sessions and then carry out the interviews. You can probably see already that there is quite a lot of pre-interview work to do, just to set things up.

Figure 6.18: Advantages and disadvantages of different types of questionnaire

Questionnaire type	Advantages	Limitations
Postal	Save on interviewing time. Reach a large number of people in a variety of locations. Respondent gets more thinking time.	Response rates can be low. Respondents can be unrepresentative of the sample. Time consuming. Expensive.
Face-to-face	Highest response rate. Interviewer is present, so can clarify questions. More likely to get full answers to open questions.	Time consuming for the interviewer and the interviewee. Can result in biased answers because of the effect of the interviewer on the respondent.
Telephone	Convenient and quick for the interviewer. Interviewer can clarify questions.	Expensive in call charges. Cannot be sure who is answering. Cannot observe non-verbal features of responses.

Identifying interviewees

There are various ways of identifying and contacting potential interviewees. You first need to define the key qualities or characteristics of the interviewees. This obviously relates to your research topic and questions. For example, if you were doing research on the topic of experiences of breast feeding and were interested in women's reasons for choosing when to stop breast feeding, key characteristics of potential interviewees would be that they were women and that they had at least one child.

How would you identify and choose people to approach? You could simply select a case study group of women whom you know fit the criteria. Alternatively, you might want to interview women you do not already know. You might attend an ante-natal class and recruit some volunteers before they give birth and arrange to interview them at some point afterwards. You could place an advertisement in a local paper or at a GP practice where women with young babies were likely to see it. Regardless of what you do, you need to find a practical method of identifying potential volunteers whilst bearing in mind the need to be objective and ethical in your approach.

Make sure that your interviewees are genuine volunteers. You must not force anyone to take part or trick them into an interview. Remember that informed consent is a key ethical principle that should always be upheld. Be positive and persuasive, and give your potential interviewees enough information about your investigation and the interview topic(s) to make up their own minds about whether or not to participate. You should also explain how you will maintain confidentiality and what you will do with the information that they give you. You will get poorer data from unwilling or reluctant interviewees.

Bailey et al., (1995) suggest a code of practice for interviews (see Figure 6.19).

Producing an interview schedule

You need to set up an interview situation that allows your respondents time and that gives them scope to talk about and develop their opinions. You should put an **interview schedule** together. This is a list of the topic areas you would like to cover and the general questions that you want to ask. An interview schedule is useful as a prompt and reminder during an interview.

You should decide how much you want to determine the focus of the interview before you put your interview schedule together. If you intend to exert some control over, and limit, the areas to be discussed, your interview will be structured to some degree. The semi-structured interview technique involves identifying general topic areas to discuss, as well as some standard questions to ask each interviewee. It also leaves plenty of scope for interviewees to take the interview in the direction of their choice. An unstructured interview, by definition, involves minimal structuring beforehand. In these situations your interview schedule might consist of just a few topic headings.

The objective of using interviews as a data collection method is to try to gain and understand the respondents' point of view, rather than to make generalisations about people's behaviour. As a result, you should make extensive use of open questions. It is

Figure 6.19: Code of practice for interviews

Code of practice

1 The aim of this interview is to obtain information and ideas on...

2 The findings will be included in a report for...

3 The identity of individuals will not be disclosed. However, the interviewees' age, sex and....may be used.

4 Interviews will take place only at these times and places....

5 All interviews will be prearranged.

6 There will be no fee for interviews.

7 Interviewees will have the right to terminate the interview at any time and/or to choose not to answer some or all of the questions.

8 The interpretation of the interview will be discussed with....before presentation in the final written report.

9 During an interview, the interviewee may ask for statements to be regarded as off the record. These must never be quoted in the final report.

your decision whether to plan and write some questions in advance or whether to think them up during the interview. The latter is a difficult and risky strategy unless you have a lot of interview experience, good knowledge of your topic and plenty of confidence!

When planning and conducting your interviews you should consider the following factors.

- Interviews take time. Both parties should be comfortable with the surroundings and should be able to talk without being interrupted.

- Think through the best way of actually recording what is said during the interview. Writing things down has considerable drawbacks. Tape recording requires permission and has ethical implications.

- In order to be successful you will need to develop a good rapport with the respondent. This is linked to data validity. We assume, rightly or wrongly, that people who trust and respect us are more likely to tell us the truth.

- You will have to know when to prompt and when to listen in the conversation that develops with the respondent. You must avoid giving your own opinions, even where you feel strongly about what the respondent says, as this is highly likely to end, or at least bias, the interview. Do your best to avoid the interviewer effect, in which the interviewer's presence or behaviour distorts the interviewees' responses.

Planning and carrying out observational research

If you want to carry out observational research for your GNVQ research assignment you will need to make an early decision about the extent to which you wish to participate in or remain separate from the research situation.

Non-participant observers need to be able to observe a situation from the outside without disturbing the natural behaviour and events that occur within the setting that they are studying. If you use video or tape recording, covert observation or one-way mirrors to collect your observational data, you face considerable ethical problems. None of these strategies are advisable in a GNVQ research project.

Participant observers need to think about how they will gain access to the group or situation that they wish to study, how they can remain in and study the group without disturbing the naturalness of the group or situation, and how they can exit. It is probably best, in your position as a GNVQ student researcher, to clearly explain your research idea and gain the informed consent of the people you wish to study, as well as permission from the authorities responsible for the setting where you wish to carry out your observations. Note that permission from the managers or authorities responsible for a care setting is not the same thing as informed consent from the research participants.

Recording data

There are various ways of recording what you see, hear and experience in your chosen research setting. Your choice of strategy will depend on the setting and the nature of what you are trying to observe. In some situations it is possible to produce an **observation schedule** in advance of undertaking the data collection. These take the form of checklists or highly structured questionnaires. However, where the observations are less predictable and unstructured, researchers produce **field notes**. Researchers write down, in diary or note form, all of the relevant and interesting things that happen or which are observed. Field notes can be written at the time of the observation or afterwards, when more time is available. Field notes provide an important source of data that can be analysed at the end of the investigation.

Triangulation

The term **triangulation** refers to the practice of using several data collection methods in the same research investigation. This can be helpful where you want to gain access to different types of data on the same topic. For example, you may want to find out about people's views and opinions on eating healthy food, but you may also want to observe what they actually eat when given a choice of healthy and less healthy meal options. By using two data collection methods, you can compare the data and see whether the findings are consistent. You might discover that people's healthy diet intentions are not matched by their behaviour! Alternatively, the observational data might confirm what they told you, allowing you to be more confident in your conclusions.

Dealing with ethical issues

Your research project is bound to raise some ethical issues. We discussed the key issues in more detail earlier (pp. 370–5). You will recall that we said that in research, ethics are applied to standards of behaviour and take the form of commonly followed procedures. We also said that researchers have an important role to play in assessing the ethical acceptability of their own proposed research. It is important to examine your research proposal critically and to try and anticipate and deal with potential ethical issues in advance of seeking approval to carry out the project.

There are two steps to making an ethical appraisal of your proposed or actual research study. First, you should critically assess your proposed research study to identify how it might infringe the interests and rights of the people who are involved in it or on whom the research may have an impact. You need to think about:

- how the research investigation will be carried out

- the possible effects on people who take part

- how the data will be presented to maintain confidentiality.

Second, you should come up with justifications for your approach and methods for dealing with the ethical issues that your particular research presents or which it might throw up unexpectedly once the research is under way. You should always seek to minimise any risks or negative impact on participants and people affected by the research.

Returning to the research proposal

Earlier (p. 380) we said that before starting any data collection you should work through the key planning stages of your research investigation. The result would be a research proposal. This is an overall plan that outlines your research idea and how you intend to carry out the research. You should now have enough knowledge to work through the various planning stages of the research process to put your own research proposal together.

BUILD YOUR LEARNING

Keywords and phrases

You should know the meaning of the words and phrases listed below. If you are unclear about any of them, go back through the last six pages to refresh your understanding.

- Bias
- Closed question
- Field notes
- Forced choice question
- Interview schedule
- Leading question
- Likert scale
- Observation schedule
- Open question
- Postal questionnaire
- Ranking
- Rating

Summary points

- Questionnaires, interviews and observational methods are relatively straightforward methods of collecting research data.

- Questionnaires are a form of structured interview schedule. To be effective, they must contain unambiguous, unbiased and appropriate questions.

- Closed questions are used to collect limited factual information. Open questions are used to elicit thoughts, feelings and beliefs.

- Researchers often use Likert scales and other forms of ranking or rating device, in questionnaires. These offer participants fixed choices of response.

- There are a number of ways of obtaining data using questionnaires. The choice depends on the extent to which the researcher feels it is important to play a part in administering the questionnaire.

- Interviews tend to be less structured and take longer to complete than questionnaires. They also involve more advance planning in recruiting participants and arranging the interview environment.

- Researchers need to be very careful to avoid breaching ethical principles or introducing bias in the way that they select interviewees and conduct interviews.

- Observational research aims to obtain data on the natural behaviour of a group in a particular situation.

- Observational researchers produce field notes and use observation schedules or checklists to record their data.

- The key difficulty for all observational researchers is to enter, remain in and study the group without disturbing the natural behaviour of participants or of the situation.

QUESTIONS

1 What problem might you face if you only used closed questions in a research questionnaire?

2 What feature of the data is compromised by the use of leading questions: reliability or validity?

3 What is a Likert scale?

4 Why do researchers who use interview methods have to concentrate on developing a rapport with their interviewees?

5 What are field notes?

Analysing and presenting research results

▲ Analysing data requires basic arithmetic and statistical skills

Analysing quantitative data

Quantitative data, by definition, consists of numerical items of information. The process of analysing a set of numerical data therefore involves some arithmetic and the use of some statistical techniques. Do not be put off by this. Student research projects usually only require fairly basic arithmetic and statistical skills.

The process of analysing quantitative data involves counting and grouping together the answers that are given to each question. Respondents may have given an actual numerical answer (for example, five cigarettes a week) or may have given an answer that is coded. **Coding** simply means allocating a number to each possible response so that similar responses can be grouped together using the common number. For example, all the yes responses to the question below would be coded 1.

Are you taking a GNVQ Advanced Health and Social Care course at the present time?

	Code
Yes	(1)
No	(2)
Don't know	(3)

Preparing the data

The first stage of data analysis involves actually preparing the data to get it into a form that is capable of analysis. The two things that you have to do with your quantitative data are to code the responses and collate them into a table of responses

The main method of collecting quantitative data in student research is usually through the use of questionnaires. Most student questionnaires have a mixture of open and closed questions. Closed questions generally produce quantitative data and are relatively easy to code.

Imagine that you were conducting a survey on older teenage attitudes to personal relationships and that you were using a questionnaire to collect data on aspects of this topic. Your first two questions require some basic demographic information, while the third question seeks data on attraction (see Figure 6.20).

Figure 6.20: Research questions

	Code
1 What sex are you?	
Male	(1)
Female	(2)
2 How old are you? (years only)	
15	(1)
16	(2)
17	(3)
18	(4)
19	(5)
3 Choose ONE response that most clearly matches your view of the statement below.	
Physical appearance is more important than personality when choosing a boyfriend or girlfriend.	
I strongly agree	(1)
I agree	(2)
I neither agree or disagree	(3)
I disagree	(4)
I strongly disagree	(5)

You will note that the three questions in Figure 6.20 are coded. That is, the potential answers have all been given a code number in advance. When the researchers have collected all of the data that they need, the next step is to produce a table of coded responses. Figure 6.21 shows a table of answers given by five hypothetical respondents to the three questions in Figure 6.20.

Figure 6.21: Table of responses

Question	1	2	3
Respondent 1	1	1	2
Respondent 2	2	4	1
Respondent 3	2	4	1
Respondent 4	1	3	3
Respondent 5	2	2	1

You should code all of your closed questions and fixed response items in your questionnaire before collecting any data. When you have collected all of your data, simply enter the response codes into a coding sheet like the one in Figure 6.21. Ideally, do this on a computer spreadsheet, as the programme will calculate a variety of simple statistics for you.

Making sense of quantitative data

Analysis means separating a whole into the component parts for study and interpretation. You will need to separate a whole data set to find patterns and relationships that make sense of, and give meaning to, the items of information you have obtained. When you have prepared your data, you can analyse it by applying a number of simple descriptive statistics techniques to it. The basic techniques that we will look at are:

- frequency distributions
- mean, median and mode
- standard deviations.

These are all forms of **descriptive statistics**. They provide a summary of the pattern of information that can be found in a sample. They do not say anything about whether these patterns are likely to apply in, or can be generalised to, the population as a whole. These three techniques allow for **univariate** (one variable) analysis. Correlations allow for **bivariate** (two variable) analysis.

Calculating a frequency distribution

A **frequency distribution** is a simple way of showing the number of times that particular items of data occur. For example, you may want to produce a frequency distribution for age to show how many of your respondents fall into particular age-bands. This kind of information can help the readers of your research understand, and put into context, the significance of your results.

Producing a frequency distribution is relatively easy. You simply need to total up the number of each type of response given to a particular question. You can use these numbers to produce a frequency table (see Figure 6.22), a bar chart (see Figure 6.23) or a pie chart (see Figure 6.24).

Figure 6.22: A frequency table

Nurses should be paid higher salaries.

	Number	%	Code
Strongly agree	12	35	1
Agree	8	23.5	2
Neutral	5	15	3
Disagree	8	23.5	4
Strongly disagree	1	3	5
Total	34	100	

Figure 6.23: A bar chart

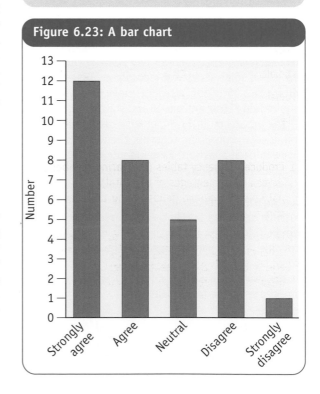

ACTIVITY

Producing frequency tables

The table below contains information on the gender, age and nationality, of users of an airport MediCentre. Study the data and then answer the questions that follow.

Gender	Age	Nationality
Male	6	French
Female	36	French
Male	32	British
Male	19	German
Female	14	British
Female	4	German
Male	18	British
Male	39	French
Male	7	French
Female	9	German
Female	19	German
Male	18	British
Female	17	British
Female	38	German
Male	16	British
Female	8	French
Male	36	French
Female	18	British
Female	44	German
Male	17	British

1 Produce frequency tables (indicating number of items and percentages of the total) for nationality, age and gender using the data set above.

2 Using data from your frequency tables, produce a bar chart for nationality and a pie chart for age to display the percentage frequency distribution graphically.

Figure 6.24: A pie chart

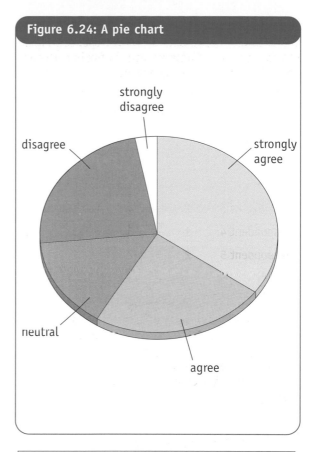

Calculating mean, median and mode

The mean, median and mode are measures of central tendency. That is, they are all ways of working out average, or central, values in the data. You have probably come across lots of headlines in newspapers and magazines that are based on these types of statistics. The average age of marriage, the average number of children born to each couple, and average life expectancy are all values that are based on a calculation of central tendency in a particular population. These types of measures are often used by researchers as a way of comparing their findings with those of other similar studies. Comparisons may be made over time, between countries or across social groups for example.

The **mean** is the numerical value around which the data is centred. It is easy to calculate. You simply have to add together all of the scores that you collect and then divide by the number of scores. The result is the numerical mean. As part of your research you might also collect data items that are not numerical. If you want to know what the most common, or midpoint, item is, you can use a different form of average measure. The **mode** is the most frequently occurring data item. The **median** on the other hand is the midpoint in a data set.

ACTIVITY

Calculating central tendency

The data below gives the waiting times (in hours) for 21 users of a hospital's accident and emergency service.

0.25, 0.5, 0.5, 0.75, 1, 1, 1.25, 3, 8, 8, 8, 8, 8, 9, 9, 10, 12, 13, 14, 16, 27,

1 What is the numerical mean waiting time in this group?

2 What is the modal and the median waiting time?

3 Which value do you think gives the best measure of central tendency?

Calculating the standard deviation

The **standard deviation** is a measure used by researchers to work out how much the data varies from the numerical mean within a data distribution. The numerical mean tells you nothing about how similar or dissimilar the individual items of data in the distribution are. This might be important in an opinion poll on closing a hospital, for example. The standard deviation value would let the decision-makers know whether there was a strong general agreement (not much variation from the average) or relatively weak general agreement (a lot of variation from the average).

To calculate the standard deviation you need to carry out the following steps.

■ Calculate the mean of the data set.

■ Calculate the difference, or deviation, between each individual response and the mean value. If the difference is higher it will produce a plus (positive) figure and if it is lower it will produce a minus (negative) figure.

■ Calculate the square of each of these deviations.

■ Add the squared figures together to get a sum of squares figure.

■ Divide the sum of squares by the number of data items to get a variance figure

■ Calculate the square root $\sqrt{}$ of the variance figure to obtain the standard deviation.

The standard deviation is a useful and important measure for identifying and showing variation within a set of data.

Analysing qualitative data

Data collection methods such as participant observation and in-depth interviews give the researcher less control over the type and range of information that respondents give. Responses to open questions and observations of natural, spontaneous behaviour are hard to predict. This can cause researchers problems when it comes to making sense of the data that they have obtained.

As with quantitative data analysis, the first thing that you need to do is to prepare the data. The two key steps of coding and collating data are again helpful to follow. The difference when working with qualitative data is that the useful items of information are usually a part of a much larger body of information, most of which is not useful with regard to the research question.

One of the strategies that researchers use to capture data during interviews is to tape record what respondents say during conversation. This ensures that the researchers get a verbatim, or word-for-word, account but also has implications in that the researchers may have to transcribe (write out) what was said. Transcribing can be very time consuming and should be avoided in a student research project where possible. Some researchers get around this by listening to the tapes over and over again and using the pause button to transcribe the most interesting and useful sections. This is one way of beginning the process of coding data. Remember to assess the data in terms of whether it is relevant to your research question.

If you have interviews on a specific topic with several people, or if you have observed a number of similar situations, it is likely that there will be patterns, themes and similarities in the data. You need to decide on some theme or pattern categories (give them a name) and allocate data items to them. Draw up a coding frame for each possible theme so that you can read through all of your data and assess the meaning of each answer. This requires a careful and sensitive approach to the data so that you retain the meaning that the respondents intended to give in their responses.

Not all answers will fit neatly into coding frame categories. You will need to make some judgements about how to deal with these items and you should acknowledge this.

Analysing qualitative data is usually quite an involved and time consuming process. This is largely because the data has to be organised into a manageable format. You may have questionnaires with written answers of various lengths to open questions. Alternatively, you may have tape recorded your respondents' answers to interview questions and have lots of tape recordings to listen to. Whatever form the data is in, you need reorganise it.

◀ Transcribing recorded responses can be time consuming and produces a large amount of data

Let's imagine that your qualitative data consists of written responses to three open questions. How can you analyse it? The first step is to make a copy of the original data. You should always keep your original, full data set to refer back to if you need to and work with the copy. In this situation, it would be best to collect together the responses to each of your questions. You might want to cut the relevant sections out of the copied questionnaires. You should then read the responses several times, thinking about possible similarities between them that could justify grouping them into distinct categories. It is best to do this several times, learning from the data as you go and looking for themes and patterns all the time. As you can probably imagine, this takes some time and mental effort.

When you have identified some themes and patterns, you need to describe them, perhaps using direct quotes as examples, in a discussion of your findings. You may also want to try to convert some of the qualitative data into a quantitative form to give you further detail to discuss.

Qualitative into quantitative data

Data that is originally collected in a qualitative form, such as written or spoken responses to open questions, can sometimes be converted into quantitative data. This can be done, for example, by counting the number of times that respondents answer in a similar way. The key preparation step is to group the responses into similarity categories. You then count the number of responses in each category. These frequency counts can now be presented in a graph or chart format.

For example, imagine that a group of respondents were asked to describe how they felt before a dental check-up. All wrote answers that were at least two sentences long. Ten people gave answers that made no reference to feeling anxious at all. Twenty people gave answers that made reference to feeling more anxious than usual and 30 people gave answers that made reference to feeling very or extremely anxious

Whilst quantifying qualitative responses can be useful, it is not always possible or desirable to do so. You must decide whether this actually adds anything useful to the understanding of the data.

Presenting qualitative data

Quantitative data is usually presented in statistical and graphical formats. It is relatively easy to present because it is numerical. Qualitative data on the other hand is not so straightforward and requires a more word-based style of presentation. Qualitative data is usually presented as a written discussion. Researchers tend to make use of short verbatim quotes of what respondents said or wrote. They do this to provide evidence of typical or particularly important responses and statements. These are often used to clarify and illustrate the key themes and patterns in the data. In addition to describing and reporting on key themes, qualitative researchers tend to also comment on what was different between respondents or what was lacking in the data.

While most qualitative research reports depend on written discussions of findings, it is also possible to make use of other devices, such as images, tape recordings, diagrams and flow charts for example. These can be used to provide evidence of, and communicate, the key findings. Whatever method is used, the validity of the data should always be preserved.

BUILD YOUR LEARNING

Keywords and phrases

You should know the meanng of the words and phrases outlined below. If you are unclear about any of them, go back through the last five pages to refresh your understanding.

- Analysis
- Coding
- Descriptive statistics
- Frequency distribution
- Mean
- Median
- Mode
- Standard deviation

Summary points

- Analysis is the process of making sense of research data. Health and social care researchers need to use different methods of analysis to make sense of qualitative and quantitative data.

- Quantitative data is prepared by counting and grouping numerical items of data so that they can be analysed statistically. Researchers code and collate numerical data and then use statistical techniques to summarise and describe the key features of the data.

- Qualitative data is less straightforward to analyse than quantitative data. Health and social care researchers who collect qualitative data look for patterns and themes in the data and then report on what they have seen, heard and observed.

QUESTIONS

1 What do researchers do when they code data?

2 Why can't qualitative data be coded easily?

3 What are descriptive statistics? Give examples of two different types in your answer.

4 What does the standard deviation tell you about a data set that the numerical mean does not?

5 Which term refers to the most frequently occurring item in a data set: the median or the mode?

Writing up your research report

WRITING UP THE RESEARCH report is one of the last stages of completing a research investigation. It is essential that the report is written in a way that communicates both the process (what you did) and the findings (what you discovered) to the people who read it. Research reports generally follow a common structure because it enables:

- researchers to outline their research investigation and findings in a logical sequence

- readers to focus on key features of the research without having to read the whole report

- other researchers to make comparisons with similar research investigations

- researchers to guard against writing an account that is biased by their personal views and feelings.

We now describe the way a standard research report is structured, giving some guidance on the content of each section.

Title

The title should be informative and refer closely and descriptively to the focus of your research. The title page should also contain the researcher's name.

Abstract

The abstract is a short summary (100–150 words) of the investigation with thumbnail details including the aims, methods and main conclusions. It should be able to stand on its own as a succinct and intelligible summary of the entire report. A clear abstract encourages people to read the entire report. It is often the last task to be completed when writing up the research report.

Introduction

The introduction explains the rationale for the research, summarises background reading about previous work in the same area, and explains the aims, research question(s) and hypothesis (if there is one) of the research. Your goal here is to establish a clear logic, building from a description and analysis of previous research and theory to a statement of the specific purpose of your own research project.

Method

This section outlines how you went about your research study. A description of your method should enable readers to assess the objectivity of your research and whether you adopted appropriate ethical standards. The goal here is to describe your sample, the data collection tools that you used and the procedures you undertook to collect your data. Your explanation should be clear enough that another person could repeat the study in the same way that you conducted it.

It is customary to divide the method section into three parts, the sampling section, the methodology section and the procedure section.

- The **sampling section** should identify the main demographic characteristics of the population (sex, age, for example), the total sample size, the criteria and method you used to select them into the sample and any criteria used to exclude others.

- The **methodology section** should identify the method of collecting your data. Any questionnaires, observation records or other data collection tools should be described. A full copy should be included in the appendix at the end of the report.

- The **procedure section** should include a step-by-step account of how you collected the data. You should refer to the conditions under which participants were interviewed or observed, as well as the specific instructions given to them. If you used a questionnaire you should explain how it was administered.

Results

The results of the research should be presented in an appropriate statistical, graphical or written form. You should not include raw data in the main body of the report. Your findings should be described without any further analysis or comment at this point.

Conclusions

You should discuss your findings in terms of the patterns, points of interest and conclusions that they lead you to draw. You must be careful to ensure that any conclusions are actually supported by the data you have obtained. You may also compare and contrast your results with those of other similar studies and with existing theories. You should critically evaluate the validity of your findings, the extent to which they provide answers to the research questions, or whether they support or refute your hypothesis, and comment on the reliability of the data.

Recommendations

You may wish to recommend ways in which your research could be extended or modified to develop or extend knowledge and understanding of the area on which you focused.

References

You must reference all of the sources of information that you use in your report. The listing should be alphabetical and follow a standard referencing system so that the source can be traced.

Appendices

These contain material integral to the research, such as a copy of the questionnaire or research and interview notes. While you should keep your original, raw data in case your teacher wishes to see it, it is not usual practice to include it anywhere in the final research report.

Finally, you should be aware of the following list of don'ts when writing your final report!

- Don't overestimate the readers' background knowledge of your topic.

- Don't use long, rambling sentences or explanations. Write simply and clearly. Stick to the structure above.

- Don't use 'I' statements. Focus on the topic and the data.

- Don't pad out your report with irrelevant information or pictures.

- Don't worry if your hypothesis is not supported by your results. You should never falsify your results or become less objective in your analysis in order to avoid saying that the hypothesis is not supported. The important thing is that you conduct the research and analysis correctly and that you can identify when your hypothesis is not supported by the data! Such a result is perfectly acceptable and is in no way wrong or incorrect.

Referencing your research

One of the final tasks you will have to undertake in writing up your research report is to check that you have correctly referenced all of the books, articles and papers that you refer to in your report. When writing research reports there are standard techniques for acknowledging the work of other published researchers and authors. Most journals that publish health and social care research indicate which referencing system they use and work must then be presented in the way they specify. The Harvard and the Vancouver systems are referencing systems that are commonly used in health and social care publications.

Under the **Harvard system:**

- references are cited in the main text of the report by including the authors surname followed by the year of publication in brackets. For example, Walsh (2000)

- where there are two authors, they should both be included in the text, for example, Walsh and De Souza (2000)

- where there are more than two authors you should name the first author and then add *et al.* For example, Walsh *et al.* (2000)

- direct quotations must be in quotation marks followed by author surname and year and the page number of the reference (in brackets). For example, 'representativeness refers to the question of whether the group or situation being studied are typical of others', (McNeill, 1990)

- references are listed in alphabetical order at end of the text in the same way as on p. 403.

A journal example using the Harvard system is Waring, T (1996) 'Prisoners with diabetes: Do they receive appropriate care?', *Nursing Times* 92 (16) 38–39. A book example using the Harvard system is Parkes, C and Weiss, R (1983) *Recovery from Bereavement*, New York, Basic Books.

Under the **Vancouver system:**

- references are numbered (number in brackets) consecutively through the text

- references are listed in numerical order at the end of the text

- journals are assigned standard abbreviations from *Index Medicus*, the American National Library of Medicine's catalogue of terms and abbreviations.

A journal example of a Vancouver reference is Waring T. Prisoners with diabetes: do they receive appropriate care? Nursing Times 1996 Apr 17–23; 92 (16): 38–39.

A book reference example using the Vancouver system is Parkes C, Weiss R. Recovery from Bereavement. New York: Basic Books, 1983.

ACTIVITY

Using referencing systems

Use the Harvard system to correctly reference each of the following.

An article from Nursing Times (pages 36 to 38) called Treating obesity in people with learning disabilities, by Michael Perry. August 1996, Volume 92, issue 35.

A paper entitled Pakistani women and maternity care: Raising muted voices, written by A.M. Bowes and T. Meehan Domokos, appeared in vol. 18, no. 1. 1996. pages 45-65 of the journal Sociology of Health and Illness.

An author called Steven Pryjmachuk had a paper published in July 1996 entitled, Adolescent schizophrenia: Families information needs. It was in Mental Health Nursing vol. 16 no. 4.

A book published in 1996 by Open University Press, Buckingham, by Loraine Blaxter, Christine Hughes and Malcolm Tight, called How to Research.

Presenting research to an audience

Health and social care researchers present the findings of their investigations to colleagues and others in a variety of settings. There is a tradition in the care professions of holding conferences and seminars at which researchers present their investigations to others who have a clinical, academic or personal interest in the kind of work that has been undertaken. These presentations provide researchers with opportunities to disseminate, or spread, their findings among a large audience and are a source of feedback on their research. Practitioners and managers who carry out research investigations into the effectiveness of aspects of their clinical practice, or the operation of their service, may be required to make an effective presentation of their findings to service commissioners and purchasers in order to secure future contracts.

Presenting research to a live audience is a test of :

- **personal skills:** coming across to your audience, creating an impression and capturing attention

- **communication skills:** speaking with clarity, making yourself understood

- **listening skills:** responding appropriately to audience feedback.

Above all, you will need to draw on expertise in your area of research: through a full understanding of what you are presenting.

In presenting research to a live audience, it is best to produce and use presentation materials such as overhead transparencies or slides, posters, leaflets or handouts to get the main information points across in a clear and succinct way. You will need to draw on your self-confidence and to hold your nerve when others are listening to and looking at you!

Before launching into presenting your research to an audience, it is advisable to practise presenting information you are completely comfortable and familiar with.

ACTIVITY

Micropresentation

In groups of five, take it in turns to stand up and tell the group about any topic you choose. It can be anything from how to make an omelette to caring for a pet hamster! Take between five and 10 minutes per person. Pay attention to:

- **voice** – pitch, tone and volume

- **posture** – how you stand, gestures, mannerisms and nervous twitches

- **facial expression** – smile, eye contact with audience

- **presence** – exude confidence.

Within the allotted time the presenter must invite questions from the floor. At the end of each presentation, group members should give constructive feedback on presentation skills.

BUILD YOUR LEARNING

Keywords and phrases

You should know the meaning of the words and phrases below. If you are unsure about any of them, go back through the last four pages of the unit to refresh your understanding.

- Abstract
- Harvard system
- Research report
- Vancouver system

Summary points

- Researchers write up their investigations in a report that explains how they conducted their investigation and what they found.

- Research reports tend to follow a standard format, beginning with an abstract or summary and moving through background information, a method section, a section on the findings, a discussion section and a conclusions and recommendations section.

- All the references cited at the end of the report must use a standard system.

- Health and social care researchers present their investigations at conferences, in seminars and in papers, or articles, in research journals.

QUESTIONS

1 **What is the purpose of the abstract section of a research report?**

2 **What material should be included in the introduction to a report?**

3 **Should the research findings and discussion be presented in one section or in separate sections of the report?**

4 **Using the author, title and publishing details of this book, construct references using the Harvard and the Vancouver systems.**

5 **Make a list of the key points that researchers should bear in mind when presenting their research findings to an audience.**

References

Bailey, V, Bemrose, G, Goddard, S, Impey, R, Joslyn, E and Mackness, J (1995) *Essential Research Skills*, Collins Educational

Bowling, A (1997) *Research Methods in Health – Investigating health and health services*, Open University Press

Farrington, D (1991) 'Childhood aggression and adult violence: early precursors and later life outcomes', in Pepler, D and Rubin, K (eds) (1991) The *Development and Treatment of Childhood Aggression*, Erlbaum, Hillsdale, New Jersey

Homan, R (1991) *The Ethics of Social* Research, Longman

McNeill, P (1990) *Research Methods*, Routledge

Index

Numbers in bold show the page on which the word is defined or used as a key word.